D1436943

CHARLES DICKENS (1812–1870)

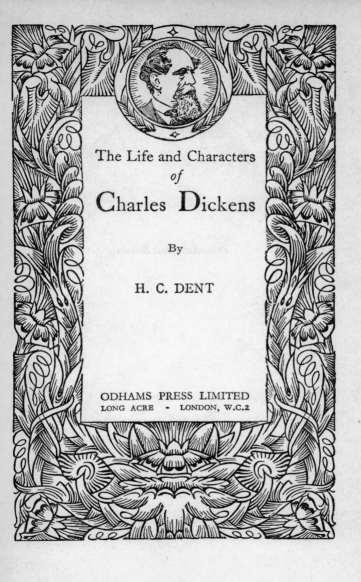

The Life and Characters
*of*
Charles Dickens

By

H. C. DENT

ODHAMS PRESS LIMITED
LONG ACRE - LONDON, W.C.2

*Printed in Great Britain*

# FOREWORD

DICKENS has universal appeal, but he cannot be entirely separated from his period. It is because some people fail to dissociate themselves from the times in which they live and the type of literature it produces that they find "The Pickwick Papers" and the rest scarcely to their taste. It is because Dickens reflected so admirably the *zeitgeist*—the spirit of the age —that his work is so useful educationally. This does not mean that his is a species of pseudo-history. Far from it. But it does mean that the reader will get an excellent idea of the Victorian period, and the knowledge will add to his store appreciably and in no wise detract from the interest of the narrative.

Fifty-eight years are not many for the life of man; they are almost insignificant in the age of a nation, yet they can be "crowded years." For those whose sense of time and events is divided into reigns, the aftermath of much confused history teaching, Dickens lived under four monarchs, George III, George IV, William IV, and Victoria. The year of Dickens' birth saw Napoleon setting out on what was to prove the beginning of the end for him, though in February 1812, the Russian debacle was not so much as foreshadowed, and the Grand Army was 680,000 strong. Wellington was no more than a Viscount, and was still fighting in the Peninsula. Great Britain and the United States were waging a foolish war that could have been averted by the use of a little common-sense on both sides. The *Comet*, the pioneer British steamer that was actually used though not the first to be built, was ploughing its way laboriously on the Clyde with paddle-wheels operated by an engine of three horse-power and filling the air with "devil's reek." Railways were things of the future, thought of but unborn, and the Bill for a horse-tramway had yet to be introduced in Parliament and thrown out because it was felt that the carriage

of goods and coal by such means would interfere with fox
hunting. The Stockton and Darlington Railway was opened
for traffic in 1825; not until 1846 did it become compulsory to
run one train a day, at a rate not exceeding one penny a
mile, provided with covered carriages instead of open trucks.

During Dickens' boyhood the land seethed with economic
unrest and discontent, brought about by diminishing wages,
the high price of food, and unemployment. Riots broke out,
and in order to prevent mass agitation large meetings were
forbidden without official sanction. A heavy stamp duty
rendered propaganda by print an expensive matter. Children
of six worked in the mills, though merciful legislation allowed
apprentices to labour for a mere twelve hours a day. By
1833 social progress had made such rapid strides that the
hours were limited to nine a day or forty-eight per week for
juveniles under eleven, and twelve a day or sixty-nine per
week for those under eighteen, and inspectors were appointed
to see that these regulations were observed. Men, women,
and children toiled in coal mines, the women doing the jobs
of the pit ponies of to-day, but whereas the animals stand
upright their predecessors were compelled to crawl or crouch
owing to the lowness of the galleries. Clad only in scanty
garments, boys and girls worked in an atmosphere often less
wholesome than that of a sewer, harnessed to a truck by a
chain fastened to a girdle round the waist, the links passing
between the legs. In one case it was found that a girl of
six years of age carried an eight-stone weight fourteen times a
day a distance equal to the height of St. Paul's Cathedral.
As for the men who worked with these unfortunates, some
wore no clothing at all. The Bill introduced by Lord Ashley
(later Earl of Shaftesbury) to amend this appalling state of
affairs met with considerable opposition in the Upper House, but
from henceforth women and girls were prohibited from working
in mines and collieries, and boys could not be employed underground until they were ten years of age. In 1847 the hours of
boys and girls under eighteen and of women in certain industries were limited to ten hours a day.

Dickens was twelve when the repeal of various Acts legalized
trade unions and free movement in search of employment.

In 1819 there were 180 offences for which a person could be hanged. In 1833 a correspondent whose watch had been stolen by a youth of twenty-one wrote to the *Times* complaining of the leniency of the sentence of seven years' transportation meted to the culprit. The Reform Bill of 1832, while it redistributed over 140 seats, gave neither the artisan nor the agricultural labourer a vote. Power shifted from the land-owning aristocracy to the middle class.

In 1833 the first national grant for education was made. It was the lavish sum of £20,000. Hitherto what crumbs of learning the poor had managed to pick up were the gifts of self-sacrificing individuals with an urge for social reform and of subscribers to the National Society, supported by members of the Church of England, and the British and Foreign School Society, the organization of Nonconformists. In 1837 it was stated in the House of Commons that 79 per cent. of the boys of England and Wales and 57 per cent. of the girls of thirteen to fourteen years of age could not read, and 67 per cent. and 88 per cent. respectively could not write. The educational grant made in 1839 was increased to £39,000. A few years later, when the employment of children was restricted to the half day either before or after dinner time, attendance at school was compulsory for three hours daily. By 1847 the State grant had reached £100,000, and twenty-two years later was five times that amount. "In 1869," says Lord Morley, "about 1,300,000 children were being educated in state-aided schools, 1,000,000 in schools that received no grant, were not inspected, and were altogether inefficient, and 2,000,000 ought to have been, but were not at school at all. The main burden of national education fell on the shoulders of 200,000 persons, whose voluntary subscriptions supported the schools." Forster's great Act, the Magna Carta of education, came into operation in August 1870, two months after Dickens' death.

When Dickens was a boy an employer paid exactly what wages he chose. If there was a deficit between the amount the agricultural worker received and what was regarded as sufficient means to enable him and his family to keep alive, the difference was paid out of the rates. In 1834, while out·

door relief could be given at the discretion of two justices of the peace on account of old age or infirmity, "the general rule," says Lord Ernle, "was to be that an able-bodied man not able to support himself and his family should only be offered the workhouse." The inevitable result was much misery until economic conditions adjusted themselves. On the other hand, rates fell appreciably, and were £2,000,000 lower in 1837, the year of Queen Victoria's accession. This fact and a revival in trade put a brighter complexion on affairs. Housing conditions in many places were appalling. It is scarcely believable, and exact statistics are not obtainable, but it was calculated that in 1837 one-seventh of the population of Liverpool and one-tenth of that of Manchester dwelt in cellars. The stringent measures of the new Poor Law undoubtedly influenced many workers to become Chartists.

The brighter outlook in commerce failed to continue, and another period of depression set in. Under Sir Robert Peel the country ceased to be highly protectionist, and hundreds of duties were either abolished or reduced. The price of bread had been kept high by the operations of the Corn Laws, the duties on foreign corn varying according to the price of the home product. Bad harvests and increasing population accentuated the urgent necessity for reform, and the Anti-Corn Law League was founded. Cobden and Bright threw themselves heart and soul into the agitation, which was accentuated by the disastrous potato famine in Ireland. Great Britain was hampered from sending corn to her distressed sister by reason of incessant rains which were rotting her own crop, and the heavy duties imposed on imported corn. After a wordy war and much bitterness the aloof but adaptable Peel succeeded in repealing the Corn Laws in 1846. Shortly afterwards the "sublime mediocrity," as Disraeli dubbed Peel, resigned and never took office again. He had probably saved a revolution.

Writing of this time Sir Spencer Walpole has this to say: "The expedients to which the poor were reduced for the sake of food almost exceed belief. The author of the 'Poor Law Catechism' said that 'Pennyworths of mutton and halfpennyworths of bread cut off the loaf are what the shopkeepers of Bolton deal out to the inhabitants of their Jerusalem.' 'I could tell you,' so ran a letter from Johnstone, 'of mothers dividing a farthing herring and a halfpennyworth of potatoes among a family of seven.' Such expedients seemed tolerable compared with others which were resorted to at the same time. Children fought each other in the streets for the offal which rich men did not allow their dogs to touch. A gentleman saw a labourer standing over his swill tub voraciously devouring the wash intended for the pigs. Twenty women begged a farmer to allow them to disinter the body of a cow, which he had buried thirty-six hours before as unfit for human food. Starving men and women, or, worse still, men and women seeing their children starve before their eyes, readily seized the vilest substances which enabled them to protract for a few hours longer their miserable lives."[1]

Among those who rendered yeoman service to the cause was Ebenezer Elliott, the Corn Law Rhymer, who not only addressed meetings but composed songs calculated to soften the stoniest heart. One of them was heard through the length and breadth of the country:

"Child, is thy father dead?"
  "Father is gone!
Why did they tax his bread?
  God's will be done!
Mother has sold her bed;
Better to die than wed:
Where shall she lay her head?
  Home we have none!

"Father clammed [hungered] thrice a week,
  God's will be done!
Long for work did he seek,
  Work he found none.
Tears on his hollow cheek
Told what no tongue could speak;
Why did his master break?
  God's will be done!

[1] *History of England*, Walpole, Vol. IV., p. 26.

> "Doctor said air was best—
> Food we had none;
> Father with panting breast,
> Groaned to be gone.
> Now he is with the blest!
> Mother says death is best!
> We have no place of rest."
> "Yes, ye have one!"

The Crimean War and the Indian Mutiny were followed by the cotton famine caused by the American Civil War. Lancashire obtained its raw material from the South, but it applauded the North and its fight against slavery. It sympathized and suffered. Thousands were thrown out of work, and a state perilously bordering on starvation was reached by many families, notwithstanding the splendid efforts that were made to alleviate distress.

This brief résumé of certain events in the troubled world of Charles Dickens' day must suffice to show something of what the novelist had to mirror. It was a time when England was suffering the birth pangs of Democracy, when aristocracy was putting up its last great fight, and the machine was marching on its progressive way, to become in the twentieth century both a miracle and a menace.

Life is the raw material upon which the novelist exercises his art, and he must know it well before he can hope to succeed. Dickens garnered a ripe harvest of experience before he essayed his first attempt at story-telling, despite the early age at which he published "The Pickwick Papers." It may be, as some critics have asserted, that he did not see life whole. If by this expression is meant that his realism did not include every biographical and biological factor, record every breath, and analyse every individual thought of his characters, the judgment is sustained. Such literary vivisection made no appeal to Dickens, and probably never occurred to him. Had he used his pen as a scalpel, according to the wont of certain ultra-modern authors, it is highly improbable that the result would have been propitious. Nevertheless he observed life in essential detail, and described it with an accuracy rarely exceeded. This, and the fact that there is fashion in fiction as in much else, accounts for the leisurely, even pedestrian way in which many of his chapters seem to amble along.

In an age when mechanization, as we understand it, was virtually unknown, there was time to breathe between sentences. In Victorian days, be it added, these were apt to wind the reader much as toiling up a long flight of stairs in a Victorian house puffed the climber. Sentences, even in the Criminal Courts, are shorter to-day. Macaulay, in the rôles of historian and essayist, sometimes found it difficult to arrive at a period, so busy was he in piling up evidence, making contrasts or parallels, and applying voluminous coats of paint of the richest colour. There was no undue hurry to develop the verbal picture. To use a simile from the cinema, "slow motion" pictures were the rule. If a passage were a little difficult to grasp by reason of its inordinate length, there was no hurry. One could go back and re-read it. The range of books was more limited than it is in a day of unrestrained production and competition. Fewer books led to a fuller appreciation of those that were available, which aided and abetted their retention in one's memory. It was not economical to be in too great a hurry because it led to a poverty of reading matter.

Nowadays the case is altered. There is too much literary matter to digest. If a questioner asks what a reader is perusing it is the usual practice for the latter to glance at the spine of the binding in order to glean the information. For the most part the professional critics were far more severe than they are now. There was a good deal of flaying. The reviewer, like the reader who perused to be amused or instructed, had more time at his disposal, and also more space to fill. It was easier to go through the eye of a needle than for a writer to receive unstinted praise at the hands of men who regarded their task rather in the light of prosecuting counsel. Possibly some of these individuals felt a keener sense of responsibility than do those who came after. Every page of printed matter had to be microscopically examined to see that it was fit for the family. The Dickens era was dominated by the fetish of the patriarchal group. What

Father read must also appeal to Mother and the children—all the children who could read, quite irrespective of age and sex. One of the tests of the worth of a book was whether it could be left lying about by the Head of the house.

We have greater liberty to-day, and any qualms of conscience in the matter are usually suffered by junior members rather than by their seniors. Not that it is usual for households to discuss the offerings of authors in the way that formerly obtained. The standardization of taste is an affair of forgotten years. To-day novels are not cast in a familiar set of moulds. Every conceivable kind of preference is catered for. Fiction still has its modes, of course. For some reason unknown even to the most erudite thinkers, there are fads and fancies in fiction that prevail for a season and pass away like the " little systems" of Tennyson. Within the last decade there have been spates of war novels, floods of detective stories, deluges of psychological studies dealing with the minutiæ of life in far greater detail than life itself is conscious of, and sex novels that are mainly pathological studies. At the moment of writing there is a strong inclination on the part of novelists to confine their books to incidents crowded in twenty-four hours or a week, the locale being an hotel, apartment house, or tenement.

It may be well to remember that when Dickens published his books there were few public libraries. Those who could not afford to buy the monthly Numbers or the completed works in volume form generally had to go without, await the favour of the loan of them from friends, or join a lending library and perhaps secure a book several months after publication. The last-mentioned and somewhat haphazard method was certainly better than nothing, but it was rather a severe tax on one's memory, more especially as Dickens was wont to crowd his stage. As Mr. Dent points out in this admirable study, it is computed that the Master's novels contain no fewer than two thousand characters.

Dickens' two outstanding talents were complementary. He was the greatest popular prose writer that England has ever known. He reached in his lifetime, and continues to reach long after his death, what the translators of the

Authorized Version of the Bible call "the common people" that is to say, the masses. Their number was appreciably fewer when the books were originally produced, but the demand increases rather than diminishes. Whereas the works of most authors decline in popularity with the decease of their writers, the spirit of Charles Dickens, like John Brown's soul, goes marching on.

Since the introduction of broadcasting the term "high-brow" has met with much favour as denoting somebody or something neither too readily understandable nor appreciated. Dickens never wrote above the heads of his public; there was nothing of "art for art's sake" about him. He was of "the common people," he loved them, and he wrote for them. Whereas many other eminent followers of the same profession have had academic honours thrust upon them, have been gowned in scarlet and introduced in Latin by the Public Orators of universities, no such distinction fell to the lot of the creator of "David Copperfield." I do not know that he would have been greatly elated by the presentation of a diploma, but I somehow feel that the seats of learning neglected an opportunity of showing that he was not un-worthy of recognition. It is perhaps a small matter, an almost insignificant trifle, but it is at least arguable that the man they missed did more to make England a brighter and happier place than some whose names are on the roll of honorary graduates.

Dickens' second outstanding talent was his ability as an actor. His Readings from his own works were not of the kind one ordinarily associates with reading aloud—a little inflection of the voice now and again to vary the monotony, and an occasional gesture. They were acted, and superbly acted, if contemporary reports speak truth. Just as Dickens lived, and moved, and had his being in each individual as he created him or her on paper, so he got into the very skin of his characters and brought them to life on the platform. Dickens was what we call a born actor. It was not the long hours at his desk, the agony and mental sweat of conception —"regular, ferocious excitement," as he termed it—alone that wore his life away, but the overstrain occasioned by his

dramatic recitals that left him a dead man at fifty-eight.
That he enjoyed this phase of his career is beyond doubt.
It is said that change of occupation is as beneficial as rest,
but in his particular case the change was in name rather than
in deed. He lived with the same characters and the same
scenes both in the study and in the lecture hall. If he did
not clench his hands on the throat of the victim when his
pen was telling the story of the murder in "Oliver Twist," he
went through the terrible scene in his mind, and when he
acted the part he merely laid his pen aside and created it
anew with added emphasis.

"His Fagin," Mr. Herman Klein tells us in his "Musicians
and Mummers," "was a masterpiece of characterization.
With his hoarse, rasping voice, his Israelitish lisp, and East-
end Cockney accent of the 'thirties, and his command of the
whole gamut of racial inflexions, he made Fagin even more
Hebrew in type than the text of the novel can suggest. In
this scene the Jew says repeatedly, '*Suppose* that lad—*suppose*
he was to do all this, what then?' But Dickens did not pro-
nounce the 'suppose' as he wrote it. He growled it out each
time with a hissing lisp—'Thuppothe,' or 'thuppothin'—and
with a snarl of concentrated hate and cunning that was
perhaps beyond his own power of verbal description. Again
and again he made his audience shudder."

On one occasion Mr. J. E. Preston Muddock, who will be
more readily recognised as the Dick Donovan of many title
pages, went to hear Dickens at the Free Trade Hall, Manchester. To quote from his "Papers from an Adventurous
Life": "The man's beautiful, sympathetic voice, the wonderfully expressive eyes, his marvellous eloquence, his magnetic
presence seemed to throw me under a spell, and I regarded
him as something more than a human being, or, at any rate,
as a man who was quite different from other men I had so
far known. The power that Dickens had over the hearts of
the people at this time was little short of marvellous. On
the occasion I allude to the great hall was literally packed
from floor to ceiling. Yet that audience was placed under the
spell wielded by the man whose voice was like a silver bell,
and who acted what he read. The pathos moved the people

to tears, the humour stirred them to roars of laughter.    There
were no accessories of music or scenery, simply one man at
a reading desk; but what a man!    What a gift to be able to
charm and sway a multitude!    Sometimes you could have
heard a pin drop, at others the roof seemed rent with the
roars of the people as they gave vent to their strained feelings.
And when it came to the peroration there was a silence which
was almost painful; even a woman's sob here and there only
served to intensify it.   .   .   ."

Lady Westmorland's account of a Dickens reading in 1862
is less complimentary to the orator, but in no way minimises
the genius of the man—accentuates it in fact by reason of
certain disabilities, as she considered them, under which he
suffered.    She was "enchanted," Dickens' rendering of the
storm in "David Copperfield" was "perfectly thrilling, and
the effect upon the crowded hall wonderful.   .   .   .    Close
to us was Fechter, a fat, clumsy-looking figure, with a very
dark, sallow face, and coarse, black hair, positively ugly, I
thought when I first looked at him; but when I saw how his
countenance reflected all he heard, and saw the tears rolling
down his face, and then his whole frame convulsed with
laughter, I recognised the beauty we saw in him as Hamlet.
.   .   .    It is certainly a wonderful triumph of genius, for there
is nothing to aid it.    Nothing can be less prepossessing than
Dickens' appearance.    His action is not graceful, his voice is
not musical, and rather hoarse; and yet he moves masses of
people of all ages and of all kinds alternately to tears and
laughter."

The suitability of a novel for reading aloud is a gruelling
test of its interest.    Mr. V. C. Clinton-Baddeley, whose wireless readings of prose and poetry are so well known to multi-
tudes of listeners-in, avows that "No actor can do anything
with unsuitable material—nor can a reader.    Just an extract
from a famous work remains just an extract: a poor amorphous
thing with nothing to commend it.    One cannot dramatize a
thing with no beginning and no end.    A reading, as much as
a play, demands a shape, and no reading is of any value unless
in itself it be complete.    Dickens is the episodic writer *par
excellence*."

He was "undoubtedly one of the sons of Toil," as he told his friend and sometime collaborator Wilkie Collins. The *Must* Demon drove him on, relentlessly and remorselessly. Had he taken things a little more calmly Westminster Abbey would not have received his tired body so soon. Truth to tell, it was not in him to "move fast slowly." Like Napoleon, he multiplied himself by his activities, and his incessant exertions wore him out in much the same way that a scuffler on a flinty road wears out the soles of his shoes. He could not rest. Was it a ride on horse-back? Then he must exert his animal to the utmost. Was it a walk? Then it must be no amble but arduous exertion. Was it a trip to the Continent? Then he must do everything and see everybody.

The generality of the public is apt to think that an author has scarcely less difficulty in writing a story than a bank clerk in using an adding machine that totals a vast array of figures by the tapping of keys. Sentences are supposed to flow from a pen almost as freely as storm water from a gargoyle. Authorship is less easy. The rhythm of a sentence is not the automatic rhythm of a spinning top. Often enough it is hewn out of the rugged rock, polished and polished again. A glance at a folio of Dickens' manuscript shows sentences scratched out, words deleted and phrases inserted. The writing is easy to follow, suggesting that the writer's thoughts are not sufficiently far ahead to preclude legible penmanship. There are no ampersands; "and" is spelled out in full. No words are joined; each word is individual and distinct. The lines are close together, as though paper were running short. With the exception of occasional sentences penned in minute characters on account of lack of space, a manuscript of Dickens presented no difficulty to the compositor.

In this, the third decade of the twentieth century, it is not considered *de rigeur* to have a title that bears any considerable relationship to the theme of a novel. If it is a little outrageous so much the better. Thousands of stories between cloth covers are published every year, and each must have a distinctive name, short and easily remembered, though these desiderata are not always obtained. Dickens went to endless trouble in this matter. "It's a great thing to have my title," he wrote to Forster, after he had chosen the subject of a story but could not think of a name by which to call it. You will read on a later page how he came by the title of "The Chimes" after days of apparently hopeless search.

It may be said without fear of contradiction that a novelist is seldom, if ever, at complete mental ease. His very livelihood depends on constant observation and sustained thought. He does not necessarily "put his friends into books," but it is evident that he must of necessity make a composite portrait of people whom he sees and meets. Gestures, appearance, snatches of conversation, peculiarities, mannerisms; all these things and much else are the data on which he works. His brain is no more a well of constant inspiration, bubbling and effervescent, pure and undefiled, than is that of a stock-broker or any other child of man. Sometimes his work comes easy, his pen is a stumbling-block rather than a stepping-stone to progress because it cannot keep pace with his ideas, but there are times when it is veriest drudgery. The plot refuses to develop, the characters are as wooden as Dickens' midshipman, words form sentences about as attractive as the coal and sticks in a cold grate. On occasion Dickens would brood fruitlessly over his manuscript for hours. What he sought would not come. "My father and I," says Sir Henry Fielding Dickens, K.C., "walked together through the streets of Rochester, and through the surrounding country time after time. During those walks I don't believe we ever exchanged a word. His mind was always absorbed, and his eye was always observant."

There is this vast and important difference between the creation of a drawing and the telling of a story. In the one the artist can see the whole of his work as he proceeds; in the other he must turn over page after page if he wishes to refer to what he has written. He cannot refresh his memory at a glance. Some of Dickens' stories run to 300,000 words. None tempers the wind to the shorn author when the east wind blows. Writing as he did with the shadow of the printer's devil athwart his threshold, with the exigencies of the press ever present at the back of his mind, and almost watch in hand, we must agree with Mr. H. P. James that Dickens was a great natural force in creative imaginative literature. Nowadays novels are not published in monthly Numbers but as a whole. This means that the author can revise and re-revise if he wishes, an opportunity denied to Dickens because his major works were completed but a few weeks before the final Part was on sale. There was no great time for final touches and varnishing. Perhaps they are all the better for it.

It leads to a fuller appreciation of a man's creations if we know something of the creator, his means and methods, his strength and weaknesses, and above all the warfare he had to wage. *Vivere est militare*—life is a fight. The truth of the Latin tag, dimly realized in its full meaning by its ancient sponsor, is confirmed by modern science and in the experience of every one of us. Dickens did not find life easy, though his success came early. He had a large family to bring up, educate, and provide for, and he fully realized the responsibilities incurred. He determined that if it were humanly possible to preclude his children from suffering in their early youth what he had undergone he would prevent it. So he chained himself to his desk, exerted the last dram of energy from a heart that was never too robust, and having achieved his purpose, left a sheaf of unfinished manuscript on his desk in the châlet, and walked into the house to die of "effusion on the brain."

This is not to suggest that Dickens failed to find pleasure, even joy, in his work. He did. When his ideas were flowing freely and he was not harassed he was in an ecstasy of delight. His characters were flesh of his flesh and bone of his bone. Work was meat and drink to him. In the quietude of his study he conjured from the realms of fancy and of reality the people who throng his books and the scenes amid which they play their parts. They inhabited no fancy places. As Mr. Dent says, Dickensland is "the most fascinatingly real country ever populated by imaginary people. Almost every place in that country is as easy to locate as one on an ordnance survey map or in a post-office directory," and he speaks from personal experience, having explored much of it on foot. A small library has been written on the haunts of the men, women and children fathered by the great novelist's brain. Not only

Kent but London is redolent of them, though many of the places once easily identified have disappeared. The City and Southwark, Fleet Street and the Strand, Holborn and the various Inns of the lawyers, Highgate and Hampstead Heath still offer shrines at which the Dickensian devotee may worship. For how long none knows, for though London endures its buildings do not. Leases fall in, bricks fall out, the National Trust has not the wherewithal to purchase every property it has the wish to buy, and present distresses are conducive to Philistinism.

Gruff, heavy-worded Carlyle got to the truth of the matter when he contrasted Dickens with Thackeray. "Dickens," he said, "was doing the best in him, and went on smiling in perennial good humour; but Thackeray despised himself for his work, and on that account could not always do it even moderately well." Kate Douglas Wiggin when a child of eight years of age met Dickens on a train during his visit to the United States in 1867. "I cry when I read about Steerforth," he told her, "I cried when I wrote it, too!" The same authoress tells us in "My Garden of Memory" that when she mentioned that she skipped "some of the very dull parts," Dickens took out a note book and pencil and gave her an exhausting and exhaustive examination on the subject.

Dickens was a democrat of democrats. He had a passion for humanity, and would have man reach out to the stars. As already noted, the England in which Dickens lived was not the England of to-day, though this is still far removed from the Jerusalem that Blake envisaged. "It was the day when, in one town," to quote Mr. Stanley Baldwin's fine tribute to "The Chronicler of the People of England," "a whole street was built along the course of a ditch, because in that way deeper cellars could be secured without the cost of digging. Those cellars were not for goods, but for human beings, and not one soul in that street escaped the cholera when the epidemic came to England. It was the period of the Sadler Report on Factory work. It was the period of which Disraeli wrote in 'Coningsby,' Mrs. Browning in 'The Cry of the Children,' and Mrs. Gaskell in 'North and South.' The economists looked on, and saw that it was good. Mr. Roebuck, whose name will never be forgotten, asked if the world had ever seen anything like it, answered: 'Nothing; and I pray that our unrivalled happiness may last.' It was an atmosphere in which plots, conspiracies, dark deeds, and poverty had a natural setting. We cannot realize the sanitary distance we are from those days—days reeking with typhus and cholera, days of bad water and the graveyard atmosphere. Into that there was projected, by the will of Heaven, a genius—one of the greatest creative geniuses of all times. No writer before him had handled our people. No one had ever written before about the poor, except as a quarry for extracting chronic criminals or humorous characters. He was the first man who had a conception of the so-called 'lower orders,' and could treat them as men and women with character, not as characters. . . . No man influenced his peers more than he."

Dickens, Carlyle, Ruskin, and Arnold, avows Sir Arthur Quiller-Couch, were the men who spent their lives to redeem England from the miseries and squalors of Industrial England. "If ever," he adds, "the forts of ugliness and commercial materialism fall in this land, theirs will be the bodies found at the apex of the bridge."

There is abundant evidence that Dickens was conscious of a mission, that he definitely started out in many of his works to reform abuses and right wrongs by means of subtle propaganda. The obvious is often the least obvious. Dickens drew attention to what people saw but did not perceive. "The magic of print" is something more than a symbolical expression. There is magic in the printed page because the words impress themselves on our minds in much the same way as the inked type impresses itself on the paper. Dickens, via his characters and the pictures of their environment, exercised a formative and reformative influence, and that he deliberately set out to achieve such an object is quite certain. He exaggerated as a caricaturist, exaggerated in order to emphasise, distorted so that the need for proper focus might be more evident, and left a picture on the mind of the reader as hard-bitten as the lines on an engraver's plate. Mr. G. K. Chesterton, the most discerning of commentators, states in his essay in "The Great Victorians" that Dickens reaches "his most earnest social philosophy in 'Hard Times,' with something of the same graver reforming spirit in 'Bleak House,'" and that "he gathered up into his last complete book, 'Our Mutual Friend,' all his growing knowledge of the realities of society, of the growth of plutocracy, and the peril now threatening the national tradition."

Reference to Dickens as a reformer naturally prompts the problem of his religious beliefs. If he has to be placed in one of the folds into which Christianity has thought fit to divide itself he may be called a Unitarian, though he never paraded his convictions. A manuscript which might shed light on the matter remains unprinted. He wrote a life of Christ for his children, and specially enjoined them that it was never to be published.

There is truth in the venerable saw that a man is known by the company he keeps. Dickens, with no social advantages, with nothing but his own brain and stout heart to help him, broke down many barriers. His famous contemporaries were many, more particularly in the wide field of literature. Carlyle, "a heaver of rocks not a shaper," to use Meredith's apt description, raised no objection to toiling from Cheyne Walk to Lincoln's Inn Fields to hear "The Chimes." Dickens, on his part, confessed that he "would go at all times farther to see Carlyle than any man alive." No two geniuses were more dissimilar, but both hated cant and would fain see humanity less vexed and troubled. They loved children. One had an ample supply of his own and the other none. The Sage of Chelsea compared the last state of the Dauphin of France in the Temple to that of English factory children; in 1858 the creator of Little Nell occupied the chair at the first festival dinner of the Playground and General Recreation Society to plead for those who could not speak for themselves. "Until the recent formation of this body," said the *Daily Telegraph*, "London was wholly destitute of public playgrounds. There are parks, unthinking people will say; but, alas! how wearily distant are the parks, in the great wilderness of London, for very many thousand little feet."

There is less astonishment at his regard for Hans Christian Andersen, "who loved him a little beyond this side idolatry," to cite Mr. Dent. The man who treasured the memory of Mary Hogarth had much in common with the Danish writer, on whose cold and still breast was found a little bag containing a letter and a withered spray of flowers that he had kept since the day of his parting with Riborg Voigt. Andersen was twenty-five when he first met his dark-eyed brunette, and he died at the age of seventy. Again there is the link of the children. In the neighbourhood of New Kent Road there is a tablet to mark the spot where David Copperfield is supposed to have rested before his flight to Dover; on the beach at Copenhagen a bronze mermaid around which the little ones gather and the sea splashes commemorates the cobbler's son whose works are still read even by the sophisticated juniors of a more scientific generation.

Dickens had the highest admiration of the genius of Edward Bulwer, afterwards first Lord Lytton, author of "Pelham," "The Last Days of Pompeii," "The Last of the Barons," "Eugene Aram," "Rienzi," and a host of other books that did not prevent him from shining as a politician, public speaker, and a figure in Society. There are certain similarities in the careers of the two friends. Dickens, sticking at his desk during his brief honeymoon at Chalk; Bulwer slaving at Woodcot, his bride seeing him "for five minutes at two or three o'clock in the morning." The lot of the wife of the literary man is not easy. His selfishness is unselfishness in disguise, but it requires a well-balanced woman to penetrate the mask. Charles Dickens and his wife agreed to part, but his wife maintained a dignified silence in marked contrast to the abuse hurled at Bulwer by the woman whose beauty veiled a distressed and recriminating mind concentrated on its own unhappiness, both real and fancied.

Harrison Ainsworth, the English Dumas whose "Old St. Paul's" fascinated most of us in youth, was one of Dickens' earliest friends and godfather to his eighth child. The Rev. Richard Harris Barham, now remembered only for "The Ingoldsby Legends," originally published in *Bentley's Miscellany* when under the editorship of Dickens, was of the select party privileged to listen to the author's reading of the proofs of "The Chimes," referred to above. There was affinity in their wit—though perhaps Barham possessed the more whimsical sense of humour—and in their fondness for Kent.

Tennyson, whom Dickens called "a great creature," was a welcomed caller at Devonshire Terrace, and his works were read again and again by his host. "How fine the 'Idylls' are!" Dickens wrote to Forster. "Lord! what a blessed thing it is to read a man who really can write. I thought nothing could be finer than the first poem, till I came to read the third; but when I had read the last, it seemed to me to be absolutely unapproachable."

Monckton Mills, later Lord Houghton, was a friend of Dickens from his early days, but there was an older tie. "When Lady Houghton was a girl at Crewe," Sir Wemyss Reid notes, "the person who filled the responsible office of housekeeper was a Mrs. Dickens, the grandmother of Charles. Lady Houghton used to tell that, when she was a child, the greatest treat that could be given to herself and her brother and sister was an afternoon in the housekeeper's room at Crewe; for Mrs. Dickens was an inimitable storyteller, and she loved to have the children round her, and to beguile them, not only with fairy tales, but with reminiscences of her own, and stories from the pages of history. It was natural therefore that when, after her marriage, Lady Houghton became personally acquainted with Charles Dickens, she should feel a peculiar interest in him." It was through the good offices of Lord Houghton that the novelist's remains were buried in Westminster Abbey.

To compile a list of Dickens' friends and acquaintances would be to catalogue most of the famous and eminent men of his generation. He breakfasted with Gladstone, dined with Disraeli, and had supper with Alexandre Dumas, visited Chateaubriand and Victor Hugo in Paris, was pictured by Samuel Lawrence, George Cruikshank, Daniel Maclise, R. J. Lane, Count d'Orsay, Ary Scheffer, W. P. Frith, and Augustus Egg. Thackeray's offer to illustrate "Pickwick" had been declined, but the introduction thus effected ripened into a warm regard, marred after many years by an unfortunate misunderstanding. George Henry Lewes, whose company

Dickens appreciated, saw fit to publish a somewhat depre-
catory criticism in the *Fortnightly Review* after his friend's
death. Sir Richard Owen, Emerson, Washington Irving,
Samuel Rogers, Thomas Hood, Douglas Jerrold, Lord Jeffrey,
Mazzini, Captain Marryat, Isambard Brunel, Sir Edwin
Landseer—he knew them all, and many others. Thomas
Moore tells how Sydney Smith decried Dickens at a dinner,
but the witty Canon subsequently confessed that at long last
Dickens conquered him.

The existence of the world-wide Dickens Fellowship is a
glowing tribute to the affection with which the great novelist's
memory is regarded, and 48 Doughty Street, London, where
part of "Pickwick" and the whole of "Oliver Twist" and
"Nicholas Nickleby" were written, is now national property.
One wishes it were possible to honour Dickens as the
Norwegians have honoured Ibsen. In the Norsk Folke-
museum at Oslo you may look through a glass door and see
the great man's study as it was when he died—the lino-
leum, chairs, desk, globe, and knick-knacks all complete.
Reproductions of the painting by Sir Luke Fildes, R.A.,
showing the empty chair in the study at Gads Hill on June 9,
1870, sold in thousands after Dickens had passed away, but a
picture, however admirable in execution, is but a poor substitute at best compared to the original. It must of necessity
lack that personal, intimate touch associated with the model.
Incidentally it may be mentioned that the apothecary's shop
at Grimstad, where Ibsen spent six years of his youth, is
preserved as a museum. Many of the prescriptions he copied,
the wooden sofa and bed, his spectacles and travelling ink-
well, and the table on which he wrote "Catiline" are preserved
in this little southern Norwegian town. Great Britain as a
State is not a whole-hearted hero worshipper, otherwise it
would have secured Gads Hill.

LATON BLACKLANDS.

# THE LIFE AND CHARACTERS

## of

# CHARLES DICKENS

## CHAPTER I

" . . . *an innocent romantic boy making his imaginative world.* . . ."—DAVID COPPERFIELD.

ON a certain May morning in the year 1866 three gentlemen were walking through the streets of Portsmouth in the direction of the Southsea front. The leader of the party was a tall, elderly man in a broad-brimmed, "wideawake" felt hat. Despite a bad cold, he was talking with boisterous good humour all the way, and, judging from the continual peals of laughter, cracking the most outrageous jokes.

As the three swung round a corner in the Landport area, a street name attracted the leader's attention.

"By Jove!" he exclaimed, "here is the place where I was born!"

Thus did Charles Dickens, in his fifty-fifth year, happen quite by accident to see again his birthplace. Which particular house had had that honour he was unable to decide. He wandered up and down the terrace, examining the dwellings one by one. All he could remember was that there had been a small front garden; but all the houses had small front gardens. The more closely one looked at them the more did each resemble its neighbour.

So the other two gentlemen thought; but Dickens could discover all sorts of peculiarities and oddities in each little residence. Each in turn he was sure was his birthplace. This one looked like the home of a man who had deserted it— and had he not done so, for over half a century? That one looked like the cradle of some poor, weak, puny child—such as he had been. A third—ah, that was surely the one. "It looks so like my father!"

His friends shouted with laughter. Whatever possible resemblance could there be between one of these prim, stolid, square-fronted little houses and the late Mr. John Dickens, so light-hearted, gay, generous and irresponsible?

So the three passed on, without deciding more than in joke the actual house. To-day, none can be in doubt as to which it is, for in 1903 the Portsmouth Corporation purchased No. 393 Commercial Road, Mile End, Landport, and opened it as a Dickens Museum.

> "To begin my life with the beginning of my life, I record that I was born (as I have been informed and believe) on a Friday, at twelve o'clock at night. It was remarked that the clock began to strike, and I began to cry, simultaneously."

So starts "The Personal History and Experience of David Copperfield the Younger," a book of which some parts at least relate very accurately something of the personal history and experience of Charles Dickens. The description of his birth, there is little reason to doubt, is one of these parts. He was actually born shortly before midnight on Friday, February 7th, 1812.

He was the first son, but the second child, of John and Elizabeth Dickens. To him were given the Christian names Charles John Huffam. The third of these, that of his god-father, Christopher Huffam, "Rigger to His Majesty's Navy," was incorrectly spelt Huffham in the baptismal register of St. Mary's church, Portsea, where he was christened. In the family rejoicing over the arrival of a son and heir possibly no one noticed this error. Even if he did, it is difficult to imagine the proud father bothering his head over such a trifle.

Mr. John Dickens was at that time twenty-six years of age,

JOHN BULL PEEPING INTO BREST

*A cartoon published in England during the Napoleonic Wars*

and a Civil Servant of some standing, having been for seven years a clerk in the Navy Pay Office. After four years' service at Somerset House in London, he had been "detached" and sent to Portsmouth to assist in the important work of paying off the men-of-war as they arrived in harbour after spells of active service.

It was a busy and exciting time. The Napoleonic wars were in full train. Portsmouth garrison and dockyards hummed with activity. Soldiers and sailors thronged the town. The Solent was crowded with ships. News, rumours and alarms poured in daily, for although since Trafalgar Britain was unquestionably mistress of the seas, Napoleon still dominated Europe, and the fear of invasion had not altogether passed from English minds.

To be "detached" and sent to so responsible a post indicated that the authorities appreciated Mr. Dickens' work and value. The young Navy pay clerk thought his prospects so good that before leaving London he decided to get married.

His wife, Elizabeth Barrow, was the sister of a fellow-clerk at Somerset House, and was at the time of her marriage less than twenty-one years of age.

John Dickens' salary was as yet very small, probably not much more than the £80 a year on which he had started in 1805. He had, however, every reason to hope that it would be raised, and there were, in addition, certain "expectations." So the young couple, with an eye to their status in Portsmouth society, rented a genteel and rather expensive little house in Mile End Terrace, Landport, as that part of Commercial Road was then called. Here they resided three years, and here were born their first two children, Frances Elizabeth, always known as Fanny, in the autumn of 1810, and Charles.

David Copperfield wrote of himself that "if it should appear from anything I may set down in this narrative that I was a child of close observation, or that as a man I have a strong memory of my childhood, I undoubtedly lay claim to both these characteristics."

Both characteristics were equally evident in Charles Dickens. From a very early age he began to observe both persons and things keenly and fully, and to store his impres-

B

sions in a singularly retentive memory. To these qualities
of mind was added a third, of perhaps yet more significant
importance. Though quite naturally his childish fancy
exaggerated the size and grandeur of inanimate objects, so
that he imagined Rochester High Street as wide as Regent
Street, his understanding of people was uncannily sure, so
much so that in later life he "unvaryingly" declared "that he
had never seen any cause to correct or change what in his
boyhood was his own secret impression of anybody, whom he
had, as a grown man, the opportunity of testing."

Doubtless the recollections of infancy recorded in "David
Copperfield" are drawn from his own earliest memories.

> "The first objects that assume a distinct presence before
> me, as I look far back, into the blank of my infancy, are
> my mother with her pretty hair and youthful shape, and
> Peggotty, with no shape at all, and eyes so dark that they
> seemed to darken their whole neighbourhood in her face,
> and cheeks and arms so hard and red that I wondered
> the birds didn't peck her in preference to apples.
>
> "I believe I can remember these two at a little distance
> apart, dwarfed to my sight by stooping down or kneeling
> on the floor, and I going unsteadily from the one to the
> other. I have an impression on my mind which I cannot
> distinguish from actual remembrance, of the touch of
> Peggotty's forefinger as she used to hold it out to me,
> and of its being roughened by needlework, like a pocket
> nutmeg-grater."

In one particular instance, however, not recorded in this
book, Dickens' memory certainly played him false. He firmly
believed and often told his friend and biographer, John
Forster, that he could remember trotting about in the little
front garden of his birthplace with his elder sister Fanny.
This could not have been so, for he was not yet five months
old when the family moved from there to 18 Hawke Street,
Portsea.

The move was a very distinct come-down. This second
house was by no means so genteel or commodious a residence
as that in Mile End Terrace. Evidently Mr. John Dickens,

THE BIRTHPLACE OF CHARLES DICKENS
No. 393 Commercial Road, Mile End, Landport, now a Dickens
Museum

The Birthplace of Charles Dickens.
See p. 35. Compiled from sketches and photographs made by G. W. Harris.

owing to his somewhat sanguine and improvident nature, had rather over-estimated his prospects, and drawn on his credit too freely. As also the "expectations" had so far failed to materialize, a policy of retrenchment and economy became absolutely necessary.

It was not, apparently, his first experience of money troubles, or "moments of difficulty," as he termed them. But as husband and father, he could no longer evade such moments by quietly disappearing, as he had been wont to do in bachelor days, until some relative or friend eased him of his difficulty by paying his debts. He was forced now to move into a smaller and cheaper house. He remained there some eighteen months, until in the spring of 1814 he was recalled to London. A third child, Alfred, was born in this house, but died in infancy.

Charles, still the baby, was barely two years old when the family left Portsmouth, but he carried thence in his memory "the exact shape of the military parade" on which he had watched the soldiers at exercise. He remembered, too, that they travelled up to London in the snow.

Though the movements of the family between 1814 and 1816 cannot be determined with accuracy, it is probable that the stay in London was quite short. Lodgings were first taken in Norfolk Street, now Cleveland Street, which is between Goodge Street and Tottenham Court Road; and either here or in some other dwelling-place in London a second daughter, Letitia Mary, was born. In 1816, or perhaps earlier, Mr. Dickens was again detached, this time for service in Chatham.

His financial position had in the meantime very decidedly improved. He was now receiving a salary of £200 per annum, and his new post carried also "extras." He could consider himself comfortably off. Accordingly, in the summer of 1817, he established himself in No. 2 Ordnance Terrace, Chatham, one of "a neat row of houses in the most airy and pleasant part of the town," and began to enter with zest into the life of the polite society in the neighbourhood.

The future must have at that time looked exceedingly rosy

to him. He was a hard-working and capable Civil Servant
whose abilities the authorities recognized and respected.
By his friends he was considered "a fellow of infinite humour,
chatty, lively, and agreeable." His wife was a "dear good
mother, and a fine woman," well able to undertake the care
and early education of her three children. These, Fanny,
Charles and Letitia, all promised to be bright and clever, and
though Charles, brightest of the three, was unfortunately
delicate and undersized, he was already developing social
accomplishments of no mean order. He could sing a comic
song, and recite beautifully. Altogether, "they were a most
genial, lovable family, with something more than a ghost of
gentility hovering in their company."

With them came to live Mrs. Mary Allen, a widowed sister
of Mrs. Dickens. She was loved by the children, who called
her Aunt Fanny, and with whose education she assisted. An
old woman acted as general servant, and for nurse the children
had "as smart a young girl then as you'd wish to see." Her
name was Mary Weller; she was, when she joined them, about
thirteen years of age, and she could tell the most hair-raising
bedtime stories.

Charles was at this time "a lively boy of a good, genial,
open disposition, and not quarrelsome, as most children are
at times." Though his frequent illnesses, which took the
form of attacks of giddiness, often accompanied by severe
pain, prevented him from taking part in the more active
games of childhood, he had no lack of entertainment, and
made plenty of friends. He adored the boy next door at
No. 1, George Stroughill, a strong, handsome, athletic
youngster rather older than himself, whose daring prowess
in outdoor sports and pastimes endeared him to the little
invalid. He fell in love with George's sister Lucy, "a peach-
faced creature in a blue sash."

The Dickens' and the Stroughill children were for ever
getting up little home-made concerts and play-actings
together, often with the help of James Lamert, son of Dr.
Lamert the surgeon at the Ordnance Hospital. James was
much older than Charles and very interested and experienced
in amateur theatricals. Then there were the young Tribes,

of the Mitre and Clarence Hotel, the best posting-house in the town, with whom visits and parties were exchanged.

Both indoors and out Charles enjoyed life to the full. He read prodigiously. The lessons taken at his mother's knee had inspired him with a love of reading which his inability to take part in outdoor games fostered and encouraged. By chance his father had become possessed of a choice selection of eighteenth century and other literature, which lay unregarded in an upstairs room until Charles happened upon it, and dragged the dusty old books into his bedroom. Among them he found "Robinson Crusoe," "Tom Jones," "Roderick Random," "Humphrey Clinker," "Peregrine Pickle," and "The Vicar of Wakefield;" "The Arabian Nights" and the "Tales of the Genii;" "Don Quixote" and "Gil Blas;" the *Tatler*, the *Spectator*, the *Idler*, and the *Citizen of the World* ; Mrs. Inchbald's "Collection of Farces"; and "certain Volumes of Voyages and Travels."

He read these books as only a small child of thoughtful mind and rich imagination can read. He "was a terrible boy to read." He used to sit on his bed of an evening, while the other children were at play in the fields, "with his book in his left hand, holding his wrist with his right hand, and constantly moving it up and down, and at the same time sucking his tongue," reading as though his very life depended upon it. It did. These books opened for him a veritable kingdom of imagination, in which he lived and moved and had his being. He was "Tom Jones (a child's Tom Jones, a harmless creature) for a week together;" "his own idea of Roderick Random for a month at a stretch;" he went about the house "armed with the centre-piece out of an old set of boot trees—the perfect realisation of Captain Somebody of the Royal British Navy, in danger of being beset by savages, and resolved to sell his life at a great price."

"A very queer small boy" indeed! Not only in his reading and his imaginings was he exceptional. The busy outdoor life of Chatham and Rochester provided for him a pageant of unfailing richness, which stored his eager mind with vivid memories that even his incredibly fertile life of authorship could not exhaust. Chatham and Rochester were in very truth "the birthplace of his fancy." They are writ large on the pages of "Sketches by Boz," the work with which he made his bow to the reading public; they recur over and over again throughout his books; they are writ equally large on "Edwin Drood," the story his death cut short.

He "peeped with interest and wonder" in all the streets and old corners, delighting in the "marine stores, hard-bake, apples, flat-fish, and oysters" he saw exposed for sale, and regarding with childish curiosity the "soldiers, sailors, Jews, chalk, shrimps, officers, and dockyard men," which Mr. Pickwick reported to be "the principal production of these towns." He wandered thoughtfully through the royal yards and saw the shipwrights, rope-makers, block-makers and anchor-smiths at work, and the gangs of uniformed convicts doing navvying jobs, "with great numbers on their backs as if they were street doors." He watched with breathless excitement "the gay bright regiments always going and coming, the continued paradings and firings, the succession of sham-sieges and sham-defences."

He sailed upon the Medway, and into the Thames even as far as Sheerness, with his father in the old Navy Pay yacht, the *Chatham*, an ancient tub nearly two hundred years old, but still a stout vessel with an occasional surprising turn of speed; and so he came to know the form and manner of ships of every kind, and the appearance of houses by the water's edge, and how the castle looked across the water, and how the sun set far up stream, where, beyond the misty distances, lay the great city of London. And he often saw the "hulks."

"And please, what's Hulks? . . ."

"Hulks are prison ships right 'cross the meshes (marshes). . . . People are put in the Hulks because they murder, and because they rob, and forge, and do all sorts of bad; and they always begin by asking questions."

He went for long walks with his father, and later by himself, through Strood and Brompton, to Chalk, Cobham, and Frindsbury; down to Snorridge (Snowledge) Bottom, and up to Gad's Hill, which is the high ground half-way between Gravesend and Rochester on the Dover Road. And here a very strange fancy possessed him.

"Presently the very queer small boy says: 'This is Gads Hill we are coming to, where Falstaff went out to rob those travellers, and ran away.'

"'You know something about Falstaff, eh?' said I.

"'All about him,' said the very queer small boy. 'I am old (I am nine), and I read all sorts of books. But *do* let us stop at the top of the hill, and look at the house there, if you please!'

"'You admire that house?' said I.

"'Bless you, sir,' said the very queer small boy, 'when I was not more than half as old as nine, it used to be a treat for me to be brought to look at it. And now I am nine, I come by myself to look at it. And ever since I can recollect, my father, seeing me so fond of it, has often said to me, *If you were to be very persevering and were to work hard, you might some day come to live in it.* Though that's impossible!' said the very queer small boy, drawing a low breath, and now staring at the house out of the window with all his might."

His father was very proud of him, and particularly of his little son's ability to sing and recite. Being a man fond of entertaining his friends and being entertained by them, he soon discovered that Charles, and his sister Fanny too, who could also sing, and was playing the pianoforte quite beautifully, were distinct assets on social occasions. So the boy was hoisted more and more frequently on to a chair or table at Ordnance Terrace, or down at the Mitre and Clarence, to recite to the company

"'Tis the voice of the sluggard,
     I hear him complain
   You have waked me too soon,
     I must slumber again. . . ."

which poem he could do "with great effect, and with *such* action and *such* attitudes." Then he and Fanny would sing together a sea-shanty. The applause of the company demanding yet more entertainment, Charles would give a comic song with his sister as accompanist, and might on occasion be induced to relate to the assembled guests a story of his own composition.

The play actings were encouraged. Led by James Lamert, the group of young actors made their own properties and stage fittings, and came quite naturally to altering and adapting the scenes and plays they performed, and so on to composing their own. Visits to the real theatre soon followed. Charles was probably not much more than six when he first visited the Theatre Royal at Rochester and saw *Richard III*. On that occasion the wicked king, backing across the stage from his dreaded adversary Richmond, actually bumped into the box in which the boy was seated, and greatly terrified him. When he was but eight he was taken up to London "to behold the splendour of Christmas Pantomime," and saw Joseph Grimaldi, greatest of all clowns.

Thus passed four very happy and lively years, the importance of which cannot be over-estimated. When, many years later, Charles Dickens described himself, in a letter to Washington Irving, the famous American author, as having been a "very small and not-over-particularly-taken-care-of boy," he could not have been thinking of the joyous days in Ordnance Terrace, but only of the experiences of later childhood which were to bite so deeply into his soul.

Without the period of neglect and hardship which he was to endure in London after leaving Chatham, the Charles Dickens that we know could never have come to be; but no less could he had his earlier years also been passed in sordid and poverty-stricken surroundings. Charles Dickens, an unusually precocious and observant child, alive to every subtle influence in his environment, was brought up until the age of eleven as a little *gentleman*, in a refined and cultured middle-class home. His abilities were recognized and encouraged. If anything, refinement and culture, or gentility, to use the nineteenth-century word, were rather too much emphasized, and the clever child was made too conscious of his cleverness. But the dominant notes of the life in Ordnance Terrace, Chatham, were easy-going prosperity and a wide variety of stimulating interests.

Thus it came to pass that when Mr. John Dickens' financial embarrassments became acute again, and finally overwhelmed him altogether, Charles knew not only the actual

WASHINGTON IRVING (1783–1859)

taste of poverty, but, what was far worse to one of his sensitive understanding, felt all the bitterness of its degradation, and realized to the full the awful narrowness and hopelessness of the life of the very poor. Had he known nothing but poverty all his life, he would have grown up more hardened to it. There can be little doubt that it was the fearful mental shock caused by a descent from comfortable prosperity into privation and neglect, rather than actual physical suffering, which hurt him, and which was instrumental in turning him into "the friend of the poor."

The decline of the Dickens' family was at first gradual. In 1821 Mr. John Dickens, though now receiving £350 a year, was forced once more to economize, and moved from Ordnance Terrace down the hill into a cottage in St. Mary's Place, called "The Brook." He lived there nearly two years, and during this time a new influence came into Charles's life. He was sent to school.

How much the boy knew or guessed of his father's "moment of difficulty" there is no means of telling, but he was now nine years old and possessed of an understanding far beyond his years. He probably knew about as much as there was to be known. In that case, it was doubly fortunate that at this juncture he was sent to school; for it would ease what must have been a strain to him while at the same time it steadied and developed his intelligence.

Chance seems to have played a large part in the selection of a school. Next door to "The Brook" stood a Baptist chapel. The pastor's son, William Giles, had recently opened a small school in Clover Lane (now Clover Street). Mrs. Dickens had chapel leanings. Neighbourliness and a community of interests no doubt made negotiations easy. Fanny and Charles were quickly numbered among "Giles's Cats," as the scholars were dubbed.

They were very lucky. Young Mr. Giles, who was twenty-three years of age, was not only a graduate of Oxford—a most unusual distinction at that time for one of his station in life—and a cultured scholar and capable teacher; he was also a very amiable and discerning man. Like his father, he was an ordained minister of religion, and he had a care for the moral and spiritual responsibilities of school-mastering as well as for the purely instructional.

His school possessed none of the characteristics of Dotheboys Hall or Salem House. Rather it resembled, except in the character of its proprietor, Dr. Strong's school at Canterbury to which David Copperfield was sent by his aunt Betsey Trotwood, and which was "very gravely and decorously ordered, and on a sound system; with an appeal, in everything, to the honour and good faith of the boys, and an avowed intention to rely on their possession of those qualities unless they proved themselves unworthy of it, which worked wonders."

Mr. Giles took at once to Charles. He recognized both his ability and his unusualness, and taught him very carefully. The two became companions and friends, spending their evenings together in informal lessons, when no doubt all the more was learnt because so much the less was taught. The schoolmaster was well read, and a practised elocutionist. He was a man too who liked all things done decently and in order, yet not gloomily; his scholars wore quiet, dark clothes, but natty little white beaver hats.

His must have been both an inspiring and a sobering influence upon Charles. The "sensitive, thoughtful, feeble-bodied little boy, with an amount of experience as well as fancy unusual in such a child, with a dangerous kind of wandering intelligence," could hardly have fallen into better hands. At the same time, the enforced economy at home had at least this beneficial effect, that the orgy of juvenile entertainment had to be given up for simpler and healthier pastimes. The play-actings certainly went on, and Charles wrote a whole tragedy, *Misnar, the Sultan of India,* in the autumn of 1821, copying rather closely, as might be expected from a boy of nine, a favourite story from his reading. He continued also to sing and recite, and to be admired for doing so; but these activities were very considerably curtailed, while outdoor sports and pastimes, rowing on the Medway, games in the hayfields, sham fights on Tom-all-alone's, with snowballing and skating in winter, took a much more prominent part.

Charles was very popular with his schoolfellows as well as with his schoolmaster. He was good-looking, full of fun and mischief, and in games as well as work of a creative and original turn of mind. He and his friends talked among themselves a nonsensical patter, or "lingo," pretending to passers-by to be foreigners. They played romantic and imaginative games based on the stories and travel books Charles had read. They had parties, and dancing. Altogether, the eighteen months at "The Brook" were for him both jolly and happy, and life was distinctly saner than in the somewhat hectic days at Ordnance Terrace.

In December 1821 occurred an event which indirectly was later to have an important bearing upon his fortunes. Aunt Fanny was married to Dr. Lamert, and James Lamert became a cousin by marriage as well as a friend. Then, about twelve months later, Mr. John Dickens was again recalled to London; and the crash came.

The move appears to have been a hurried one. It certainly marked a crisis in Mr. Dickens' affairs. He had been some seven years in Chatham; and shopkeepers were easy-going and gave long credit in those days to anyone of established position and assured income. But they expected to be paid, nevertheless, and doubtless the news of his impending departure caused them to become insistent upon the settlement of their accounts.

There was a sale of goods and furniture at "The Brook." Mary Weller's sweetheart, a young shipwright, bought the rush-seated parlour chairs, two of which may still be seen in the Eastgate House Museum at Rochester. Mary herself had to be left behind, though there were babies enough to be looked after, and the sole domestic taken with the family was the "orfling" of "David Copperfield," a young waif from the Chatham Workhouse.

In London, Mr. Dickens could do no more than rent one of a row of cottages in Bayham Street, Camden Town. Camden Town was at that time almost a country suburb of London; the district was still moderately pleasant, but on the downgrade. Into it was flowing an artisan and labouring population, which would later turn it into a slum area. But in

1823 it was emphatically not a slum; it was a mixed grill of a place in which quiet, tree-shaded avenues were to be found cheek by jowl with rows of jerry-built cottages, and where rather well-to-do poverty was rubbing shoulders with faded and shabby gentility. To this latter state had Mr. Dickens descended; he had at 16 Bayham Street a washerwoman as next door neighbour, and a Bow-Street officer across the way. There were almshouses at the top of the street, and an area of waste land given over to dust-heaps, docks and stinging nettles.

Charles did not move with the family. At the last moment it was suggested that he should remain for a while in Chatham, probably to finish his term at school. There is a passage in "David Copperfield" describing the departure of the Micawber family from London which is no doubt an almost literal description of what happened on this occasion.

> "I think, as Mrs. Micawber sat at the back of the coach, with the children, and I stood in the road looking wistfully at them, a mist cleared from her eyes, and she saw what a little creature I really was. I think so, because she beckoned me to climb up, with quite a new and motherly expression in her face, and put her arm round my neck, and gave me just such a kiss as she might have given to her own boy. I had barely time to get down again before the coach started, and I could hardly see the family for the handkerchiefs they waved. It was gone in a minute. The Orfling and I stood looking vacantly at each other in the middle of the road, and then shook hands and said good-bye."

Though Charles was soon afterwards summoned to rejoin his people, this parting was in a very real sense a final one. He lived with his parents again after this, and shared some of their most trying experiences, but mentally and spiritually he was to be from that moment completely alone. If indeed the Micawber incident quoted above carry more than an external resemblance to truth, then this isolation had been growing upon him during the last part of his stay in Chatham. His mother and father, obsessed with material troubles, had been failing for some time to realize their responsibilities towards their delicate and exceptionally gifted son, and he with his keen perception had been aware of the injustice of their neglect, and perhaps had realized a little more than vaguely how this neglect would stand in the way of and frustrate his burning ambition to grow up "a learned and distinguished man."

When, about the end of 1822 or the beginning of 1823, he left Chatham for London, it was as though the fates had conspired to prepare for him as abrupt and terrible a shock as possible. The journey was depressing.

". . . have I ever lost the smell of the damp straw in which I was packed—like game—and forwarded, carriage paid, to the Cross Keys, Wood Street, Cheapside, London? There was no other outside passenger, and I consumed my sandwiches in solitude and dreariness, and it rained hard all the way, and I thought life sloppier than I had expected to find it."

A baby sister had died, and he was called home to attend the funeral. But that was not all.

". . . there was Debt at home as well as Death, and we had a sale there. My own little bed was so superciliously looked upon by a power unknown to me, hazily called "The Trade," that a brass coal-scuttle, a roasting-jack, and a bird-cage, were obliged to be put into it to make a Lot of it, and then it went for a song—so I heard mentioned, and I wondered what song—and thought what a dismal song it must have been to sing."

Though these are quotations from works of fiction written by Charles Dickens, they almost certainly describe the exact state of affairs he found in Bayham Street when he arrived there. "No man's imagination," he wrote in later life, "can over-step the reality," and he himself rarely attempted to do so. His real experiences had been so varied and so poignant that there was no need for him to try; he could not improve upon an exact relation of them. Here lies one of the main secrets, if not, indeed, the fundamental secret, of his amazing success and still more amazing popularity as a writer. He wrote his books straight out of his own life; they are all, in substance, and often line for line and word for word, fragments of his autobiography.

He found in Bayham Street what was potentially even worse than debt and death; he found his parents in a state of paralysed confusion. In a desperate endeavour to placate his creditors, Mr. Dickens had signed away to them most of his income. That done, matters were simply being allowed to drift, though the fear of want, if not actual want, was staring the family in the face. There were now five children, not counting the little one who had just died, of whom the eldest, Fanny, was but slightly over twelve. But the disastrous march of events seemed to have bereft Mr. Dickens of all initiative or sense of responsibility towards his family. He did not even seem to know what to do with Charles when the latter returned from school.

"So I degenerated into cleaning his boots of a morning, and my own, and making myself useful in the work of the little house; and looking after my younger brothers and sisters . . . and going on such poor errands as arose out of our poor way of living."

Those errands, Charles discovered, were soon to include frequent visits to the pawnbroker's. The description of these visits makes a richly humorous passage in "David Copperfield," but they must have been exquisitely humiliating to the sensitive and gentlemanly little boy, so suddenly and cruelly torn from an ordered life full of variety and beauty, and thrust fathoms deep into one of strain, want and neglect.

Small wonder that he "seemed to fall into a solitary condition apart from all other boys of his own age." He was of another race from the boys he met in Camden Town. The only kind of boys he knew had been left behind in Chatham. He could as yet see nothing hopeful in this new and awful way of life. "As I thought," he said long after to Forster, "in the little back-garret in Bayham Street, of all I had lost in losing Chatham, what would I have given, if I had anything to give, to have been sent back to any other school, to have been taught something anywhere!"

It was the utterly purposeless and wasteful inactivity of his life, and the calamitous, and apparently callous, neglect of his abilities, that galled him worst. No doubt he performed willingly enough the household tasks that fell to his share, and was even glad of the occupation that they gave him, but he felt bitterly, and continued so to feel throughout his life, the fact that he could have been "so easily thrown away at such an age. A child of excellent abilities, and with strong powers of observation, quick, eager, delicate, and soon hurt bodily or mentally. . . ."

It has been suggested that Charles Dickens in later life exaggerated his sufferings during this period and the even more tragic one which was to follow. It has been said that he worked himself up to a fury of self-pity over them. Such suggestions show utter ignorance of the mind of a child.

Dickens was eleven years of age when the Bayham Street catastrophe fell upon him. He stood upon the threshold of adolescence, with a mind developed beyond his years. He was not only precocious but keenly ambitious. More than most boys he dreamed of and believed in the glorious future that lay before him. Like all boys of his age he was incapable of thinking of anyone but himself; and the keener the intelligence, and the more sensitive the understanding, the more completely egotistical is the young adolescent.

Take away suddenly, then, from an extraordinarily intelligent and sensitive small boy all that has made his life worth living for him, dash from him all his prospects, so that he sees his every ambition crumble and collapse, and offer him no ray of hope for the future—and you have the measure of young Charles Dickens' tragedy. "A lost child," wrote Mr. G. K. Chesterton when dealing with this period of Dickens' life, "can suffer like a lost soul." In no words could the essence of this tragedy be more truly expressed.

An incident, happy in itself, seemed to reveal to the boy the ultimate depths of his miserable state. His elder sister, Fanny, was in April 1823 elected a pupil at the Royal Academy of Music. Even Fanny, his "beloved Fanny," his comrade and intimate from his earliest days, was to have her chance. She would go away and be educated and make a career and be famous; but he was left. Someone had been interested enough to help Fanny, but nobody in the whole wide world cared what happened to him. He had nothing to hope for.

But his was too strong and resilient a mind to sink under misfortune, however grievous. He began to find compensations. He sought happiness first in dreamy meditation, brooding for hours together on the waste land near Bayham Street, whence he could see the great dome of St. Paul's rising above the mist and smoke of London. But, though egotistical, he was not introspective; his mind craved activity. Thinking about London soon inspired in him a desire to see it, and he began to get people to take him into the city. Amid its crowded streets and busy scenes he recommenced his peeping "with interest and wonder," loving especially the area in and around the Strand and Covent Garden, and, strangely enough, by what Forster has called "a profound attraction of repulsion," the squalid but intensely lively district of the Seven Dials. "Great Heaven!" he used to exclaim later, "what wild visions of prodigies of wickedness, want, and beggary, arose in my mind out of that place!" The visions were to be faithfully recorded in various of the "Sketches by Boz," and in scores of passages in other works.

James Lamert proved himself at this juncture a real friend; later he was to show his interest in Charles in a way less appreciated by the latter, though ultimately far more valuable. Having been through Sandhurst, and while waiting for a commission, he came to live in Bayham Street with the Dickenses, and in his spare time constructed and decorated a toy theatre, on which the two played puppet shows, greatly to the amusement of the younger children, and which was a great joy to the lonely little boy.

Charles was also invited to pay visits to his godfather, Christopher Huffam, who lived in Limehouse, and to his uncle, Thomas Barrow, eldest brother to his mother, who was at the time nursing a broken leg in Soho. These visits were beneficial to the boy in several distinct ways. In his godfather's house, which was a comfortably prosperous one, foregathered the boatbuilders, riggers, and master-mariners of the district. To them Charles began to sing the comic

THE DEMOLITION OF OLD LONDON BRIDGE

*After the Engraving by E. W. Cooke, 1832*

songs learned in happier days, and from them to receive adulation which must have helped considerably to restore his self-esteem. They thought him a "progidy." In Limehouse, too, he first became acquainted with the Thames riverside he was afterwards to know so intimately. At Mr. Barrow's he was lent exciting books to read; while from thence he explored Soho, then really a queer, mysterious, foreign place, full of interesting, odd, comic, tragi-comic and tragic figures.

Stimulated by these varied experiences, he began in secret to commence author. He wrote a description of the eccentric barber who shaved his uncle, and other descriptions of other people. He was very proud of his compositions, but was too shy to show them to any one. Then, just as the horizon seemed to be lightening on every hand, fate dealt him another cruel blow. He fell seriously ill; and recovered to find the family in the throes of another crisis, and one graver than any which had preceded it.

His father's resources were practically exhausted, yet his creditors were still unappeased. Something had got to be done. Mr. Dickens was apparently incapable of doing it. So Mrs. Dickens, with the desperate but all too often unhappily futile courage a wife and mother will display in an extremity, decided to take matters into her own hands, and to save the family from ruin. She decided to open a school and to make a fortune. Charles, with the pitiful trustfulness of childhood, believed in her, at least to the extent of hoping that "perhaps even I might go to school myself."

Mrs. Dickens' determination was heroic; her execution of her project too feeble for words. Actually, she never got properly as far as execution. The venture proved a complete fiasco; its sole material result was a move into a much more expensive house.

The episode affords an illuminating insight into the hopelessly unbusinesslike attitude of Charles's parents towards financial affairs. At a moment when there was practically no money in the house, nor any obvious likelihood of obtaining any, and while Mr. Dickens was in imminent peril of being arrested for debt, they launched out upon a scheme involving as a start £50 a year in house rent, on the ridiculously improbable chance that an inexperienced woman, hampered by a family of small children, would make a resounding success of a private school. True, anyone could open a school in those days; all that was necessary was a brass plate and discreet advertisement; but fees were small and competition keen. Mrs. Dickens would have required some score of certain pupils to have justified the rent alone; and even the East Indian connection of Mr. Christopher Huffam, upon which she was relying for a supply of children from over the seas, could hardly have guaranteed that. As it was, Mr. Huffam went bankrupt himself, and thus even that faint hope was extinguished.

The story is told, exactly as it happened down to the veriest details, in Chapter XI of "David Copperfield." Most of this chapter was written by Charles Dickens as autobiography some months before the book was thought of, and the autobiographical material was incorporated bodily in the story, with only the change of names and of a few words here and there.

"The centre of the street door was perfectly covered with a great brass-plate, on which was engraved 'Mrs. Micawber's Boarding Establishment for Young Ladies:' but I never found that any young lady had ever been to school there; or that any young lady ever came, or proposed to come; or that the least preparation was ever made to receive any young lady. The only visitors I ever heard or saw of, were creditors. *They* used to come at all hours, and some of them were quite ferocious."

The only person who appears to have done anything really strenuous on behalf of the proposed school at 4 Gower Street North, was Charles himself, who "left, at a great many doors, a great many circulars calling attention to the merits of the establishment."

The Gower Street house was taken at Michaelmas, 1823. By February of the next year the inevitable had happened. John Dickens was arrested and carried off, first to a sponging house, and then across the Thames to the Marshalsea prison; and the Dickens family was left destitute.

The father went off to prison declaring wildly that the sun was set upon him for ever; and no doubt, like Mr. Micawber, was cheerfully playing skittles by noon. The mother, aided by her eldest son, aged just twelve, was left behind to grapple with the problem of keeping the home going and the children from starvation. There was only one way.

"'I have parted with the plate myself,' said Mrs. Micawber. 'Six tea, two salt, and a pair of sugars, I have at different times borrowed money on, in secret, with my own hands. . . . There are still a few trifles that we could part with. . . .'

"I began to dispose of the more portable articles of property that very evening; and went out on a similar expedition almost every morning. . . .

"Mr. Micawber had a few books on a little chiffonier, which he called the library; and those went first. . . ."

They were the very books which Charles had dragged out of the lumber room at Ordnance Terrace, and upon which his youthful fancy had feasted in those happy days. That they went first is not in itself surprising; books usually do under such circumstances, but the fact that Charles Dickens noted and recorded it is evidence that their early disappearance hurt him, and convinced him yet more clearly that his personal interests were more than ever forgotten.

"At the pawnbroker's shop, too, I began to be very well known. The principal gentleman who officiated behind the counter, took a great deal of notice of me; and often got me, I recollect, to decline a Latin noun or adjective, or to conjugate a Latin verb in his ear, while he transacted my business."

Even a pawnbroker's clerk could recognize the boy's unusualness. Only his parents would not.

But daily sale of the "more portable articles of property" in a house could not continue indefinitely. The time came when there was nothing more that Charles could carry away, and then:

"I don't know how the household furniture came to be sold for the family benefit, or who sold it, except that *I* did not. Sold it was, however, and carried away in a van; except the bed, a few chairs, and the kitchen table. With

these possessions we encamped, as it were, in the two
parlours of the emptied house in Windsor Terrace: Mrs.
Micawber, the children, the Orfling, and myself; and lived
in those rooms night and day. I have no idea for how long,
though it seems to me for a long time."

No doubt it did; to a child a day can be an eternity.
Actually, it was at most a few weeks. Mrs. Dickens soon
gave up the hopeless struggle; she relinquished the tenancy
of the Gower Street house on Lady Day, 1824, and moved
with her family to join her husband in the Marshalsea.

Charles did not accompany them. Shortly before the
move a wage-earning job had been offered to him, and his
parents had "accepted very willingly."

James Lamert, sick of waiting for a commission that never
came had gone into business as general manager for his
cousin and brother-in-law, George Lamert, who had purchased
a blacking manufactory at 30 Hungerford-stairs, Strand.
Not forgetful of his little playmate, James, "seeing how I
was employed from day to day, and knowing what our
domestic circumstances then were, proposed that I should
go into the blacking warehouse, to be as useful as I could, at
a salary, I think, of six shillings a week."

It was a kindly and generous offer. It could even be
called a remarkably good opportunity for any ordinary boy
situated as Charles then was. The wages were, for a boy
going to his first post, substantial; the hours, judged by the
standards of the 1820's, not over long. The warehouse
closed at 8 p.m., and the employees had an hour off for dinner
and half an hour for tea. This, in an age which tolerated
the employment of babies of five in factories, and allowed
children of eight to work fourteen and sixteen hours a day in
coal mines, could be considered most reasonable. Moreover,
James Lamert promised to teach Charles during the dinner-
hour; and, as the boy was a relative, if only by marriage, of
both proprietor and general manager, there was the possibility,
however remote, of his succeeding eventually to the business.

In order to appreciate the true significance of this episode
in Charles Dickens' life, it is necessary always to bear in
mind the character of the boy who went through it, the life

he had been used to beforehand, and, particularly, the high value he had come, quite rightly, to set upon himself. To understand his deep and lifelong bitterness about it, one has to think almost exclusively in terms of mental, not physical, suffering. While it is no doubt unaffectedly true that during his time in the blacking warehouse—which, be it remembered, did not last more than a very few months—Charles Dickens "worked from morning until night, with common men and boys, a shabby child, (and) lounged about the streets, insufficiently and unsatisfactorily fed," it is not so true that " but for the mercy of God, I might easily have been, for any care that was taken of me, a little robber or a little vagabond." During the time his mother was still in Gower Street he was living with her, and so no worse off than the other children as regards food. When she went into the Marshalsea, he was lodged with a Mrs. Roylance, in Little College Street, Camden Town, where he did not have to pay for his lodgings, and was found in clothes.

He had his "own exclusive breakfast, of a penny cottage loaf and a pennyworth of milk, (and) another small loaf, and a quarter of a pound of cheese. . . . to make my supper on when I came back at night." This, as he said, "made a hole in the six or seven shillings" he was paid, but it was good wholesome food, and it still left him three to four shillings with which to buy dinners and teas. It was not a luxurious nor even a satisfactory standard of living for a growing boy who was still rather delicate, but it was very far from starvation, and considerably above serious malnutrition. He could have his plate of beef and his glass of beer every now and then. He had pennies enough to buy Hunt's roasted corn, a popular coffee substitute, for Sundays, and to carry home his weekly magazine, the *Terrific Register*, or the *Portfolio of Entertaining and Instructive Varieties in History, Science, Literature, the Fine Arts, Etc. Price Twopence.* He could even, on one famous occasion, tip a waiter—though he wished the man hadn't taken it!

His physical sufferings were not grave; his mental sufferings undoubtedly were. He "held some station" at the blacking warehouse. James Lamert "did what a man so occupied, and dealing with a thing so anomalous, could, to treat me as one upon a different footing from the rest," though the dinner-hour lessons soon ceased. The boy did his work well, and "soon became at least as expeditious and as skilful as either of the other boys," but, "My conduct and manners were different enough from theirs to place a space between us. They and the men generally spoke of me as 'the little gentle-man.'"

That was the trouble. He was alone, and alone in the most awful of lonelinesses, the loneliness of despair. He has described his feelings in words so poignant that no commentary can better them.

> "No words can express the secret agony of my soul as I sunk into this companionship; compared these henceforth every-day associates with those of my happier child-hood . . . and felt my hopes of growing up a learned and distinguished man crushed in my bosom. The deep remembrance of the sense I had, of being utterly without hope now; of the shame I felt in my position; of the misery it was to my young heart to believe that day by day what I had learned, and thought, and delighted in, and raised my fancy and my emulation up by, would pass away from me, little by little, never to be brought back any more; cannot be written."

When these words were written as autobiography, before being incorporated in "David Copperfield," Dickens added also, "My whole nature was so penetrated with the grief and humiliation of such considerations, that even now, famous and caressed and happy, I often forget in my dreams that I have a dear wife and children; even that I am a man; and wander desolately back to that time of my life."

It needs only to add that he received "no advice, no counsel, no encouragement, no consolation, no support, from any one that I can call to mind," and that "My rescue from this kind of existence I considered quite hopeless, and abandoned, as such, altogether," to understand why he "never for one hour was reconciled to it, or was otherwise than miserably unhappy."

The memory of his experiences haunted him all the more dreadfully in after life because, from the moment of his escape from the blacking warehouse to the moment of his death, he hugged his secret to himself, hiding it from even his nearest and dearest. A chance encounter in 1847 led to a confession to Forster and to his writing down for his own comfort an account of it; this in its turn led to "David Copperfield," in which he told the story to all the world in the guise of fiction; but his wife and children never knew the truth until the publication of Forster's "Life" in 1872.

The account in "David Copperfield" is, with slight variations of detail, a full and accurate description of his life in 1823 and 1824. He did not wash empty wine bottles; his work actually was ". . . to cover the pots of paste-blacking; first with a piece of oil-paper, and then with a piece of blue-paper; to tie them round with a string; and then to clip the paper close and neat, all round, until it looked as smart as a pot of ointment from an apothecary's shop. When a certain number of grosses of pots had attained this pitch of perfection, I was to paste on each a printed label; and then go on again with more pots."

His boy companions, called in "David Copperfield" Mick Walker and Mealy Potatoes, were in real life Bob Fagin and Poll (Paul) Green. Bob Fagin's name was borrowed later for one of his most famous characters; and it was Poll Green's little sister who "did Imps in the Pantomimes." Gregory the foreman, and Tipp the carman, were actually called Thomas and Harry.

During the Marshalsea period he called every Sunday at nine o'clock at the Royal Academy of Music for Fanny, and the two spent the day with their family in the prison. The Dickenses were living there quite comfortably, more so, in fact, than since they had come to London; and no doubt it was the contrast between the cosy sociableness of the family's prison lodgings and his own bleak and lonely quarters in Mrs. Roylance's child farm in Camden Town which led him to protest to his father against existing arrangements.

The latter was quite surprised that everything was not all as it should be; the point had not struck him before. But he saw it, and Charles was immediately moved to quarters near the prison. An attic was rented for him in Lant Street, in the Borough. It had "a pleasant prospect of a timber yard," and he "thought it was a Paradise." From that time he could breakfast and sup with his family; and he could, when he arrived at the gates too early in the morning, thrill the "orfling," who was also lodged outside, with "quite astonishing fictions about the wharves and the Tower."

He had not been in Lant Street very long before his father was released from prison. A relative died, and left a considerable legacy, some hundreds of pounds, to Mr. John Dickens. The "expectations" could not have matured at a more opportune moment; enough money was at once paid into court to enable the debtor to go free. Mr. Dickens was released on May 28, 1824, after having been in the Marshalsea just over three months.

He had in that short time become popular and respected among the shabby population of the prison. He had been elected Chairman of the committee of debtors which had some say in the internal arrangements. He was, after all, a Government servant, and still drawing his £350 a year; quite a major star in the dingy constellation of the Marshalsea. He was also a gentleman of culture and considerable eloquence, with a leaning towards the stage. To celebrate his release he drew up a petition, the whole story of which is deliciously, and accurately, told in "David Copperfield"—with one significant alteration. Mr. Micawber "composed a petition to the House of Commons, praying for an alteration in the law of imprisonment for debt." Mr. John Dickens drew up a petition "praying, not for the abolition of imprisonment for debt . . . but for the less dignified but more accessible boon of a bounty to the prisoners to drink his majesty's health on his majesty's forthcoming birthday."

Charles got special leave of absence from his work to attend the signing of the petition, and established himself in a corner "near the petition." From thence he observed every detail, even to his father's "listening with a little of an author's vanity."

Whatever was comical in this scene, and whatever was pathetic, I sincerely believe I perceived in my corner . . . quite as well as I should perceive it now. I made out my own little character and story for every man who put his name to the sheet of paper. I might be able to do that now, more truly: not more earnestly, nor with a closer interest. Their different peculiarities of dress, of face, of gait, of manner, were written indelibly upon my memory. I would rather have seen it than the best play ever played.

Truly, from earliest days, the "divine reporter!"

The family, after a brief stay in lodgings with Mrs. Roylance, moved into 29 (now 13) Johnson Street, Somers Town. This house was in a poorer though more countrified quarter than Bayham Street. Evidently some influence was restraining Mr. Dickens from plunging immediately into fresh extravagance. Perhaps it was the same influence, one suspects that of Mrs. Dickens, which kept Charles on at the blacking warehouse; for, to the boy's pained surprise, he "never . . . heard a word of being taken away, or of being otherwise than quite provided for."

This must have plunged him into the deepest depths of despair. The future was indeed without hope, save from his own efforts, if, now that his father was clear of his embarrassments and even possessed of a little capital, no one so much as thought of releasing *him* from his degradation, or considered the continuance of the education of so obviously brilliant a boy. It is hardly fanciful to date from this moment the birth of that almost savage determination to succeed by his own endeavours which was evidenced in the superhuman labours of a few years later.

But release was to come, and quite soon. Quite unexpectedly, too, unless one makes allowance for the temperament of the elder Dickens. Suddenly, that worthy quarrelled violently with Mr. James Lamert. The quarrel was about Charles. It was probably about the boy's having to work exposed to public view. The story is too good not to be true.

The blacking manufactory had been moved from the

"crazy old house with a wharf of its own" at Hungerford-stairs to larger and better premises in Chandos Street, Covent Garden. Here, for the sake of the light, the boys used to work by a window looking on to Bedford Street, and the dexterity of Bob Fagin and Charles Dickens in particular caused people to stop on the pavement to watch them. "Sometimes there would be quite a little crowd there." One day Mr. Dickens came to the warehouse and observed this; and Charles saw him, and "wondered how he could bear it."

Evidently he could not. Mr. Dickens was wonderfully slow to notice things, but when he did he acted promptly, even rashly. The boy might have gone on working all his days in the blacking warehouse; but he could not be allowed to work under the gaze of the vulgar mob. As became a man who always avoided personal contact with trouble, Mr. Dickens went home and composed a letter to Mr. James Lamert, in which he told him without reticence, and no doubt with considerable eloquence, what he thought of him. With exquisite forethought, he made Charles the bearer of the letter.

At the warehouse there was a most distressing scene. James Lamert, on reading the letter, said outright, in front of Charles, exactly what he thought of Mr. Dickens, and told the boy, in kindly but unmistakable words, that he could not possibly keep him there any longer. Charles broke down; the sudden snapping of the strain and Mr. Lamert's language about his father were too much for him. He cried a good deal, was comforted by old Thomas the foreman, who told him it was no doubt all for the best, and then, "with a relief so strange that it was like oppression . . . went home."

Mrs. Dickens was furious. She went straight down to the warehouse next day, patched up the quarrel—who knows at what cost to her pride?—and returned with a glowing report of the boy's character and work, and a request that he should resume the day after.

Twenty-three years later her son was to write, "I never afterwards forgot, I never shall forget, I never can forget, that my mother was warm for my being sent back."

THOS OLLEYS
[MILK]

TOLLEY COW...

HUNGERFORD MARKET, WITH THE RIVER AND HUNGERFORD STAIRS

*After an old Engraving*

He was not sent back.    Mr. Dickens had suddenly become proud of his son again.    Charles was to go to school.

Modern psychologists have invented the term "arrested development."    It signifies a state in which, owing to some great shock in youth, or to prolonged error in nurture and education, the growth of the mind is stopped short before maturity, though the body continues to develop normally. The phrase exactly fits Charles Dickens.    Like Peter Pan, he never grew up.    That he did not do so was doubtless due to the shock of the awful experiences of 1823 and 1824, and more particularly those of the blacking warehouse.

His mind remained brilliantly adolescent, in the first flush of its glowing youth, to the end of his life.    He retained throughout every characteristic of adolescence; extraordinarily keen powers of observation; the vivid "picture" memory of childhood; a childish gusto in all he did; the adolescent habit of setting himself impossible tasks.    He remained egotistical, overmastering, resentful of interference, rash, aggressive, tempestuous.    All of his life he loved passionately the centre of the stage, the glitter of the limelight, the sound of applause ringing in his ears.    He never lost the tender affection of childhood, nor its trustfulness, nor its feeling of inferiority and dependence; behind all the swagger of his crashing success, he longed for home, and love, and some one to comfort him. He never forgot how to laugh—nor how to cry.    All of which is typical of adolescence.

Had he grown up mentally he might still have been a great writer; he would more probably have been a great social reformer.    But he could never have written "Pickwick," or "Bleak House," or "Great Expectations," to choose at random books from his early, middle, and later life.    He would never have remembered so well; he would never have taken that childish delight in exact description of detail which has given us that most marvellous composite picture of lower-middle class and rather-below-lower-middle class England in the early nineteenth century which is revealed in his books.

It is commonly said that Dickens exaggerates, that his characters are too funny, or too quaint, or too tragic or monstrous or absurd to be true.    Childhood always does exaggerate; everything appears to childhood rather bigger or funnier or sadder than it does to adults. But that does not mean that the picture is not true. The adult may see it in better proportion, but the grown-up eye misses all sorts of eccentricities and oddities of detail that the childish eye snaps up at once, and which are essentially part of the picture; often the most interesting part.

Therein lies the charm of Dickens; to him was given to see, and to relate, all the interesting parts of a life passed amid most varied surroundings during the last years of an epoch, when eccentricity and oddity and the grotesque could still play prominent parts in human affairs, before the social services and big business combined to sweep them out of existence.

Charles Dickens went on observing omniverously all his life, and he forgot nothing that he observed; but most of what is vital and enduring in his work, most of what still endears him to countless readers, so that he remains to this day a better seller than any modern author, has its roots in his personal experiences during childhood and youth, in Chatham and Rochester and London. To select but at random an instance here and there in proof: the autobiographical portions of "David Copperfield" are the simplest told yet the most unforgettable. Mr. Wilkins Micawber towers high above all other characters, save only Mrs. Micawber. Mrs. Roylance became Mrs. Pipchin of "Dombey and Son." The Marshalsea pictures in "Little Dorrit" rival the King's Bench pictures in "David Copperfield." In Lant Street Charles lodged with Mr. and Mrs. Garland, and met Bob Sawyer. Mr. Tony Weller drove the "Commodore" coach from Chatham to London, and his immortal son Sam, one strongly suspects, in spite of all the alleged living originals, had more than a resemblance to one Mary Weller, a child's nurse, a jolly girl who could tell the most thrilling bedtime stories. . . .

## CHAPTER II

*"Surely there are some ways in which I might begin life with hardly any outlay, and yet begin with a good hope of getting on by resolution and exertion?"*—DAVID COPPERFIELD.

CHARLES went back to school, probably in June 1824, at a place called the Wellington House Academy, which stood at the corner of Granby Street and Hampstead Road. It was not a good school, though it had achieved an excellent reputation. The proprietor, a Welshman called Jones, was an ignoramus whose main occupations seem to have been ruling ciphering books and thrashing small boys; he was cunning enough, however, to use his ruler and cane chiefly on his boarders, and to spare the day-boys, of whom Charles was one. Perhaps this explained in part the reputation of the school; boys rarely see more than one side of a question, and day-boys and boarders are traditional foes. But Charles, though by reason of his day-boyishness more or less immune from corporal punishment, saw through his headmaster, and did not spare him when he painted his picture as Mr. Creakle of Salem House.

Among the chief features of the school were white mice and an assistant master with gentlemanly manners, whom the boys believed knew everything. The schoolroom was apparently a Zoo in miniature, the pupils keeping all sorts of live pets, bees, birds, mice, and puppies in desks, lockers, hatboxes and the covers of Latin dictionaries. White mice were easily first favourites; and "the boys trained the mice much better than the master trained the boys." The gentlemanly usher, who incidentally played the flute, was always, on account of his manners, detailed to call at parents' houses to enquire after sick pupils. Mr. Jones may have been ignorant, but he was evidently no fool; one begins to see why his school was well thought of. Pets for the boys and compliments for the parents; with the stick reserved for boarders. It was an ideal arrangement—from Mr. Jones's point of view.

Charles, at any rate, enjoyed himself there hugely. Even to be at school again was very heaven. Just at first he felt a little nervous at coming once more into the companionship of boys of his own standing, but that soon wore off, and he became as merry and jolly as anyone there. His experiences during the dismal eighteen months which intervened between Mr. Giles's school at Chatham and Mr. Jones's in Mornington Place, Hampstead, had impaired neither his boyish health nor his temper, and in the relief from the strain of the blacking warehouse and of straitened home circumstances, his pent-up animal spirits broke forth in joyous activity and an increased self-confidence. Handsome and well-proportioned, though rather small for his age, he held his head higher than most boys do, and was somewhat more full of fun; his dress was rather smarter, and he wore clothes which made him look older than he actually was. He was, after all, more of a man than the others, for they had only known the schoolroom, while he had known life. More, had he not just escaped from life?

He quickly became, if not exactly a leader, at least a leading light among his schoolfellows. He did not distinguish himself at lessons, unless indeed the account he wrote later in *Household Words* of *Our School* is more accurate than the reminiscences of his schoolfellows. But probably no one could be distinguished in school-work at Mr. Jones's; there was too much thrashing and too many white mice, and it does not matter in the least whether Charles Dickens ever won a prize there or no. If he did it was probably because the proprietor made a point of awarding to every day-boy at least one prize during his school career.

What Charles did do was to be cheerfully in evidence in all fun and harmless pranks; to be strong in talking "lingo" or "gibberish," as he had been at Chatham; to edit—with a partner called Bowden—an "almost weekly" newspaper, the single copy of which was circulated to subscribers of marbles, slate pencils, toffee, and the like; and to be very prominent in amateur theatricals. He also attempted to learn the violin, no doubt in emulation of his sister Fanny, but making no progress, wisely gave it up.

It is quite clear that, dunce and brute though Mr. Jones himself may have been, some strong cultural influence was playing upon his school throughout the time Charles Dickens was a pupil there. It was almost certainly that of Mr. Taylor, the gentlemanly usher who knew everything, who was "writing master, mathematical master, English master," as well as general secretary and factotum for the establishment. The boys wrote, recited, and performed tales and plays, while some of the older pupils formed themselves into a literary society or club for the reading and study of current fiction. All this can hardly have come to pass without considerable encouragement from someone on the staff. What Dickens owed to Mr. Taylor cannot be known, but when this gentleman left Mr. Jones to set up a school of his own, a younger brother was sent there in preference to the Hampstead Road establishment; a fact which speaks for itself.

One of Dickens' schoolfellows, Dr. Henry Danson, says that while at school Dickens began writing small tales, which were circulated among members of the literary club. He certainly had a great deal to do with the play production, which was quite out of the ordinary for such a school. The boys made their own stage and "very gorgeous scenery," the the latter no doubt thanks to young Beverley, then a pupil there, who was later to achieve fame as a scene painter. They produced pieces which had been popular on the professional stage, no mean feat for any group of amateur players, and quite an extraordinary one for boys of fourteen and fifteen in days long before dramatics became a feature of school life. One of these pieces, *The Miller and his Men*, which fascinated Dickens for many years, was played with a mill so constructed as to fall to pieces when fireworks were let off in it during the final scene. The dénouement was so realistically achieved that on one occasion the police came rushing to the house to interfere.

Charles remained at this school about two and a half years, and was then considered fit to make a second start in life. He left either at Christmas 1826 or Easter 1827, that is, when he was just under or just over fifteen years of age.

His father was not in a position to help him financially. Mr. Dickens had retired, or had been retired, a year previously from Somerset House with a small pension, upon which, astonishingly enough, he appears for the moment to have been making ends meet. But only just, of course; there was no question of affording the premium necessary to give Charles a decent start in a respectable profession. So the boy was given the respectable profession without the decent start; he was put into a lawyer's office, without articles. In plain language, he began life this time as a dignified office boy, with scarcely a hope of rising in his profession above the rank of salaried clerk.

After a very short time with Mr. Molloy, solicitor, of Symond's Inn, he was placed in May 1827 with the firm of Ellis and Blackmore, solicitors, of Gray's Inn, through the influence of Mr. Edward Blackmore, the junior partner, who was known to the Dickens' family. His commencing salary was ten shillings a week, his duties those of a very junior clerk. He remained in this post for exactly eighteen months, dividing his time between the law, exploring London, and the theatre.

He evidently did his work in the office conscientiously and well, since his salary was twice raised, first to thirteen and six, and later to fifteen shillings. The petty-cash book kept by him from January to March 1828, is neatly made up and carefully checked. It contains, incidentally, the names of Mrs. Bardell, Corney, Newman Knott, Rudge, and Weller. The desk at which he worked here can be seen at the Dickens House, 48 Doughty Street, W.C.1., with the name "Charles Dickens" carved in block capitals on the lid.

How thoroughly he explored the town is shown by a re-collection of one of his fellow clerks, Mr. George Lear, who said, "Having been in London two years, I thought I knew something of town, but after a little talk with Dickens, I found that I knew nothing. He knew it all from Bow to Brentford." And not only the town, apparently, but the

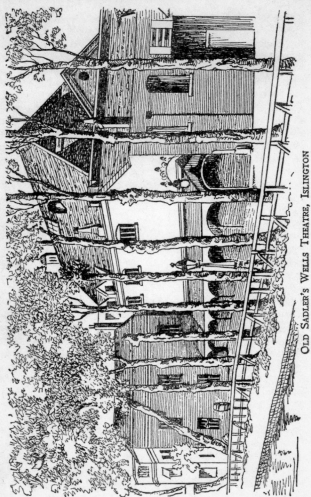

OLD SADLER'S WELLS THEATRE, ISLINGTON

townspeople also, for "he could imitate . . . the low population of the streets of London in all their varieties."

Already that restless energy which he was to exhibit all his life was possessing him. He acquired this knowledge during a period in which offices remained open until 8 p.m., when there were no fleets of motor-buses and tramcars, but only occasional horse coaches to facilitate exploration of London streets. Yet he was all this time assiduous in his attendance on the theatre, which was indeed his chief love. He and another fellow clerk, called Potter, went as often as they could, and, it is said, sometimes actually appeared on the professional stage, with the result that Dickens at least, "could give us Shakespeare by the ten minutes, and imitate all the leading actors of that time." Other and livelier adventures of the two are related in an early Sketch by Boz, entitled, "Making a Night of It," while Potter, *alias* Jones, but not unlike the yet unborn Mr. Jingle, dominates another, "The Misplaced Attachment of Mr. John Dounce."

Though he was apparently having a gay time about town, young Dickens was thinking hard during these eighteen months. When he actually made his decision one cannot say, but in November 1828, at the age of sixteen years and nine months, he left Ellis and Blackmore's office, and started out on his own as a free-lance shorthand writer, with a view to becoming eventually a parliamentary reporter.

His father had given him the idea. Mr. John Dickens, finding his pension much too small for his needs, and having had yet another son born to him, had, with a determination and energy quite remarkable in a man round about forty upon whom the stoutness and leisureliness of middle-age were already growing, qualified as a newspaper parliamentary reporter in order to increase his income.

The passage in "David Copperfield" in which Charles Dickens described his own struggles with the "savage stenographic mystery" has often been quoted; but it is worthy of some note that his father must also have coped with the "almost heartbreaking" task of learning shorthand, complete mastery of which, a friend told Dickens, was "about equal in difficulty to the mastery of six languages." John Dickens succeeded so well that, even assuming that he began to learn shorthand directly after he relinquished his post at Somerset House in 1825, he reached the parliamentary gallery within three years, an exceptional feat achieved only by the most able and expert shorthand writers.

He had, it is true, journalistic connexions. This may have helped, though nothing but his own ability and persistence could have enabled him to become a master of shorthand. It is true that he finally obtained employment on the staff of the *Mirror of Parliament*, a newspaper founded and conducted by John Henry Barrow, a brother of Mrs. Dickens. On the other hand, the Barrows by this time knew Dickens so well, and for the most part were so tired of his financial vagaries, that it is more than probable that he had to obtain the post on his merits. The fact that he was on the parliamentary staff of two papers previously seems to suggest that he did; at any rate, Charles Dickens told Mr. George Lear that his father was a "first-rate shorthand writer . . . and a capital reporter," and nearly twenty years later, when the son founded the *Daily News*, he put his father in charge of the reporting staff, an important post the latter retained, and the duties of which he punctiliously performed, until his death in 1851.

Everything seems to suggest that Mr. John Dickens made a persistent and brilliantly successful attempt to rehabilitate himself in life between the years 1824 and 1828; and as both before and after this period he may be said to have been at most times a capital hindrance and positive danger to his son's ambitions and prospects, it is more than cheering to find that both by the example he now set and the profession he chose he was directly instrumental in pointing to his son the way he should go.

In this connexion it is perhaps not so clearly recognized as might be how narrowly Dickens escaped a career on the stage. From earliest days he had been play-acting; and as he grew up the theatre more and more enthralled him, till by the age of sixteen he was an accomplished mimic and an amateur actor of no mean ability, gladly accepted, if well-grounded report speaks truly, in "walking-on" parts at minor theatres. At the age of twenty he made definite application to the stage-manager at Covent Garden for a trial, and was given an appointment with a readiness which seems proof positive of his acceptability. A bad cold prevented his keeping the appointment; and before his application could be renewed the possibilities of journalism had become so attractive that he had abandoned all idea of the stage as a career.

Had not his father become a journalist, and risen quickly to the height of his profession—a lucrative one—and thus incited his son to follow his example, it is more than likely that young Charles would have become in his early twenties, not "the inimitable Boz," but the inimitable somebody-or-other at Covent Garden or Drury Lane Theatre. Whether he would have remained an actor is much more doubtful; but in any case he would have been side-tracked for years, and the glorious work of his early period of authorship would have been lost.

Exactly how or where young Dickens occupied the months between November 1828, when he left Mr. Blackmore, and the beginning of 1830, can for the most part only be conjectured. It is certain that they were full of desperately hard work. First, there was the mastery of shorthand, during which time, as is related in "David Copperfield," after the actual learning of the system itself, there were weeks and weeks when every night "Traddles" came and dictated parliamentary speeches for the benefit of the young reporter, and "often and often we pursued these debates until the clock pointed to midnight, and the candles were burning down."

The system he learned, Thomas Gurney's "Brachygraphy, or an easy and compendious System of Shorthand," was an old one, having been invented in 1750, and even then based on a still older system of 1707; and it was by no means so easy as the title suggested. Moreover, he was self-taught; he just bought the half-guinea manual, and ploughed steadily through its "sea of perplexity." He undoubtedly took up this system because his father and an uncle, Edward Barrow, both reporters of distinction, employed it. Gurney's shorthand, incidentally, remained popular in spite of the competition of simpler systems for many more years, an edition of the manual being called for as late as 1884.

Once he had become competent in the use of shorthand, he began to make a living by it. For some considerable time he did not obtain a regular appointment; as for the parliamentary gallery, that was as yet far beyond his reach. For two years or more he led what must have been a somewhat precarious existence as a free-lance. As became an ex-lawyer's clerk, he specialized in legal work, becoming "a shorthand writer for the proctors," that is, picking up commissions from proctors to take down verbatim reports or notes of cases.

He visited also the police courts, Bow Street and the Old Bailey, in search of copy; and there used to come into the office of the *British Press*, a newspaper on the staff of which John Dickens was for a time employed, "a smart, intelligent, active lad, who brought what was then called 'penny-a-line stuff:' that is to say, notices of accidents, fires, police reports, such as escaped the more regular reporters, for which a penny a printed line was paid." Young Dickens' comprehensive knowledge of London would be invaluable to him in the collection of such material.

He prospered. Wisely, he consolidated his position. On his eighteenth birthday, that is, on the first possible date, he applied for a reader's ticket at the British Museum, and the very next day began to study there. He continued to do so for practically three years. Sometime also in 1830 he set up his own office at No. 5 Bell Yard, Doctors' Commons, as a professional shorthand writer. This step, though plucky enough for a boy of eighteen, would not only greatly facilitate his work, but would add considerably to his prestige among the proctors who employed him, and from whom he was deriving the greater part of his income.

It did not entail, or even suggest, the abandonment of his determination to become a parliamentary reporter. But by this time he was living at a very high pressure. He had made up his mind to get on, to make a big material success of life, that is, primarily, to earn large sums of money. With wisdom and foresight rare in one of his age, aided by his tremendous nervous energy and his keen, able intelligence, he neglected no opportunity. To become a parliamentary reporter was his chief ambition, for such a man was not only paid what must then have seemed to him a princely salary, namely fifteen guineas a week, but one often used the position as a jumping-off point for a yet more distinguished career. But the parliamentary gallery was not easily accessible, so meanwhile he slaved in the law-courts, dull and dreary though the work was, acquiring an intimate knowledge, not only of the forms and procedures and ceremonies of the law, but also of its very essence and real being; and he kept much more than half an eye upon the stage.

"I went to some theatre every night, with very few exceptions, for three years," he told Forster: "really studying the bills first, and going to where there was the best acting. . . . I practised immensely (even such things as walking in and out, and sitting down in a chair); often four, five, six hours a day; shut up in my own room, or walking about in the fields. I prescribed to myself too, a sort of Hamiltonian system for learning parts: and learnt a great number." He took in addition regular lessons from an actor of note, Mr. Robert Keeley.

Three spurs to his ambition urged him on, his temperament, his unbounded vital energy, and the remembrance of the blacking warehouse. But during 1830 and 1831 these were fused and sublimated into one single and dominating impulse. He fell in love.

So do we all; and we all imagine that never was there love like ours, never did a lover love so utterly and so devotedly. It is a universal belief. But there was in Dickens such intensity, such fixity of purpose, such strong emotional capacity, that when he wrote to Maria Beadnell, some time in 1832, that "I have never loved and never can love any human creature breathing but yourself," he was probably nearer the truth than many of us are when we make this assertion.

She was the daughter of a Lombard Street banker, a dark-eyed, rosy-lipped, winning little beauty about a year older than Charles, with plenty of admirers, and a roguish tendency to flirtation. But there is much more to the story than that.

It is a tangled skein which will never be unravelled satisfactorily. Charles was introduced to the family about

Christmas 1829 by Henry Kolle, who was engaged to one of Maria's sisters. He was favourably received. He was at the time tall, slenderly handsome, with charmingly shy manners but an unmistakable distinction of personality. He had very considerable social gifts, could sing a good song, mimic a coster, imitate all the popular actors, tell a merry yarn, and on occasion knock off a pretty set of doggerel verses for the amusement of the company. Unfortunately, he had no social status.

That was undoubtedly the first snag. The Beadnell family liked the delightful and accomplished youth well enough. As a pleasant and entertaining visitor he could hardly have come to the house too frequently. As a serious suitor for the hand of one of the daughters it is probable that he was never considered by the Beadnell parents to be at all eligible. He was the son of a nobody, he had no profession to speak of, his income, compared with that of a bank manager's, was negligible, and looked likely to remain so.

Maria's conduct remains inexplicable. She was certainly attracted at first, but whether it was on her part a mere fleeting interest, or whether she was really in love with Charles, but yielded to parental pressure or was beguiled out of love by the intrigues of the mysterious Mary Anne Leigh, one of her friends, cannot be decided. Most biographers have inclined to the view that she never was in love with Dickens; and this may very likely be the case, but it seems beyond question that for a long time she was very much under the spell of his intense devotion.

The part that Mary Anne Leigh played cannot either be settled satisfactorily. She was either the accomplice of a very cruel little woman in getting rid of a too troublesome suitor, or she was desperately in love with Dickens herself, and determined at all costs to stir up trouble between the two and so to separate them. The latter seems more probable.

The only certain points in the whole painful episode are that Charles Dickens loved Maria Beadnell with all the intensity of his passionate and emotional personality, that his love spurred him on to greater feats of energy and

WILLIAM COBBETT (1762–1835)

persistence than ever before, and that the incident had a deep and lasting impression upon him.

For more than a year he persisted in his suit. He did every mortal thing that man could do to please his love. Though Maria was by turns capricious, cold, disdainful or haughty, he returned to her over and over again, humiliating himself as only a man who is passionately in love can do. " I have positively stood amazed at myself ever since," he wrote to Forster in 1855: "—So I suffered, and so I worked, and so beat and hammered away at the maddest romances that ever got into any boy's head and stayed there, that to see the mere cause of it all now, loosens my hold upon myself."

It could not last. Charles pleaded, Mary Anne Leigh uttered poisoned insinuations, Maria—no one knows what Maria felt or wanted. Even her sister, at the very height of crisis, was forced to tell Charles that she had no inkling as to the state of Maria's affections. At last, having tried every expedient to win her love, young Dickens penned one of the most manly and pathetic letters ever made public.

" . . . I have considered and reconsidered the matter, and have come to the unqualified determination that I will allow no feeling of pride, no haughty dislike to making a conciliation to prevent my expressing it without reserve. I will avert to nothing that has passed; I will not again seek to excuse any part I have acted or to justify it by any course you have ever pursued; I will revert to nothing that has ever passed between us,—I will only openly and at once say that there is nothing I have more at heart, nothing I more sincerely and earnestly desire, than to be reconciled to you. It would be useless for me to repeat here what I have so often said before; it would be equally useless to look forward and state my hopes for the future—all that anyone can do to raise himself by his own exertions and unceasing assiduity I have done, and will do. I have no guide by which to ascertain your present feelings and I have, God knows, no means of influencing them in my favour. I have never loved and never can love any human creature breathing

but yourself. We have had many differences, and we
have lately been entirely separated. Absence, however,
has not altered my feelings in the slightest degree, and the
Love I now tender you is as pure and lasting as at any
period of our former correspondence. I have now done
all I can to remove our most unfortunate and to me most
unhappy misunderstanding. The matter now of course
rests solely with you, and you will decide as your own
feelings and wishes direct you. I could say much for
myself and I could entreat a favourable consideration on
my own behalf but I purposely abstain from doing so because it would only be a repetition of an oft told tale and
because I am sure that nothing I could say would have the
effect of influencing you in any degree whatever. . . ."

Dickens knew when he wrote that what the decision would
be. He was already prepared to face it. His romance was
ended; and while he left its formal closure to the lady, he
had buried his own hope, and was ready to stride forth again
without it. This is no broken-hearted, despairing, passionate
appeal; it is a carefully thought out, logical, and absolutely
final statement of the position, possible only to a wearied man
who has endured and suffered until passion is exhausted and
the very light of love grown dim. He loves still; but it is
with a smouldering love, not unwilling to be extinguished.
If she would have him still—good; if not—also good.

The expected happened. Maria answered "coldly and
reproachfully," and so Charles "went his way."

Many years later Charles Dickens told the whole world in
"David Copperfield" how his early romance might have been
transformed into an idyll. The courtship and marriage of
Dora Spenlow and David Copperfield is one of the most
beautifully human love stories ever written; but it is significant that the author had by then realized the necessity for
Dora's early death, and for a loyal, patient, tenderly resource-
ful Agnes Wickfield in the background, before the richer
harmonies of human love could be sounded. Happily for
him, he did not marry Maria Beadnell; but alas! there was to
be for him, in real life, no Agnes.

GLADSTONE AT THE AGE OF 31

His education was by now almost complete. A little of it had been gained in school, but most of it from actual contact with real life. He had known joy and suffering, pleasure and pain, prosperity and poverty; had wandered in happy childhood through the narrow streets and quiet lanes of an old-fashioned country town and its rural neighbourhood, and miserably through the crowded streets and noisome alleys of poorer London. He had soared aloft on aërial wings of fancy, had trudged the muddy depths of humiliation and despair; had known the fierce exultation of clambering by his own strong efforts from an almost hopeless obscurity into at least the first warm light of advancement; and had passed through the fire, heated seven times hot, of a grand but unrequited passion. One further apprenticeship was required of him before he was to embark on that career of unbroken triumph, unparalleled in the literary history of England, which he was to pursue for over thirty years.

On the 5th of March, 1832, a new evening newspaper, the *True Sun*, made its appearance. On the staff of this *True Sun* Dickens obtained an appointment, though possibly only as a supernumerary reporter. His editor was Laman Blanchard, afterwards a dear friend of his; and on to the staff came also John Forster, that "gruff man with the kindest heart in the world" who was, for thirty years or more, Dickens' most intimate friend, his guide and counsellor in all his affairs, to whom, many years before the novelist's death, was to be entrusted the task of writing his biography. Forster's "Life of Charles Dickens," published in 1872 and 1873, is one of the greatest biographies of all time, and, in spite of petty inaccuracies here and there, especially in relation to Dickens' early life, remains the standard and indispensable record from which all other biographies must largely draw.

The two did not become acquainted at once, though Forster says he noticed Dickens as "a young man of my own age whose keen animation of look would have arrested attention anywhere." He makes this statement, however, in connection with a reporters' strike headed successfully by Dickens, and as this strike, it has recently been proved, did not take place among the staff of the *True Sun*, as Forster declares, but four years later, it is possible that they did not meet at all as yet.

Dickens did not apparently remain long with the *True Sun ;* by August of the same year he was reporting for the *Mirror of Parliament,* his uncle's publication.

He had achieved his ambition; he was a parliamentary reporter. He had joined the select few who sat in the back row of the old House of Commons, or stood in the "preposterous pen" allotted to the press in the House of Lords, to take down the weighty words of Britain's legislators. He was getting his fifteen guineas a week during the session.

If he had expected to be thrilled, he was profoundly disappointed. He entered the gallery at a critical period of the Empire's history, the passing of the great Reform Bill of 1832. He reported some historic debates, and listened to some magnificent oratory. It is recorded of him that on one occasion he was so overcome by a moving description of Daniel O'Connell's of an Irish peasant woman searching for her son among the dead after a tithe riot that he could not continue his reporting. He must have seen and listened to many giants of Victorian statesmanship—Lord John Russell, Palmerston, Wellington, Melbourne, Sir Robert Peel, Earl Grey, William Cobbett, young Mr. Gladstone, the "rising hope of the stern unbending Tories."

Moreover, in his own words, he "made a great splash" in the gallery. There never was such a reporter, declared more than one of those who knew his work. Dr. Charles Mackay, a colleague of a year or two later, avowed that Dickens was "universally reported to be the rapidest and most accurate shorthand writer in the gallery." Mr. James Grant, a writer in the gallery with him, stated that "Among its eighty or ninety reporters he occupied the very highest rank, not merely for accuracy in reporting but for marvellous quickness in transcribing," and added the following remarkable tribute: "Literary abilities of a high order with reporting capacities of superior kind are seldom found in conjunction. They were so in the case of Mr. Dickens in a measure which I venture to say they never were in any other man since parliamentary reporting was known." His skill indeed

VISCOUNT PALMERSTON (1784–1865)

became legendary, and stories anent it were circulated which finally became too good to be true. Twenty years later Dickens himself told an audience, half-jokingly, that he was even then probably the best shorthand writer in the world; and his claim, whether meant seriously or not, was very likely justified.

But his resounding success in the gallery failed to satisfy his ambition. By December 1833 he had made two fresh bids for fortune, one of which was to alter the whole course of his career. He had applied for another job which would give him a wider scope, and he had had printed in that month's issue of the *Old Monthly Magazine* an original article.

His first attempt to get on to the staff of the *Morning Chronicle* was unsuccessful, in spite of influential recommendation, and he had to wait a further six months before he achieved that ambition. But his first little sketch of London life, "A Dinner at Poplar Walk" (afterwards entitled, when it was republished in the second series of "Sketches by Boz," "Mr. Minns and his Cousin"), which he dropped "with fear and trembling, into a dark letter-box in a dark office up a dark court in Fleet Street," was at once accepted by the editor. No payment was made; but for the moment what did that matter? He was in print!

Dickens, of course, had often been in print before; it was his daily business to fill the columns of his newspaper. But this was altogether different. As a reporter he was no more than a trained machine. As an author he was a creator, a parent.

The appearance of his first sketch affected him profoundly. He bought a copy of the magazine in the Strand, and walked with it down to Parliament Square, where he turned into Westminster Hall and remained there for half an hour, "because my eyes were so dimmed with joy and pride, that they could not bear the street, and were not fit to be seen there."

"A Dinner at Poplar Walk" is an amusing little description of how a bachelor uncle, very reserved and prim, is inveigled to a dinner party by a vulgar cousin in the hope that he may become so enamoured of the cousin's son that he will make him his heir. Needless to say the plan goes all wrong, and poor Mr. Minns ends a night of misery by missing the last coach from Poplar and having to walk back to the city through pouring rain.

It is all very cleverly done, perhaps a shade too cleverly, as is apt to be the case with the work of quite young men. It is the production of a smart youngster not unconscious of his smartness. It ends abruptly; one can as one reads it picture the young author, having carefully polished the beginning paragraph so as to catch the editor's eye, getting more and more absorbed, and writing on and on, quite capable of going on for hours—then suddenly remembering that it is a short story he is writing; and, being quite unable to cross out anything he has written, because it is all so good, drawing hurriedly to a close, and hoping that the editor will have become so interested in the middle that he will not notice the weakness of the ending.

When all that has been said about "A Dinner at Poplar Walk," there is this to add: that it has Charles Dickens written all over it. In his best days the novelist could hardly improve upon the opening to his first sketch.

"Mr. Augustus Minns was a bachelor, of about forty as he said—of about eight and forty as his friends said. He was always exceedingly clean, precise and tidy; perhaps somewhat priggish, and the most retiring man in the world. He usually wore a brown frock coat without a wrinkle, light inexplicables without a spot, a neat neckerchief with a remarkably neat tie, and boots without a fault: moreover he always carried a brown silk umbrella with an ivory handle. He was a clerk in Somerset House, or, as he said himself, he held 'a responsible situation under government.'"

And so on, in the unvarying Dickens' style.

From first to last Charles Dickens never put a character on to his stage without clothing the body and stripping the soul in an introductory paragraph, so that from the moment of their appearance we know his people intimately, and are ready to love or to hate them from the start. In the same way he always described his places accurately down to the last detail, and with an uncanny twist that exposed the character of the owners or habitués. The cousin's house at Poplar was "a yellow brick house, with a green door, brass knocker and doorplate, green window frame, and ditto railings, with a 'garden' in front, that is to say, a small loose bit of gravelled ground, with one round and two scalene triangular beds, containing a fir tree, twenty or thirty bulbs, and an unlimited number of marigolds." It only needed to add that at each side of the front door stood a Cupid on a heap of chalk flints decked out in pink cone-shells to complete an exquisitely accurate picture of small suburban pretentiousness.

The editor liked the first sketch, so there followed it in the January issue of the *Monthly Magazine* a second, "Mrs. Joseph Porter over the Way," in February "Horatio Sparkins," in April "The Bloomsbury Christening," and in May "The Boarding House." All these are reprinted in the first series of "Sketches by Boz."

"The Boarding House" was a longer piece than its predecessors, and appeared in two parts, the first in May 1834, and the second in August. This second part was signed "Boz." Previous contributions had been unsigned.

"Boz" was Charles Dickens' affectionate nickname for his youngest brother, Augustus, born in 1827, of whom he was extremely fond. He had first called him Moses, after the hero of the "Vicar of Wakefield"; this became—no doubt thanks to somebody's bad cold—Boses, and was finally shortened to Bose.

In the same month that he reached the dignity of a signed contribution, Charles Dickens joined the staff of the *Morning Chronicle.*

This was an old-established daily journal, nearly twenty years older than the *Times ;* and until recently it had enjoyed a very high reputation, largely on account of its full and accurate reporting of the parliamentary debates. In that field it was for many years unrivalled. But when a new proprietor decided to change its politics and transform it into a Liberal paper, its circulation decreased so much that a thorough reorganization of the staff was decided upon. This brought Dickens his opportunity.

While in the parliamentary gallery he had been courteous, but shy and reserved, with his colleagues. He had made one friend only, Thomas Beard; with him he had been on the closest terms of friendship. When, therefore, Mr. Beard was appointed to the *Morning Chronicle* and asked to recommend another shorthand writer, he had no hesitation whatever in recommending Dickens, since in addition to being the latter's friend, he knew him to be beyond question the "exceptionably able shorthand writer" the *Morning Chronicle* was looking for.

Charles Dickens was engaged at the "Fleet Street minimum" rate of £5 5s. per week, which all the newspapers except the *Times* had agreed to pay. This salary was continuous throughout the year; on the *Mirror of Parliament* he had been paid at a higher rate, but was only regularly employed during the Parliamentary sessions.

He celebrated the occasion of his appointment by buying in a stock of new clothes, and was shortly afterwards to be seen in "a new hat and a very handsome blue coat, with black velvet facings, the corner of which he threw over his shoulder *à l'espagnole*." All his life he was to love fine and rather daring clothes.

He had before this, some time in 1833, set up his own bachelor establishment; certainly in order to be nearer the offices of his paper, and perhaps also to be further from his father. For Mr. John Dickens was playing the old game once more. As adversity had stiffened that gentleman's character, so prosperity relaxed it, and he became again the charming man of property, elegantly entertaining his friends in genteel and generous style. He had moved from the squalid obscurity of Somers Town, where there had been some horrid adventures, including an eviction, not to be recalled without a shudder, into a more desirable area, and was living at 18 Bentinck Street, Manchester Square. Unfortunately his ideas of his estate were as improvidently vague as ever, and quite early on he had exceeded the patience of his wine-merchant and been arrested a second time for debt.

SIR ROBERT PEEL

*Reproduced from a contemporary engraving*

But he had now a grown-up son, who was earning good money. . . . Charles settled the matter; and had to live very carefully himself for a long while afterwards. Mr. John Dickens, regrettably, took shameful advantage of his son's generosity; he began to disappear whenever money troubles got pressing, and to remain away from home until Charles put things right. He did it quite frequently. "I own," wrote Charles Dickens to Thomas Milton, the solicitor friend who assisted him to liquidate these "moments of difficulty," "that at present his absence does not give me any great uneasiness, knowing how apt he is to get out of the way when anything goes wrong." Probably he was more uncomfortable on his father's return.

One can well understand Charles's desire to get away from home. He was twenty-one, and so of age; a promising young man with a growing reputation. His life was becoming increasingly busy. He was making his own circle of friends. He wanted liberty; and above all, one may guess, to escape from an atmosphere of what Mr. Micawber called "pecuniary liabilities." At all costs he was not going to be dragged back into blacking warehouse times again, even in thought. Accordingly, he took rooms in Cecil Street, Strand, but being there badly looked after and having "too much water in the hashes," he moved to the top floor of No. 15 Buckingham Street, Strand, the very rooms he gave young David Copperfield to live in. In 1834 he moved to Furnivall's Inn, High Holborn, and remained there until his marriage in 1837, living first at No. 13 for a year, and then at No. 15.

His work on the staff of the *Morning Chronicle* carried him all over the country. He still reported parliamentary debates during the session, but while the Houses were up, he and Beard were sent chasing hither and thither after statesmen to take down their utterances in their constituencies, at banquets, great public meetings, and so forth. He travelled to Edinburgh (by sea), to Salisbury, Bath, Bristol, Exeter and elsewhere. It was a hard life, made harder by the keen competition which existed between the leading papers. In days when the *Times* called the *Morning Chronicle* "the squirt," and the *Morning Chronicle* replied that the *Times*

D

was conducted with "a reckless disregard of principle which can only be equalled by its utter want of dignity," the representatives of the papers could be excused if they practised every conceivable dodge to steal a march on their rivals.

Being first with the news then depended largely upon the reporter's courage and skill, his powers of physical endurance, and the speed with which he could transcribe his shorthand notes and carry or get them carried to his paper. Neither train nor telegraph was as yet sufficiently developed to be of use to him; the telephone was still unknown. It was a case of the open road, and good luck to the fastest man. "I have often transcribed for the printer," Charles Dickens told a gathering of newspaper men in 1865, "from my shorthand notes, important public speeches in which the strictest accuracy was required . . . writing on the palm of my hand, by the light of a dark lantern, in a post-chaise and four, galloping through a wild country, and through the dead of the night. . . ."

No expense was spared by the paper, no feat was too arduous for the reporter. When Charles Dickens went with Beard to Edinburgh to report the speeches at a banquet on Earl Grey's retirement, the expenses for the two amounted to £84; the same occasion cost the *Times*, which sent four reporters, £250. As for the trials of the reporter of those days, Charles Dickens told the journalists of a later and easier generation that "I have had to charge for half-a-dozen breakdowns in half-a-dozen times as many miles. . . . I have had to charge for all sorts of breakages . . . broken hats, broken luggage, broken chaises, broken harness—everything but a broken head, which is the only thing they would have grumbled to pay for."

Because, of course, a broken head would have meant a disabled reporter; and in this work, as in the parliamentary gallery, Dickens quickly rose to the peak of his profession. As instance of his speed, on one occasion he reported a speech at Exeter on the Friday night, and got it so swiftly to London that it was printed in the first edition on Saturday morning. Exeter is 172 miles from London, and the roads were not nearly so good as they are now.

Meanwhile, his original work was still being published; and

THE HOUSES OF PARLIAMENT, BURNED TO THE GROUND IN 1834. HERE DICKENS WORKED AS A REPORTER

*From a contemporary engraving*

a further important opening along this line presented itself in January 1835. The *Morning Chronicle* decided to start a companion evening paper, and the editor invited Dickens to contribute some original work to the opening number. Dickens grasped the opportunity with both hands. He wrote in reply:

"MY DEAR SIR,

"As you have begged me to write an original sketch for the first number of the new evening paper, and as I trust to your kindness to refer my application to the proper quarter, should I be unreasonably or improperly trespassing upon you, I beg to ask whether it is probable that if I commenced a series of articles, written under some attractive title, for the *Evening Chronicle*, its conductors would think I had any claim to *some* additional remuneration (of course, of no great amount) for doing so? . . ."

The reply was prompt and profitable; his suggestion for a series of articles was approved, and his salary was raised from five to seven guineas a week.

"Boz" was fairly launched.

Week by week the "Sketches of London," published in the *Morning* and the *Evening Chronicle*, for they appeared in both papers, grew in popularity, and as they did Dickens, by the foresight of his editor, John Black, was in consequence relieved of much of the hack work of the office. He continued to report as before, but the odd reviewing of books and notices of plays handed over to reporters in their idler hours was kept from him. "Any fool," said Black, "can pass judgment, more or less unjust, on a book or a play, but 'Boz' can do better things; he can create works for other people to criticize. . . . Keep 'Boz' in reserve for great occasions. He will aye be ready for them."

The "great occasions" were much nearer at hand than Mr. Black or perhaps even Charles Dickens could imagine.

## CHAPTER III

" . . . *the inimitable Boz* . . ."—WILLIAM GILES.*

THERE is a period in the career of nearly every successful author when, before becoming widely known to the general public, he begins to acquire a certain reputation in the small, but to him extremely important, publishing world. He is regarded as a coming man, an author of promise, on whose work it would be wise to keep a watchful eye. It might even be advisable to get in touch with him now, while his work is still unknown, and he is ready to accept almost any terms. If he does come off, the profits may be prodigious; if not—there is that risk, of course; but . . . well, a publisher's life must consist largely of speculations.

This stage Charles Dickens had now reached and, alive to its possibilities, he began to explore them. "No one but a fool ever writes except for money," honest Dr. Johnson had declared; and Dickens, kept continually and sometimes desperately short of money by his "prodigal father's" frequent disappearances, naturally turned his attention to the financial side of original authorship. He approached the editor of the *Monthly Magazine,* to which he had now contributed nine sketches, but that periodical was not sufficiently prosperous to make any payment to its contributors. Dickens would have been content with half a guinea a printed page; but even this was impossible. So contributions to the *Monthly Magazine* ceased; the last appeared in the issue of February 1835.

His first original sketch in the new *Evening Chronicle* had appeared a few days previously. The close proximity of the

* Inscription on a snuff-box sent to Dickens by his old teacher, Mr. William Giles, to commemorate the success of " Pickwick."

EARL GREY (1764–1845)

dates cannot be pure coincidence; obviously the raising of his salary by the *Chronicle* on account of this work decided him to close his account with the *Monthly Magazine*.

His "Sketches of London Life" continued regularly in the *Chronicle* until August, when they suddenly ceased. They were later resumed, but in the meanwhile a certain "Tibbs" had contributed a dozen sketches to "Bell's Life in London," then edited by an ex-gallery colleague of Dickens, Mr. Vincent Dowling. Evidently the work of young Mr. Dickens of the *Morning Chronicle* was being sought after, and he could begin to pick and choose his employers.

Although he ceased for a while to contribute original work to the *Evening Chronicle*, his personal relations with the editor, George Hogarth, were not adversely affected. Quite otherwise, in fact; some time in 1835 Charles Dickens became engaged to Mr. Hogarth's eldest daughter, Catherine.

It has been suggested that Dickens, sad and lonely after his final parting with Maria Beadnell, found comfort and distraction in the cheerful society of the four young Hogarth girls, fell in love with them all simultaneously—and unfortunately married the wrong one. There is perhaps more than a grain of truth in this somewhat cynical suggestion.

He had loved Maria Beadnell with that grand and consuming passion which a man experiences but once, if at all, in a lifetime. When he parted from her, there passed from him the possibility of his ever loving with like fervour again. But such bereavement does not necessarily prevent one from falling in love a second time. It often rather tends to throw a man into the arms of the first companionable and sympathetic woman he meets.

It would be grossly inaccurate to suggest that this was what happened to Charles Dickens. But we are all, at one time or another, the sport of circumstances; and circumstances might conceivably at this moment have conspired rather more favourably for his ultimate happiness.

To abandon all hope of winning Maria must have been a terrible blow for him. Life in bachelor chambers had its periods of intense loneliness for the ardent, lively young man; the family atmosphere in Bentinck Street was uncongenial, full of petty strains and squabbles; by contrast, the jolly, friendly Hogarth house in Chelsea, and the attractive Hogarth sisters, with their obvious admiration of the handsome, clever young author-journalist, must have drawn him like a magnet, soothing his nerves, flattering his self-esteem, and stimulating his wounded and repressed emotions.

Catherine Hogarth was twenty; the next sister, Mary, was not yet sixteen; the others were mere children, good for a romp and a game. Charles fell in love with Catherine; but he worshipped Mary. He was of an age when a man naturally connects love with marriage; Mary was but a child; an angel child.

The engagement was approved. Only, it would be advisable for Charles to be earning rather more than seven guineas a week before marriage should be contemplated. He is moving, one sees, among people with more discreet financial ideas than his father. John Dickens at twenty-three married on £80 a year; Charles Dickens at twenty-three was probably making all told about £400 a year, but was not considered to have quite enough yet to marry on. Of course, there is no saying how much of that £400 a year was being swallowed up by the "prodigal father."

Very soon a modest but gratifying opportunity presented itself. Mr. William Harrison Ainsworth, author of "Rookwood" and the most popular novelist of the day, wrote to Dickens commending his "Sketches" and suggesting that they might be collected and published in book form. He offered to introduce him to a thoroughly good publisher—his own, in fact. Dickens was not slow to respond; so Ainsworth introduced him to Mr. John Macrone, a young and energetic publisher whose advertisements were to be seen everywhere in the journals and magazines, and to Mr. George Cruikshank, a celebrated illustrator of books, and an agreement was soon reached.

Dickens was to sell the copyright of his published sketches, which so far he had wisely retained, to Mr. Macrone, and to supply eight more to make up sufficient "copy." He was to receive in return a single payment of £150. Mr. Macrone was to publish the sketches in two volumes at half a guinea each.

Mr. Cruikshank was to enliven the volumes with "improvements," that is, illustrations, in his own well-known and popular style. It was indeed a very handsome agreement. The young author ran no risk, was paid a lump sum down, and received the assistance of one of the best-known illustrators of the day. This last was in itself no small advertisement, the book illustrator being in those days often more important than the author.

In January 1836 the two volumes of "Sketches by 'Boz,' Illustrative of Every-Day Life, and Every-Day People," duly appeared, neatly bound in dark green cloth. But before this had happened, a much more momentous proposition, as it was to prove, had been made to Charles Dickens.

One Wednesday morning very early in 1836 a certain Mr. William Hall called at Furnivall's Inn to speak to Mr. Dickens. He represented Messrs. Chapman and Hall, a young and not very well-known, but distinctly enterprising, firm of publishers. Curiously enough, he was the man who had sold Charles Dickens his copy of the *Monthly Magazine* containing his first sketch just two years previously; in those days bookselling and book publishing were frequently combined.

Dickens was known to Chapman and Hall through his work on the *Monthly Magazine*, and had already written for them two humorous sketches for their Library of Fiction, entitled "The Tuggses at Ramsgate," and "A Little Talk about Spring and the Sweeps."

What Mr. Hall had to propose was this: Mr. Robert Seymour, an artist noted for comic illustrations, chiefly of the sporting variety, and who had recently illustrated for the firm a book called the "Squib Annual," had suggested to them that he would very much like to do a distinctly superior series of pictures illustrative of cockney sporting life. They had talked over the matter together, and come to the conclusion that the idea would go down with the public very well if the drawings could be published in a series of monthly magazines, each of which should contain also a story or running commentary written attractively round them. What they had thought of was the central idea of a Nimrod Club, consisting of cockney sportsmen, who should go out on various

hunting, fishing, shooting, and similar expeditions, in all of
which they would, being sportsmen in intention rather than
by practice, entangle themselves in ludicrous and awkward
situations, which would be presented by the artist and enlarged upon by the author. Would Mr. Dickens care to entertain the idea of supplying the letterpress? Mr. Hall was
very sorry to have to ask Mr. Dickens to make a very quick
decision, but the fact was that the matter had been held over
for some time owing to the author they had first written to
not having replied, and Mr. Seymour had informed them that,
as another good job had just been offered to him that would
occupy all his time if he accepted it, he would be much obliged
if they could at once come to a decision.

Dickens was at least the second man to whom Messrs.
Chapman and Hall applied. That fact exactly indicates his
position at this moment in the world of letters. His was not
yet the name that would naturally spring to the mind of a
publisher directly any piece of work in his line was suggested.
But as unfortunately Mr. William Clarke, the popular author
of "Three Courses and a Dessert," had not seen fit to reply to
their communication, they must get somebody else. Why not
"Boz"? He might be just the very man! It would be a real
chance for the youngster, and he would be so very keen that he
would probably make quite a good job of it.

Dickens was more than pleased to entertain the idea.
That same night he wrote to his fiancée:

"MY DEAREST KATE,

"The House is up; but I am very sorry to say that I must
stay at home. I have had a visit from the publishers this
morning . . . they have made me an offer of fourteen
pounds a month, to write and edit a new publication they
contemplate, entirely by myself, to be published monthly,
and each number to contain four woodcuts. I am to make
my estimate and calculation, and to give them a decisive
answer on Friday morning. The work will be no joke,
but the emolument is too tempting to resist."

Obviously a hurried and rather excited note. Kate must
know at once of this splendid opportunity. But the young

man kept his head. A chance like this, of course, simply could not be let slip; but there was a great deal, of the utmost importance, to be thought out most carefully. There were at least three main obstacles to be considered and negotiated before he could safely walk out of Messrs. Chapman and Hall's office on Friday morning with a signed contract in his pocket. First, except as a walker, and more or less as a horseman, he was not a sportsman, and so would be at a disadvantage in trying to deal with field sports; second, he thought the idea of the Nimrod Club a decidedly stale one, sporting club prints, anecdotes and so forth having been in considerable vogue for rather too long a time; and third, he was himself of the very decided opinion that it was the place of the author to come first, and the artist second. It was the author's part to write the book, the artist's to embellish it, and not vice versa; at any rate, if he was to be the author.

Sometime between the Wednesday and Friday mornings Dickens must have gone over the whole matter very carefully and critically in his mind. "I am no sportsman," he began. " I am not even greatly interested in sport as sport, so I should probably make a ghastly failure if I tried to be funny about drawings the subjects of which would be alien if not distasteful to me. Also, I do not like the idea of having my subjects suggested to me. I don't believe I could possibly confine myself within the bounds of any other person's suggestions. I am too full of ideas myself. . . . Now, what I really would like to do would be to take three or four congenial characters, and start off with them on a roving journey about England. They could meet all sorts and conditions of people—just as I have done—go to all sorts of places—as I have—have every kind of adventure on the road—Heaven knows I've had plenty —stop at hotels, inns, coaching houses, boarding houses, lodging houses, farm houses—I know the whole gamut— be present at weddings, elopements, funerals, christenings, Christmas parties, picnics, banquetings, parliamentary elections; be fooled, swindled, robbed; fall in love and fall out of it, fall into debt—fall into prison if necessary. Why, what with my own personal experiences and all I've listened to and reported in Doctor's Commons, the law courts and up and

down the country, I don't believe there's a single variety of
human adventure possible in England that I couldn't describe
to the very life! . . . That's the idea. I could make a hit
with that. Hang the Nimrod Club and suchlike fatuities!
. . . I'll put it to the publishers."

He put it; no doubt with considerable eloquence, and
certainly convincingly, for the publishers agreed with all he
said. And so, "my views being deferred to, I thought of Mr.
Pickwick."

"My views being deferred to," indeed! Here was a young,
inexperienced author, offered his first big commission, practically throwing overboard all his publishers' suggestions and
substituting his own; and in addition coolly relegating a well-
known and popular artist of established renown, for whom in
fact the whole project was being planned, to the subordinate
and inferior position of illustrator to a mere hack author.
That in effect was what Dickens did; and it gives a first taste
of the real quality of the man.

And the publishers agreed. It sounds incredible. But
equally incredible was to be their reward. The young man
"thought of Mr. Pickwick."

He wrote the first number. Mr. Seymour, handed the
proofs, drew pictures of "a long, thin man." Mr. Chapman
thought he would prefer a podgy man, and described a friend
of his "at Richmond, a fat old beau who would wear, in spite
of the ladies' protests, drab tights and black gaiters." Mr.
Seymour had not long before, in a book on fishing he had
illustrated in 1833, sketched a somewhat similar figure. If
Mr. Chapman preferred a portly man, there was the model
ready; a touch here and there, and the thing would be done.

Thus, by almost a series of accidents, did chance provide
for the birth of the "immortal Pickwick."

On the 26th of March, 1836, an advertisement in the *Times*
announced:

THE PICKWICK PAPERS. On the 31st of March
will be published, to be continued monthly, price one
shilling, the first number of the POSTHUMOUS PAPERS
OF THE PICKWICK CLUB, containing a faithful record

of the Perambulations, Perils, Travels, Adventures and Sporting Transactions of the Corresponding Members. Edited by Boz. Each Monthly Part embellished with four illustrations by Seymour. Chapman and Hall, 186 Strand, and of all Booksellers.

The first number came out quietly, on the 31st of March, as advertised. It made no "splash." The publishers thought four hundred copies enough to order from the printer.

On the 2nd of April, at St. Luke's Church, Chelsea, Charles Dickens was married, quietly, to Catherine Hogarth. The marriage was by licence, and the ceremony was performed by the curate. (The rector of the parish, incidentally, was the Rev. Charles Kingsley, father of the author of "Westward Ho!") The bride, who was not yet twenty-one, "was dressed in the simplest and neatest manner." To the wedding breakfast sat down only the two families and Mr. Beard of the *Morning Chronicle*, who was best man. "A few common, pleasant things were said, healths drunk . . . all things passed off very pleasantly, and all seemed happy, not the least so Dickens and his young girlish wife." The honeymoon was spent near Gravesend, at Chalk, a quiet little village five miles from Rochester, and not quite so far from Gads Hill.

Altogether, a modest little affair, without a touch of pretentiousness or ostentation. Quite in keeping for a young reporter with only seven guineas a week certain, even though he had just published a collected edition of "Sketches," and was engaged upon his first book. Dickens had as yet no right to bank upon the future. The "Sketches by Boz" were no more than reprinted newspaper articles, of which the copyright had been sold outright; and "Pickwick" was a piece of literary hackwork, contracted for and paid by the yard. When he married, Charles Dickens was but a *Morning Chronicle* reporter—of excellent ability and most highly thought of certainly—who had recently begun to add to his income by contributing here and there short humorous articles, which were proving acceptable to editors, and were rather fancied by one or two good judges. But he had no fame; the general public neither knew nor cared who "Boz" was.

Moreover, there was always in the background the "prodigal father."

Mrs. Craddock's cottage at Chalk was quiet and secluded. The honeymoon couple stayed there a fortnight. Charles put in a good deal of work on his book. He had made an agreement with Messrs. Chapman and Hall on February 12th to supply twenty-four pages of approximately five hundred words for each number of "Pickwick," that is, some 12,000 words of original writing per month. This was no slight undertaking for a busy reporter who might at any time be kept at work in the House till the early hours of the morning, or sent by his paper on a journey that backwards and forwards could last anything up to a week. Further, Messrs. Chapman and Hall had requested that "copy" should be delivered to them by the author two months before the date of publication, and though for this period Dickens had substituted five weeks, it is quite obvious that, what with the necessary preparations for the marriage and the possibly heavy demands on his time afterwards, there was every danger that unless the greatest diligence and care were exercised he would be unable to deliver the "copy" to time.

Before his marriage he had discovered this danger. "I want to get them," he wrote to Kate, referring to Mr. Pickwick and his friends, "from the ball to the inn before I go to bed; and I think that will take until one or two o'clock at the earliest. The publishers will be here in the morning, so you will readily suppose that I have no alternative but to stick at my desk."

Charles, no doubt, welcomed the opportunity to get on with his work during the long, quiet days at Chalk; but one wonders whether Mrs. Dickens was not just a little disappointed at finding herself married to a husband who considered he had no alternative but to stick at his desk even on his honeymoon.

She had no idea yet what a volcano of energy she had married. Nor probably had Charles himself. He had done pretty well so far in the matter of hard work, but he had never yet been all out. He had not even come into his strength. Success was to call out in him many qualities which were still lying dormant, and not least an almost herculean capacity for hard and sustained work.

This is not to belittle what he had done before his marriage. He had worked long hours as a child in the blacking warehouse; his hours in Mr. Blackmore's office were not short, and he had filled his nights with systematic sight-seeing and theatre-going. He had mastered shorthand in an incredibly short time, a feat that must have meant intense application. He did not live for two years as a free-lance reporter on trade union hours of work; he must have been up early in the morning and to bed late at night. Parliamentary reporting often meant sitting in the House until three or four a.m.; speeches were longer in those days. Political reporting when the House was up could mean travelling and working continuously for twenty-four hours.

The early nineteenth century conception of "work" was almost inconceivably different from any held now. It is possible that at no time in English history did men toil so laboriously. The industrial revolution had by this time destroyed much of the peaceful leisureliness of life without as yet offering any compensation in the way of amenities. It had vastly increased the possibilities of reward for the successful, but it had in no way smoothed the road to success. Rich or poor, man had literally to live by the sweat of his brow and the fatigue of his body. A sinecure was the only escape from incessant and tiring work for all who had to earn their living.

It was the age of get on or go under. Competition was fierce and unrestricted. To rise from the ranks one required savage courage, inflexible determination, and tremendous powers of endurance. To go under was to sink to a life of squalor.

The result was that all men of ambition were accustomed to think of life in terms of hard and unceasing endeavour, to take as in the ordinary course of events feats of endurance that now seem superhuman, to propose to themselves, and to achieve, literally colossal tasks. The conditions of the age imposed this manner of thought upon them, and caused them to call upon their physical strength to an extent that is hardly possible to-day, because for two generations or more modern invention has been rendering it less and less necessary. Only the very courageous and the very strong won through.

All this must be taken into consideration before one can make a just estimate of the early life and work of Charles Dickens. Up to the time of his marriage his labours had been those of a keenly ambitious youngster, not too well, yet not too badly, placed at the start. He had been somewhat handicapped by illness in early life, and to a less degree later, and the blacking warehouse episode had been a most unfortunate retrogression; but from the moment he entered Mr. Molloy's office a career had always been possible for him, and in the one he had carved for himself he had followed more or less the normal upward route of a clever boy determined to succeed. His labours had been severe, but not exceptional, except by virtue of being exceptionally successful. That they certainly had been; he had reached by his twenty-fourth birthday a standing most men starting as he did would have been happy to have attained by thirty-four.

Yet he had been working all this time well within his strength. His body had been trained to endurance of hardship and to sustained activity by growing up in an age that knew nothing of labour-saving devices and was eased of little toil by machinery, that was as yet ignorant of trains, motor-cars, telegraphs, telephones, typewriters, fountain pens —or steel pens even—electric light or gas light—though gas was just beginning feebly to make its way as an illuminant— that took for granted uncomfortable and arduous working conditions, and regarded muddy, ill-lighted streets and pot-holed roads out-of-doors and frowsty, crowded, unhygienic quarters indoors as being all in the normal and accepted order of things. The strength of his mind had never been properly tested, for, as John Black had so sagely observed, it was a creative mind; and so far it had not been called upon to create. It had assimilated marvellously; it had thrown off a few bright, flashing sparks in the "Sketches" by "Boz" and "Tibbs;" but it had never as yet been stirred to real exertion.

Success, and that came almost simultaneously with marriage, was to lay upon him the burden of creative work, a burden from which he was never afterwards to escape. He welcomed it at first unhesitatingly, and with too great eagerness; and steadfastly refused to throw it off later because, from the moment the public began to demand it from him, he regarded himself as their servant, and sternly set himself to fulfil every self-imposed obligation, though the number of these obligations grew greater with every year, and their demands more arduous.

The change that this wrought in him can be traced quite clearly by comparing the "Sketches by Boz" with "Pickwick," leaving out for the purposes of this comparison the earlier chapters of the latter work. It is necessary to make this exception, for the opening chapters of "Pickwick" are little more than an extended "Sketch," and, to say truth, not an overpoweringly interesting one at that. It is not surprising that at first the public preferred the "Sketches."

The earliest work of a successful author does not always repay attention, but the "Sketches by Boz" are worthy the closest study. They are youthful, crude, sometimes (though rarely) artificial, often clumsily constructed, and generally weak in the ending. But not only do they give a marvellously accurate and interesting picture of London and, less often, country life during an age now completely passed, but they present in all his freshness the young, witty, carefree and untrammelled Dickens before he has been compelled to think, and while he is still the "divine reporter" and no more, seeing everything, noting everything, remembering everything, flicking off, as it were, without effort superlatively brilliant cameos, and enlivening and irradiating all he writes by a most original and humorous turn which never seems to falsify description, but rather, by holding up the subject at a quaintly unusual angle, and treating it in whimsically playful fashion, appears to make the truth stand out more truly.

Forster's description of the "Sketches" as "the first sprightly runnings of his genius" can hardly be bettered, nor can his comment that "There is laughter and fun to excess; there are the minute points and shades of character, with all the discrimination and nicety of detail. . . . The observation shown throughout is nothing short of wonderful."

Quite so.   Pure observation, unadulterated by thought.   A book of pictures sketched in words, accurate in every detail, and with a laugh on every page.   Consider his titles, picking one or two at random: "The Parish," "Greenwich Fair," "The River," "Vauxhall Gardens by Day," "Astley's" (the famous circus), "Seven Dials," "Shops and their Tenants," "London Recreations"—exactly the type of title that is set daily to children in school for their English composition lesson, and which can be justified outside a school only by a writer possessing exceptional powers of observation and more than usual nicety of description.   Provided one does possess these, and has a flair for seeing the unusual in things, there is no reason why one should not go on for ever producing such sketches.   There is always a market for them.   Dickens, by reason of his keen eyes and sure memory, his vast experience in London and elsewhere, his sense of humour, and with his skill as a writer trained by the sternest of all disciplines, that of writing up facts for a newspaper, would appear peculiarly fitted for such work.

No place was too insignificant, nor any happening too ordinary, to attract his attention, to divert him and so enable him to divert his readers.   He did not require of necessity such general subjects as those above; anything could set him going; he could be equally entertaining about a "Pawnbroker's Shop," "Gin Shops," "Brokers and Marine-Store Shops," about "Omnibuses," "Early Coaches," and "Hackney-Coach Stands," things one saw every day but never dreamed were interesting.

He could meditate in Monmouth Street, "the only true and real emporium for second-hand wearing apparel," whose inhabitants, a "peaceable and retiring race," "immure themselves for the most part in deep cellars or small back parlours," and "seldom come forth into the world, except in the dusk and coolness of evening"; or he could attend a public dinner and notice  the waiters place the decanters of sherry "at very respectful distances," and comment that "people who can carve poultry are great fools if they own it"; or he could stop to watch two girls of fourteen and sixteen put into a prison van, and observe "that they were sisters was evident from the resemblance which still subsisted between them, though two additional years of depravity had fixed their brand upon the elder girl's features as legibly as if a red-hot iron had seared them."

There was little that escaped "Boz," whether of grave or gay, though to be sure it was usually the funny side of things that he saw.

It was not only things that he saw. He could ink in a character as neatly as one could wish. He had stored in his mind the memories of all sorts of funny folk he had observed here and there right from his infancy, and he could at any moment recollect one of these, imagine a ludicrous little adventure for him (or her), sketch in the setting, apply, if the story required it, a slight dash of pathos, and lo! there was a genuine phase of real life to chuckle over. So deliciously funny—and so true! So exactly what *would* happen with "Mrs. Porter over the Way," or "Our Next Door Neighbours," or Miss Amelia Martin, "The Mistaken Milliner," thirty-two years of age, and "what ill-natured people would call plain, and police reports interesting." And how one could appreciate the discomfiture of "Mr. Horatio Sparkins," the fascinating young man about town unfortunately discovered by his lady admirers—on the last page—behind the counter of a third-rate haberdashery shop; or those so amusing "Passages in the Life of Mr. Watkins Tottle."

No wonder the "Sketches" appealed. No wonder the two half-guinea volumes sold—not in large numbers, because after all a guinea is a guinea, and a guinea for books is the equivalent of two guineas for anything else—but steadily, so steadily that Mr. Macrone began to talk about a second edition, was issuing a second edition, and was offering the author no less than £200 for the MS. of a book—a real book this time—not yet written, but to be called "Gabriel Vardon, The Locksmith of London," and was making it quite clear that this £200 was for a first edition of 1,000 copies only, and that if further editions were called for all profits then ensuing would be shared by author and publisher. And "Boz" was, naturally, accepting, and mentioning November 30th as the date by which he hoped to have the MS. completed. This in May.

"Boz's" stock was distinctly on the up grade. The collected "Sketches" had been well worth while. They had made no big hit, but they were evidently appreciated by the book-reading public; they were selling steadily. And why not? It was all such excellent fooling, light, witty and neat, yet most instructive, because it told one about real people and real places; and every now and then there came a gentle tug at the heartstrings. A "Sketch" was just the very thing to pass away an idle quarter of an hour, say after dinner; it was interesting, it made one smile, at times it made one lay one's book down and laugh outright; one chuckled over the lovely little "naughty" hits at people, and called one's wife to listen —My dear, isn't this too exquisitely funny? . . . Here's "Boz" describing a proctor in Doctors' Commons, and he says he "spoke rather fast, but that was habit; and rather thick, but that was good living"—doesn't that exactly describe old So-and-So? Or,—Now doesn't this just show up our dreadful government and the laziness and incompetence of the idiotic numskulls who get into Parliament nowadays? "Boz" tells us in this "Sketch" how our rulers—rulers, mark you!—sit guzzling in the dining-room when they ought to be attending the debate; and how the whips, when a division is about to come off, drive them into the lobbies—listen, "to give their 'conscientious' votes on questions of which they are conscientiously innocent of knowing anything whatever, or to find a vent for the playful exuberance of their wine-inspired fancies, in boisterous shouts of 'Divide.'" . . . Wine-inspired fancies, ha! ha! ha! that's rich!

"Boz's" work is rich; it has a flavour to it. And that flavour is appreciated among the rather small circle of comfortably well-off people who do not mind putting down a guinea every now and then for a new book, provided it has got something in it. "Boz" is making his way among the book tasters.

True, here and there an occasional person with a shade more gentility than the rest, a slightly keener sense of Refinement (with a capital R), will be heard to murmur that, isn't he, well, a little low? Doesn't he deal rather too much with common, vulgar people? But there are not many of these critics; and all will agree that there is nothing spiteful or wounding in "Boz's" humour; it is all good, clean, generous fun that leaves no taste of malice or injury behind it.

And "Pickwick"? What about Mr. Pickwick, in his green paper covers, at one shilling monthly, with "embellishments" by the well-known artist Mr. Seymour? "Pickwick," issued cheaply with a view to catching small fish as well as large, though to be sure the publishers have not as yet thrown their net very widely!

At first there is a bit of a mystery about "Pickwick," and behind the scenes a shocking tragedy. . . .

The more one learns about the early history of "The Posthumous Papers of the Pickwick Club," the more one stands amazed that that marvellous history ever struggled through to real life. Its start was unpropitious. Mr. James Grant went so far as to say that the early numbers proved "a signal failure," and superficially it would not have been surprising had the venture fizzled out altogether at an early date.

The publication originally planned was to have consisted of a series of humorous engravings designed and executed by Mr. Robert Seymour. Mr. Seymour had himself suggested the project, and, as his was a name that could be relied upon to draw, Messrs. Chapman and Hall had readily listened to what was obviously a reasonably safe proposition. Any book embellished by Mr. Seymour would be pretty sure to sell sufficient copies to cover expenses and leave a margin of profit.

In accordance with common practice, and to concentrate people's attention on the pictures, a certain amount of printed matter would be supplied with the pictures. Every picture tells a story, but readers prefer to have the story told for them. So an author was engaged to tell the story.

It is true that the particular author engaged in this case, Mr. Charles Dickens, had by some extraordinary feat of persuasiveness induced the publishers to reverse the rôles of author and artist; but the public, on whose willingness to purchase depends ultimately the success or failure of any book, could know nothing of that—and would not have cared one jot on March 31st, 1836, if they had. It was the name Seymour on the advertisements, and not the name "Boz," that would tempt them to risk their shillings.

So the first number sold like an ordinary Seymour publication. Just a few hundred copies. Later, no doubt, sales would increase, as people got to like the engravings and perhaps grew interested in the story. This was only the first number of a new venture; and, all things considered, it was not doing too badly. "Pickwick" was, of course, only one of many irons Messrs. Chapman and Hall had in the fire, and not a particularly large or important one.

The author was not doing too badly, either, for a beginner.

And that, looking at the matter with a dispassionate eye, is about all one can say. For, to tell truth, however great an initial impression Dickens made upon Messrs. Chapman and Hall, and it must have been considerable or they would never have acceded to his suggestions as they did, the opening pages of "Pickwick" reveal him as very young, very nervous, rather overweighted by the formidable nature of his task, and more than a little in awe of the great Mr. Seymour. The first chapter of "Pickwick" is conventional and dull.

Dickens had pooh-poohed the idea of the Nimrod Club, but he opens with the Pickwick Club; and the Pickwickians in club assembled are very poor fish. Mr. Pickwick is in Chapter I merely silly, with his "gigantic brain" and his "Tittlebatian theory"; Mr. Tracy Tupman is the stale old traditional rather stout middle-aged and perpetually amorous bachelor, familiar since fiction began, born only to be the butt and sport of younger rivals; Mr. Snodgrass is an equally conventional figure, that of the cloudy young poet, "poetically attired," but giving little other evidence of poetry beyond a general mooniness and insipidity; while Mr. Winkle has been included because, well, after all, Mr. Seymour had made and maintained his reputation on his pictures of sporting life, and it would be hardly playing the game not to give him at least one sportsman, or would-be sportsman, among the party. The first chapter is artificial and elaborately boring because Dickens is completely out of his element; he has never met Mr. Pickwick and his friends in their club, and he does not know them, and has not the least idea what they would be likely to do and say.

In Chapter II the author, with a sigh of relief, gets his party out into the London streets. Here he is on old familiar ground, and a lively little Bozian sketch ensues. Yet the Pickwickians are still lay figures, mere puppets set up to be knocked down by cab-driver No. 924, who takes Mr. Pickwick for an informer, and who is more than equal, in interest as well as in fisticuffs, to the whole four of them, Pickwick, Snodgrass, Winkle and Tupman.

The interest quickens, though. Dickens recalls Potter, that theatre-loving friend of his in the Blackmore days, whose dashingly amateur manner had so appealed to him, and who has already figured in two of his sketches. In the nick of time Potter appears on the scene, just as he used to do in real life, master of any situation, and just the man for a street row, to extricate the Pickwickians from their most awkward predicament.

Precisely what Potter would have done. He has saved the situation—and the plot. He cannot be allowed to pass out of the story; so he receives a full paragraph of accurate description, and emerges fully clad, save that all his clothes are too small for him and he shows no sign of a shirt, as Alfred Jingle, Esq., of No Hall, Nowhere, and for the time being, of no name either. Mr. Jingle's life has been so full of vicissitudes that he has cultivated the habit of concealing his identity until he is quite sure of his company. Even then, as time will prove, he does not always use the same name, for "accidents will happen, even in the best regulated families" —or circumstances.

Before "the stranger," as Mr. Jingle continues to remain for some days, has been with the Pickwickians for more than a few moments, he has struck the first vital spark out of Mr. Pickwick.

"'I was ruminating,' said Mr. Pickwick, 'on the strange mutability of human affairs.'

"'Ah! I see—in at the palace door one day, out at the window the next. Philosopher, sir?'

"'An observer of human nature, sir,' said Mr. Pickwick."

With those words there begins to disappear the "learned" Mr. Pickwick of the "gigantic brain" and the "Tittlebatian theory," to be replaced gradually by the benevolent and golden-hearted child of nature beloved by all readers of Dickens. The author will still make one or two bad mistakes over Mr. Pickwick, in particular the stupid and ridiculous BILST UM PSHI S. M. ARK episode, but he is discovering that there is a man behind the spectacles and the tight gaiters; and is beginning to like him a little.

Meanwhile the party has bundled on to the "Commodore" coach, and is already on its way to Rochester. As Dickens knows this coach and its coachman, old Cholmondely (Chumley), from Chatham days, and is well acquainted with the road, and has decided to make Alfred Jingle a travelling companion for the Pickwickians, the journey and the story both go on "swimmingly," as Dickens himself described it, until with the aid of "an occasional glass of ale," Rochester is reached, "by which time the notebooks of both Mr. Pickwick and Mr. Snodgrass were completely filled with his (Jingle's) adventures."

At Rochester Dickens is thoroughly at home; Mr. Pickwick can observe the inhabitants of the four towns, dine his friends and the "stranger" at the Bull Inn in the High Street, and sleep off his wine in company with Mr. Snodgrass and Mr. Winkle while Mr. Tupman and the "stranger" slip upstairs to the charity ball; and at the ball Mr. Tupman and Mr. Jingle, the latter clandestinely attired in Mr. Winkle's dress suit, can meet Dr. Slammer, surgeon to the 97th, who is the exact image of Dr. Lamert who married Aunt Fanny, and all the fashionable society, military and civilian, of the garrison.

Dickens knows them all intimately, from the Commissioner downwards; he used to be stood on a table to sing to them. And so the remainder of the first number of the "Posthumous Papers" rattles merrily on through a quarrel at the ball and all the preliminaries of a duel that does not come off, but which allows the author to make great fun of sportsman Winkle, to an end that leaves the reader pleasantly anticipatory of further humorous adventures in No. II.

The author has not done too badly. He has got his story fairly under way, he has provided Mr. Seymour with some excellent material for drawings, he has done two or three descriptions in the best "Boz" style, and he has introduced at least one live character, Mr. Alfred Jingle. But, though his heart has begun to warm towards them, he has not yet really got to know Mr. Pickwick, Mr. Snodgrass, Mr. Tupman and Mr. Winkle.

The general public is not terribly interested. Four woodcuts by Seymour, accompanied by the usual agreeable chatter; it is not too good a bargain for a shilling, especially as this sort of book, picture plus story to match, has been done so often before. The general public on the whole prefers to keep its shillings in its pockets at present, and to wait and see whether there is going to be anything unusual enough in the series to justify a subscription.

Then, on April 20th, before the second number was out, before the plates for the second number had been completed, Mr. Seymour shot himself.

This is not the place to rake over the ashes of the unhappy controversy which arose out of this most distressing event. Suffice to say that the family of Mr. Seymour claimed, and tried to secure monetary satisfaction of their claim, that the idea of Mr. Pickwick was entirely the artist's, and that the author had appropriated it and unfairly made profit out of it. Dickens, who allowed the claim to distress him unduly, went so far as to publish a refutation of the charge as long as ten years after, in the preface to an edition of 1847, when his statement was amply substantiated by Mr. Chapman; but from time to time, right down to the present day, champions have arisen on behalf of Mr. Seymour.

Nor is it meet here to open the still more painful and delicate question of whether Dickens was in any way responsible for Seymour's suicide. The facts are these: On his return from Chalk, Dickens examined the drawings Seymour had submitted for No. II of "Pickwick." He found the

one designed to illustrate "The Stroller's Tale" in Chapter III
not quite to his liking. He wrote and told Seymour so, and
asked him to be good enough to alter it. He explained in
detail the alterations he desired, and included in the letter
an invitation to Furnivall's Inn, where he and his wife were
living, for the next Sunday evening. The invitation was to
a social, not a business, gathering. Of course, as Messrs.
Chapman and Hall were coming, they would no doubt discuss
things generally over their wine and cigars. But quite
informally.

Mr. Seymour came. It was the first time he and Dickens
had met. The publishers were not present, after all. The
party consisted of Charles Dickens and his wife, his young
brother Frederick, aged sixteen, and Mr. Seymour. They
talked over the drawing to be altered, Dickens explaining,
and Seymour agreeing and offering "no suggestion whatsoever." It sounds a cordial enough evening.

On the Monday night Seymour worked very late on the
picture of the drink-sodden actor's death-bed, which is in
point of vivid interest the best of the seven he produced for
"Pickwick." Having completed it, in the early hours of
Tuesday morning he destroyed himself, being depressed
through overwork and worry.

This untimely death raises the question of the mystery,
why did "Pickwick" continue? So far as the public was concerned there was no reason whatever for going on with the
publication; those people who had bought No. I had bought
it, presumably, for the sake of Seymour's engravings, and
Seymour being dead, as they were told in an "Address to
the Public" in No. II, what possible inducement was there to
buy further numbers?

No. I had made no popular hit. Nor did No. II. No
one could have blamed the publishers had they dropped the
venture. But they did not. They pushed on with it, in
spite of all discouragement, with a determination that on the
face of things seems astonishing. For Seymour's death was
not the only setback they received.

They experienced considerable difficulty and vexation over
securing an artist to take Seymour's place. An appoint-

ment had to be made urgently, for engravings had to be prepared at once for No. III, due for publication in just over a month. Several candidates appeared, including William Makepeace Thackeray, then thinking of draughtsmanship rather than the craft of writing. Thackeray visited Dickens at Furnivall's Inn, "with two or three drawings in my hand, which," he commented dryly at a Royal Academy dinner long after, "strange to say, he did not find suitable." Messrs. Chapman and Hall would very much have liked to secure George Cruikshank, who had illustrated the "Sketches by Boz," and whose name was considerably more of an advertisement than Seymour's. Mr. Cruikshank was far too busy; he sent along, however, a young man called John Leech, who might possibly fill the post. Leech, though afterwards to become famous and intimately connected with Dickens, was very young at the time, only nineteen, and had not yet really learned how to draw. So Mr. Jackson, engraver to Messrs. Chapman and Hall, was applied to for advice, and he recommended Robert Buss, a man of thirty-two, and an engraver of established reputation.

Mr. Buss submitted drawings and was engaged. Unfortunately he had done previously only wood engraving, and the publishers required metal engraving. He did his best. He toiled "night and day, for at least a month" to learn the technique of metal engraving, but succeeded in producing only two engravings which he admitted later were "abominably bad." He was paid off at once, and "Pickwick" was again without an artist. This, one would think, was the final blow.

No. I of "Pickwick," with four illustrations by Seymour, had made little impression; No. II had to appear with three engravings only by Seymour, and an announcement of the artist's death; No. III came out "embellished" only by two "abominably bad" engravings by Buss. It was enough to kill any publication depending upon pictorial appeal.

But was "Pickwick" depending upon pictorial appeal? Obviously not, in the publishers' opinion, or it would certainly have died. Whatever attitude the public took towards the story during the first three months, and there is every reason

to believe that it was a more favourable one than has usually
been represented, the publishers were quite clearly not basing
their hopes of ultimate success entirely, or even mainly, on
the illustrations.

Before Seymour's death they had been considering increasing the letterpress from twenty-four to thirty-two pages per
number; they had also listened sympathetically to Dickens'
suggestion that his rate of remuneration should be increased.
He had agreed in February to receive £9 9s. per sheet of
sixteen pages, with the proviso that if the publication proved
very successful, the publishers would "be happy to increase
the amount in a proportionate degree"; he was in April asking
that this amount should be increased to £10 10s. In May
or June he was writing to thank his publishers for the "very
handsome terms" they were now offering, £25 for each number
of thirty-two pages after No. VIII, or £4 a sheet more than he
had asked for in April.

Before "Pickwick" had shown any visible signs of becoming
a popular success the publishers were backing their young
author with might and main. This fact appears to dispose
of the suggestion, often made, that owing to Seymour's
death and Buss's failure, they were "desperate" about "Pickwick," or even that they were seriously anxious about its
ultimate success. They acted strangely if they were. All
the evidence suggests that they had, at an early stage, transferred their hopes from artist to author, and were so far
confident that their expectations would be justified that
they raised his salary almost monthly, and began to plan
six months ahead.

They were more right than they could ever have imagined.
In July "Pickwick" literally blazed into flame.

It is useless, especially after a lapse of practically one
hundred years, to attempt to say exactly why "Pickwick"
suddenly became a best seller, and much more than a best
seller, became indeed so universal a household favourite
that, as Mr. Ralph Straus says, "over every dinner-table,
whether it was standing, beautifully polished, in a West End
Mansion or a plain thing of deal in a country cottage, two
people, a master and a man, neither of whom had ever

existed outside the covers of a book, were monopolising the conversation."

The usually accepted explanation is that at this point Sam Weller entered the story.

Sam appears on the scene in Chapter X, which was the second chapter in No. IV, published June 30th, 1836. His entry is the reverse of dramatic; he is introduced quietly into the quiet courtyard of an old inn, which has been described in soothing, if not actually sleepy, terms. It is the yard of the White Hart Inn, High Street, Borough, once a celebrated coach headquarters, but by this time "degenerated into little more than the abiding and booking-places of country wagons"; the time is the peaceful early morning before the inn is more than half awake. Mr. Jingle has, it is true, arrived during the night with Miss Rachael, after successfully escaping from the pursuit of Mr. Wardle and Mr. Pickwick, but Sam knows nothing of this. He is discovered "busily employed in brushing the dirt off a pair of boots." Nothing could be more prosaic.

He is, of course, at once described.

> "He was habited in a coarse-striped waistcoat, with black calico sleeves, and blue glass buttons; drab breeches and leggings. A bright red handkerchief was wound in a very loose and unstudied style round his neck, and an old white hat was carelessly thrown on one side of his head. There were two rows of boots before him, one cleaned and the other dirty, and at every addition he made to the clean row, he paused from his work and contemplated its results with evident satisfaction."

And immediately springs into life, and wit:

"'Sam!'

"'Hallo,' replied the man with the white hat.

"'Number twenty-two wants his boots.'

"'Ask number twenty-two wether he'll have 'em now or wait till he gets 'em,'" was the answer. He goes on imperturbably cleaning other boots, explaining, with one of those quaintly far-fetched illustrations for which he is to become famous, "No, no, regular rotation, as Jack Ketch (the hangman) said wen he tied the men up."

He soon shows that his gift of repartee is equal to any occasion.

"There was another loud ring; and the bustling old landlady of the White Hart made her appearance in the opposite gallery.

"'Sam,' cried the landlady, 'where's that lazy, idle—why, Sam—oh, there you are; why don't you answer?'

"'Wouldn't be gen-teel to answer, till you'd done talking,' replied Sam gruffly."

And that he knows his London intimately:

"'Boots,' said the gentleman (Mr. Jingle).

"'Sir,' said Sam, closing the door, and keeping his hand on the knob of the lock.

"'Do you know—what's a name—Doctors' Commons?'

"'Yes, sir.'

"'Where is it?'

"'Paul's Churchyard, sir; low archway on the carriage-side, bookseller's at one corner, hot-el on the other, and two porters in the middle as touts for licences.'"

And that he is no mean judge of character:

"'My friend,' said the thin gentleman.

"'You're one of the adwice gratis order,' thought Sam, 'or you wouldn't be so werry fond o' me all at once.' But he only said, 'Well, sir.'"

Was the mere appearance in the story of Sam Weller, delightful as he is, quite sufficient to make a periodical publication jump suddenly from comparative neglect into fame? Hardly, one thinks. Say, rather, that the appearance of Sam Weller, or, to speak more truly, his second appearance in Chapter XII (the first chapter in No. V, in which he is engaged as personal servant to Mr. Pickwick), breathes into the story just that extra spark of vitality which was required to transform an already well-kindled and warmly-smouldering fire into a blazing conflagration.

The publishers had been confident from the start. The fact that the first three numbers of "Pickwick" sold only in hundreds was not so conclusive of failure in 1836 as it would be to-day. Newspapers and magazines passed from hand to hand then in a way unknown at the present time, so that a single

copy might have a score or more of readers. Reading aloud was
very much practised, even in literate circles, and was often a
necessity, seeing that over half the population was illiterate.
The probability is that "Pickwick" was much better known
and more popular during the first three or four months than
is usually suggested, but that it was as yet a restrained
popularity; more and more people were borrowing copies or
hearing the story read to them, but it did not yet compel them
to go out and buy it.

There is no sudden marked heightening of interest upon the
appearance of Sam Weller. The story has been growing in
strength all along. Mr. Pickwick has long ceased to be a
mere figure of fun, and has become the most genial and lovable of elderly gentlemen. Mr. Jingle first galvanized him
into life, old Wardle of the Manor Farm, Dingley Dell, at
once recognized his good nature and simple honesty of
character, a couple of horses which ran away revealed his
human frailty and showed that he was rather old and rather
stout, and could feel quite tired, hungry, dusty and cross, the
arrival of the Pickwickians at Dingley Dell proved that he
never could be cross for long, and that only very exceptional
vexations could disturb his sunny cheerfulness. From the
moment he so charmingly made friends with deaf old Mrs.
Wardle his picture is complete. He is a "dear." Definitely
one of the older generation, yet not too old to enter
in spirit, and now and then actively, into the fun and
frolic; by reason of his age and his unobtrusive yet definite
leadership of his party he is looked up to and respected
by all; but chiefly, by reason of his kindliness, his benevolent charm and his childlike and transparent simplicity,
he is beloved.

There is something more. By Chapter X Mr. Pickwick has
become a great deal more than an agreeable character in a
story. He has become the story itself, not so much in the
sense that the plot depends upon him, though in so far as
there is one it does, but much more, and this is infinitely
important, in the sense that the whole atmosphere of the
story depends upon him, and that it is an atmosphere which
is redolent of goodwill and good humour. One feels that

E

envy, hatred, malice and all uncharitableness simply cannot exist where Pickwick is.

In such an atmosphere his companions simply could not fail to come to life and to become likeable.  Mr. Tupman is caught in the grip of a real romance—and such a human one, too, with a spinster aunt of uncertain age—and, though he remains rather funny, he also becomes rather sweet and rather pathetic.  Mr. Winkle's exploits with horse and gun arouse laughter, but they arouse sympathy as well.  One gets the impression that Mr. Winkle is more sinned against than sinning; it is not his fault that everyone always takes it for granted that he can do this, that, or the other in the sporting way.  He has never said so.  Emily Wardle and the dinner at the Blue Lion in Muggleton have begun to make a man of Mr. Snodgrass—

"'Is anything the matter with Mr. Snodgrass, sir?' enquired Emily, with great anxiety.

"'Nothing the matter, ma'am,' replied the stranger. 'Cricket dinner—glorious party—capital songs—old port— claret—good—very good—wine, ma'am, wine.'

"'It wasn't the wine,' murmured Mr. Snodgrass, in a broken voice.  'It was the salmon.'"

And, naturally, what jolly and companionable people Mr. Pickwick gathers round him.  Old Wardle, bluff, genial and full of hospitality; his deaf, would-be cross but really good-natured old mother; Aunt Rachael, quite ready for a flirtation even at her age; Mr. Wardle's daughters; the old clergyman. . . .  Even the "careworn-looking man" with "sallow face and deeply sunken eyes" finds himself telling "The Stroller's Tale," which, to be sure, is sad enough; but would "Dismal Jemmy" ever have opened his mouth in less cordial company? The very serving girls at Dingley Dell are buxom and blithe, and the "large-headed, circular-visaged" farm hands, one feels sure, expand into large, bucolic smiles in the warmth of Mr. Pickwick's genial presence.

Then there is that gorgeous monstrosity, the fat boy.

"'Come along, sir.  Pray, come up,' said the stout gentle-man.  'Joe!—Damn that boy, he's gone to sleep again.'"

The fat boy is utterly impossible; he is an outrage upon

nature, conceived, surely, by his author in a fit of diabolical merriment, and never meant seriously to remain in the story. In no other story could he remain, except as a grotesque caricature, a mere rotund puppet introduced as comic relief to draw laughter from the audience. Everything is becoming possible in "Pickwick," thanks to the amazing gift Dickens is developing of describing a fairyland in the exactest terms of everyday reality. So the fat boy can stay, must stay; and is presently discovered to be no fool, and not nearly so sleepy as he looks, and, above all, a real boy.

People come pouring into the story. It is all perfectly natural; exactly as it would happen in real life. Every mile brings fresh companions, every day new friends. Always friends; nothing but hail-fellow-well-met comradeship is possible in the Pickwick atmosphere. Meanwhile adventure follows adventure, one hilarious scene tumbles on the heels of the other. The encounter with the coachman, the ball, the duel, the military manœuvres, the lunch on Wardle's coach, the ride to Dingley Dell that became a walk, the rook-shooting expedition on which Winkle shoots Tupman, the cricket match between Dingley Dell and All Muggleton, the Blue Lion dinner and its shocking sequel, three sadly tipsy Pickwickians, Tupman's love affair, Jingle's daring elopement, and a roaring pursuit of the eloping couple through a night of storm and rain. . . . The author is well under way, and a rollicking, rattling, clattering, breathless stage-coach of a comedy it is, ever broadening into farce, occasionally sobering into drama, but never losing for one instant, save in the interpolated stories—and why Dickens put those in none knows—its dominant note of invincible good nature.

One touch was necessary yet to transform this exuberantly boisterous chronicle into a work of genius.

Mr. Pickwick has emerged as the central figure, nay more, as the very life and soul of the story. Everything has come to depend upon him. Mr. Pickwick, however, began life in Chapter I as an amiable simpleton; and, for all the outward change that has taken place in him, the essence of his nature has not changed one atom. He has developed and become altogether lovable, but he is still a simpleton. He is

possessed, as Mr. G. K. Chesterton says, of a "god-like gullibility." So far, nearly all has gone well, and more than well,
because he has fallen in with such jolly, good-hearted people,
who would never dream of mocking at or abusing his simplicity, who are most of them, indeed, not less simple
than he. What is going to happen, though, if he meets one
or two more Jingles? Or many more ostlers like the one
who provided the horses for the journey from Rochester to
Dingley Dell?

He will, of course, be shamelessly and ignominiously
fooled, cheated and robbed. He will be taken in by every
rogue and sharper on the road; and the English roads abounded
in Pickwick's days with shifty characters always on the
look-out for a greenhorn. He cannot stand it; after two or
three such adventures all his dignity will be gone; he will be
merely a ridiculous old fool. Once strip Mr. Pickwick of his
quaint, childlike, ageless dignity, and you will leave him
helpless, and the story empty. He will not even continue to
be funny for long; there is little fun in baiting the defenceless.
It is when the animal bites that the fun begins.

Mr. Pickwick must have a protector. He needs someone
who is as sharp as he is simple, as wise in the ways of the
world as he is ignorant; who can prevent his being imposed
upon, and taken in at every turn, as he undoubtedly would be
if he rambled on his way unguarded. His present companions
are quite out of the question; Snodgrass, Tupman and Winkle
are quite as simple as he, and without his dignity. To introduce a fifth companion would be to upset the balance of the
group altogether. A new Pickwickian introduced to look
after Pickwick, would snuff out Messrs. Snodgrass, Tupman,
and Winkle altogether. But a valet? That idea would fit
exactly.

So Dickens searched among his memories and fished up
Sam Weller.

There were at one time, so it is said, at least three living
persons claiming to be the original of Sam Weller. Their
claims need not be disputed; they simply do not matter.
The only thing that does matter is that in Sam, Dickens has
found the one and only complement of Mr. Pickwick. Sam

could stand alone in any history; his ready wit would make a name for him anywhere, but alone he would be no more than a keen-eyed, wide-awake Cockney "Boots" possessed of the not uncommon Cockney gift of humorous repartee.

It is the perfect opposition of the two, and the exquisite dovetailing of their characters that have lifted Mr. Pickwick and Sam Weller clean out of the ruck of clever fictions, and ranked them among the immortals.

In a sense they are only one character, Pickwick-Weller. For Mr. Pickwick is as necessary to Sam as Sam is to Mr. Pickwick. If Sam protects his master from rogues and vagabonds, Mr. Pickwick keeps Sam straight, and brings out in him a loyalty, a sense of responsibility and an almost maternal care and love for his master, characteristics that could never have developed in the "Boots" at the White Hart Inn. In spite of the character given him by the landlady, one strongly suspects that Mr. Sam Weller's early life had been by no means so blameless as that the good lady would have Mr. Pickwick believe; he is allowed to leave the White Hart at a moment's notice, and apparently without regrets, and one cannot forget that the landlady, wanting him on that first morning of his appearance, called, "Sam!—where's that lazy, idle . . . ?" No, Sam has not been an irreproachable character; he would not be so sharp as he is if he had been. It needed a Pickwick to bring out his real worth.

That Mr. Pickwick undoubtedly did. Sam caught the public eye much more at first than his master. This is not surprising, for Mr. Pickwick has to be seen whole to be appreciated; the book has to be read again and again before it is realized how thoroughly he informs it, how it is impregnated with his spirit. Try to analyse Mr. Pickwick and he falls to pieces; one cannot by taking any single scene get from it the essential Pickwick. Nor, for that matter, can one obtain the quintessence of Wellerism from any extract, but one can pick up Sam at any point, and not fail to be at once interested and amused. That cannot be said of Mr. Pickwick. The following extracts from a review written in March 1837, when twelve out of the twenty numbers of "Pickwick" had been published, will perhaps make the point clear.

"Sam (the younger, we mean), who is undoubtedly the prime character of the whole book, is admirably conceived, and as admirably sustained. He unites in about equal measure, shrewdness and honesty; great attachment to his benefactor and master, with a very sagacious perception of his own interests; abundance of mother-wit, and a warm and honest heart. . . . Sam is about the most perfect example, in fictitious literature, of the very best specimens of the English lower classes.

"About Mr. Pickwick . . . there is a very grievous want of keeping and consistency. Nobody can reconcile the instances of absurdity and good sense which are alternately displayed in the conduct of Mr. Pickwick. Sometimes he is represented as saying or recording in his 'Note Books' . . . things which an idiot would not have believed, and at other times acting and talking like a person of excellent sense. . . ."

That description of Mr. Pickwick is perfectly just. No one *can* reconcile his inconsistencies; no one now ever wants to. It is they alone which make the book possible. No consistent man could possibly have gathered unto himself such a glorious mixture of "Perambulations, Perils, Travels, and Adventures" as did Mr. Pickwick. Nor could any consistent man have called forth the sterling qualities of Sam Weller.

Perhaps Sam himself expressed the truth more nearly than all the critics when, on taking his seat in the coach for Eatanswill, in the full glory of his new Pickwickian attire, he said to himself, "I wonder wether I'm meant to be a footman, or a groom, or a gamekeeper, or a seedsman. I looks like a sort of compo of every one on 'em. Never mind; there's change of air, plenty to see, and little to do; and all this suits my complaint uncommon; so long life to the Pickvicks, says I!"

Yes, long life to the Pickwicks! When Dickens made Mr. Pickwick and Sam Weller join forces he created an irresistible combination, which immediately caught the popular imagination and captured the hearts of all good English people. "Not a man, woman, nor schoolboy," says Mr. Ralph Straus, "but wanted to shake Mr. Pickwick by the hand and listen to Sam's Cockney wisdom." Not only was the combination irresistible, it was impregnable also; for while Sam made Mr. Pickwick safe by interposing his "Cockney wisdom" between his master and the "tricks i' the world," Mr. Pickwick's natural benevolence and good humour, thus shielded, could shine forth in all their splendour, irradiating everything and everyone, including Sam, cleaning away the dross, and leaving only the pure gold of kindliness and goodwill.

At the same time Fortune chose to smile upon the enterprise, and added a final blessing. Dickens found the perfect artist.

In this same year, it may be in the very month he created Sam Weller, "Boz" had found time to write, under the name of "Timothy Sparks," a serious little pamphlet entitled "Sunday under Three Heads," attacking certain parliamentary proposals which had been put forward, happily without success, to enforce a more rigid observance of the Sabbath. "Sunday under Three Heads," incidentally, is a most interesting piece of work, for it reveals an utterly different Dickens from the author of the "Sketches" and "Pickwick," a Dickens in dead earnest, hard, bitter, cynical, without a jest on his lips, a fierce defender of the scanty rights of the poor, and pouring scorn, contempt and invective upon the hypocritical rich who retained their own luxurious privileges but would deprive the workers of their only opportunity for healthy recreation by closing restaurants and shops, and forbidding travel in public vehicles on Sunday. It is Dickens the social reformer.

"I would to God," he exclaims in the first part, "that the iron-hearted man who would deprive such people as these of their only pleasures, could feel the sinking of heart and soul, the wasting exhaustion of mind and body, the utter prostration of present strength and future hope, attendant upon that incessant toil which lasts from day to day, and from month to month, that toil which is too often protracted until the silence of midnight, and resumed with the first stir of morning. How marvellously would

his ardent zeal for other men's souls diminish after short
probation, and how enlightened and comprehensive would
his views of the real object and meaning of the institution
of the Sabbath become!"

This pamphlet had been excellently illustrated by a young
man of twenty, Mr. Hablot Knight Browne. Whether
Dickens himself thought of him after Buss's dismissal, or
whether Mr. Jackson recommended him, is immaterial.
H. K. Browne was appointed to the vacant post of artist to
"Pickwick," took the pseudonym "Phiz," drew Sam Weller
brushing the boots in the White Hart courtyard, and a partnership, comparable only with that of Gilbert and Sullivan
later, had begun.  It was to last almost twenty-five years.

True, Dickens was always very much the senior partner; the
relation actually was that of director and assistant, with the
director very autocratic and extremely exacting, and the
assistant at times expected to make quite a lot of bricks from
very little straw, "Phiz" frequently having to draw illustrations for Dickens' works from a verbal description of what the
author intended to write.  But it was an eminently happy
partnership from the point of view of results; and in considering the resounding fame Dickens achieved through "Pickwick" and his succeeding works, it is only fair at this point to
pay tribute to the artist whose illustrations certainly rounded
off that success, if they did no more.

## CHAPTER IV

*"To understand the colossal fame of Dickens you have to go outside literature altogether now ; Charlie Chaplin is the only rival worth mentioning."*—J. B. PRIESTLEY (1928).

BY August 1836 "Pickwick" had definitely achieved a permanent success, and "Boz" was famous. The pseudonym was retained, and it was not until the publication of No. XVII of "Pickwick" that the author's real name was officially revealed to the public, though by that time most people knew what it was.

Sudden success, especially if coupled with popularity, is always liable to be intoxicating. Dickens would have had more excuse than most men had he become drunk with popularity. He was impulsive and ardent, emotional to a degree; he had had a hard struggle; he was newly married; and his success and popularity, as well as being sudden, were phenomenal.

In the best sense, he kept his head. He did not rush into extravagance or excess. He became neither arrogant nor conceited. Throughout his life, which from this point onwards was to consist of one crashing success after another, he remained, in spite of a certain imperiousness, a liking for rather gaudy attire, and a love of show and excitement, so essentially modest that his friends never failed to remark this quality in summing up his character.

In another, and most important sense, he lost his head completely. He accepted right and left commissions of work which publishers began to shower upon him, and quickly saddled himself with more promises than it was possible for him to fulfil. Forster says in his defence that "what the

sudden popularity of his writings implied, was known to
others some time before it was known to himself," and that
he "unwittingly sold himself into a quasi-bondage, and had
to purchase his liberty at a heavy cost, after considerable
suffering."

The "others" were, of course, the publishers, particularly
those who had already handled his work. Naturally they
were watching his progress carefully. Mr. John Macrone,
advised no doubt by William Harrison Ainsworth, who seems
to have had a very keen perception of the potential value of
"Boz," had already, as has been seen, secured the promise of
an early book by Dickens. He now made proposals for a
second series of "Sketches by Boz," which should be, as
before, first published in the *Chronicle*, and afterwards issued
in book form.

Messrs. Chapman and Hall were for the moment too fully
occupied in coping with the sudden popularity of "Pickwick."
Meanwhile, Dickens was being approached by Mr. Richard
Bentley, a well-known printer and publisher with a sound and
established reputation, who had already gathered round
himself a circle of distinguished writers. With Mr. Bentley,
Dickens signed a contract on August 22nd for two novels, his
fee for these to be £1,000, and in October he agreed with him
to undertake the editorship of a new monthly periodical to be
started in January 1837, and to be called *Bentley's Miscellany*.
His salary for this was to be £20 per month, and the first of
his novels was to commence in an early number. The name
of this magazine, by the way, was originally to have been
"The Wit's Miscellany," and when the change of title was
made, a critic, Richard Barham Harris, was heard to ask
plaintively, "But why go to the other extreme?"

In addition to undertaking all this, Dickens became this
autumn desperately interested in the theatre. It was only
four years previously that he had seriously considered making
his way on to the stage as an actor. Now he could afford to
look at the theatre from a very different angle. Instead of
working upwards, so to speak, from the stage door to a
share in the limelight, he could now propose to descend in full
shining glory upon the auditorium in the capacity of a popular

dramatist. Managers, it appeared, were only too glad to
welcome him in the part. Before the end of the year two pieces
by "Boz" had occupied the London stage; a farce called *The
Strange Gentleman*, adapted from a "Sketch" called *The
Great Winglebury Duel*, and described on the bills as a "comic
burletta"; and a comic opera, *The Village Coquettes*, to which
he had contributed the libretto, a friend of his own age, John
Hullah, being responsible for the music.

Of these pieces, the former, produced September 29th, the
opening day of the theatrical session, ran for sixty nights, a
long run in those times. This success, it must be admitted,
was chiefly due to the impressive acting of John Pritt Harley
as "The Strange Gentleman."

This actor, well-known and celebrated in particular for his
impersonations of low-comedy Shakespearean characters, was
in all probability the cause of the production of *The Strange
Gentleman*. It was *The Village Coquettes* which was originally
to have been produced on September 29th at the new theatre
of St. James's, but circumstances preventing it being ready for
presentation by that date, it was no doubt Harley who suggested to Mr. and Mrs. Braham, the owner-managers, that his
friend "Boz" had among his manuscripts an excellent little
farce which was quite certain to make a popular hit.
Incidentally, it was one that would, and did, provide Harley
himself with a part allowing for full exercise of his particular
genius.

Both pieces had been written some time previously, *The
Village Coquettes* in 1835, and *The Strange Gentleman* probably
during the early days of 1836. *The Village Coquettes* arose
out of a request for help from John Hullah, who had probably
become acquainted with Dickens through the latter's sister
Fanny. Hullah was engaged in 1835 upon an opera called
*The Gondolier*, and was having trouble with the libretto.
Dickens having agreed to help, objected to the whole of the
libretto, threw it out, and substituted an entirely new story
of his own. It sounds singularly like what he was to do only
a few months later with a Nimrod Club proposed by Messrs.
Chapman and Hall.

Though both farce and opera had actually been written

beforehand, they occupied a great deal of Dickens' time during
this autumn. He went frequently to the theatre, even, it is
said, taking a part in *The Strange Gentleman*. He altered *The
Village Coquettes* considerably at the request of Mr. Braham,
who wanted "a low comedy part introduced—without singing
—thinking it will take with the audience," in other words, just
such a part as "Boz" was elsewhere popularizing rapidly.

This theatrical work occupied not only much of his time,
it occupied his attention also and greatly excited him. It
was not very long before he was to become thoroughly
ashamed of these early dramatic efforts and to seek to prevent
their revival, an attitude he never subsequently abandoned;
but during the latter part of 1836 and the early months of 1837
he was tremendously in earnest about them, and it is quite
conceivable that at moments he quite seriously saw himself
playing the glittering rôle of England's most popular playwright.

He wrote to John Hullah to say that Braham was "speaking
highly of my works and 'fame' (!), and expressing an earnest
desire to be the first to introduce me to the public as a
dramatic writer"; and later to tell him that Harley had
written of *The Village Coquettes* that "It's a sure card—
nothing wrong there. Bet you ten pounds it runs fifty
nights," that Mr. and Mrs. Braham were "far more enthusiastic than Harley," Mr. Braham going so far as to declare
that "there has been no such music since the days of Sheild,
and no such piece since *The Duenna;* while Stansbury, "by
no means an excitable person," had had the opera *sung* right
through to him, and had been *charmed.* He had, as early as
February of this year, written to tell Messrs. Chapman and
Hall that he was anxious to publish *The Strange Gentleman;*
and *The Village Coquettes* was actually published by Bentley
in December, the month of its production at St. James's.

The publication of this play was to mark an epoch in the
life of Dickens. He sent a copy with an accompanying letter
to a man to whom he had just been introduced, namely
John Forster, no doubt mainly because he happened to be
the chief dramatic critic of *The Examiner.* This letter marks
the opening of the lifelong friendship between the two.

Dickens was a man who needed friends. Only in the warm sunshine of friendship could his genius mellow and come to full ripeness. Without being a hothouse plant, his nature was keenly sensitive to the winds of opinion, and required the utmost of that sincere kindliness, encouragement and sympathy which true and loving friends alone can give. Given that, he had in his turn a rich wealth of friendship to offer, the friendship of an open, generous, and warm-hearted man.

He needed friends also for another reason, to protect him, and chiefly from himself. Like his own Mr. Pickwick, he was possessed of a "godlike gullibility," which in his case consisted of an infinite capacity for self-deception. He was never properly to understand the limits of his strength, which he was constantly to undermine by making impossible demands upon it, nor could he save himself from the worries and vexations to which his impulsiveness laid him open. As has been seen, by the time he made acquaintance with Forster, he had already taken upon himself more work than any author could perform except at the risk of degenerating into a brain-weary hack journalist, frantically scribbling long hours to turn out his daily quota for the publishers, and steadily losing all freshness and originality in his work.

There was, of course, another way out of the difficulty in which Dickens was at this time involving himself. Contracts could be broken. The manuscript of "Gabriel Vardon" was to have been delivered to Mr. Macrone "on or before the 30th day of November [1836], or as soon after as I can possibly complete it." When Dickens wrote to Forster in February 1837 he sent to him his "Sketches," for which the arrangement had been made after that for "Gabriel Vardon," but there is no mention of this latter book. Actually, it was never written. It may be quite without significance, but it is worth noting that in this second letter to Forster, Dickens refers to his "obligations" to him. It was a word that was to be frequently applicable to their relationship.

Dickens was happy in his friends, of whom he made a great number, including many of the most illustrious men and women of the century. He was never more blessed than in his friendship with John Forster; and he was most singularly fortunate in the moment of its inception. There is no saying what follies he might not have committed in 1837 in the way of overwork or expensive quarrels with publishers had not Forster been on hand to be a companion to him, to advise him and to conduct business negotiations on his behalf.

John Forster, who was born on April 2nd, 1812, was a lawyer by profession who had devoted himself entirely to literary work and journalism. Although a member of the Inner Temple, and actually called to the Bar in 1843, he never practised. At the time when he met Dickens he was contributing to *The True Sun*, *The Morning Chronicle*, *The Courier*, and *The Athenæum*, and was chief literary and dramatic critic to *The Examiner*. He was in addition making a start upon biographical work with his "Lives of the Statesmen of the Commonwealth," part of which appeared between 1836 and 1839 in "Lardner's Cyclopædia," and which was published as a whole in 1840. Later, Forster was to produce other biographies, including one of Goldsmith. A "Life of Swift" was interrupted that he might write his "Life of Charles Dickens," and then cut short by his death in 1876, a death hastened, it may be, by his labours on the biography of his friend. He published also historical studies, and from time to time edited various reviews and newspapers, until an appointment in 1861 under the Lunacy Commissioners enabled him to devote himself fully to more literary pursuits.

All Forster's other compilations have passed into oblivion; they are now unread save by the research student. His "Life of Charles Dickens" remains, monumental, invaluable, indispensable, comparable only with Boswell's "Life of Samuel Johnson."

The relationship between Forster and Dickens had, however, nothing whatever in common with that between Boswell and Johnson. Boswell was, to put it bluntly, a hanger-on and a toady, a horrid little man whose almost only merits were that he refused to be shaken off, that he had a most persistent habit of asking questions, and a most industrious one of chronicling the answers. Forster was, from 1837 until the day of Dickens' death, in a very peculiarly intimate sense the novelist's confidential friend, from whom no secrets were hid; he was also his literary critic and proof-reader, legal adviser and business man in chief.

"There was nothing written by him after this date" [early 1837], says Forster, "which I did not see before the world did, either in manuscript or proofs." By the summer of this year Dickens was already writing to Forster, "I look back with unmingled pleasure to every link which each ensuing week has added to the chain of our attachment. It shall go hard, I hope, ere anything but Death impairs the toughness of a bond so firmly riveted."

The bond held, though it went very hard many a time, and the strains placed upon it later by Dickens' outbursts of temper, intense fits of depression, impossible demands, and other eccentricities of genius would have snapped the links of any friendship less devoted than that of John Forster; but Forster had for Dickens, so it has been aptly said, "a love amounting to jealousy."

Even so, as the years lengthened, while Forster became more than ever necessary to Dickens, what the world ordinarily calls friendship imperceptibly diminished, as indeed it was bound to do in time between men so opposite in temperament. As Mr. Edmund Yates has written, "Forster . . . was almost as much over, as Dickens was under, their respective actual years; and though Forster's shrewd common sense, sound judgment, and deep affection for his friend commanded, as was right, Dickens' loving and grateful acceptance of his views, and though the communion between them was never for a moment weakened, it was not as a companion 'in his lighter hour' that Dickens in his latter days looked on Forster."

Those days were as yet far ahead, and at present Forster was the constant companion of Dickens' 'lighter hour,' oftener indeed, Forster half-plaintively records, "than I could well afford the time." He relates amusingly how he would receive abrupt messages from Dickens. "I start precisely—precisely mind—at half-past one. Come, come, *come*, and walk in the green lanes. You will work the better for it all the week. COME! I shall expect you." More often the command was for an expedition on horseback, Dickens being in these days passionately fond of riding. "A hard trot of three hours?" would come a laconic note, Dickens' idea of a good ride being fifteen miles out, "ditto in and a lunch on the road." The demands of genius, even in lighter hours, are apt to be somewhat overwhelming; and it must have been no small responsibility for an orderly, methodical, and business-like man, with plenty of work on his hands, to have an exuberant friend who would brook no denial, and who might at any hour of the day send round an imperative bidding to an outing which would end goodness knows when.

Dickens in the first flush of his glorious youth, with all his splendid faculties quickened and his giant energies unleashed, spurred and stimulated by success, must at times have been an exacting companion, with his thirty-mile rides and his ten-mile walks to shake off the effects of his days of continuous and concentrated work. But if he was exacting, he was also irresistibly fascinating. Forster's description of him at this time is memorable:

"A look of youthfulness first attracted you, and then a candour and openness of expression which made you sure of the qualities within. The features were very good. He had a capital forehead, a firm nose with full wide nostril, eyes wonderfully beaming with intellect and running over with humour and cheerfulness, and a rather prominent mouth, strongly marked with sensibility. The head was altogether well-formed and symmetrical, and the air and carriage of it were extremely spirited. The hair so scant and grizzled in later days was then of a rich brown and most luxurious abundance, and the bearded face of his last two decades had hardly a vestige of hair or whisker; but there was that in his face as I first recollect it which no time could change, and which remained implanted on it unalterably to the last. This was the quickness, keenness, and practical power, the eager, restless, energetic outlook on each several feature, that seemed to tell so little of a student or writer of books, and so much of a man of action and business in the world. Light and motion

flashed from every part of it. *It was as if made of steel,*
was said of it, four or five years after the time to which I
am referring, by a most original and delicate observer, the
late Mrs. Carlyle."

Truly, a young god among men! Add to all this an
impulsive good nature, a generous warm-heartedness, a full
and boisterous enjoyment of life, a radiant flow of animal
spirits, flashing wit, and an immense capacity for friendship,
and one must find in the Dickens of 1837 a youth compellingly
attractive not only in person but in personality also. No
wonder Forster loved him. Happily for Dickens, Forster
concealed behind that brusque, gruff manner of his, not only
love, but the kindest and staunchest heart in the world.

Dickens was at this time literally soaked in success; his
whole being was permeated with the rich joy of hard work and
abundant reward. The strain of his work had hardly begun
to be noticed, and he could throw it off at any moment. He
felt equal to all demands. True, the printers were for ever
at his heels; he could never get a week ahead of them, but
what did that matter? He could work till his brain reeled,
pouring down upon paper the teeming fancies of his brain, till
for a brief space the greedy hunger of the printing presses
would be appeased, and then he would scribble exultantly to
John Forster, "To be heard of at Eel-pie-house, Twickenham!"
and gallop off light-heartedly through the glorious morning
air.

For was ever success like unto this? Forster, writing soberly
and critically thirty-six years after the event, could still say of
the popularity of "Pickwick" that "For its kind, its extent,
and the absence of everything unreal or factitious in the causes
that contributed to it, it is unexampled in literature;" and
he goes on to say, almost with an air of not even at that date
having got over his first dazed surprise, and being still at a
loss to explain the phenomenon, "Here was a series of sketches,
without the pretence to such interest as attends a well-con-
structed story; put forth in a form apparently ephemeral as
its purpose; having none that seemed higher than to exhibit
some studies of cockney manners with help from a comic

artist; and after four or five parts had appeared, without newspaper notice or puffing . . . . it sprang into a popularity that
each part carried higher and higher, until people at this time
talked of nothing else, tradesmen recommended their goods
by using its name, and its sale, outstripping at a bound that
of all the most famous books of the century, had reached to an
almost fabulous number."

Forster does not exaggerate in any one particular. "Pickwick" began as a piece of literary hackwork, of a kind moreover quite common in those days; it had no unity of purpose,
no strong thread of interest running through it, no plot; not
£10 was spent in advertising it; such reviewers as noticed it
were distinctly cool—and within a few months the whole
country was talking about it, the printers were working day
and night shifts to cope with the demand, in country towns
people were queueing up at the newsagents to secure a copy,
from country villages folk were tramping miles to buy or
borrow one, in London and the big towns Pickwick Clubs
were being formed, "Boz" cabs were for hire on the streets,
and the public omnibuses were plastered with pictures of the
young author; the ladies were buying Pickwick chintzes and
Pickwick biscuits, young men were swaggering in Weller
corduroys with Pickwick hats and gaiters, swinging Pickwick
canes, and smoking Pickwick cigars; manufacturers and
tradesmen were advertising everything from blacking to
brandy on quotations and illustrations from "Pickwick";
correspondents were addressing letters to friends with Pickwick pens on Pickwick notepaper, and striking the match to
heat the sealing-wax for the envelope on a Bill Stumps
matchbox. Judges on the bench were slyly rebuking counsel
in Wellerisms, and learned counsel were gravely retorting
with quotations from the memorable case of Bardell *versus*
Pickwick. Men and women, old and young, boys and girls, were
flinging catchwords from "Pickwick" at each other in their
homes and in the streets, and the very cats and dogs were
being christened "Mrs. Bardell," "Job Trotter," "Jingle,"
and "Sam Weller."

Of all the amazing stories told of this incredible popularity,
perhaps the best is that related by Thomas Carlyle in a letter

to Forster as having been told to him by "an archdeacon with his own venerable lips," of how a solemn clergyman, having administered holy communion to a sick person in his house, heard, to his unspeakable horror, as he left the bedroom, the patient exclaim, "Well, thank God! 'Pickwick' will be out in ten days any way!"

Then, before "Pickwick" had reached the acme of its popularity, "Oliver Twist" began to appear.

January, February, and March, 1837, must have been wonderful months for Charles Dickens. On January 6th a son and heir was born to him. In February he and his wife managed to snatch a brief holiday at Chalk in their honeymoon lodgings; and in the same month "Oliver Twist" commenced publication. On March 6th a third play of his, a comic burletta entitled *Is She His Wife? or, Something Singular*, was presented at St. James's Theatre. A few days later he moved from Furnivall's Inn to his first real home, 48 Doughty Street, Mecklenburgh Square, W.C.1, while at the end of the month a grand celebration dinner was held in honour of the first anniversary of "Pickwick," at which feast, in addition to many compliments, his publishers handed him a cheque for £500 over and above his salary.

No. 48 Doughty Street, it may be mentioned here, is now national property, held in trust as a permanent Museum and Library, and called the Dickens House. It contains the finest library and collection of Dickensiana in the world, and is the headquarters of the world-wide Dickens Fellowship, which raised the money for its purchase in 1923. Dickens lived here from 1837 to 1839, and here wrote the latter part of "Pickwick," and the novels "Oliver Twist" and "Nicholas Nickleby." The fabric of the house is as it was during Dickens' occupation, save that the basement kitchen, which was in a very bad state of repair when the trustees took possession, has been transformed into a replica of the Manor Farm kitchen at Dingley Dell. Doughty Street, which runs South by East from Mecklenburgh Square towards Theobald's Road, just west of Gray's Inn Road, was closed at either end in Dickens' time by gates which have long since been removed.

The first number of "Oliver Twist" appeared alongside the

eleventh number of "Pickwick," and for ten months these stories were being produced concurrently.

It is difficult at this date to dismiss even for a moment from one's mind that image of Dickens which is familiar throughout the English-speaking world, being yearly reproduced in countless pictures and prints; that of the bearded, elderly Dickens of the 1850's and 1860's, the beloved "Master," the writer of international reputation, whose strong, powerful, experienced face radiates a settled confidence, yet is scored by deep lines of suffering, and marked by years of heavy and exacting toil. It is necessary to do so, however, if one is to realize to the full what an astounding achievement was the writing of "Pickwick" and "Oliver Twist" side by side, day in and day out, throughout ten months of serial publication.

Even the painting by Maclise does not reveal quite the youth one must imagine, for it shows Dickens as he was in 1839, when both "Pickwick" and "Oliver Twist" were completed, and he was pressing on to win fresh laurels. In that portrait one can see already the beginning of that look of certain confidence which can spring only from a realization of acknowledged and unquestioned power. A drawing by S. Laurence of "Boz" in 1838 is better, for it seems to hint at eyes still questioning, probing, as yet not quite sure; but even that is not quite young enough.

Dickens was barely twenty-five when he began to drive this strangely assorted pair in double harness. He was still very much a beginner in the world of letters; for all his fame, for all the applause that greeted him on every hand, he was no more than a youngster with half a book, some reprinted articles, and a stage farce or two behind him. His immense popularity, viewed dispassionately, seems based on a slender enough foundation; it was the quality, not the quantity, of his work which had brought success, and that quality would have to be sustained if popularity were to continue.

There was in his published work as yet little to indicate to the general public the Dickens that was to emerge from the writing of "Oliver Twist" and the second part of "Pickwick," though there might be sufficient to reveal to a few far-seeing minds the possibility of such emergence. He had won his reputation as the king of laughter, who had set all England rocking with mirth, and as the very prince of observers, who had played with his powerful searchlight on the lives of the great mass of middle-class and lower-middle-class people— hitherto of no great interest to writers of fiction—and for the first time since Shakespeare had made these lives stand out as real and interesting. He had done something new.

This was no mean achievement for a beardless "boy" of twenty-four. A much greater was to follow. The piercing weapon of laughter and the impregnable shield of accurate and acute observation were to be shown in the hands of a warrior, who could fight on the battlefield as well as run his course on the tournament yard, and whose real heart was in the battle and not in the jousts.

It is perhaps unwise even to suggest that there was any conscious idea of social reform in Dickens' mind when he began to write "Oliver Twist." In all probability there was not. Dickens' work was developing him faster than he knew, and his power of spontaneous creation was well ahead of his judgment. He was to remain all his life a man of feeling rather than of thought, and it was pure feeling, stored up during those impressionable years in which he had lived among and observed the poor, the humble, the lowly, the wretched, and the ill-used, that was now to come pouring out of him.

It has been emphasized in an earlier page that the boy Charles Dickens never himself experienced the real depths of poverty, never knew personally starvation, or rags, or utter destitution. He came near enough to it, though, to be able, with his keen senses, to appreciate what it meant, and was aided to this appreciation by the fact that in the London of the 1820's poverty, hopeless, filthy, and frightful, with its dreadful concomitants of disease, drunkenness and vice, walked openly through the streets, beholden by all, while its squalid courts and festering tenements clustered noisome at the very back doors of the mansions of the rich.

A more enlightened and better-policed age has purged the streets of our great cities, reduced poverty and vice, pulled down most of the worst slums and hidden the rest, so that comfort and prosperity are no longer exposed to contact with the suffering poor, but that has happened since the days of Dickens' childhood. Then, wherever one went, wherever one lived, in London at any rate, barefooted, hungry and vicious poverty leaned against the street lamp, hawked and thieved on the pavement, and lived just round the corner.

All this Dickens had seen; and in his heart had grown up a fierce smouldering rage that such things could be. Like all true idealists, all great reformers, he saw the uselessness of palliatives, and searched for fundamental causes, and so his anger became directed against the indifference and hypocrisy, the blindness and selfishness of society, and the bribery and corruption and rottenness in officialdom, as the main reasons why such misery could be and was allowed to continue. For poverty itself he had nothing but pity, for he saw only too plainly that it was not the fault of the poor that their lives were often slovenly and miserable, drink-sodden and vice-besotted, that it was the fault of the appalling conditions in which they were born and bred, the hopeless monotony of the incessant and unprofitable toil by which alone they could snatch from life a bare subsistence, and that it was the elemental, irrepressible desire of human nature to seek any outlet, to escape by any means from an intolerable weariness and boredom, that drove them to theft and murder and bestial excesses. He saw, too, the unflinching bravery, the indomitable courage and the resolute determination of those—and they were found in their thousands—who refused to sink under the weight of circumstances, who fought hunger with a jest, laughed at rags, found consolation in suffering, happiness in privation, and lasting solace in the simple loves of family and home.

The thought of all this had long been fermenting in Dickens' mind, and to those who can look down upon his early work from the profound elevation of almost one hundred years there are not lacking in it indications that sooner or later he must give his indignation full expression.

That he had any conscious idea of doing so when he began "Oliver Twist" is much too rash a hypothesis to put forward. The evidence is all to the contrary. He set out to tell a story; his unconscious mind pointed the way of that story; Oliver and his associates became so real to their author, grew so upon him, that he could hardly bear to leave off writing; and thus, without a thought of moralizing, without the slightest intention on Dickens' part to preach, great social evils were exposed in the ruthlessly accurate pictures he was compelled to draw, and the desire was kindled in many hearts to sweep them away.

It would be fascinating to try and trace in detail the steps which led up to this apparently sudden development of Dickens. Months beforehand, in his first series of "Sketches," he had lightly attacked some abuses and injustices to which the poor were exposed, in his pictures of "The Beadle," "The Broker's Man," "The Schoolmaster," "The Pawnbroker's Shop," "The Prisoners' Van," and elsewhere, while in "Gin Shops" he had almost fiercely suggested that the way to fight drunkenness was to attack, not the public houses, but the hunger and misery upon which they throve. In "Sunday under Three Heads" he had spoken out unrestrainedly, had let loose a bitter denunciation of the self-indulgence and hypocrisy of the rich, and of legislation proposed by and on behalf of the privileged classes.

"Pickwick" was begun, of course, as a purely comic book; it had no other purpose than to amuse. Yet even in the first half of "Pickwick," all bustle and laughter, it is not long before a deeper note begins to recur. "The Stroller's Tale" in Chapter III is a terrible picture of a drunkard's death, and the stroller himself is a "Dismal Jemmy," a man of "all sorts of miseries." This sudden peep into the squalor of a broken-down actor's life is quite out of place in the story, and its insertion can only be explained by the theory that Dickens' subconscious mind was all the time revolving this problem of poverty.

With the introduction of Sam Weller into the book, one is bound sooner or later to come into contact with low life, for Sam has known what it is to have to sleep in the arches of Waterloo Bridge. The moment Messrs. Dodson and Fogg appear, it is certain that the law's delays and circumlocutions and sharp practices are going to be exposed and ridiculed, for young Dickens has never attempted to conceal the fact that he thinks the law an ass, and lawyers humbugs.

Old Wardle's beautiful legend of Gabriel Grub, the sexton who was stolen by the goblins, is pure sermon. It tells of the awful fate reserved for "the man with the sulky face and the grim scowl," who throws "evil looks at the children," and strikes an innocent youngster "in the envious malice of his heart, because the boy could be merry and he could not." The pictures shown to Gabriel Grub in the goblins' cavern have all the same theme, happiness, contentment and peace found in hard work, endurance of privation, and the love of children.

Like all great-hearted men, Charles Dickens could not help loving children; their innocence, their trustfulness and their simplicity appealed irresistibly to one who was himself essentially childlike in nature. It is singularly happy, but not remarkable, that the first of those great books by Charles Dickens which, by their laughter and ridicule, and their exact and unexaggerated description of injustice and suffering, were to blast out of existence abuses that had flourished unchecked by solemn legislation, had for its hero a child, and, superb stroke of genius and of daring, an orphan child, a workhouse brat.

This is no place for a dissertation upon the way in which children brought up by the parish in the earlier part of the nineteenth century were treated. Those who wish to learn how they were driven in droves like cattle (only much worse handled) into factories and mines, there to grow twisted and deformed, will find it all written down in the sober pages of the reports of one Royal Commission after another published during the first half of the nineteenth century. Suffice to say that the early life of Oliver Twist, as related in the first seven chapters of the book, far from being an exaggerated account of impossible hardships and sufferings, is that of, on the whole, a very fortunate workhouse child. He was not starved to death; he does not seem to have been beaten with anything more serious than fists and canes; he escaped being apprenticed to Mr. Gamfield, the brutal chimney sweep, and he was finally indentured to a master who was "as far as his power went—it was not very extensive—kindly disposed towards the boy."

It was hardly to be expected that the writing of "Oliver Twist" and the development of Dickens' powers that this book reveals could be without effect upon "Pickwick." The effect is clearly obvious; and Dickens had to face the criticism that "Pickwick" ended as an altogether different book from that which he began. The criticism is just, and the world is greatly the gainer from the fact.

The first half of "Pickwick" is, in spite of occasional graver notes, rollicking comedy throughout. The fainting of Mrs. Bardell in Pickwick's arms, the glorious Eatanswill election, the Leo Hunters, Mr. Pickwick's adventures in the garden of the boarding school at Bury St. Edmunds, and at Ipswich in the bedroom of the middle-aged lady in yellow curl-papers, the arrest, interrogation and release of the Pickwickians by the majestic and impartial Mr. Nupkins, and Sam's pilgrimage to Dorking, have all provided scenes of richest farcical comedy. The treatment is episodic; except that the same main characters figure in each, the adventures are unrelated, the merest thread of plot stringing them together.

The culminating comic (as opposed to tragic) episode in "Pickwick" is the magnificent Dingley Dell sketch covering Chapters XXVIII to XXX, in which Dickens fairly lets himself go over a coach ride, a grand Christmas party, complete with wedding, and a comic skating expedition that nearly ended in tragedy. All that is good-humoured and jolly and cheerful in Dickens is poured out in abundance in these wonderful chapters, which for light-hearted merriment and pure fun are unrivalled.

After that, "Pickwick" ceases to be episodic, and settles down to be a story, the story of the memorable action of Bardell against Pickwick and of what ensued upon Mr. Pickwick's refusal to pay the damages assessed against him. Of the second half of the book, one-quarter is devoted to Mr. Pickwick's experiences in the Fleet Prison.

This great account of a debtors' prison is easily the finest and most moving piece of sustained descriptive writing in the whole book. It can take its place without fear alongside the story of Mr. Micawber in the King's Bench prison and the Dorrit family in the Marshalsea.

But what, precisely, has it to do with "The Pickwick Papers"? If one compares it with the account of the trial of Bardell against Pickwick, which is told in the purest Pickwickian style, one will realize how far Dickens has travelled away from the road on which he started. He has travelled, in fact, into the world of "Oliver Twist," and in that world he will henceforth remain.

All the wit and humour, the laughter and the merriment and good fellowship that sent England raving over "Boz" are still there, but there has come also a deep tenderness, a pathos, and a burning indignation now veiled in laughter, now choking with tears, running like an undertone throughout. It is always remembered that Dickens made, and still makes, the whole world laugh; it must not be forgotten that he also made those of his own generation weep. We have in these days grown ashamed to shed tears, and may feel inclined to scorn our grandparents for shedding them so readily and copiously; but we cannot penetrate into the secret of Dickens' extraordinary hold upon his readers unless we recognize that it was due as much to his ability to wring their hearts as to his genius for provoking mirth.

Dickens is often reviled by twentieth-century critics for his sickly sentimentality. Tastes change; our grandparents liked a good cry, and no doubt it benefited them, but the point to be noted here is that the "sickly sentimentality" of Dickens always has its roots in indignation. His most pathetic pictures are always of those who have suffered cruelty or injustice or privation. It is never sentimentality for the sake of being sentimental; and for that reason alone, much as we may dislike it personally, we cannot but defend it. Had he remained pure humorist he might have turned cynical and hard; there are signs indicative of this in "Sketches by Boz," and it is clearly evident in "Sunday under Three Heads."

In "Oliver Twist" Dickens found his full stature; hitherto, for all his well-deserved success, he had been no more than

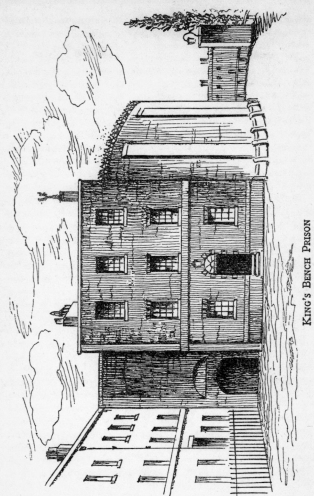

King's Bench Prison

brilliantly experimenting. Like Shakespeare, he began with a comedy of manners, and like him, quickly found himself absorbed by the humanity of which manners is but the cloak. As he himself put it, "though the mere oddity of a new acquaintance was apt to impress one at first, the more serious qualities were discovered when we became friends with the man."

Before he had been engaged for more than a few months on "Oliver Twist" he suffered an overwhelming grief. Mary Hogarth, the younger sister of his wife, whom he loved so deeply, had come to live with them in Doughty Street, and here one night in May she was taken suddenly ill and died within a few hours. She was only seventeen years old. Her death, which was quite unexpected, for she had returned from the theatre that same evening apparently quite well, so upset Dickens that he was unable to continue his work. The publication of both "Pickwick" and "Oliver Twist" was interrupted, and he went out to Hampstead to seek rest and peace.

It is indicative of the excited state into which the reading public of England had been thrown that the non-appearance of the "Pickwick" number caused the most absurd rumours to spread, as that the book was being produced by a syndicate and the "editor" was an inmate of the King's Bench debtors' prison. Another suggested that the author was a boy of eighteen, who had gone mad as the result of overwork. These "idle speculations and absurdities" caused Dickens to publish addresses to his readers on the resumption in July of the publication of "Pickwick" and "Oliver Twist," explaining the reason for the interruption.

In the autumn of this year, 1837, Messrs. Chapman and Hall announced in the XVIIth number of "Pickwick" that they had "completed arrangements with Mr. Dickens (thus first introduced to his readers in his proper name) for the production of an entirely new work, to be published monthly, at the same price and in the same form as the 'Pickwick Papers.'" In the contract made between publishers and author, dated November 19th, 1837, it was agreed that Dickens was to be paid £150 for each of the twenty monthly numbers, the first of which was to be delivered on March 15th, 1838, and that five years after the completion of the work the entire copyright was to revert to the author. This book, produced in accordance with the contract, was "The Life and Adventures of Nicholas Nickleby."

Before this, however, for six months or more Dickens had been reaping the harvest of his rash agreements of 1836, and been taught a sharp lesson as to the meaning of the words copyright and contract.

It has sometimes been said that he was an excellent man of business. The truth is more nearly got at by saying that he had excellent business acumen without comparable business ability. He realized very quickly after the success of "Pickwick" the greatly enhanced financial value of his work, and began to chafe at the thought of the unsubstantial rewards he was to receive under agreements entered into while his fame was still in the making. He could, unfortunately, see only one side of the question—his own. He could not understand that publishers who had speculated on his probable success were entitled to the full reward of their courage. He even persuaded himself that they had no right to hold him to contracts which he considered, in view of his now undoubted fame, to be unfair.

The first dispute was over "Gabriel Vardon." Mr. Macrone naturally wrote for it towards the end of 1836 and, finding that it had not even been begun, threatened legal proceedings. Dickens, having no shred of defence, hurriedly compromised by handing over to Macrone the entire copyright of all his "Sketches," first and second series, in return for a payment of £100 and the cancellation of his agreement to write "Gabriel Vardon."

In the summer of 1837 he heard that Mr. Macrone was proposing to re-issue the "Sketches" in monthly parts, in a form similar to that in which "Pickwick" was appearing. On receipt of this information he wrote indignantly to Forster asking him to go at once to Macrone and use every argument he could against the scheme, pointing out how cheaply the "Sketches" had been purchased, the profits the publisher had already made from them, and how injuriously this new form of publication would affect the author, who would appear to be thrusting old work upon the public in order to fill his pocket to the utmost.

Forster went, no doubt fully realizing that Macrone was perfectly within his rights. He found the publisher deaf to all arguments, and finally had to suggest the repurchase of the copyright by the author. Mr. Macrone asked so large a sum that Forster would not consider it, but broke off negotiations, and advised Dickens to do nothing about the matter for a while.

This was impossible for Dickens. Any vexation worried him into such a state of excitement that he was unable to work. He had to find an immediate solution. The very next day he sent to Forster, failed to find him, and in his absence concluded, conjointly with Messrs. Chapman and Hall, an agreement with Mr. Macrone to repurchase the copyright of "Sketches by Boz" for £2,000, with the express purpose that Messrs. Chapman and Hall should publish them in monthly parts, and in the hope that his own publishers, by reason of their better equipment, would reap a larger profit than could Mr. Macrone, and so recoup him for the great expense of buying the copyright.

Dickens' conduct in this matter cannot be defended. He had surrendered unconditionally the copyright of the "Sketches," and Macrone was perfectly entitled to do whatever he pleased with what was, in every sense, his own property. The only plea one can possibly advance for Dickens is that he was young, that owing to his rising household expenses and his father's now frequent "disappearances," he was not too well off, and that his highly strung, nervous temperament caused him to brood and worry over what appeared to him to be unjust until it became monstrously unfair. No author, having disposed of a copyright, ever ceases to regard his work as his own; and it must be remembered that Dickens' popularity was immense, that his publishers were undoubtedly making fortunes out of him, and that they had certainly got from him contracts which time had quickly proved to be very favourable to themselves, and very unfavourable to him. Still, they were contracts; and so no more can Dickens be defended in the dispute with Mr. Bentley which ensued, and which dragged on from midsummer until September, being then closed for a time by a compromise in which he was very generously treated.

Under his agreement with Bentley of August 1836, Dickens had contracted to write two novels at a fee of £500 each. At the time when it was made, this agreement was a very handsome and profitable one for Dickens; it contrasted most favourably with the £200 offered by Mr. Macrone for "Gabriel Vardon" only a month or two previously. Dickens, however, appears to have forgotten all about the terms until the following midsummer, by which time "Pickwick" was booming as never before, and "Oliver Twist," the first of the Bentley novels, gaining monthly new admirers, and then suddenly awakened to a realization that not only was he being miserably underpaid for "Oliver Twist," but that when that was completed he was still under contract to produce a second novel on the same terms. There was also a third tale in the offing somewhere. This was unendurable!

As before, Forster was called in to clear up the mess. The second novel had been promised for a date which by this time had become manifestly impossible; its production was now postponed on the undertaking that it should be completed by November 1838. Mr. Bentley gave up his right to the third novel, on terms which Forster says were favourable to Dickens. The remuneration for "Oliver Twist" was increased from £500 to £750.

Even with these accommodations, Dickens was still faced with the prospect of being desperately overworked for a very considerable period. "Pickwick" was not yet completed; the end of "Oliver Twist" was still many months ahead, its run in the *Miscellany* not being due to close until March 1839; "Nicholas Nickleby" had to start in March 1838, and "Barnaby Rudge" to be completed by November of the same year. In addition, Dickens had his editing of the *Miscellany* to do monthly, and had further agreed to edit for Bentley a "Life of Grimaldi." He was also writing from time to time occasional small pieces elsewhere.

Under such conditions of taskmastership, it appears

marvellous that his work could possibly have retained freshness and originality. The mere bulk of what he turned out in 1837–8 would have swamped an ordinary writer; at a moderate estimate he was composing some 30,000 words of original matter every month, an average of one thousand words per day, Sundays included, not counting editorial and journalistic work. Unremitting industry might faithfully perform such a task, but to inform the work with genius— was that possible? No wonder the *Quarterly Review*, in a notice on the completed "Pickwick," gravely warned that "Mr. Dickens writes too often and too fast. . . . If he persists much longer in this course, it requires no gift of prophecy to foretell his fate—he has risen like a rocket, and he will come down like the stick."

The answer is to be found in a survey of what he achieved. From January 1837 to November of the same year "Pickwick" and "Oliver Twist" were pouring from his pen; during almost the whole of 1838 "Oliver Twist" and "Nicholas Nickleby" ran side by side. Throughout these two years he was very seriously editing *Bentley's Miscellany*, and contributing thereto the "Mudfog Papers," a series of articles humorously descriptive of "the proceedings of the Mudfog Association for the Advancement of Everything." He wrote in addition a small book called "Sketches of a Young Gentleman" and a play called *The Lamplighter*, and edited the "Life of Grimaldi."

The mere quantity is impressive, though it will be noted that "Barnaby Rudge" has not yet appeared. That had proved the one straw too many for the camel's back, and its production had been a second time postponed. Quantity by itself, however, is valueless; it is the amazing quality, the vitality, the reality and the vividness of the three great books of these two years, "Pickwick," "Oliver Twist," and "Nickleby," their freedom from any signs of strain or artificiality, their fertile inventiveness, buoyant humour, deep genuine pathos, and intensely dramatic scenes, which gives back the real answer, one that confounds the critics and doubters, and leaves the ordinary reader dumbly wondering at what seems superhuman power.

F

The achievement becomes all the more remarkable when one considers that Dickens was at all times capable of being driven to distraction by the slightest worries or vexations, that for two months in 1837 he was prostrate with grief over Mary's death, that for months and months he was liable to agonies of suspense and infuriation over quarrels with his publishers, which caused one major and a number of minor interruptions to his work. It becomes yet a little more remarkable when one reads of constant visits to the theatre, frequent dinners and parties, hypnotic séances at Doughty Street, a hustling sightseeing tour of Belgium, seaside holidays at Broadstairs, and endless rides and walks with Forster and Ainsworth.

Such an achievement was only possible to a man of great strength and energy, full and lively mind, and extreme powers of concentration. To say that Dickens possessed all these is to make a mild statement of an extraordinarily dramatic fact. He had in addition that something more which transforms talent into genius. Few writers have ever possessed to the extent that Dickens did the gift of living in the world of their own imaginings. Hardly any writer has so absorbed reality, so richly stored his mind with varied experiences from every-day life. No writer has been more successful in combining in his work photographic accuracy of details with an alluringly imaginative handling of them. To put it paradoxically, Dickens did not write his novels: he lived them, and the novels wrote themselves. This is apparent in every page of his earlier books.

Read the memorable trial of Bardell against Pickwick. It is like no trial on earth. No lawyer ever states his case in quite such extreme terms as did Serjeant Buzfuz; never was evidence quite so irrelevant made to appear so significant, never were witnesses quite so funny as Mrs. Cluppins or the unfortunate Mr. Winkle; never did one quite so bamboozle learned counsel as did the imperturbable Mr. Sam Weller. But it is all intensely real, so real that eminent jurists have declared that there is no aspect of the law which is not faithfully reflected in the proceedings. It is minutely real, because Dickens is sitting there in the court room every

WILLIAM HARRISON AINSWORTH

*From the drawing by Daniel Maclise, R.A., 1834*

moment of the time, just as he had sat over and over again in his youth listening intently to and reporting endless cases of Bardell against Pickwick.

Or follow Mr. Pickwick into the Fleet prison. It is not Mr. Pickwick only who follows Mr. Roker into the warden's room—there is a boy, Charles Dickens, whose father has just been arrested for debt, and who, in spite of his eyes brimming with tears and his heart burning with shame, is yet curious enough to peep into the other rooms along the corridor, and to wonder at the tobacco smoke and the beer and the cards, and the indescribable filth of everything.

It is this small boy who has listened to the story of "Number Twenty," whose comprehensive gaze has taken in, "all at the same time," the "cap, feet, head, face, legs, and whiskers," of the rakish but down-at-heels and out-of-elbows Mr. Smangle, and the maudlin toady, Mr. Mivins. It is this precociously observant child who has absorbed the weirdly haunting, jaunty, devil-may-care atmosphere of this aimlessly busy, reckless, feckless, dingy and dirty prison world, the only genuine emotion in which, not to be observed save in secluded corners and unguarded moments, is gaunt despair.

It is this boy, grown man, but still a boy at heart, who is living again through all the false hopes and real fears, the nightly drink-begotten jollity and the cold morning terrors and awful hopelessnesses of a debtors' prison—until at last his rising indignation can no longer be restrained, and he bursts clean away from the story he is writing to cry out his wrath in his own proper person that "we still leave unblotted in the leaves of our statute-book, for the reverence and admiration of succeeding ages, the just and wholesome law which declares that the sturdy felon shall be fed and clothed, and that the penniless debtor shall be left to die of starvation and nakedness."

This is no fiction, he exclaims vehemently. It is not. The greatest passages in Dickens are never fiction.

Little Oliver Twist is born in the workhouse. His father is unknown; his mother dies in giving birth to him. From that moment though, he has a constant, watchful champion, who lives with him, day in day out, feeling his every sorrow and knowing his every grief more nearly than himself. It is Charles Dickens-Twist who starves in Mrs. Mann's child farm, is scared stiff by the pompous, bullying Mr. Bumble, the "porochial" beadle, who plucks up courage to ask for more gruel, and who is beaten for demanding it. With what savage joy does the author, in the person of his diminutive hero, rise up and smite the hateful Noah Claypole, that "large-headed, small-eyed youth, of lumbering make and heavy countenance," who, aided and abetted by Charlotte, the slatternly maid-of-all work at the Sowerberry's, has made the workhouse boy's life so miserable! How carefully Oliver is guarded from mortal harm when he falls among thieves! He is a favourite of Fagin's, Nancy takes pity on him, even Bill Sikes carries away the wounded boy from the house they have unsuccessfully tried to burgle. With what charming and kindly folk does he fall in both times that he escapes from Fagin and his associates. How considerate of his worthless brother to have left, in spite of his wicked and wasteful career, just sufficient money to start Oliver comfortably in life. This is not simply the Victorian desire for a happy ending; it is Charles Dickens carefully protecting the child he adopted long before Mr. Brownlow did.

By common consent, the characters Oliver Twist meets in the thieves' den in London are among the greatest Dickens ever created. One hesitates to say they are the greatest in all English fiction, not because this would be an exaggerated statement, but because Fagin, Bill Sikes, Nancy, Jack Dawkins "the Artful Dodger," Charley Bates, and Flash Toby Crackit, so obviously and patently belong to the world of fact. They are Sam Wellers gone wrong. Theirs are idealized portraits, as was the portrait of their prototype, for never was a wicked Jew quite so cunning, so smooth, so gentle, and so villainous as old Fagin; housebreaker so callously brutal and reckless as Sikes; pickpocket so nonchalantly master of his trade as the Artful Dodger; but they are real, deadly real, because Dickens is seeing them all just as he has seen them in the streets and slums and police-courts of London.

No doubt he achieved this extraordinary knowledge of London's underworld during his free-lance reporting days.

In any case it is abundantly clear that every scene is stamped with the impress of absolute truth, from the moment when the Artful Dodger led Oliver through Islington past the Angel into St. John's Road, and thence by Exmouth Street, Coppice Row, Hockley-in-the-Hole, and Little Saffron Hill, into Saffron Hill the Great, and to a house near Field Lane, right on to that marvellously told flight of Bill Sikes out of London to Hatfield, back, terror-haunted, to London, and into the unknown depths of Rotherhithe, filthy, decaying, desolate, there to be trapped by the infuriated mob and at the very moment of seeming escape to be caught and hung by the very rope that was to ensure freedom; and the yet more marvellously told trial of Fagin, followed by the terrifyingly vivid description of the Jew's night in the condemned cell. This is no fiction; years before, at the Old Bailey and at Newgate, there used to sit in the public gallery a boy reporter with piercingly keen eyes who saw man after man condemned to be hanged by the neck until dead, who noted every change of feature, every gesture—a boy who could follow in spirit into the cells, and live with the unhappy wretches doomed to execution through their awful last night, and who had never been able to forget.

It was not achieved without cost, this fidelity to life. Mr. G. K. Chesterton does well to remind one of Dickens' "raging and sleepless nights, his wild walks in the darkness . . . his nerves in rags." To relive memories one must suffer.

For what? Why, one may ask, this lavishing of power, this superhuman straining after truth, this reckless spending of body and mind? Because he was in bondage to his publishers? Not at all; Dickens would have defied or evaded all the publishers in London had he been so minded. He could easily have satisfied them with work that would have taken much less out of him.

Because he was an artist, driven on to creation by that irresistible urge which possesses every artist, impelling him, with his will or against his will, to some form of self-expression? Partly. Dickens lived a completely realistic emotional life in his books; he laughed, wept, loved, and hated with the children of his mind, who were to him, as they became to his readers, as real as the folk he met in the flesh. Yet it is impossible to believe that this was the fundamental reason. Scarcely any writer had less of what are called artistic ideals than Dickens; praise or criticism of his work as literature moved him far less than did praise or criticism of it as a picture of life.

Because he loved the work? No doubt he did, when once he had lost himself in it; but in these earlier years at any rate he had far too many engagements to allow him to regard his writing with unmixed pleasure. The thought of each book, as the time for its beginning drew near, hung like a "hideous nightmare" over him. When he had summoned up courage to start, there were always so many "slips" to be written each day. Authorship, he said, was his pleasure, as it was his trade. Except when he was actually writing, the trade aspect was apt continually to unnerve and terrify him.

Because he was popular? Strange, disappointing as it may at first sight appear, here one approaches the root of the matter. Dickens' genius, his energy, his tremendous creative power, were called out in all their greatness, and urged relentlessly on by a stupendous, all-compelling command— the voice of the people.

He had captured the hearts of all England. He had won them to laughter; he could move them to tears. He had to go on and on. The people needed, demanded, clamoured for him. Not so much the rich and the powerful and the privileged, though they liked him and could laugh with him, but the great mass of ordinary folk, the poor, the lowly, the humble and meek. In a word, his own people. Because he was of them, he belonged to them; he was their slave.

It was his business to tell of their joys and their sorrows, to picture their daily life in all its drabness and its heroism, to laugh at their oddities and chide gently their failings, to raise outcry against the wrongs which oppressed them, to hurl mighty bolts of ridicule and indignation at the foul abuses and injustices and cruelties that rode roughshod over them and trampled them down into the mire and the filth.

This was the destiny he took upon himself. Not perhaps so

consciously as has been analysed here; but his warm, generous, overflowing love for humanity caused him to undertake the responsibility he felt his popularity had laid upon him. From the moment of the success of "Pickwick," whether he knew it or not, Dickens ceased to be his own master and became the servant of his people.

Great was his reward. His people bought his books in ever increasing scores of thousands. The order for the XVth number of "Pickwick" exceeded 40,000 copies, that for the first number of "Nickleby" 50,000. These numbers must be multiplied by twenty at least if one is to gain any adequate idea of the popularity such a circulation implies. The population of England and Wales was in 1837 only about fifteen millions, as compared with forty millions to-day, and vast masses of the people were illiterate.

His popularity was immense. His people loved him as never was author loved before or since. They made of this young man of twenty-six a god. They walked and talked with his characters, ate, drank and made merry with them, cried over their sufferings, suffered agonies of suspense over their fates. They filled his letter-box with appeals begging for more of this one, imploring him not to kill that one.

Dickens took it all with perfect seriousness. He held long arguments with his friends, who were as serious as he. That Charley Bates and the Artful Dodger might not suffer the fate of Fagin, but live on to see happier and more honest days, Mr. Serjeant Talfourd could plead "as earnestly . . . as ever at the bar for any client he most respected."

That was long ago. Dickens still remains England's best-loved author. His fame as a writer has suffered many vicissitudes, but the love he first inspired in English hearts nearly one hundred years ago has never grown cold. Critics may attack his literary faults, which were many; mudrakers may delight to expose his faults as a man, which also were many; but while his works remain, nothing will ever diminish the steadfast affection with which he is regarded by thousands upon thousands of plain, ordinary men and women. He is one of us.

If there be any one simple answer to the question, Why?

it is this, that in 1837 young Charles Dickens, a writer of popular humorous sketches, while grappling for the first time in his life with a serious book—"Oliver Twist, or The Parish Boy"—realized that the people of England wanted, and could get, from him something more than mirth; and he resolved at all costs to give them what they wanted—themselves. And so, he is "for ever England."

# CHAPTER V

*"His characters are a part of knowledge, they are a part of laughter and sorrow, they are a part of melancholy. They have become words in the English language because they are a part of thousands of English memories."*—MICHAEL SADLEIR.

"PICKWICK" came to a triumphant end in November 1837, the last two numbers appearing simultaneously. In the same month a complete edition, entitled "The Posthumous Papers of the Pickwick Club" by Charles Dickens, and dedicated to Mr. Serjeant Talfourd was published by Messrs. Chapman and Hall. To celebrate the event there was a dinner at the "Prince of Wales," in Leicester Square, at which were present Dickens, Talfourd, Forster, Chapman, Hall, Harrison Ainsworth, William Jerdan, editor of the *Literary Gazette*, and Macready, the famous actor. Everybody was "in hearty good humour," and Dickens received a second "extra" cheque from his publishers, this time for £750.

Messrs. Chapman and Hall, it is only fair to say, shared the spoils most generously with their author. True, they had netted a profit of £14,000 from "Pickwick," but whereas Dickens' original agreement would have brought him a little over £300 for writing it, he actually received from the publishers little short of £3,000. In addition, in the "Nickleby" agreement they conceded to him, after five years should have elapsed, a one-third share in the copyright of the "Pickwick Papers."

In January 1838, Dickens, accompanied by Phiz, went north to collect material for his forthcoming story, "The Life and Adventures of Nicholas Nickleby," which was to contain "a Faithful Account of the Fortunes, Misfortunes, Uprisings,

Downfallings, and Complete Career of the Nickleby Family."
This full title was in obvious imitation of that of "Pickwick,"
and the story was to be, by agreement, of a similar character.
It was to prove a very different book. Dickens could not now
write another "Pickwick." He had advanced beyond that
stage.

"I do not," said Forster, ". . . think the 'Pickwick
Papers' comparable to the later books." The opinion is
just. "Pickwick" is unique; it is the sort of book a man can
write only once in his life—when he is very young. Afterwards, he must either repeat himself unsatisfyingly, or press
on to greater heights.

Dickens pressed on. "Oliver Twist" came to grips with
humanity in its more poignant aspects, moving "Pickwick"
to do the same. From "Oliver Twist," which, realistic as it
was, dealt mainly with types of life unfamiliar to most
readers, Dickens advanced to "Nicholas Nickleby," the
universal appeal of which touched and conquered all hearts,
even the professional critics.

"Oliver Twist" had had for hero a child, but one born
into unusual circumstances, to whom came quite out-of-the-
ordinary adventures. It was not surprising that during the
writing of this tale Dickens should have been drawn to consider what sufferings chance might bring to any ordinary child
born under more or less normal circumstances. He was
never, in all his life, to lose his deep love for children, and a
sympathy which persistently urged him to strive to protect
childhood led him again and again to the creation of beautiful
studies of childhood and youth which must be ranked among
his finest and sincerest achievements. One has only to recall
little Nell of "The Old Curiosity Shop," David Copperfield,
Paul and Florence Dombey, Pip in "Great Expectations,"
among many others, to realize how irresistibly his mind was
attracted by this great theme.

Although Nicholas Nickleby, a youth of nineteen, and so
hardly to be considered a child—though Heaven knows he is
childlike enough in character—is the eponymous "hero" of
Dickens' third book, he is, for all his attractiveness, no more
than the peg upon which the story is hung.

"Nicholas Nickleby" is a very remarkable achievement. In it two stories both of enthralling interest run side by side, that of Nicholas and that of his sister Kate Nickleby. It contains a rich galaxy of character of most varied types, Mrs. Nickleby, Newman Noggs, Miss La Creevy, Madame and Mr. Mantalini, the Kenwigses, the brothers Cheeryble and Tim Linkinwater, Messrs. Pyke and Pluck, and the superb Mr. Vincent Crummles, who, of course, is not to be mentioned without Mrs. Vincent Crummles, Master Crummles, Master P. Crummles, and Miss Crummles the infant phenomenon, who had been ten years of age, "certainly for five good years," and was likely to remain so for at least another five. What renders the book supremely great, however, and has placed it among the best-known of all Dickens' works, is its ruthless exposure of the cheap Yorkshire boarding schools of the time, contained in the dreadful picture of school life at Dotheboys Hall under the sly and brutal Mr. Wackford Squeers and his no less brutal wife.

From Chatham days Dickens had remembered vaguely the story of a boy who had returned home to Rochester from a Yorkshire school, emaciated, bearing every sign of prolonged neglect, and with a fearful suppurated abscess on his head, "in consequence of his Yorkshire guide, philosopher and friend having ripped it open with an inky penknife." From time to time other shocking stories of these northern schools had come to light. In 1823 a Mr. William Shaw had been the defendant in a lawsuit over boys who had gone blind through alleged neglect and cruelty, and had had heavy damages assessed against him. There had been, too, more recent cases. A boy of nineteen had died in one school, the result, it was said, of years of cruelty and neglect. In 1832 Mr. Shaw had again been in the courts.

Dickens determined to visit Mr. Shaw and other Yorkshire schoolmasters, and to learn the truth for himself. Warned that "those gentlemen might, in their modesty, be shy of receiving a visit from the author of the ' Pickwick Papers,' " he travelled incognito as a gentleman making inquiries on behalf of a widowed mother who wished to select a school for her little boy. From a Malton solicitor, Mr. Charles Smithson,

he obtained a bogus letter of introduction to Mr. Richard
Barnes, attorney, of Barnard Castle, who came to the inn
where Dickens and Browne had put up, and was jovial and
talkative—on all subjects but Yorkshire Schools. About
these he evaded inquiry, and was uncomfortable whenever
the subject was approached.

When the time came for him to leave, however, the honest
Yorkshireman, moved no doubt as all Dickens' friends were
by his cordiality and honesty, could not restrain himself,
and looking him full in the face, he begged him not to send the
boy. . . . "Ar wouldn't mak' ill words amang ma neeburs,
and ar speak tiv'ee quiet loike.  But I'm dom'd if ar can gang
to bed and not tell 'ee, for weedur's sak', to keep the lattle
boy from a' sike scoondrels while there's a harse to hoold in a'
Lunnon  or a goother to lie asleep in!"

On February 2nd, Dickens and Browne visited Mr. Shaw at
the Bowes Academy, Greta Bridge.

"Mr. Squeers," wrote Dickens in the preface to the first
edition of "Nicholas Nickleby," "is the representative of a
class and not of an individual" . . . [he] "and his school are
faint and feeble pictures of an existing reality, purposely
subdued and kept down lest they should be deemed impossible."  He declared in this preface that there was on
record evidence of "such offensive and foul details of neglect,
cruelty, and disease, as no writer of fiction would have the
boldness to imagine."  He had, in addition to making personal investigation, carefully studied the reports of the lawsuits, and during the publication of the book received from
unimpeachable sources "accounts of atrocities . . . very
far exceeding any that appear in these pages."

Only ten years later he was able to write in the preface
to another edition of "Nicholas Nickleby," "There were,
then [1838], a good many cheap Yorkshire schools in existence.
There are very few now."  No words can speak more
eloquently of his tremendous influence on public opinion.

That influence, gained in the first place by his irresistible
humour and unfailing veracity of description, was immeasurably strengthened by the force and absolute sincerity of his
hatred of cruelty and oppression.  "He hated," said T. A.

Trollope, "a mean action or a mean sentiment as one hated something that is physically loathsome to the sight and touch. And he could be angry, as those with whom he had been angry did not very readily forget."

The greatest passages in Dickens, as has been said in an earlier page, are never fiction. Nor are the greatest characters; nor, one would dare to affirm, are any of his characters. Much research and ingenuity have been expended in discovering the "originals" of Dickens' characters; and both during and after his lifetime an extraordinary host of people believed themselves to have been honoured, flattered, slighted, insulted, or ridiculed by being put into one of his books. In many cases they were more or less right in believing that they had been used as models. Dickens wrote always from real life, and would without the slightest hesitation or compunction borrow a father or a mother, a relative, a friend, an acquaintance, or a mere passer-by, for incorporation in his story if it suited his purpose. A living model having been found from which to draw his inspiration, his genius worked upon it until there emerged from the dull clay of a very ordinary person a brilliant and unforgettable work of art. The "original" might be so little altered as to remain clearly recognizable, or might be so transformed that no person in the world could say from whom the portrait had been drawn. Nowhere is this more evident than in "Nicholas Nickleby."

Several Yorkshire schoolmasters claimed the dishonour of being Mr. Wackford Squeers, either by threatening his author with libel actions or personal assault, or by carefully explaining how unlike that hero they really were. Public opinion fixed upon Mr. William Shaw as the genuine original, a conclusion to which the Dotheboys Hall chapters, and more particularly the earlier ones, certainly pointed.

Dickens began to write "Nickleby" the day after he returned to London from Yorkshire. Burning with indignation, with all the terrible memories of the expedition seething in his mind, he could stay to do no more than cast what he had seen into story form. The setting he recorded as faithfully as any reporter. The incidents of the journey of Squeers and Nicholas from London to Greta Bridge are, down to the very weather, practically identical with those of the journey he and H. K. Browne had just made. The snow, the George Inn at Grantham, the "very fastidious lady" who had expected a green chariot to meet her, and the inn at Greta Bridge, figure in both. Mr. Squeers' advertisement of his school is only a slightly altered version of the one Mr. Shaw actually inserted in the *Times*. Both pedagogues, the real and the imaginary, started north from the Saracen's Head, Snow Hill (near Holborn Viaduct), the time of departure being altered by only a bare half-hour. The description of the Dotheboys Hall buildings tallies with that of Bowes Academy, and Phiz's drawing of Squeers is said to portray Shaw with fair accuracy. On his way home Dickens stopped at York, visited the Minster, and was shown the famous "Five Sisters" window by the organist, Dr. John Camridge, who told him the stories connected with it, material which Dickens employed for the grey-haired gentleman's story in Chapter VI of "Nickleby."

All this does not necessarily imply that William Shaw exactly resembled Mr. Wackford Squeers. He is said, on the contrary, to have been kindly and humane in private life, and there is no getting away from the fact that on his death in 1850 his fellow-worshippers erected to his memory a stained-glass window in the parish church. Memorials and monuments, it is true, have been known, like charity, to cover a multitude of sins, but it is difficult to imagine any village folk subscribing to a memorial window for Mr. Squeers; though the point is worthy of note that that gentleman gets Mr. Snawley to supply a reference that he is "a highly virtuous, exemplary, and well-conducted man in private life."

The question of the resemblance has been endlessly discussed. The answer is probably that Dickens, having seen Shaw's and other schools, and with the details of the various lawsuits in his mind, concentrated all his skill and indignation upon a deadly accurate, though restrained, composite picture, which exposed the gravity, if not the deepest infamies, of the evil. That the picture of Dotheboys Hall is a composite one is surely certain beyond doubt; for even if Wackford Squeers be William Shaw to the life, it is impossible that he could have possessed at one and the same time so amazing a counterpart as Mrs. Squeers, his equal in crime and his superior in audacity, such a love-making and letter-writing genius of a daughter as Fanny Squeers, and such a vicious little beast of a son as Master Squeers.

So far as the truth with regard to Dickens' characters and their originals can ever be got at, it can be amply demonstrated by two stories concerning the composition of "Nicholas Nickleby." "The brothers Cheeryble live," wrote Dickens in his original preface, ". . . their liberal charity, their singleness of heart, their noble nature, and their unbounded benevolence, are no creations of the Author's brain." They were David and William Grant, Manchester merchants and self-made men, who actually gave away hundreds of thousands of pounds in charity. On the other hand, Mrs. Nickleby's character was undoubtedly derived from that of Dickens' mother; yet, when he was commenting some years later in a letter on the doubts people were casting upon the reality of some of his characters, Dickens declared "Mrs. Nickleby herself, sitting bodily before me in a solid chair, once asked me whether I really believed there ever was such a woman!"

How far Dickens' characters are exact individual pictures of their living "originals" is a question that can never be solved; even Dickens himself could not have given any satisfactory answer, for no picture of a man or woman, be it in words, on canvas or in stone, can ever be more than a partial reflection of a picture which has crystallized in the artist's mind, and which is itself in its turn both a reflection and a transmutation of the original; and during the complicated mental processes of reception, crystallization, and reproduction of an image the line between fact and fancy becomes inevitably blurred. What is quite certain, and this is what alone matters, is that however "true" or "false" to their living originals Dickens' characters were, they were true to life; and equally, that in passing the images of living people through the crucible of his mind, Dickens purged them of all their dreariness and commonplace aspects.

The Yorkshire schoolmasters he visited were no doubt dull, vicious brutes; Squeers is at least witty, and a pioneer of "practical" education. There is never a dull moment in his company. Life at Dotheboys Hall for the pupils must in reality have resembled life in the trenches during the Great War, as once described by a British soldier—"months of intense boredom punctuated by moments of intense fear." Dickens' description of the school is absolutely realistic, but it lives in the memory of all readers by virtue of having so vividly brought into relief the moments of intense fear and so subtly suggested the intense boredom.

No mention of Dotheboys Hall is complete without reference to Smike, the poor deserted boy whom the Squeers' neglect and cruelty have driven half-witted, who runs away to follow Nicholas, accompanies him in many adventures, and finally dies in his arms. Smike talks as no boy could ever have talked, but in spite of this artificiality—which would be far less so a hundred years ago than now—his personality is absolutely real, and brings to the whole sordid picture that final touch of utter hopelessness and irreparable wrong which damns beyond reprieve Mr. Wackford Squeers and all his pitiless associates.

Dotheboys Hall would by itself have been sufficient to immortalize any book; but Dickens paints in lighter vein at least one other picture of equal force and veracity, that of the exploits of the travelling theatrical company of Mr. Vincent Crummles. In describing the persons and experiences of a third-rate company of actors he is, of course, able to work from intimate knowledge of the theatre, but it is typical of his passionate love of exactitude in description that he acquired a huge collection of newspaper cuttings in order to assist and correct his memory. Incidentally, among the many legends which accumulated round Dickens was one to the effect that he was actually for a time a member of the Crummles' company.

Equally effective in their way are the descriptions of the Kenwigses, in whose home we get the first of the many gloriously funny but yet tenderly sympathetic full-length pictures of lower-middle class domestic life Dickens was to present in his books, of Kate's experiences under the Mantalini régime, of the generous, kind-hearted Cheeryble brothers and their dear old clerk, Timothy Linkinwater, of Newman Noggs, first of a long line of oddities—always so tenderly treated—and of poor, distracted, muddle-headed, weak-willed Mrs. Nickleby, so foolish, so well-meaning, and so dangerous to the happiness of those she loved.

As compared with "Oliver Twist," "Nickleby" shows great deepening and widening of sympathy; the main characters are much more numerous and far more varied, and, with the exception of the Fagin group in the former book, they are drawn with more precision and far greater fullness. As regards the construction of the story, that is another matter. Dickens has been told over and over again by his critics how badly constructed are his novels. It may be admitted that they are; that he uses coincidence to a ludicrous degree to make his plot hang together; that he sacrifices coherence ruthlessly to obtain dramatic effect; that he often forgets what has gone before; and that no matter what the injury to artistic ideals, he will make virtue triumph in the end and rub the nose of vice well into the ground. Having conceded all that to the critics, one may then ask how much better they would have succeeded had they been compelled to spread the writing of a story over twenty months, to supply each monthly part to hard-pursuing printers, to write it always with an eye to its being "continued in our next," to be constantly over-worked, usually to have two full-length stories on hand at the same time, and finally, to have to please all Victorian England with the result.

"Nicholas Nickleby" completely reassured those friends who doubted lest Dickens might not be able to follow up his previous successes, and finally won over the critics who, like Lockhart, Walter Scott's great biographer, thought "Pickwick" "All very well, but damned low," and who had entertained serious doubts as to whether such wicked and vulgar characters as Fagin and Sikes were permissible in polite literature. It did not put an end to a species of annoyance from which the novelist suffered all his days, the incessant imitation and pirating of his stories.

This took two forms: the publication of stories purporting to be similar to or sequels of those he was actually writing, and the production of stage plays based on his current book. Thus, one journalist who pursued him very closely during these early years called himself "Bos," and produced "The Posthumous Notes of the Pickwickian Club," "Oliver Twiss," and "Nichelas Nickelberry"; while a "Penny Pickwick" sold in thousands among the poorer classes. Two dramatists, Edward Stirling and W. T. Moncrieff, fell upon every book as it was being published, and produced garbled stage versions, making their own adaptations, and adding conclusions long before the author himself had done so, or even knew how he was going to do so! The law of copyright at that time gave the author very little protection against plagiarism, and none at all against stage adaptations of his work.

Dickens was from the first stung to irritation by this impudent parasitism, but though he engaged in violent quarrels with the pirates, whom, as usual, he took too seriously, he could not restrain their activities, and was generally worsted in the argument. He went to see representations both of "Oliver Twist" and "Nickleby." After a few moments of "Oliver Twist" he lay down on the floor of his box and refused to get up until the curtain fell; with "Nicholas Nickleby" he was much better pleased, even writing to the actor Yates, who played Mantalini, that he could not object when "the thing is so admirably done in every respect as you have done it in this instance."

Just before the appearance of the first number of "Nickleby" Dickens made an attempt to frighten the pirates by the publication of a "Proclamation" in a number of magazines and reviews, in which, after declaring himself to be, "the only true and lawful 'Boz,'" he pretended to have "at length devised a mode of execution for them, so summary and terrible" that if they dared to touch "Nickleby" he would "hang them on gibbets so lofty and enduring, that their remains shall be a monument of our just vengeance to all succeeding ages."

The pirates laughed both at this and at Serjeant Talfourd's efforts in Parliament to get the copyright law amended, and carried on merrily. By November 1838, ten months before Dickens completed the writing of "Nickleby," Stirling had

No. 4 Ailsa Park Villas, Isleworth Road, Twickenham
Where Dickens spent the summer of 1838

his play ready for production at the Adelphi Theatre. With brazen impudence he dedicated it to Dickens. It ran for 160 nights. Other plays adapted from "Nickleby" were used for years in the provinces, while dramatizations of "Oliver Twist" remain popular to this day.

The pirates, however, were but a minor trouble. A much more serious one which assailed Dickens early in 1838 was the thought of having to complete "Barnaby Rudge" by November. He had filled his spare time between the completion of "Pickwick" and the commencement of "Nickleby" in writing for Messrs. Chapman and Hall "Sketches of Young Gentlemen" as a humorous counterblast to "Sketches of Young Ladies," by Quiz (E. Caswall), in producing his promised edition of "Grimaldi" for Bentley—not a heavy task, certainly, as he did no more than write a preface and dictate alterations in the manuscript, which had been prepared by a Mr. Egerton Wilks, using his father as shorthand writer —and in making his journey to Yorkshire. He was all this time deeply immersed in the writing of "Oliver Twist," and was in addition being swamped by his editorial work for the *Miscellany*. So he wrote to Bentley in February suggesting that the present agreement concerning "Barnaby Rudge" should be cancelled, and that that tale should follow "Oliver Twist" as a serial in the magazine. It was July before publisher and author could agree; in the end Dickens got his way.

It must not be imagined from the foregoing that Dickens' life at this time was unhappy. Far from it. There is, indeed, only one word to describe a life such as his; it was intense. He crowded into it far more activity than can the ordinary man, and emotionally he always lived at exceptionally high pressure. In whatever mood he happened to be, and he was essentially a man of moods, he was extreme. His gaiety was uproarious, his tenderness overflowing; he quarrelled impetuously and stridently, and could be driven almost to madness by trifles.

At present happiness and joyous fun predominated. Life was going very well. He could fall upon both work and play "with tooth and nail"; he could hale Forster out any day (or night, as he did at midnight on the day of the publication of No. I of "Nickleby") to ride with him through long hours; he could find time for theatre-going in abundance, for dinner parties and long evenings with his friends. Life was growing steadily more full of interests, and more spacious. His circle of friends grew rapidly; his social position improved; he bought his carriage, banked with Coutts, and was elected to the Athenæum and Garrick Clubs. He played Lord Bountiful to his family, and became to them an object of respect, if an easy prey for plunder.

On 6th March, 1838, his eldest daughter, Mary (Mamie) was born. For the summer Doughty Street was abandoned for a cottage at Twickenham, 4 Ailsa Park Villas, Isleworth Road, and here, as at Elm Cottage (now Lodge), Petersham, the summer retreat of 1839, great sportings and high jinks took place, in which Dickens, though perhaps in individual feats occasionally beaten by various of his friends, always outstayed the rest. Bowling, quoits, leaping, battledore, and bagatelle were among the pleasures to which he called his friends, and there is a story of a great game of leap-frog played boisterously by Literature, Art, Criticism, and the Stage, to wit, by Dickens, Maclise, Forster and Macready. A round of incessant gaiety. "Even the lighter recreations," says Forster, ". . . were pursued with relentless activity." Even in these halcyon days there is a note of perpetual restlessness.

Some time during this year Daniel Maclise, R.A., now in the inner circle of Dickens' friends, and much beloved, painted the picture of Dickens which is usually called the "Nickleby" portrait, of which Thackeray, also a frequent visitor at Twickenham, declared that "as a likeness it is perfectly amazing . . . here we have the real identical man Dickens." The drawing done by Samuel Lawrence two years previously is said, however, to be an even better likeness.

In August and September the family were holiday-making at Broadstairs, to which they were to return year after year; and during November, Dickens made a short tour of North Wales, noting on the way there, between Birmingham and Wolverhampton, "such a mass of dirt, gloom, and misery, as

I never before witnessed." During the autumn and early winter he was making final arrangements for the publication of "Oliver Twist," which thus appeared in book form some five months before the tale concluded in *Bentley's Miscellany*. Publication was slightly delayed by his having to ask Cruikshank, who was his illustrator for this story, to re-design the plate showing Rose Maylie and Oliver. Cruikshank, incidentally, was many years later to be responsible for a story, first circulated in America, that his drawings suggested the whole plot of "Oliver Twist" to Dickens. The story has been disposed of long ago, but it is really immaterial; twenty men might suggest the plot, or even the characters, of "Oliver Twist," but only a Dickens could have written the book.

In January 1839 the shadow of "Barnaby Rudge" began again to fall heavily upon him, and he wrote to Bentley suggesting a further postponement. It seems fairly clear that he was now seriously feeling the strain of overwork, though his letter to Forster on the subject is a bitter complaint of the financial return he was getting from his books. Yet phrases such as "the slavery and drudgery of another work," and a passionate declaration that, "It is no fiction to say that at present I *cannot* write this tale," certainly suggest something more than exasperation at an inadequate monetary reward. He asked for a reprieve of six months; the outcome of the matter was that immediately on the conclusion of "Oliver Twist" he was allowed to relinquish his editorship of the *Miscellany*, and became, comparatively speaking, a free man for a few months.

He used part of his leisure time to arrange for the pension-ing-off of his father. The old man had had persistent attacks of "moments of difficulty" during the past few years. He had also developed an uncomfortable habit of borrowing money from Messrs. Chapman and Hall. No doubt he was all the time dipping frequently into Charles' purse, probably by now without the formality of regarding a remittance as a loan. Anyhow, in March his son took and furnished for him a good-sized cottage at Alphington, just outside Exeter. "I don't think," he wrote to Tom Mitton, "I ever saw so pleasant and cheerful a spot." Nor, he may have added privately to himself, one so difficult to "disappear" with impunity from.

Mr. John Dickens was none too pleased. What on earth, he asked, was he expected to do with himself in a place like that? But he went. The head of the family was now Mr. Charles, not Mr. John Dickens, and it was not wise, the family had found, to offend the new head.

Throughout the year "Nicholas Nickleby" pursued its triumphant career, bringing Dickens an ever wider, yet a definitely changing, popularity. While his humour retained all its freshness and originality and lost some of its cruder aspects, it was his pathos, his hatred of wrong, and his tenderness which were now winning the stronger hold upon his readers. Sympathy and insight compel a firmer bond than laughter. His Pickwickian characters had been the most delightful and original of companions, but Oliver Twist and the children of Dotheboys Hall, Smike in particular, brought nearer home to anxious hearts the pain and grief that had touched, or might touch, them. Do not kill Smike, was the prayer of scores of letters addressed to Dickens. Your beautiful story . . . my own son whom I lost . . . was the theme of scores of others.

His remuneration for "Nicholas Nickleby" being considerably more than that for his previous books, he could now afford to indulge in a more ample style of living, especially as, at its conclusion, Messrs. Chapman and Hall came down with their usual "extra" cheque, this time to the tune of £1,500. In November 1839, Dickens, now the proud father of three children, a second daughter, Kate Macready, having been born to him a month previously, moved from Doughty Street to No. 1 Devonshire Terrace, Regent's Park, near the York Gate. It was, he said, "a house of great promise (and great premium), undeniable situation, and excessive splendour."

It was all that, and more. The move was out of one world into another. He had, in fact, arrived. He was now an author of established reputation, secure in fame, with a firm hold upon a vast public. He was practically free from his entanglements with publishers; he had only "Barnaby

Rudge" to write, and that he had at last started, and it was going well. Otherwise, publishers were practically offering him blank cheques for his work. He could afford to launch out.

If one takes the comparatively short walk from Doughty Street north-west to Devonshire Terrace, one will realize something of the significance of this move. Doughty Street has no doubt declined since Dickens' days; but at its best it was no more than the home of modest gentility, a neat enough little house, but rather cramped, rather shut in, rather *bourgeois*. Whereas on the outskirts of Regent's Park one could breathe not only great gusts of pure air but an eminently aristocratic atmosphere. Everything was on a large scale, more ample, more luxurious; mansion houses, with Corinthian-pillared front doors, spacious gardens, trees with room to grow.

All his life Dickens played his part. An actor to the very marrow, he played, as really great actors do, instinctively, with unerring touch for dramatic effect. His move to Devonshire Terrace was perfectly timed. However personal and private he may have considered his reasons for leaving Doughty Street, and they were no doubt the very ordinary ones given by every successful business man who is rising rapidly from modest beginnings to affluence, his translation to the house near Regent's Park was a magnificent gesture to his readers; and they did not fail to be impressed. As Mr. Ralph Straus has very aptly put it, ". . . its occupation by Dickens may be said to have marked the beginning of that curiously reverent attitude henceforth paid to him by the public. He was no longer the mirth-provoking 'Boz'; he was Dickens, without the Charles; a great moral force in the land; in fact, an institution."

He occupied No. 1 Devonshire Terrace for twelve years. During that time he was to prove himself even more than "a great moral force in the land," more even than "an institution." He was to become "the Master."

## CHAPTER VI

*"And then, while round them shadows gathered faster*
*And as the fire-light fell,*
*He read aloud the book wherein the Master*
*Had writ of ' Little Nell.' "*—BRET HARTE.

ALTHOUGH the much postponed "Barnaby Rudge" was
actually commenced in the autumn of 1839, it was not destined
to be completed yet awhile.   A new and most exciting project
seized upon and possessed Dickens' mind.

"Nickleby" was running towards the end of its course.
After "Nickleby," what then?   There must be no mistake;
he had no longer a reputation to make, but one to maintain.
He had also to maintain a large and expensive establishment.

His popularity was assured.   Yet public favour is a fickle
jade.   The public taste can so easily become cloyed.   What if
his readers should tire of a too oft-repeated "twenty monthly
numbers"?   What if they should find the strain of waiting a
whole month for each instalment too great, should wander
off in search of fresh distraction?   They might be caught by
the glitter of some new toy, they might forget.

That must never happen.   He would prevent it.   He would
himself prepare a new and tasty meal that should tickle
the public palate.   He would give them, not one number a
month, but four; they should have a weekly paper, devised
and edited by himself, and so cheap that no pocket could
refuse.   A new sort of weekly paper, providing a light and
varied menu instead of the solid one-course meal of a serial
story.   A most original and novel repast, to cater for all
tastes; a paper that should offer anecdote and information,
fiction and fact, entertainment and social service, advice

salted with wit, and inspiration seasoned with humour—in short, as Mr. Micawber would have said, a miscellany.

It is entirely characteristic of Dickens that no sooner had he decided upon the project than he threw himself into it body and soul, utterly regardless of all other considerations. It mattered not that he was under contract to produce very shortly a full-length novel, of which as yet hardly any was written; it was of no consequence that a bare six months previously he had been groaning under the strain of editing a monthly periodical, and that now he was proposing to edit a weekly one. It never occurred to him to ask whether his public would like the scheme. How could such a question arise in his mind? He had swept the British public right off their feet by his originality, humour and pathos; they were at his mercy. All he had to do was to go on being original, and humorous, and pathetic.

"Barnaby Rudge" went by the board; the "waves of each month's work" that had threatened to drown him in a "sea of manuscript" during his editing of *Bentley's Miscellany* were forgotten.

"Nicholas Nickleby" got on as best he could. Dickens could think of nothing but this new project. Aided and abetted by the indefatigable (and invaluable) Forster, he laid his plans carefully. It was essential that this projected periodical should not only greatly strengthen his hold upon his readers, but also ensure a really adequate financial return to its editor, and that with less expenditure of time and energy than he had been compelled to give to previous enterprises. Obviously, he must choose his publishers carefully. Messrs. Chapman and Hall had been very fair, but he must be quite certain of them. So off went Forster under orders to ascertain from Messrs. Chapman and Hall what they had in mind as an honorarium for the author at the conclusion of "Nickleby," and to discover how liberally-minded they might be expected to feel towards a future enterprise of the kind Dickens had in mind. To assist them to make a more ready and agreeable decision, Forster was sent, metaphorically speaking, with a well-loaded revolver in his pocket. "If," Dickens warned him, "if they do something handsome, even handsomer

perhaps than they dreamt of doing, they will find it their
interest, and," he added, with gracious condescension, "will
find me tractable."

And if not? Well, he would be "unwilling to leave them";
they have only to be prepared to "behave with liberality"
towards him, and he will not think of doing so, "on any
consideration," but if not, he knows that "to a certain extent
I certainly and surely must gain by it," and the obvious
inference is that he would not hesitate to do so.

Strange words these from a young man of twenty-seven,
who not four years previously was writing to thank these same
publishers for their "very handsome terms" of twenty-five
guineas per 16,000 words! Strange until one thinks of
"Pickwick," and "Oliver Twist," and "Nicholas Nickleby,"
and their great popularity; and of his treatment of Mr.
Macrone, and of Mr. Bentley waiting year after year for
"Barnaby Rudge," and of Dickens' attitude towards publishers
in general, and of Devonshire Terrace, and all its great promise
and great premium, and its magnificent significance. Not so
strange when one remembers that "Oliver Twist," by the
author of "Pickwick," and, like its predecessor, easily the
most popular and most talked about book in England, circu-
lating in its scores of thousands, had been produced for a mere
£750—about as much as the ordinary novelist then expected
if he sold fifteen hundred copies of a story! Still less strange
when one learns that there were lying on his desk "straightforward offers from responsible men to publish anything
for me at a percentage on the profits, and take all the risk."

Was Dickens greedy? Emphatically, no. Genius cannot
be measured by the foot rule by which one measures ordinary
men. However much it may have been his own fault, he had
toiled like a slave for four years; he had conquered all England;
yet he had been paid, except possibly for "Nickleby," like
any hack journalist. He knew his value now, and was
perfectly entitled to demand it.

Surely though it was a little hard on Messrs. Chapman and
Hall? They had never been anything but liberal; and the
relations between them and Dickens had been throughout
marked by the utmost cordiality. Well, look at it from

Dickens' point of view for a moment. Messrs. Chapman and Hall had treated him very fairly so far, and had remunerated him on a distinctly more satisfactory scale than anyone else; but it was absolutely necessary at this point that they of all people should clearly realize that from now onwards they had to deal, not with an aspiring young writer, not even with the "mirth-provoking 'Boz,'" but with "Dickens," acknowledged and unquestioned monarch of the world of books, the idol of the public, a great national figure. He has burst the bonds of his earlier contractual mistakes, and from henceforth will dictate, not accept, terms from publishers.

So Messrs. Chapman and Hall, having been sounded by Forster, and approved by him as sufficiently liberally-minded, have laid before them an elaborate scheme, complete in every detail, for a threepenny weekly, edited by Dickens, to commence on March 31st, 1840, and to resemble in plan the famous eighteenth-century periodicals, Addison and Steele's *Spectator* and *Tatler*, and Goldsmith's *Bee*, though much more popular both as to subjects treated and the method of treating them.

There would be a "little club or knot of characters," after the fashion of Sir Roger de Coverley and his famous associates; into which club, if required, Mr. Pickwick and Sam Weller could easily and naturally step. There would be club evenings, and "Sketches, essays, tales, adventures, letters from imaginary correspondents, and so forth"—not all to be actually written by Charles Dickens, but all contributed strictly under his direction. There would be certain established features to which the public could look forward weekly, such as Chapters on Chambers, a series of articles on London, past, present and future, with the City giants, Gog and Magog, in the rôle of narrators, "satirical papers, purporting to be translated from some Savage Chronicles," in which the editor could watch over the interests of his readers by keeping "a special look-out upon the magistrates in town and country, and never leave those worthies alone." For these special features Dickens would himself be responsible.

In every question of make-up the decision of the editor was to be final. The contents of each number were to be entirely under his control. He alone would "pursue *these*

*ideas.*" Of course, he would need assistance, but "I should
stipulate that this assistance is chosen solely by me." He
would be good enough to allow himself, however, to be
pledged and bound, after "discussion and arrangement," as
to the amount he should contribute with his own hand to
each number. Finally, with an absolutely supreme touch of
benevolent despotism, he would offer, "in order to give fresh
novelty and interest to this undertaking," "to contract to
go at any specified time " (say midsummer or autumn)
"either to Ireland or to America," to collect for the magazine
descriptions, tales, legends and traditions, likely to be of
interest. There was, he might mention, one simple condition
to be observed in respect of any such contract; he would
"wish the publication of these papers in a separate form," a
condition, he added incidentally, which would attach to any
series of articles he undertook.

It was a truly regal proposition, and—a wonderful scheme;
a sort of mixture compounded of essence of "ArabianNights,"
"Robinson Crusoe," "Gulliver's Travels," and Addison's
*Spectator*, or, to provide as near a modern parallel as
possible, a periodical combining the leading features of *The
Wide-World Magazine*, *Punch*, *The Quiver*, *Tit-Bits*, and
*John Bull*.

As to the financial side of it he was equally precise and
equally dictatorial. He was to be made a part-proprietor
and sharer in the profits. No mention was made of possible
losses, but then, "I say nothing of . . . its chances of success.
Of course I think them great, very great; indeed, almost
beyond calculation. . . ." For his contract as contributor
he was to be remunerated separately. His assistants were
to be paid for their work on an agreed scale, and immediately
on publication, or, if Messrs. Chapman and Hall liked it
better, they could hand over to the editor the total amount
due each week for contributions, and he would distribute
his largess as he thought fit, on condition that he would not
be held "accountable in any way." "I need not add," he
concluded, "that some arrangement would have to be made if
I undertake my Travels, relative to the expenses of travelling."

Truly, a veritable "monarch-of-all-I-survey" scheme!

Mr. G. K. Chesterton has summed it up in an illuminating sentence: "He thought of the thing as a kind of vast multiplication of himself, with Dickens as editor opening letters, Dickens as leader-writer writing leaders, Dickens as reviewer reviewing books, Dickens, for all I know, as office-boy opening and shutting doors." And, he might have added, Dickens as owner-director, entirely surrounded by cheques.

The valedictory passage of this astounding document sums up the position beautifully. Dickens could not have done it better in a novel.

"Now I want our publishing friends to take these things into consideration, and to give me the views and proposals they would be disposed to entertain when they have maturely considered the matter."

After such words Messrs. Chapman and Hall could remain in no possible doubt whatsoever as to exactly where they stood. Almost less than the dust.

Messrs. Chapman and Hall accepted the position. What else could they do? Dickens was a gold mine to them, and one which showed as yet no sign of exhaustion; and they could not fail to see that unless they signed, sealed, and settled this bond, whatever their private doubts might be as to its wisdom, they might incontinently dismiss from their minds any hopes of further participation in any riches the mine should produce in the future.

They agreed to pay Dickens £1,500 as his honorarium on the conclusion of "Nickleby." They agreed to take all the risks of the projected undertaking, and to pay the editor weekly, whatever the sales of the magazine might be, the sum of £50. They agreed further to hand over to him half the profits on each separate number, and to carry forward no loss to the general account. They agreed to do all this for a period of twelve months; at the end of which time, if they decided to continue, which naturally they would only do if the venture was proving successful, the editor would consent to bind himself to the enterprise for five years, on the condition that the ultimate profits and copyrights were to be equally divided between editor and publishers.

G

Thus was launched *Master Humphrey's Clock*, the first of Dickens' essays in autocratic editorship. The scheme as proposed was adopted practically without modification, though it was agreed in discussion that for the first few numbers at least Dickens had better be the sole contributor; and the suggestion that at some time, in some way, a serial under his name ought to figure in the contents seemed to express the general opinion of the meeting. No arrangement for this, however, was made in the agreement. Mr. George Cattermole and H. K. Browne (Phiz) were engaged as illustrators, and early in 1840 Dickens sat down to write the first number.

The periodical was to be novel in every particular, and not least, so Dickens planned, in the account that should be put forward of its genesis and the origin of its contents. He had devised a quaint and pleasing fiction of a solitary old man, a dreamer and philosopher, living alone in a queer shadowy old house, with his books and his memories, and an "old quaint queer-cased" grandfather clock that he had come, by reason of his loneliness, to regard almost as a living companion and friend; and from its "old, deep, dark, silent closet where the weights are" he would from time to time draw odd manuscripts he had accumulated there in days of yore. Round this old man the "club or knot of characters" was gradually to form, and Master Humphrey would reminisce and read his manuscripts, and the members of the club would also reminisce and read their manuscripts, and (imaginary) correspondents, fond memories stirred by these ancient tales, would write to the editor their reminiscences, and so *ad infinitum*.

It is perhaps hardly necessary to say that all this flood of inspiration had its source in a tiny well of fact. While on his visit to Yorkshire, Dickens had crossed the Durham border, and in Castle Barnard had come across the shop of a Mr. William Humphreys, a watch and clock maker, where he had seen behind the door "Master Humphrey's clock," a beautiful old timepiece built by the horologist himself some years previously. After a lifetime of considerable fame, this clock now rests in the Dickens House, Doughty Street.

There was an old-fashioned, melancholy fragrance about the whole idea of Master Humphrey and his clock that was very charming. "All our sweetest songs are those which tell of saddest thought." Dickens was, in fact, though he knew it not, groping his way towards a supremer expression of his great, generous, loving nature than he had yet, in spite of all his triumphs, manifested.

In theory *Master Humphrey's Clock*, contained every element necessary for overwhelming success. In practice it immediately encountered an insuperable obstacle. It did not please the public. What the public wanted from their Dickens was a story, a real story, and nothing but a story. Their instinct was a true one, and it is to their obstinate perversity on this occasion, aided by a divine accident, that the world owes "The Old Curiosity Shop."

The first number of *Master Humphrey's Clock*, "now wound up and going, preparatory to its striking," as the advertisement humorously put it, came out on Saturday, April 4th, 1840. The public rallied round to the magnificent tune of 70,000 copies; then they discovered that there was no serial story by Dickens.

One cannot blame the public. Dickens himself had educated them up to expecting from him something far better and of much more sustained interest than "Sketches" by "Boz," and that was, in effect, what he was giving them in *Master Humphrey's Clock*. Wiser, wittier, more varied and more mature work certainly than had been contained in the original "Sketches," but "Sketches" none the less.

Not without reason the public objected, as rapidly decreasing sales soon showed. Even the introduction of Mr. Pickwick and Sam Weller, the latter accompanied by his father and anecdotes of a precocious infant son, who plays all day with a quart pot and would not take a pint pot if it were offered to him, failed to mollify the public to any comfortable extent. To say truth, there was little reason why it should. Mr. Pickwick and Sam are but caricatures of their former selves. Mr. Pickwick, not to put too fine a point on it, fairly oozes benevolence, while marriage has made Sam prosy. The elder Weller, so delightfully poised in

"Pickwick" between cuteness and thick-headedness, has gone definitely over to stupidity and a widow-complex.

To what extent "The Old Curiosity Shop" was due to the perversity of the public, or to the happy impulse that moved Master Humphrey to relate the story of his meeting with the child from the old curiosity shop, it would be idle to speculate.

In February Dickens and his wife, accompanied by Forster and Maclise, travelled to Bath to visit the poet Walter Savage Landor, and spent with him at 35 St. James's Square three very pleasant days. During this time an idea for a short story began to mature in Dickens' mind, and a few days later he wrote to Forster to say that he was throwing out of No. III of the *Clock* a witch-story, and concluding "with the little child-story, which is SURE to be effective," especially as it was to be told by quiet old Master Humphrey.

Thus was begun the story of little Nell. It was at first to be no more than one of the miscellaneous contributions to *Master Humphrey's Clock*. This accounts for the title; for, as numberless critics have pointed out, the old curiosity shop speedily disappears from the story. The fact that it was being related by Master Humphrey accounts for the opening, which is perfectly attuned to introduce a reminiscence of his. The conclusion of the first chapter shows that even at that early stage little Nell has wound her way into her author's heart. Master Humphrey found he could not dismiss her image from his thoughts. "It would be a curious speculation," he mused, "to imagine her in her future life, holding her solitary way among a crowd of wild, grotesque companions: the only pure, fresh, youthful object in the throng. It would be curious to find"—and there he checked himself, for "the theme was carrying me along with it at a great pace, and I already saw before me a region on which I was little disposed to enter."

Or rather, should one say, a region into which Dickens felt he dare not at present enter, seeing that he was on the very eve of the launching of this colossal new venture of his, this weekly magazine that was to contain everything except a serial story? It has to be remembered that the first

SAMUEL ROGERS (1763–1855), TO WHOM DICKENS DEDICATED
"MASTER HUMPHREY'S CLOCK"

*After the Portrait by Sir Thomas Lawrence, P.R.A.*

chapter of "The Old Curiosity Shop" was written before the publication of No. I of *Master Humphrey's Clock*.

When, however, the non-success of succeeding numbers made it clearly evident that the public strongly disapproved of the snippety character of the contents of the new periodical, the whole situation altered. It was obvious that the public wanted a serial. Here was one throbbing in his mind. What could be more opportune? "He resolved," says Forster, "to throw everything else aside, devoting himself to the one story only."

So, within a few weeks of the impressive first chimes of *Master Humphrey's Clock*, he had abandoned the whole elaborate scheme, and was back again at his old familiar task, the sole difference being that he was now furnishing weekly instead of monthly instalments. As a considerable amount of other matter had been prepared for the magazine which, incidentally, was being published in Germany and the United States as well as in the British Isles, it was a week or two before "The Old Curiosity Shop" could get properly going, but as he naïvely explains in the preface to the completed work, "I cheerfully set about disentangling myself from those impediments as fast as I could." There was an interval of three weeks between the appearance of Chapters I and II; there were breaks between the fourth and fifth, and eighth and ninth chapters, but with these slight early interruptions "The Old Curiosity Shop" ran continuously until its conclusion in January 1841.

It requires an immense effort of imagination at this date to conceive the effect the story had upon the minds of the English-speaking world. There are to-day popular authors and best-sellers among books; every now and then a novel becomes something more even than a best-seller, it becomes "the rage," and for a few weeks, possibly months, its characters are seriously discussed in literary and lending-library circles. But no one ever forgets that they are only characters in So-and-So's book.

No one in 1840 ever thought of Dickens' people as belonging to a book. To put it paradoxically, they only read the book to learn more about people who were as real as themselves.

When Dickens created little Nell he set a real child in every home. When he introduced Dick Swiveller in "The Old Curiosity Shop" every young clerk in the city drank his beer with a grander air, talked about the "rosy," and called his sweetheart the Marchioness.

"I am not acquainted," says Forster, "with any story in the language more adapted to strengthen in the heart what most needs help and encouragement, to sustain kindly and innocent impulses, to wake everywhere the sleeping germs of good."

Those words will perhaps illustrate the enormous distance we have travelled away from the 1840 conception of a novel. We do not now ask of a work of fiction that it shall do any of this for us. We do not expect it; we are content that it shall amuse, or interest, or intrigue us. We have neither time nor inclination to take novels seriously. There are too many of them, and it may be that they are all too much alike.

The early Victorian age was a solid and serious one. Its very newspaper columns were essays in philosophy; its novels were ponderous efforts in three volumes, their pages breathing morality in long paragraphs, and sustaining innocence and virtue and condemning vice in chapters of intolerable length. Good people to-day are sometimes heard to declare that they have to "skip" parts of Dickens because they find them dull; though they do not realize it, they are paying him the highest compliment. The passages they find "dull" were the very meat and drink of a novel to the early Victorians; they loved to gorge themselves upon such stuff; they could not have too much of it. Imagine such readers: and then imagine what a triumph it was on Dickens' part to conquer their affections with "Pickwick!"

It was an eminently formal age. Its inhabitants were divided strictly into three classes: the aristocracy, the middle-classes—with upper and lower compartments—and the poor, deserving and undeserving. There was for each of these classes a separate justice, a separate morality, a separate life. Between each two classes there was a great gulf fixed, which hardly anyone ever thought of bridging.

The gulf that separated the poor from the rest of society was almost fathomless in its breadth, depth and height. As regards morals, it was so enormous that while the middle-class, especially the upper division, could not under any condition be thought of except as patterns of virtue and uprightness, it was hardly conceivable that the poor could be anything but dishonest, drunken, and immoral. There was, it may be said, much reason in this view; the middle-classes had little temptation to be unrighteous: the poor had little chance to be anything else.

It was this gulf which Dickens bridged.

It is because this gulf no longer exists (thanks, among others, to Dickens) that many people to-day find it difficult to appreciate the story of little Nell. She is impossibly good, they say. Yes, she is, for the sufficient reason that the appalling conditions of life which alone could develop such goodness as hers have been swept away by that great wave of social reform which in 1840 was only just beginning to surge upon the foul disgrace of England's festering poverty and malodorous ignorance.

Little Nell is not a child; she is the apotheosis of mal-treated childhood. Dickens explains her quite carefully in the first chapter of "The Old Curiosity Shop," and once one can understand this explanation, the rest of the story follows as naturally as the day the night. It is the night of our non-comprehension of how childhood could be, and was, treated in the 1840's which prevents us to-day from seeing her clearly. "I love these little people," says Master Humphrey, and, "It always grieves me to contemplate the initiation of children into the ways of life, when they are scarcely more than infants. It checks their confidence and simplicity—two of the best qualities that Heaven gives them—and demands that they share our sorrows before they are capable of entering into our enjoyments."

"It will never check hers," replies little Nell's grand-father, "the springs are too deep."

There is the whole theme; what one has to do in order to appreciate it is to fill in the background; an England forty years before elementary education became compulsory, when children were chattels, and the children of the poor were beasts of burden from the day they could stand upright, and long before they were strong enough to bear their harness, when the voice of Lord Shaftesbury calling aloud for some protection by law of these little ones was like the voice of one crying in the wilderness.

Fill in, too, the personal background. "This delicate child, with so much beauty and intelligence . . . so very young, so spiritual, so slight and fairy-like . . . holding her solitary way among a crowd of wild grotesque companions." It was not yet three years since Mary had died, Mary Hogarth, sister of Mrs. Dickens, "young, beautiful, and good," whom God had "numbered . . . among His angels at the early age of seventeen"; Mary, whose image had never left Dickens' mind, who, dead, yet lived with him wheresoe'er he went and whatsoever he did. "Is it not extraordinary," he wrote from Greta Bridge, "that the same dreams, which have constantly visited me since poor Mary died, follow me everywhere? . . . I have dreamt of her ever since I left home. . . . I should be sorry to lose such visions, for they are very happy ones. . . ." In the diary he began to write in January 1838, there are constant references to her, and among them this: "She is sentient, and conscious of my emotions *somewhere*. . . . I have seen her. . . . I know but too well how true all this is."

Can it be wondered that the story possessed him as no other he had written had done, that as he drew towards its conclusion the thought of the approaching death of little Nell, which the logical Forster had pointed out to him was the only possible end to his story, cast "the most horrible shadow" upon him, and rendered him "the wretchedest of the wretched," so that at last he cried aloud in his agony in a letter to Cattermole, "I am breaking my heart over this story, and cannot bear to finish it"?

He broke his readers' hearts over it, too; in scores upon scores of letters he was implored not to "kill" little Nell; her story literally dissolved the United States—then, as now, an intensely sentimental nation—in tears. Daniel O'Connell, the great tender-hearted Irish patriot, protested, with tears in his eyes, "He should not have killed her. She was too good!" while Francis, Lord Jeffrey, editor of the *Edinburgh Review* and most devastating of literary critics, pleaded earnestly for her life to be spared, and wept without shame over her death.

However one may feel over little Nell, and it is all a matter of feeling, there can hardly be two opinions over Dick Swiveller. Dick is one of the lads. His author liked him from the start, and meant to make much of him. Incidentally, it was not always a good augury when Dickens made up his mind to devote especial care to a character; sometimes the more he toiled the less effective was the result. But Dick, with his great mouthfuls of words, is incomparable, because he so perfectly expresses one of Dickens' outlooks upon life. "But what," said Mr. Swiveller with a sigh, "what is the odds so long as the fire of soul is kindled at the taper of con-wiviality, and the wing of friendship never moults a feather! What is the odds so long as the spirit is expanded by means of rosy wine, and the present moment is the least happiest of our existence!" Exactly what Dickens himself would have said, and thought, on any one of those riotous days at Petersham.

There must have been an almost breathless excitement in reading Dickens in the days when his works were appearing in their monthly or weekly numbers. There must have been endless palpitating discussions as to whatever would happen next, whatever queer sort of person would turn up in the next number. All his best people were so different from those in other books. (It will be noticed that whenever Dickens creates a conventional character, such as Mr. Brownlow, Rose or Harry Maylie, that character rarely impresses). Oliver Twist, a workhouse boy, Fagin, a wicked old Jewish thief, Bill Sikes, burglar and murderer, Jack Dawkins and Charley Bates, pickpockets, Mr. Wackford Squeers, a brutal schoolmaster, Mr. Vincent Crummles, manager of a third-rate touring theatrical company, Miss La Creevy, an elderly and obviously third-rate painter of miniatures, Dick Swiveller, a down-at-heels, disreputable clerk, distinguished by "a prevailing greasiness of appearance—" and then, with superb audacity, Dickens descended into the dark basement of the

Brasses' house, and unearthed the Marchioness as companion for Dick Swiveller.

The stroke was as happy as it was daring. Had it been suggested to any Victorian householder in the early months of 1840 that within a few weeks all England would be talking rapturously about a small servant girl, so ignorant that she did not know her own age, and (what appeared far worse to Mr. Swiveller) had never tasted beer, that householder would either have had a fit or gravely requested the speaker not to refer to such low topics. Yet so it happened.

A poor little starved slavey with a perpetual cold in the head through living in a damp dungeon of an underground kitchen, common, vulgar, dirty, a thief in intention if not in fact, all the time watching at keyholes "to know where the key of the safe was hid," though she would not have taken much, "only enough to squench my hunger." Of such stuff are heroines made when a Dickens is in the field. The devotion of the Marchioness to Dick Swiveller and her nursing of him through his illness are as fine as anything in the book.

Daniel Quilp, the revolting, ugly and cruel dwarf, naturally strikes many people now as merely a grotesque monstrosity. He certainly does sound as though he had strayed by mistake out of the "Arabian Nights." Yet Quilp is probably far nearer a photograph than most of us now can realize. The age of oddities is past, swept out of existence by popular education, trade unionism, and the dole. Both ogres and fairy-godmothers were quite possible in the 1840's, when neither private charity nor private cruelty were much interfered with by the State. Dickens' pictures of eccentric and grotesque people are far too numerous and too realistic to be purely imaginary. The same applies to some extent to his "villains."

He was born into a moral world of hard and fast colours. Black was black, and white was white, and never the twain could meet. If a person was good, his virtues rose up to heaven with a sweet (and rather overpowering) savour; if he was bad, his vices stank in the nostrils of all the righteous. One reason, a minor but still a strong one, why Dickens was so popular with Victorian readers, and has become so un-

popular with some sections of very modern people to-day,
is that he carried this doctrine to extremes.  His good people
are, like little Nell, too good; his villains have not a dog's
chance from the start.  They are born only to flourish
unholily for a brief space, and then to go to their just, and
generally eternal, damnation in the closing chapters of the
book.

Their ultimate doom is writ large upon them from the
moment of their entry.  Who could doubt the fate of Mr.
Sampson Brass, "an attorney of no very good repute," from
the moment one learns that he had "a cringing manner but
a very harsh voice," and that "his blandest smiles were so
extremely forbidding, that to have had his company under
the least repulsive circumstances, one would have wished
him to be out of temper that he might only scowl"?  Or
of his "clerk, assistant, housekeeper, secretary, confidential
plotter, adviser, intriguer, and bill of cost increaser," his
sister Miss Sally Brass, "a kind of amazon at common law"?
This quite apart, of course, from the fact that it was far
easier for the scriptural camel to pass through the eye of the
needle than for a lawyer to find favour in the eyes of Charles
Dickens, though the miracle does happen occasionally; it
happens in "The Old Curiosity Shop."

The villains of "The Old Curiosity Shop," however, are by
no means the most interesting characters.  Quilp's seizure
of old Trent's belongings, and the decision of Nell and her
grandfather to steal away from their old home "early and
softly, that we may not be seen or heard" gives Dickens an
opportunity of which he takes glorious advantage.  He gets
them out on to the broad highway, and there follows an epic
of vagrancy scarcely surpassed in English literature, during
the first half of which Mr. Thomas Codlin, the misanthrope,
and Short, who appears to be the friend, but is not (according
to Codlin), and Mrs. Jarley with her immortal waxworks,
step up to take their place alongside Mr. Vincent Crummles
among Dickens' strolling heroes of the open road.

Mr. Codlin, "who had a surly, grumbling manner" and
"the air of a discontented philosopher," and Mr. Harris,
known as Trotters, or Short Trotters, "by reason of the small

size of his legs," and usually as Short, " a little merry-faced
man with a twinkling eye and a red nose," the itinerant
Punch showmen, are inimitably drawn, in perfect contrast.
They are exactly what a hard and not too profitable life on
the road would have made them; the worse things are the
more Short smiles, and does all the work; the better things
are the more anxiously Codlin counts the ha'pennies Short
has earned. But then, as Codlin points out, Short has not
got to "stand in front of the curtain and see the public's
faces," as he does. If he did he would "know human natur'
better." Kind-hearted, both of them, but the life compels
them always to keep wide open a watchful eye to the main
chance. It is Short who conceives the idea of detaining
little Nell and her grandfather, and of restoring them to their
friends, "who I daresay have had their disconsolation pasted
up on every wall in London by this time." Codlin understands
him perfectly; but Codlin likes to have things said and
arranged precisely. He agrees that "it's possible that there
might be uncommon good sense in what you've said. If
there is, and there should be a reward, Short, remember
we're partners in everything!"

Mrs. Jarley, of course, moves in very different circles.
Her horror at Nell's innocent question as to whether she
knows Codlin and Short has behind it a whole lifetime of
superiority. "Know 'em, child! . . . Know *them*! But
you're young and inexperienced, and that's your excuse for
asking sich a question." Mrs. Jarley, stout, comfortable,
and prosperous, is one of the aristocrats of her profession;
she tours the country in a "smart little house upon wheels,
with white dimity curtains . . . and window-shutters of
green picked out with panels of a staring red," and her
unrivalled collection of waxwork images travels ahead of
her in "wans."

Mrs. Jarley exhibits in "assembly-rooms, town-halls,
large rooms at inns, or auction-galleries. There is none of
your open air wagrancy at Jarley's . . . no tarpaulin and
sawdust. . . .'' As for any connection with a Punch!—
"a low, practical, wulgar wretch, that people should scorn
to look at. . . ." The idea! Mrs. Jarley's waxworks are

"calm and classical . . . with a constantly unchanging air of coldness and gentility." They are patronized by Royalty (do not her placards say so?) and are the "delight of the Nobility and Gentry." Mrs. Jarley has her posters and her handbills; she can calmly pay for poetry in her advertisements; and while her menials are distributing "pathetic effusions" among the private residents and the tradespeople, and doggerel rhymes in the public-houses, she is calling in person upon the young ladies' boarding schools, "with handbills composed expressly for them, in which it was distinctly proved that wax work refined the mind, cultivated the taste, and enlarged the sphere of the human understanding."

Withal, she is a dear, kind, bustling, clever old lady, whose good-natured heart is immediately conquered by little Nell; and could little Nell and her grandfather have stayed with Mrs. Jarley their lives would have been happy and prosperous. But alas! the old man's passion for gambling drives them from this earthly paradise, and from the moment of their leaving Mrs. Jarley the child's doom is certain. Dickens' power of creating an atmosphere, especially of tragedy, to accompany events, is often remarkable, and never more so than in this last long journey of little Nell's, with its endless dragging trail through the dreary and desolated industrial area, with the road lying "through miles and miles, all lighted up by fires . . . a strange black road," and so on and on "through cold, wet, hunger, want of rest, and lack of any place to lay her aching head," befriended once by a strange fire-keeper, then on again, past homes laid waste by starvation and crime, to be found at last by the poor schoolmaster and carried away into the pure, quiet, restful countryside . . . to die; peacefully, all toil and weariness and suffering past, but still, to die.

While the story of little Nell dominates the book, there are in "The Old Curiosity Shop" three quite distinct threads of interest, and these keep on colliding with each other (there is no other word for it) in the cheerfully irresponsible way that Dickens' plots always do. The stories of little Nell, Kit Nubbles, and Dick Swiveller have, of course, a common origin; they all begin from the old curiosity shop, though Mr. Swiveller is certainly rather dragged there against his will. The story of Kit, that "shock-headed shambling awkward lad, with an uncommonly wide mouth," who is errand boy and assistant to old Trent before the shop is broken up, gives Dickens the opportunity to portray kindly benevolence in the persons of Mr. Garland, that "little fat placid-faced old gentleman," Mrs. Garland, as plump and placid as her husband, and Mr. Abel Garland so exactly like his father, even to the club-foot. It gave him, too, the chance to prove the sterling worth and honesty of the deserving poor. Kit, given a shilling for a job worth only sixpence, does return, as he promises, the following Monday morning to work it out, thereby thoroughly upsetting Mr. Chuckster, the notary's clerk, who was "blessed if he could make out whether he [Kit] was 'precious raw' or 'precious deep,' but intimated by a distrustful shake of the head that he inclined to the latter opinion."

Kit gives his author the opportunity to display the interior of a poor, hardworking home, and to show what it can cost to maintain decency and cheerfulness under such conditions. Mrs. Nubbles, Kit's mother, is a widow, with two infant children besides her eldest boy; and when Kit gets home, after eleven at night, she is "still hard at work at an ironing-table," and so, though Kit "was disposed to be out of temper, as the best of us are too often," he looked at his brothers, and he looked at his mother, "who had been at work without complaint since morning, and thought it would be a better and a kinder thing to be good-humoured," and "What a one you are!" says he to his mother, "there aren't many such as you, *I* know," and when his mother declares that there are many better, "or ought to be, accordin' to what the parson at chapel says," he bursts out in one of those pregnant sentences in which Dickens speaks his own mind without fear or favour. "Much he knows about it. . . . Wait till he's a widder and works like you do, and gets as little and does as much, and keeps his spirits up the same, and then I'll ask him what's o'clock and trust him for being right to half a second."

There are a dozen more people in the story who, though minor characters, amply repay attention; old Mrs. Jiniwin,

Mrs. Quilp, Miss Sophy Wackles—second daughter to Mrs. Wackles, who kept the "Ladies Seminary" in Chelsea, and sister to Miss Melissa Wackles and Miss Jane Wackles—who was courted by Mr. Swiveller but decided to marry Mr. Cheggs, "who was bashful before ladies," but a very substantial market-gardener none the less, and was moreover strongly aided in his courtship by the determined Miss Cheggs; Mr. Witherden, that strange phenomenon in Dickens' works, an honest lawyer, and the aforementioned Mr. Chuckster, his clerk, who is again bitterly disappointed when Kit Nubbles proves not to have stolen the five-pound note, "inasmuch as his guilt would have had in it something daring and bold, whereas his innocence was but another proof of his sneaking and crafty disposition" and who remains his deadly foe for years on this account; the "single gentleman," so obviously mysterious, and so obviously the god out of the machine who is to settle the hash of the various villains; Barbara, "very tidy, modest and demure, but very pretty too," and Barbara's mother, like Kit's mother, a widow, and so "We must have been made to know each other" she says to Mrs. Nubbles; George, Mrs. Jarley's caravan driver; Jerry, proprietor of the performing dogs; Mr. Vuffin, called Sweet William, "probably as a pleasant satire upon his ugliness," the landlord of the Jolly Sandboys, and Mr. Slum, the writer of poetical advertisements.

Two delightful animal pictures may be included in this gallery: the dog that Jerry punished, and Whiskers, the Garlands' pony. Dickens was a great dog-lover and owner, yet he did not introduce many dogs into his books, though Bill Sikes's is famous. When he does, their portraits are as real as those of his human characters.

"'That dog,' said Jerry, pointing out the old leader of the troop, and speaking in a terrible voice, 'lost a halfpenny to-day. *He* goes without his supper.'" The unfortunate dog is set to play the barrel-organ while the rest are called up and fed from their master's plate, and "When the knives and forks rattled very much, or any of his fellows got an unusually large piece of fat, he accompanied the music with a short howl, but he immediately checked it on his master looking round, and applied himself with increased diligence to the Old Hundredth." One can only hope he did not know the words set to that immortal tune.

Whiskers, "a little obstinate-looking rough coated pony," with a habit of inspecting lamp-posts, and of stopping every now and then to meditate, is evidently drawn from the pony of Mrs. Dickens' first conveyance, as it is related that that animal had a habit of rushing off up side-streets whenever the fancy took it.

"The Old Curiosity Shop" definitely set the seal upon Dickens' fame. It reveals him for the first time at the very height, breadth, and depth of his powers. All that had made his previous books attractive to such large numbers of people was present, the lively and unforced wit, the humour so fresh, so original, and always so akin to tenderness, the brilliant and minutely accurate characterization which marshalled before his readers the most varied, the most novel, and most real army of people they had ever met, the descriptive ability which caused places to appear as though photographed, and the power in narrative of always enveloping his people in the appropriate atmosphere; and with all this there had come the full flowering of his pathos—foreshadowed in "Oliver Twist," greatly developed in "Nicholas Nickleby," and realized in towering and almost unbearable grandeur in "The Old Curiosity Shop."

Owing to revolutionary changes in social conditions in England, and no less revolutionary changes in our educational, moral, and religious ideas, the main story, that of little Nell, which lifted the book right out and beyond his previous ones, does not now hold readers spellbound as it used to do; but even if admiration be confined to other aspects of "The Old Curiosity Shop," Dick Swiveller, the Marchioness, Codlin and Short, Mrs. Jarley, and Sampson and Sally Brass are in themselves sufficient to place it among the finest of his works.

Dickens loved it himself; he delayed as long as he could its conclusion, and grew daily more miserable as the end approached. At last. . . . "I took my desk upstairs; and writing until four o'clock this morning, finished the story.

It makes me very melancholy to think that all these people are lost to me for ever, and I feel as if I could never become attached to any new set of characters."

That was on the 17th January, 1841. His letters during the next month show the very real difficulty he had in transferring his affections to his next book. It had to be done, of course; the successor to "The Old Curiosity Shop" had already been advertised in *Master Humphrey's Clock* (the original name of the magazine had been retained), and was due to commence in February.

The next book was the many times postponed "Barnaby Rudge," the contract for which was now held by Messrs. Chapman and Hall. In the previous May Mr. Bentley, apparently despairing of ever receiving this novel from Dickens, had decided to make the best of a bad job, and opened negotiations which resulted in the transfer to Messrs. Chapman and Hall of the agreement on their purchase on Dickens' behalf of the copyright and remaining stock of "Oliver Twist" for £2,250.

There is a humorous note in the letter in which Dickens confirmed the details of this transaction which shows that at times he could laugh at himself, even when the laugh was seriously against him. ". . . this £2,250," he wrote, "is to be deducted from the purchase-money of a work by me entitled 'Barnaby Rudge,' of which two chapters are now in your hands, and of which the whole is to be written within some convenient time to be agreed upon between us. But if it should not be written (which God forbid) within five years. . . ." That mention of five years must have sounded somewhat ominous to Chapman and Hall; but their hearts were no doubt cheered by the gift of an antique silver-mounted claret jug sent to them by Dickens to express his gratitude at being freed at long last from the net of unprofitable entanglements with publishers.

"Barnaby Rudge" was to consist in bulk of the equivalent of ten monthly numbers of "Pickwick," that is, about 160,000 words; for this Dickens was to receive £3,000, and the entire copyright was to revert to him six months after the publication of the last number.

He began upon it in good earnest towards the end of January 1841, and completed it by the end of October, in spite of a serious illness during the autumn, and a number of other vexations and distractions. In some respects it was the most difficult book he had yet attempted. He was working upon historical data, of which he had collected a large amount since 1838, and thus to some extent was compelled to curb his riotous fancy; he did not thoroughly "warm up" to the work for quite a long time. When he did the story carried him away with it, so that "the interest with which the tale begins," as Forster says, "has ceased to be its interest before the close." He bestowed more than usual care upon its writing, no doubt to ensure historical accuracy, and in so doing found himself caught up by as moving a theme as any he had yet approached, with the result that the story of the private lives of his characters was swept into and absorbed by the great tumultuous and heartrending public story of the "No Popery" riots of 1780.

Critical opinion does not rank "Barnaby Rudge" very high among the novels, the general feeling being that it is "Not quite Dickens." Yet the critics are strangely divided in their judgments. Forster speaks of defects which "supervened in the management of the plot," apologizing for these on the grounds that the book had been started a long time previously and then laid aside, and that a different design shaped in the author's mind when he took it up again. George Gissing, on the other hand, while admitting that the two parts of the story, the historical and the private, are not well knit together, thinks that "Barnaby Rudge" "is free from Dickens' worst vices of construction." Mr. G. K. Chesterton says it is "no more an historical novel than Sim's [the boy conspirator, Simon Tappertit] league was a political movement, but," he adds, "they are both beautiful creations." Mr. Bernard Darwin, a later biographer of Dickens, remarks justly that "it lacked characters that became part of the reader's life," and agrees with Forster and most other critics that "its merits lay rather in that creation of an ominous and darkling atmosphere," to which Forster has referred in such moving words.

"There are few things more masterly," says the latter of
the sustained descriptions of the riots, "in any of his books.
From the first low mutterings of the storm to its last terrible
explosion, the frantic outbreak of popular ignorance and rage
is depicted with unabated power. The aimlessness of idle
mischief by which the ranks of the rioters are swelled at
the beginning; the recklessness induced by the monstrous
impunity allowed to the early excesses; the sudden spread
of drunken guilt into every haunt of poverty, ignorance, or
mischief in the wicked old city, where such rich materials of
crime lie festering; the wild action of its poison on all, without
scheme or plan of any kind, who come within its reach; the
horrors that are more bewildering for so complete an absence
of purpose in them; and, when all is done, the misery found
to have been self-inflicted in every cranny and corner of
London, as if a plague had swept over the streets: these are
features in the picture of an actual occurrence, to which the
manner of the treatment gives extraordinary force and
meaning."

The book is, in fact, precisely what one might expect
from the conditions of its genesis and composition. It was,
as has been seen, originally promised to Macrone way back
in 1836 as the story of "Gabriel Vardon, the Locksmith
of London." What its contents were then to have been one
can only conjecture. Before it was begun, it was transferred
to Bentley in 1838 as "Barnaby Rudge," and, remaining
still unwritten, proved itself the desolating blot upon the
happiness of Dickens' existence. He put off beginning it
time and again; and quite as much, one ventures to suggest,
because the very idea of writing an historical novel—that is,
one in which his imagination could not have free play—was
repugnant to him as because of the actual labour of composing it.

The agreement for it passed into the hands of Messrs.
Chapman and Hall in the summer of 1840. It was an opportune moment. Dickens, who was absorbed in the writing
of "The Old Curiosity Shop," was overcome with gratitude
to them for freeing him finally from the last threads of the
web of his injudicious agreements, signed gladly the terms of

the new contract and then, one imagines, forgot all about "Barnaby Rudge" for several months in the tumultuous emotional excitement of the story of little Nell.

When the time arrived, towards the end of 1840, to make plans for a successor to that story in the *Clock*, the thought of "Barnaby" came, no doubt, not as something repugnant but almost as a relief. Emotionally, Dickens was still bound up in the story of little Nell; the image of the child was pursuing him even in his dreams, and he was delaying, with a very luxuriance of grief, the conclusion of her story.

Both mentally and emotionally, one can safely surmise, he was for the moment thoroughly exhausted; he had given so copiously of both his creative ability and of his love and sympathy to this tale that his soul must have cried out for a quiet period of rest and relaxation in which to refresh itself from its hidden springs of feeling, to recuperate after a well-nigh intolerable strain. Yet he had another novel to begin immediately.

In "Barnaby Rudge" there lay work, ready to his hand, which would no doubt satisfy his public, yet would not make undue demands upon his higher powers. He had accumulated abundance of material for it; the book would be in a sense more of a compilation than a novel. Several chapters were already written, and happily these contained, in Solomon Daisy's story, the outline of the plot. There only remained to work it out.

He started, ploughed his way steadily and laboriously into the melodrama, the prologue to which he had, a year or more previously, caused to be related in the Maypole Inn near Chigwell, and then—with a start, dare one say?—found himself back once more in the dear old familiar dirty London streets and alleyways, with the exciting prospect of a tremendous tumult brewing in their dark holes and corners. His imagination quickened, began to riot with the rioters; in his mind, well stored with contemporary accounts, the dreadful scenes of the 1780 outbreak began to re-enact themselves with a vividness only possible to one who had such power of imagery as he, and who knew low life in London through and through.

After that, it was but the inevitable that happened. Dickens with his brain on fire was incapable of writing a dull word, and it was on fire now with two consuming themes: one picturesque, one moral: the streets of London and their mobs, and the awful futility and waste and savagery of the unhappy Gordon riots. What could provide greater incitement to his powers? So there follows that steadily accumulating storm of description which begins "one wintry evening, early in the year of our Lord one thousand seven hundred and eighty," when "a keen north wind arose as it grew dark, and night came on with black and dismal looks," swells with the fury of the ignorant, misguided mob, and culminates in the shocking execution scenes and that awful curse of Maypole Hugh, the illegitimate ostler son of Sir John Chester, just before he is hanged for his share in the riots, and which sums up all the bitter hatred of disillusionment:

"Upon these human shambles, I, who never raised my hand in prayer till now, call down the wrath of God! On that black tree, of which I am the ripened fruit, I do invoke the curse of all its victims, past, present, and to come. On the head of that man, who, in his conscience owns me for his son, I leave the wish that he may never sicken on his bed of down, but die a violent death as I do now, and have the night-wind for his only mourner. To this I say, Amen, amen!" Through all this torrential spate of description, which never falters, there run the deep undertones of Dickens' understanding of and sympathy with the wretched, ignorant, misguided rioters, the tools of crafty plotters, misled by their so-called leader, who are wantonly excited to deeds of violence, and then butchered by revengeful powers that troubled to lift no finger to restrain them before grave harm was done.

Among the characters that figure in "Barnaby Rudge," Maypole Hugh, ostler and general man at the Maypole, "a dreadful idle vagrant fellow, sir, half a gipsy," who "in his fits of laziness . . . sleeps so desperate hard," according to his master, "that if you were to fire off cannon balls into his ears, it wouldn't wake him, sir," and who becomes, on account of his great strength and demonic energy, a leader

among the rioters, is a powerfully drawn figure, who reaches
the height of tragedy in his death. Old John Willet, landlord of the Maypole, ignorant, obstinate, slow and stupid, is
a hundred comfortable, opinionated, sluggish landlords rolled
into one. Safely in possession of a fine old well-spoken-of
country inn on the road to London, he cannot help growing
rich and regarding himself as the most important man for
miles round, especially as he has a small circle of cronies
which unites to keep him of that opinion.

Gabriel Vardon, the locksmith, originally to have borne
the responsibility of the title of the book, is of the tribe of
the Cheeryble brothers and the Garlands, a "round, red-
faced sturdy yeoman, with a double chin, and a voice husky
with good living, good sleeping, good humour, and good
health," whose kindly and hearty benevolence shines through
the tale, and blesses many a person, including Barnaby
himself, who is saved from execution through his efforts.
Mr. Vardon is at first unfortunately afflicted with having as
wife "a lady of what is commonly called uncertain temper,"
but he is rewarded later by a remarkable change for the better
in her, and is all the while comforted and consoled by his
pretty daughter Dolly, who had "the loveliest pair of sparkling eyes," which lit up her laughing, dimpled, fresh and
healthful face.

His apprentice Sim, "as he was called in the locksmith's
family, or Mr. Simon Tappertit, as he called himself, and
required all men to style him out of doors, on holidays, and
Sundays out," is the finest piece of characterization in the
book. This "romantic guttersnipe," as Mr. Chesterton
terms him, "in years just twenty, in his looks much older,
and in conceit at least two hundred," is born of the same
stock as Mr. Dick Swiveller, but without the latter's greatness. The essential difference between them is that though
Dick is flowery and ornate and pretentious, he knows it, and
is doing it all for the fun of the thing, to keep at arm's length
the boredom and uneasiness of a shiftless and poverty-
stricken life; while Simon Tappertit, comfortably apprenticed
to a sound trade, and serving an honourable and kindly master,
is in dead earnest over his pretentiousness. He is the founder

CHARLES DICKENS

*After the Drawing by Count D'Orsay, 1841*

and captain of the United Bulldogs, a society of apprentices who have banded themselves together, as idle and adventurously-minded boys will do, to fight for the suppression of their masters and perpetual holidays for themselves. His foolish and bombastic mind is easily deluded into the belief that Lord George Gordon's is a crusade his Bulldogs must join and assist. He suffers for his fondness of imagination by losing both his legs in the riots, but is rewarded for general liveliness of disposition by being transformed later into a very successful shoeblack and married to the widow of an eminent bone and rag collector.

Barnaby Rudge, the half-wit "hero" of the book, is in essence the ill-starred child of Dickens' imagination all over again. Though actually grown up (he is twenty-three), he is doomed to perpetual childishness by the most terrible curse of all, that feebleness of mind which deprives one of the right to be ranked as equal among one's brothers and sisters in society, that "absence of the soul" which, as Dickens says, "is far more terrible in a living man than in a dead one." Barnaby, more helpless in many ways than a child, and threatened, though he knows it not, by the return of a murderer father, is guarded devotedly by his mother, but in spite of her care is swept into the riots by his friend Maypole Hugh, and goes through it all, even to the very foot of the scaffold, without any true understanding of what it is all about.

Inseparable from Barnaby is his raven, Grip, a famous character drawn from famous originals, Dickens' own pet ravens. There were two of these: the first died, or was poisoned, and the second took its place while the story was actually being written. The Grip of the story is drawn with lifelike precision, even down to the biting of ankles, except that probably his language was toned down considerably. Dickens, pre-eminently Victorian in most of his morality, had little sympathy with those who would prohibit either strong liquors or strong language, and in the preface to the first cheap edition of "Barnaby Rudge" he tells how, after the death of Grip the First, a friend sent him "an older and more gifted raven," who, after "disinterring all the cheese and halfpence" his predecessor had buried in the garden, "applied himself to the acquisition of stable language" with such assiduity that he "would perch outside my window and drive imaginary horses with great skill all day."

It is perhaps as well, in view of the close proximity of Devonshire Terrace to the Marylebone Parish Church, that Dickens was unable to follow the advice of the raven's previous master, who said that if he wished him "to come out very strong" he should "show him a drunken man." Grip the Second, however, seems to have come out quite strongly enough in a variety of other ways, and judging from Dickens' account of him, the reiterated cry of Barnaby's bird, "I'm a devil, I'm a devil, I'm a devil," probably expressed what most people living near No. 1 Devonshire Terrace thought of him. After Grip the Second's early death three years later, Dickens thought it prudent to give up ravens as pets.

Keeping ravens was by no means the only fun Dickens enjoyed in these merry, strenuous, and well-filled days. Forster speaks of his capacity to indulge the two men in him, the wise and the foolish, "to give rest and relief to what was serious to him, and, when the time came to play his gambols, [to] surrender himself wholly to the enjoyment of the time." He played at least one gambol so wholeheartedly that it had vexatious, and might have had very serious, results. He wrote a distracted letter to Landor at Bath, pretending to have fallen madly in love with the young Queen Victoria (married the previous day) and, she being quite beyond his reach, to be planning to run away "to some uninhabited island" with any likely maid-of-honour, "to be entrapped by conspiracy for that purpose," and begging Landor's assistance in his scheme.

In a further letter to Forster, he hinted at various forms of suicide and murder, and other horrors. It may not actually have been as a consequence of this practical joke, but a few months later a report was spread widely to the effect that he was insane, and was being detained in an asylum. A few days later another rumour found its way into the papers, goodness knows why or how, that he had turned Roman Catholic. The reports annoyed Dickens—which report annoyed him more it would be difficult to say—and the first

THOMAS CARLYLE (1795–1881)

at least distressed a great many people. It must be admitted that Dickens' riotously exuberant behaviour on many occasions, notably at the seaside, was quite well calculated to encourage rumours of insanity.

He had yet not really begun to learn the disadvantages of being famous.

In spite of the anguish of concluding "The Old Curiosity Shop," which was very real and at moments overpowering, it is probable that the years 1840–1 were among the happiest of his life. "No one," says Forster, "so constantly recalled to his friends the description Johnson gave of Garrick, as the cheerfullest man of his age."

He was still young, and, in spite of recurrent attacks of illness, the *sequelæ* of his childish complaint, able to indulge freely and joyously in riding, walking, seaside junketings, and social entertainments with his numerous friends, the circle of which had now extended to include almost all the aristocracy of intellect, including, in addition to those previously mentioned, Proctor (Barry Cornwall), D'Orsay, Landseer, Bulwer Lytton, and Thomas Carlyle. For Society with a capital "S" he never had much taste; he preferred brains, and he openly detested bores. His growing family—there were four children by 1841—was giving him great joy. He was free at last of the rash engagements of his earlier days of authorship, and as a result could enjoy more leisure than ever before. He was comfortably installed in a big house in a fashionable neighbourhood, reasonably well-off, with a steadily rising income. His popularity with his readers, far from diminishing, was increasing by leaps and bounds. Not only from all parts of Britain but increasingly from abroad, and notably from America, were coming tributes to his fame.

He began to act as a man of affluence and established position. The habit of summer residence out of town grew upon him. He spent two considerable periods at Broadstairs in 1840. Travel and change of scene had always attracted him; he now began to indulge his fancy in this direction much more liberally than before. He made a tour of the Shakespeare country to celebrate the first publication of *Master Humphrey's Clock* (the party had to pawn their watches in

Birmingham to raise funds to get home), explored Devonshire in August, ran down to Brighton the following February for a week's quiet work, and set out in June for a tour in Scotland. All these journeyings, needless to say, implied very considerably more time and money than they would to-day, when a motor-car can make nothing of a hundred miles or so in an afternoon.

Two or three anecdotes of this period related by Forster well illustrate other aspects of his character. His trip to the Midlands was in keeping with the practice he had formed of being always out of town whenever a new venture was launched. This was not superstition, but an exaggerated sense of orderliness which was to grow more and more upon him as the years passed. He had been away from London when No. I of "Pickwick" came out; therefore, to do all things decently and in order, he must always be out of London when any book was published, any story started. In the same way, there had always to be a dinner on the conclusion of a novel.

Equally illustrative of this love of order is a letter from Broadstairs in June 1840. "Before I tasted bit or drop yesterday [the day of his arrival], I set out my writing table with extreme taste and neatness, and improved the disposition of the furniture generally." This passion for regularity and orderliness, both in time and arrangement, was a main factor later in enabling him to get through the colossal amount of work he did. Dickens was no eccentric genius as regards his manner of work; he never, from his earliest years, worked by fits and starts. As he grew older he trained himself, like any athlete, to consistent performance, till he sat down to his daily task as regularly and as punctually as any clerk.

In 1840 he was summoned as juryman in a case in which a mother was accused of having murdered her new-born babe. Being made foreman of the jury, he exerted his influence, and with the aid of the coroner, got returned a verdict only of concealment of birth. The pitiful protestations of her innocence made by the accused woman so moved him that he had her looked after in prison, and saw that she was provided with counsel at her trial; with the result that she received a light sentence. It was the only time he ever served on a jury: the case affected him so much that he positively ignored every such subsequent summons, and, being Charles Dickens—one can only assume that to have been the reason —no complaint was ever lodged against him for his quite unjustifiable neglect of his duty as a citizen. For civic responsibilities he had in general no great desire; he was twice during this year invited to become a candidate for Parliament, in May by the Borough of Reading, and later by a Scottish constituency, but happily declined both invitations quite decisively. He told the people of Reading that it was much against his will, and solely on account of the expense, that he refused, but it is more than likely that his whole inclination was against the proposal. Dickens in Parliament would have been miserably unhappy, and probably ineffective.

The year 1841 was to mark a culminating point in his career. The trip to Scotland, planned mainly as a holiday, on which various friends, including Lord Jeffrey, were to be visited, and a public dinner was to be attended in Edinburgh, turned out to be, in Edinburgh at least, something after the nature of reception of royalty. In Edinburgh, Fame caught up with him in person; and was never afterwards to desert him. After 1841 Dickens ceased to be a private individual, and became, as it were, national property.

He had thought originally of going this year to Ireland, but a letter from Lord Jeffrey announcing that he was coming to London, and saying that Edinburgh was desirous of welcoming Dickens, made him change his mind. Jeffrey came to London in April, and the visit was fixed for June.

His reception at Edinburgh staggered him. The first day after his arrival he wrote to Forster that "I have been this morning to Parliament House, and am now introduced (I hope) to everybody in Edinburgh. The hotel is perfectly besieged, and I have been forced to take refuge in a sequestered apartment at the end of a long passage, wherein I write this letter. They talk of 300 at the dinner."

The public dinner surprised, as it delighted, him still more. "The lord provost, council, and magistrates voted me by acclamation the freedom of the city, in testimony . . . of

H

the sense entertained by them of 'your distinguished abilities as an author,'" but this was not the sole marvel. "It was the most brilliant affair you can conceive. . . . The room was crammed, and more than seventy applications for tickets were of necessity refused yesterday. . . . I wish to God you had been there, as it is impossible for the 'distinguished guest' to describe the scene. It beat all natur'. . . ."

He wrote Forster a list of his engagements, told him how he had circulated false rumours to avoid a similar dinner at Glasgow, and added the following, strange sounding in view of his huge delight in and hunger for popularity and acclamation, yet strangely true, "The moral of all this is, that there is no place like home; and I thank God most heartily for having given me a quiet spirit, and a heart that won't hold many people."

Dickens slipped away at last from Edinburgh to enjoy a somewhat adventurous tour in the Highlands, loving and admiring the scenery, being appalled by Glencoe Pass, getting into all the bad weather possible, doing huge journeys, narrowly escaping being overturned with his wife in their coach while crossing a dangerously flooded stream, refusing an invitation to Glasgow, but promising to return later in the year, and always longing for home—"I am dying for Sunday, and wouldn't stop now for twenty dinners of twenty thousand each."

He returned to London in July, and was back at Broadstairs in August, bathing and writing doggerel rhymes in his spare moments; and in his more serious ones arranging to discontinue publication of *Master Humphrey's Clock* after the conclusion of "Barnaby Rudge," and not to begin another story until November 1842. The *Clock* was too much for one man; but no other man could share its labour with Dickens, so there was only one thing to be done; to wind it up for the last time.

Dickens had previously agreed with his publishers to start a fresh story in March 1842. Forster thought this unwise. So did Dickens by now, though not for the same reason as his friend. A far greater and more exciting project than a mere book was surging, seething, and boiling in his mind.

WILLIAM CHARLES MACREADY (1793–1873)

He was, in short, deciding to go to America. Forster had his suspicions of him when the agreement with Messrs. Chapman and Hall releasing him from all work for twelve months was signed, and only a week later, on the 13th September, he received a letter which amply confirmed them. "I am still haunted," wrote Dickens, "by visions of America, night and day. Kate cries dismally if I mention the subject. But, God willing, I think it *must* be managed somehow."

It was managed, of course. Kate might cry her eyes out, there might be four young children to dispose of—or forty, for that matter—there might be a thousand and one obstacles to surmount, but once Charles Dickens had made up his mind, no difficulties could be insuperable, and he would be "in his usual fever" until they were disposed of. The final decision took place, in capital letters, on September 19th—"I HAVE MADE UP MY MIND (WITH GOD'S LEAVE) TO GO TO AMERICA—AND TO START AS SOON AFTER CHRIST- MAS AS IT WILL BE SAFE TO GO." He had come, he said a day or two later, to persuade himself it was "a matter of imperative necessity." Kate continued to weep. But it was useless; the volcano had begun to erupt.

Dickens, finding the American preliminaries "necessarily startling" and, to a "gentleman of my temperament" destructive of "rest, sleep, appetite and work, unless definitely arranged," rushed to and from Broadstairs and London, feverishly making arrangements, wringing a reluctant consent from Kate, accepting Macready's offer to take care of the children, reconciling Kate to the idea of going, working her up to the pitch of talking quite gaily about it, writing almost every day to Forster, and generally feeling "so amiable, so meek, so fond of people, so full of gratitude and reliance, that I am like a sick man." He started to count the days— amazing inconstancy!—not to the date of his departure, but to the date of his return from America!

He racketed himself into a serious illness necessitating an operation, and had barely recovered before two domestic bereavements struck the family, Mrs. Dickens' maternal grandmother and her younger brother dying in quick succession. Their loss reopened the wound of Mary Hogarth's

death, more particularly as Dickens felt compelled to give up
the ground next her grave, where he had long decided to be
buried himself.

He suffered grievously. Charles Dickens was always moved
by death, and his sorrow was genuinely deep and sincere.
Yet in spite of everything the arrangements for the visit to
America went forward. He endured his grief in private,
forced himself to regain his health and strength, went to
Richmond and afterwards to Windsor to convalesce during
November, and immensely fortified and excited by "all sorts
of cordialities, anticipations, and stretchings-forth of hands"
which the Christmas mail-packet brought from America, was
ready to sail on the 4th January, 1842, in the British and North
American Mail Steam Packet Company's * first transatlantic
steamer, the *Britannia*, 1,154 tons, Captain John Hewitt.
He was accompanied by his wife, who took with her her lady's
maid, Anne.

He had already arranged with Messrs. Chapman and Hall
to publish a notebook on his return.

* Now the Cunard Steamship Co. Ltd.

## CHAPTER VII

*" Have a passage ready taken for 'Merriker . . . then let him come back and write a book about the 'Merrikins as'll pay all his expenses and more, if he blows 'em up enough."*—MR. WELLER, SENIOR, in the "Pickwick Papers."

*"Americans can't bear to be told of their faults.  Don't split on that rock, Mr. Dickens, don't write about America ; we are so very suspicious."* *

MANY writers have risen up to "explain" Dickens.  Some have attempted the task in long books; others have achieved it in short newspaper articles.  It can be done in a single sentence.  Dickens was a very human man, possessed of exceptional abilities, great energy, and strong convictions, very deep emotional capacities, and a number of exceedingly human frailties.  All the rest is but commentary on this statement.

One obvious comment is that his frailties—or faults, or failings, call them what you please—were as evident as his virtues.  They obtruded; they could not be hid.  They were inherent in his genius.  To record them is not pleasant; to conceal them would be to present an imperfect picture of the man—not that any picture of Dickens could ever be near perfection; he was too many-sided for that.  But concealment or diminution of his faults and failings and of the blunders and mistakes these caused him to make would be to obscure the reason why he was the author who, above all others in English literature, could understand, and sympathise with, and cause others to sympathise with, the common

* American advice quoted by Dickens in a letter written from Baltimore to Macready, March 22nd, 1842.

frailties of mankind. There is nothing of the objective artist in Dickens; it was quite beyond him to stand away from his work, to view it with critical detachment. His novels are intensely subjective; the humanity that is poured into them is all his own.

The story of his first trip to America does not make altogether agreeable, though it certainly makes lively, reading. Across the Atlantic he was received and entertained like royalty, only with much more cordiality; the highest and the lowest of the land united with spontaneous unanimity to pay him such homage as had never been accorded to author before, and scarcely to human being. In return, he insulted his hosts, aroused their just resentment, and, returning to England, wrote books describing their manners and their customs which, however true they may have been, contained passages that would have been in bad taste if written by an ordinary traveller, and were, coming from one who had been treated as he had, an offence against all English laws and traditions of hospitality and common courtesy.

That is stating the case baldly and crudely. The statement needs considerable amplification. Much of his trip was thoroughly enjoyable and without friction. In spite of what he said, he made and kept many true friends in the States. To these, to the better qualities of the average American, and to a number of American public institutions he paid the warmest and sincerest tributes, which should have gone far to soften the sting of his adverse comments on other aspects of American private and public life. The fault was not entirely on his side; various elements in America proved themselves unduly sensitive to criticism, and viciously out-spoken in reply. The same elements exhibited intolerable self-conceit, a vulgar inquisitiveness, and disgusting rapacity. Finally, the expectations aroused on both sides were altogether excessive, so that, granted an emotional man like Dickens on the one hand, and an emotional nation like the United States on the other, some degree of disillusionment and some recriminations were inevitable.

In essence, however, the case is as first stated. Dickens was received in America as the nation's guest, and one cannot

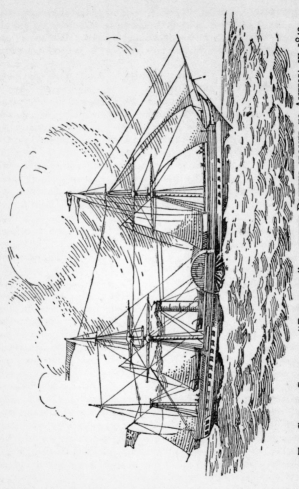

The Cunard Steamship "Britannia" in which Dickens crossed to America in 1842

defend an attack upon one's host over the dinner table, nor a published satire on his failings upon one's return home. It is pleasant to recall that twenty-five years later, at the conclusion of his second visit to America, Dickens made a very frank and honourable apology by promising to have printed, so long as he or his descendants held the copyrights, as an appendix to "American Notes" and "Martin Chuzzlewit," his public testimony to the courtesy he received on this latter occasion.

Perverse though the suggestion may sound, it would not have been Dickens had the first tour gone otherwise.

If there was one virtue Dickens emphatically did not possess, happily for us, it was that of keeping his eyes open and his mouth shut. He kept his eyes open wider than most men, and to better purpose, but not to have spoken of what he saw and thought would have been as impossible for him as to have refrained from breathing. He could have no more gone to America and not written a book about it than he could have kept Mr. Micawber, alias Mr. John Dickens, out of "David Copperfield." No more could he have resisted speaking out his mind on the subject of international copyright so soon as he realized what the existing state of affairs meant to him, not though the whole of the United States as one single man had begged him or commanded him to stay silent. In that case he would probably have said all the more.

He was to the very core both reporter and reformer. These are both dangerous trades; they become particularly dangerous when one tries to combine them, and yet more dangerous still if one succeeds in so doing. As Dickens combined them with greater success than any other English writer, it is not surprising that in his lifetime he offended many people. It is rather surprising that he did not offend more; but for his irresistible humour he might easily have become the best-hated man in England.

It is not in the least surprising that he offended the Americans. In Great Britain the saving grace of humour can carry off most situations. We are, as a race, so ready to laugh at ourselves that, provided a speaker or writer can

amuse his audience, he can say almost anything he likes to
it. We are also so soaked in tradition, and as a result so
opinionated, that we can hardly ever be persuaded to take
reformers seriously. We do not mind in the least their telling
us our faults because we do not really believe them. If they
grow too earnest, we either get bored or we laugh at them.
Trying to reform Englishmen is like trying to reform ele-
phants; they have the toughest skins and the most massive
obstinacy in the world. The Americans whom Charles Dickens
met had, on the contrary, the thinnest skins and the most
easily pierceable vanity possible.

Dickens had by 1842 been saying what he liked to Englishmen for a matter of five years. They had loved him for it.
The Americans had loved him for it, too, but for rather different reasons. The English had loved him primarily for his
superbly English wit and humour, and because, as their fancy
was taking them in that way at that time, he could make them
cry as heartily as he made them laugh. They loved him also
because at all times they loved fair play and a sporting chance
for the under-dog, and they realized in him a doughty champion of various classes of people who were getting anything
but a sporting chance. They were even moved in some
instances to do something about it, though chiefly as yet
where it most nearly affected them in their own private
lives, as in the case of the Yorkshire schools.

It is difficult, on the other hand, to believe that the
Americans, save the intellectuals and such as were of sufficiently recent English-born stock, fully appreciated Dickens'
humour. They certainly appreciated his pathos, because
theirs was in many instances a life in which emotion and pathos
lay very close to the surface. The Wild West was still very
much of a reality, full of dangerous Red Indians and hardly
less dangerous forests. America was a land of pioneers;
men had still to work and women to weep as the most wonderful civilization in the world was being hazardously carved out
of the primitive prairie. All the strongest elemental passions,
love, devotion, anger, hatred, curiosity, acquisitiveness, pride,
were constantly evoked in their arduous and often perilous
task.

One ideal above all others inspired the breasts of the strangely heterogeneous nation which then inhabited the United States of America—Liberty. Its expression took many forms; but in every form, even including the sordid, it represented a genuine ideal. America was the land of freedom and the free; there one shook off all the shackles which held hidebound Europe in bondage, and stepped forth as God's free man—always provided one had a white skin. Government was "of the people, by the people, and for the people," as Abraham Lincoln was to say. America was the first great experiment in democracy.

It was as the Apostle of Freedom that the Americans chiefly worshipped Dickens. Did he not pour ridicule upon all the effete institutions of government in Europe, the institutions they regarded with contempt and hatred as the instruments of tyranny? Did he not pillory official pomposity and titular pride and aristocracy and snobbishness, vices from which they had freed themselves? Did he not thunder against all the old traditional stupidities and oppressions and abuses which kept the able poor man from taking the place his abilities warranted? Had he not revealed, as never European had done before, the sterling qualities to be found in the masses of the people? Had he not "done more already to ameliorate the condition of the English poor than all the statesmen Great Britain had sent into Parliament?" Was he not, in short, the embodiment of all that the United States stood for; was he not the Democrat of democrats?

They were very nearly right; and Dickens, for his part, entirely reciprocated the sentiments. He regarded the United States as the nation which had begun with a clean slate, which had not even allowed to enter her gates those abuses which were so strongly entrenched in England and oppressed it, which especially oppressed his England, the England of the poor and the meek and the lowly. In America all men were free, he thought; a man was a man for a' that, and all were equal in God's sight, living gloriously as brothers in the sunshine of democratic institutions. The Republic of the United States of America seemed to him the apotheosis of Liberty—except, of course, for slavery. That was the only

blot on an otherwise stainless 'scutcheon.  He never dreamed,
until he visited America, how the doctrine of freedom could
work out in practice.

So, with hopes "wonderful, wonderful, and most wonderful
wonderful" on both sides, Dickens crossed the Atlantic,
touched at Halifax, Nova Scotia, and came to Boston.

The passage was a very bad one.  It was so bad that for
two or three hours at any rate they gave up all hope of coming
safely to land.  "I never expected," he wrote, "to see the
day again, and resigned myself to God as well as I could."
His fears were not exaggerated.  It was the worst weather
officers on board could remember; but the stout paddle-
steamer, her funnel kept upright by innumerable lashings,
with men lashed to masts and rigging to hold it in place, held
truly on her course in spite of terrific gales and mountainous
seas, and hove in sight of Newfoundland on the fourteenth
day after their departure from Liverpool.  Even then
disaster almost befell them, for they ran aground, the pilot
lost his head, and for an hour and a half all believed themselves in imminent danger of death.  Happily the captain
kept perfect command of himself and his crew, and it turned
out that they had struck the only soft patch in an area sown
with rocky reefs.  The grateful passengers subscribed £50
to present the captain with a piece of plate recording their
appreciation of his coolness and skill.  Dickens was the
secretary and treasurer of this fund, and quite likely the
prime mover in this graceful act.

After a few hours at Halifax, where Dickens was cheered
through the streets, taken up to Government House and to
the Houses of Parliament, where, "the observed of all
observers," he listened "with exemplary gravity to the
queerest speaking possible," yet could not help breaking into
involuntary smiles at the "thought of this commencement
to the Thousand and One stories in reserve for home," the
party moved on to Boston, where they landed at 5 p.m. on
Saturday the 22nd of January.

Dickens' first shock was to discover that what he thought
were newsboys rushing on to the boat to sell papers were the
editors of the Boston journals!  His dislike of American habits

had its tiny commencement in this very first hour, before he had landed on United States' soil. There was a most objectionable man, "in very dirty gaiters, and with very protruding upper teeth," who, having been introduced to him, would keep on saying to all who came after him, "So you've been introduced to our friend Dickens—eh?" How Dickens hated that man! There was also, however, a very useful and obliging man among the editors, Dr. Palmer of the *Boston Transcript*, who ran two miles to book rooms and dinner—unaccountably this had not been done—at the Hotel Tremont, Boston, then reckoned one of the best hotels in the United States.

The party landed, and were conducted "through cheering crowds" to their hotel. Throughout the whole of their stay the cheering never ceased. "How can I tell you," Dickens wrote to Forster a few days later, "what has happened since that first day? How can I give you the faintest notion of my reception here; of the crowds that pour in and out the whole day; of the people that line the streets when I go out; of the cheering when I went to the theatre; of the copies of verses, letters of congratulation, welcomes of all kinds, balls, dinners, assemblies without end?"

In a letter to Tom Mitton, dated 31st of January, 1842, he gave further details. "There never was a king or emperor upon the earth so cheered and followed by crowds, and entertained in public at splendid balls and dinners, and waited upon by public bodies and deputations of all kinds. . . . If I go out in a carriage, the crowd surround it and escort me home; if I go to the theatre the whole house (crowded to the roof) rises as one man, and the timbers ring again. You cannot imagine what it is." It made him feel, he remarked in his letter to Forster, "a more retiring, sober, tranquil man." "The best aspects of this welcome," he said, "seemed to have in them something of the presence and influence of that spirit which directs my life." Then he added, in words which sound strangely in view of what was so soon to follow, "if I know my heart, not twenty times this praise would move me to an act of folly."

If it did not move him to an act of folly, it moved him to

an extremely injudicious and ill-timed one. It seems reasonably clear that the overwhelming cordiality, the lavish
hospitality, and the universal spontaneity and sincerity of
his welcome by all classes led him into the very grave mistake
of supposing that he might tell the Americans, as he had told
the British, anything he pleased. By the worst of all possible
mischances, he told them what he thought of international
copyright.

For the moment there were no clouds on the horizon, save
that the perpetual receptions began very soon to make both
himself and his wife deadly tired at times. At present
everything was so novel and so exciting and so gratifying
beyond all expectations that he gloried in it all. The queer
American houses, with their central heating which made them
so "infernally hot," their curtainless windows and beds, and
their tiny wardrobes; the quaint streets, the individuality of
the people in dress, their good manners and good nature; the
universal deference paid to ladies—who "are very beautiful,
but they soon fade"—the prosperity of all classes, the absence
of beggars and the rareness of illiteracy; the splendid schools
and prisons and asylums, in all of which institutions he took
especial interest; the factories and workshops; everything
delighted him.

He breakfasted, lunched, dined and supped with the best
people. He met all the intellectuals; Longfellow, then a
professor at Harvard University, Prescott the historian,
James Russell Lowell, Oliver Wendell Holmes, Richard Dana,
author of "Two Years before the Mast," Charles Sumner,
John Kenyon, friend of Coleridge and of Lamb, and Cornelius Felton, who was to become one of his dearest friends,
and to whom he was to write the most entertaining and
delightful of all his letters. His photograph was taken, his
picture was painted, his bust sculptured—with admirers,
chiefly women, crowding into the very studio. Once he got
over-nervous and bolted from them. He had to engage a
secretary to cope with his correspondence, and so numerous
were the invitations which poured in upon him from all parts
of the States that he had to refuse three-quarters of them.

There was a magnificent ball in his honour; there was a

HENRY CLAY (1777–1852)

Dickens play and a Dickens pageant at the theatre; there was a grand public dinner on February 1st, for which guests were charged fifteen dollars, but given a choice of over forty dishes—a "most superb affair, and the speaking *admirable*." Boston, indeed, went to such lengths in its homage and its hospitality that some wit christened it "Boz-town," while the New York papers began to talk about "liquorice doses" and the "beslavering of Boz."

Leaving Boston on the 5th of February Dickens travelled via Worcester, Springfield, Hartford, Wallingford and New-haven to New York, which he reached on Saturday, February 12th. Everywhere there were receptions and levees, with endless handshakings—up to five hundred people at a time. At Hartford, where he stayed four days, there was a public dinner, at which the guests were offered a choice of seventy dishes! Here, incidentally, Dickens for the second time spoke his mind on the subject of international copyright, as he had done at the Boston banquet. There were serenades at Hartford and Newhaven, and at the latter place, though the party embarked at an early hour, there was a crowd on the harbourside to give "three times three for Dickens" as the boat put off for New York. It was roses, roses all the way, with a terrific storm brewing and muttering in the rear. Already indignant editors were attacking him whole-heartedly over his copyright speeches.

What did a few editors matter? The citizens of New York had forwarded to him the most impressive welcomes and invitations. In particular as a "slight, tho' thankful, tribute" to his genius, which, they said, had secured to him "a passport to all hearts," he was asked to meet them at a public dinner; as a mark of appreciation for his "labours in the cause of humanity" a public ball was being arranged in his honour.

The ball took place first, on the following Monday, February 14th, at the Park Theatre. "There were three thousand people present in full dress," wrote Dickens to Forster; "from the roof to the floor, the theatre was decorated magnificently; and the light, glitter, glare, show, noise, and cheering, baffle my descriptive powers." The opening ceremonies were tremendous; a general in full uniform took charge of Mrs. Dickens,

the M.C. of Dickens, and the party of four marched in state
through the "centre of the centre dress-box" on to the stage,
where Dickens was formally received by the Mayor and the
civic dignitaries; and then twice "all round the enormous
ballroom," "for the benefit of the many-headed." After
that, they all began to dance; and the guests of the evening
danced until they could no longer stand, and then they slipped
quietly back to their hotel, leaving, presumably, their hosts
and the other guests still dancing.

Royalty could not have wished for more.

Within a week the storm burst in all its fury. It is a pitiful
story, of mistaken honesty, obstinacy, and complete lack of
taste and tact on Dickens' part, incredibly vulgar abuse on the
part of the American Press; and, to say the whole truth, of a
sorry exhibition of greed on both sides.

The public dinner at New York, the most important function to which Dickens was invited, took place on Friday,
February 18th. All the most distinguished men of the day
in art, literature, science and education were present. Washington Irving, the famous author of "Rip Van Winkle," long
a friend by correspondence, and to meet whom had been one
of Dickens' main inducements to visit America, was in the
chair. The enthusiasm was colossal. The chairman, trembling with emotion, broke down as he had foretold he would,
and could not continue his speech of welcome; but he managed
in a few faltering sentences to convey the spirit of all that was
best in America, to acquit it of the charge of being "sordid
and mercenary," a charge, he said, given the lie to by "this
burst of enthusiasm, which has been echoed from city to city
. . . and has spontaneously arisen in one wide scene of homage
paid to intellect." He proposed the toast of "Charles Dickens,
the Literary Guest of the Nation."

In reply, Dickens not only spoke out his mind more freely
than before on international copyright, but actually proposed
it as a toast at the conclusion of his speech.

He had been begged not to mention it. The whole dinner
committee had implored him not to do so. He had been pursued since he left Hartford by anonymous letters, newspaper
attacks and personal communications, advising, warning,

threatening and abusing him. He knew perfectly well by
now where he stood in the matter. Educated America agreed
with him, but thought it wiser not to say so in public; the
editorial world was, with few exceptions, ranged against
him, quite naturally, since he was attacking a substantial
source of income; the gutter press, which lived largely on
literary piracy, was metaphorically foaming at the mouth.
Opposition merely stiffened his obstinacy. As always, the
thought of injustice burned and throbbed and swelled in his
mind until it had blotted out all reason. He began to think
of himself as a Crusader, to see himself as the solitary
courageous Knight of the Copyright, *sans peur et sans
reproche*, fighting a lone battle against the powers of evil
for the sacred rights of authorship. Nothing should deter
him, nothing should move him. When he got home he would
write about it; while he was here he would speak of it. No one
else dared, but he would dare; and he would not mince his
words. "Accordingly, when the night came," he told Forster,
"I asserted my right with all the means I could command to
give it dignity, in face, manner, or words; and I believe that
if you could have seen and heard me, you would have loved
me better for it than ever you did in your life."

It was tragic. All this heroism, this misplaced reforming
zeal, this flying in the face of the most cordial, admiring, and
respectful hosts on earth—for what?

To-day when a British author's book is published in the
United States, he receives his royalties on its sale in accordance
with his contract with his American publishers just as he does
from his British publishers. In 1842, a British author had
no copyright in America; any publisher there could get hold
of a copy of his works and publish them for his own private
profit. He could edit them, cut them, mangle them if he so
desired: the author had no means of restraint or redress.
The same conditions applied to the works of American
authors in Britain.

Dickens' books had sold in thousands all over America.
When he got there he realized at once that he had lost a for-
tune through there being no law of international copyright.
Had he been protected by such law he must have received

thousands of pounds from America. As it was, all the money he had ever been offered from the States had been £25, or some such sum, for advance proofs in order to enable an enterprising publisher to forestall his rivals.

Dickens had every reason to feel disgruntled. He had had, from his own point of view, a hard enough struggle in England to secure adequate financial return for his extraordinarily successful labours: and now, to find that these Americans had been making fortunes out of him without ever thinking of sending him a penny, was too much altogether. It must not be too rashly assumed that had the question been one entirely of his own pocket he would have taken up the cudgels so violently and at such unfortunate moments.

What moved him especially to wrath, and confirmed him in his fatal obstinacy, was that every author of repute in America, and practically all his distinguished hosts, entirely agreed with him. Many of them were suffering in the same way as he was. Every English author whose works crossed the Atlantic was also suffering. Yet here in the United States no one dared to lift up his voice against this monstrous outrage. In England valiant attempts were being made by Talfourd and others to amend the copyright law; in America —land of the free!—no one dared to do anything! One courageous American editor alone, Cornelius Mathews, ventured at the dinner to declare that Dickens had proposed "the only honest turnpike between the readers of two great countries." The fact that Mathews' mind was obsessed chiefly by the thought that the American market was being so flooded with European works that American authors were standing no chance, does not detract from his bravery.

Why, one may ask, this conspiracy of silence? Why dared not American authors assert their own rights or even support the rights of their European brothers? Because, in 1842, two other gods were worshipped in the United States besides the goddess Freedom; the "almighty dollar " and "smartness," or as it is now better termed, "slickness."

The American intellectuals were a very distinguished but very small minority of the United States population. Outside their ranks was surging the most heterogeneous mob of a nation the world has ever seen. A native-born nucleus had been, for long, daily reinforced by immigrants from all over the world, honest, dishonest, thrifty, shifty, sober, dissolute, weak, strong, young and old, but all burning with one desire, to make money. As the never-ceasing hordes of immigrants settled down they became rapidly Americanized; and so to make money became the consuming ambition of almost every citizen. It could be made by almost anyone at that time in that land of rapid development. The nobler Americans made it laboriously, by long years of toil, and so laid strongly the foundations of America's greatness. A vast army of scamps realized the opportunities of making it in less difficult and less scrupulous ways, and corrupted the morals of the nation—a corruption from which it has even yet not recovered. The idea spread, and became a belief, that it did not matter how money was made, provided it was made; and, as unscrupulousness generally demands some degree of cunning, "smartness," on account of its glittering rewards, grew to be considered an eminently desirable virtue. Naturally, the majority of the press pandered to the ideals of the majority of the people.

To get hold of a popular European book, rush it across the Atlantic, publish it before your neighbours, and so reap a large profit, achieved both ends. It was smart to get in first with the goods, and it was a certain method of raking in the dollars. It was absurdly easy; the only consideration was speed, while in the case of an author so popular as Charles Dickens, the second and third publishers, and even the "also-rans," might expect excellent returns for very little outlay. No wonder the American newspapers hit back when Dickens attacked.

At Boston, Dickens had merely expressed the hope that before very long American authors would "receive of right some substantial profit and return in England from their labours, and when we, in England, shall receive some substantial profit and return in America from ours." He added that England had done her part, and it was now up to America—or words to that effect. By the time he got to Hartford—it is so typical of Dickens—his blood was boiling at the thought of the "monstrous injustice," and he "thrust it down their throats" that "if there had existed a law in this respect, Scott might not have sunk beneath the mighty pressure on his brain." By New York, so incensed had he become, he was resisting all prayers, bribes and threats to keep silent, and was asserting that he had "a most righteous claim" to speak upon the subject.

It all seems very sad. The American newspapers fell upon him with their unrivalled outspokenness; he was a fool, a liar, a mercenary scoundrel, worse than a murderer (they selected one for comparison); he had entered the country under false pretences and with sinister designs; he had better get out before he was shot out—to be merely shot, one imagines, the baser press considered far too great an honour for him.

A wrong impression of how matters stood at this stage of his visit must not be given by over-estimating the extent of the hostility towards Dickens. His popularity, in the widest sense of the term, remained undiminished; if anything, people wanted to see him all the more because of the uproar he had created. There was no cessation in the stream of invitations and deputations that poured in on him; the lionizing of him continued with unabated fervour; the "more respectable" newspapers and reviews fought his battle for copyright as vigorously as the other sort fought against him.

Dickens was already tired in body; and he was bitterly disappointed and disillusioned. The salt had lost its savour, and everything had turned to dust and ashes and bitterness. He was nauseated with adulation: "I can do nothing that I want to do, go nowhere where I want to go, and see nothing that I want to see. If I turn into the street, I am followed by a multitude. If I stay at home, the house becomes, with callers, like a fair. . . . I take my seat in a railroad car, and the very conductor won't leave me alone. I get out at a station, and can't drink a glass of water, without having a hundred people looking down my throat when I open my mouth to swallow. . . ." And so on.

The main cause of his disappointment lay far deeper. America had failed him. The shining ideal of an unstained liberty had been shattered; and instead, "I believe," he wrote to Forster, "there is no country on the face of the earth, where there is less freedom of opinion on any subject in reference to which there is a broad difference of opinion than in this." "My dear Macready," he wrote in March, "I desire to be so honest and just to those who have so enthusiastically and earnestly welcomed me, that I burned the last letter I wrote to you. . . . Still it is of no use. I *am* disappointed. This is not the republic I came to see; this is not the republic of my imagination. . . . In everything of which it has made a boast—excepting its education and its care for poor children—it sinks immeasurably below the level I had placed it upon." There follows shortly after in this letter a warm and comprehensive appreciation of the better qualities of the American people, but he comes "back to the point upon which I started," to conclude that "the man who comes to this country a Radical and goes home again with his opinions unchanged, must be a Radical on reason, sympathy, and reflection, and one who has so well considered the subject that he has no chance of wavering."

Under such circumstances it was not surprising that both sides should begin to get on each other's nerves. The incessant tobacco-chewing and spitting revolted Dickens; the eternal talk, limited, it seemed, to the "almighty dollar" and the slave question, bored him; the perpetual questions irritated and infuriated him. For their part, American society circles were shocked by Dickens' gaudy waistcoats, and his gaudy conversation—he actually declared a Duchess to be "kissable!" It will be recalled that New England was colonized by the Puritans.

Dickens determined to escape. His wife was ill, and he himself practically voiceless from continual speaking. He decided not to accept any further invitations to public functions but to continue his travels, as far as was possible, as a private gentleman; and he kept to this decision throughout an extended tour, in which he visited Philadelphia, Baltimore, Washington, Fredericksburgh and Richmond. Only at St. Louis, his westernmost point, did he give way. Yet he could not avoid publicity, nor exhausting receptions. "In every town where we stay, though it be only for a day," he wrote Mitton, "we hold a regular levee or drawing-room, where I shake hands on an average with five or six hundred people, who pass on from me to Kate, and are shaken again by her. . . . Think of two hours of this every day, and the people coming in by hundreds all fresh and piping hot, and full of questions, when we are literally exhausted and can hardly stand!"

Yet there is in this same letter an exquisite reminder that the child who "peeped with interest and wonder" in Chatham and Rochester and the boy who knew London "from Bow to Brentford" was as keenly alive as ever. "I go into the prisons, the police offices, the watch-houses, the hospitals, the work-houses. I was out half the night in New York with two of the most famous constables; started at midnight, and went into every brothel, thieves' house, murdering hovel, sailors' dancing places and abode of villainy, in the town." On that night, one may be sure, it was not the Americans who asked all the questions.

His experiences by road, rail and river on this tour are fully described in the "American Notes for General Circula-tion" which he published on his return home, and which may be described as a record of Dickens' American experiences with all the Dickens part left out—that is to say, with little or no reference to the "literary-guest-of-the-nation" side, and none whatever to world copyright. "American Notes" is a lively traveller's chronicle, with touches such as only Charles Dickens could have penned, but not differing in essentials from any other reliable and interesting travel book. The last chapter but one, on Slavery, would have been better published as a separate pamphlet, as it is not in tune with the rest of the book. The last chapter contains some exceedingly unflattering remarks upon American people in general; but it also con-tains a tribute which cannot be too often quoted, that "they are, by nature, frank, brave, cordial, hospitable, and affec-tionate. Cultivation and refinement seem but to enhance their warmth of heart and ardent enthusiasm; and it is the posses-sion of these latter qualities in a most remarkable degree, which renders an educated American one of the most endearing and generous of friends. I never was so won upon, as by this class; never yielded up my full confidence and esteem so readily and pleasurably, as to them; never can make again, in half-a-year, so many friends for whom I seem to entertain the regard of half a life."

All of which words are true to-day. There are still two American peoples, the educated and the half-educated, the cultured and the crude. Dickens clearly perceived the distinction; yet he flung his grievances against the crude in the faces of the cultured, he descended to battle with the uneducated while he was being entertained like a monarch at the tables of the educated. That is the tragedy of his visit to America.

On the 25th of April he thankfully crossed the border into Canada and began once again to feel himself. His last experience in the United States had been peculiarly unfortunate. At Cleveland, Ohio, at six o'clock in the morning, "a party of 'gentlemen' planted themselves before our little cabin, and stared in at the door and windows *while I was washing, and Kate lay in bed*." Then a Cleveland newspaper had recently advocated "war with England to the death" and promised "all true Americans that within two years they should sing 'Yankee-doodle' in Hyde Park and 'Hail Columbia' in the courts of Westminster." Dickens was so enraged by all this that he refused to be received by the mayor, and angrily shook the dust of all Yankee-doodle-dom from his feet.

He stayed some days at an hotel on the English side of the Niagara Falls, enjoying "a blessed interval of quiet in this beautiful place," of which he wrote glowing and beautiful descriptions home. "Great God!" he is said to have exclaimed to himself when he first saw the Falls, "how can any man be disappointed at that!" They gave him "peace of mind—tranquillity—great thoughts of eternal rest and happiness—nothing of terror." From his hotel window he could see them "rolling and tumbling, and roaring and leaping, all day long, with bright rainbows making fiery arches down a hundred feet below. . . . When the sun is on them, they shine and glow like molten gold. When the day is gloomy, the water falls like snow. . . ."

He relieved his mind by writing to his friends exactly what he thought about the copyright question, and about the "vile, blackguard, and detestable" American newspapers, "so filthy and bestial that no honest man would admit one into his house for a scullery door-mat" by exulting in the fact that "the greatest men in England have sent me out, through Forster, a very manly, and becoming, and spirited memorial and address, backing me in all I have done." He sent this to Boston for publication, but hugged to himself the thought that "my best rod is in pickle."

Then, thoroughly refreshed in body, mind and soul, he travelled to Montreal, to become the "stage manager and universal director" in some amateur theatricals being got up for charity by the officers of the Coldstream Guards, and in which he had promised Lord Mulgrave, a fellow passenger in the *Britannia*, and an officer in the Coldstreams, to take part. Here he had the time of his life, with his coat off, "urging impracticable ladies and impossible gentlemen on to the very confines of insanity, shouting and driving about . . . and struggling in such a vortex of noise, dirt, bustle, confusion, and inextricable entanglement of speech and action"; subjecting his unprofessional players to "the most iron despotism"; persuading Mrs. Dickens to take a part, which she did, and, to his evident amazement, played "devilish well"; and finally, playing on two nights (one private and one public performance) with huge success leading parts in all three plays presented.

A glorious wind-up to one of the most astonishing journeys ever made by mortal man.

On the 7th June he embarked at New York on the sailing ship *George Washington* en route for "home—home—home—home—home—home—HOME!!!!!!!!!!!" as he had described it in his last letter from America, and in anticipation of which he was "FEVERED with anxiety." Throughout the whole period, from the moment he left Liverpool, the longing to be back at home had never left him. Among all the eccentricities of this weird and wonderful tour, there is none stranger yet more typically Dickensian than that Dickens borrowed an accordion on the voyage out, bought one of his own in America,

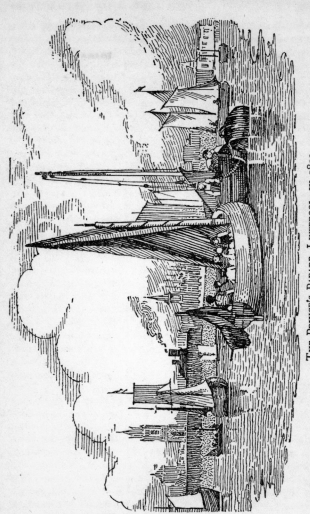

THE PRINCE'S PARADE, LIVERPOOL, IN 1832

*After the Engraving by R. Brandard*

and played "Home, Sweet, Home" with intense feeling nightly to the ladies, making them and himself most "pleasantly sad." Mrs. Dickens had a lot to put up with.

They returned by sailing vessel because Dickens had sworn never to trust himself in a steamer again. His experiences on the outward journey had convinced him that if the funnel went overboard in a gale the whole ship would instantly be on fire, and as he says that solid fire could be seen at night two or three feet above a funnel forty feet high, it is quite probable he was right. As a result of this decision the voyage home took them twenty-three days, during which time Dickens organized a United Vagabonds Club, the members of which dined apart from the other passengers, with much mock-solemn ritual. As the chief vagabond, Dickens made daily processions round the ship disguised as a doctor, with Bob Sawyer and Ben Allen accompanying him armed with large surgical scissors and huge rolls of dressings!

The party landed at Liverpool on July 1st, and left the same day for London. There was a rapturous reunion with the children, who, apart from their natural joy at seeing their parents again, had found "Creedy's" (Mr. Macready's) ideas of discipline a trifle too strict for their liking, and were heartily glad to be away from the "prim, gloomy, unjoyful house," as Dickens' eldest daughter, Mamie, had called it. The baby had cried and sobbed while she was being dressed, and declared she would "not doe," and all had pined for Devonshire Terrace with its guinea-pigs and rabbits, and Grip the raven, and the swing in the garden, and the laughing, joking father who sang funny songs to them every evening before bedtime, imitating so comically the old man who had caught cold in an omnibus, "and rheumatiz, as well as a stiff neck."

How exciting it was to make friends with the new little dog, "Timber," who had come all the way from America! How jolly it was again to be called by those gorgeous nicknames daddy had invented for them—Mild Glo'ster, Lucifer Box, Flaster Toby, and Young Skull; and what a relief to creep once more into the arms of a father who never frightened them nor punished them harshly, but who would reason gently and

sweetly, who would charm away all their childish fears, and
who "understood and felt for *every* childish suffering." Mamie
Dickens relates of her father that "the shyest baby would hold
out its tiny arms to him with perfect faith and confidence."

What a long way this is from international copyright, the
degraded American press, and even the whirlwind of the
Montreal theatricals! This is the Dickens of little Nell,
Oliver Twist, Smike, and home. It was always the same;
behind the Dickens squabbling with his publishers, behind the
obstinate misguided Dickens hurling defiance at the United
States, behind the Dickens of the gaudy waistcoats and the
limelight and the big reputation, behind even the slightly
ludicrous Dickens who solemnly inflated lifebelts for his
party on the American river boats, there was always this
kind, loving, sympathetic, perfectly understanding father,
utterly devoted to his children, and inspiring in them that
greatest love which casteth out all fear.

Work was calling from the moment he landed, and after
a week or so's rest with his family to work Dickens addressed
himself with his accustomed energy. The "American Notes"
were to be published in October, and apart from the actual
labour of reducing his letters and memoranda to book form,
there was much anxious thought to be taken over the material
to be published. That the book would offend many shades of
American opinion Dickens well knew; nor did he much care.
What he was anxious about was that it would not offend any
of the true friends he had made across the Atlantic, and to
whom he was intending to dedicate it. Every word was
scrutinized by himself, by Forster, and by others. At the
very last moment Forster persuaded him not to issue with it
the introductory letter he had already written, in which, among
other things, he had said, "I can scarcely be supposed to be
ignorant of the hazard I run in writing of America at all . . .
I know perfectly well that there is in America . . . a
numerous class of persons so tenderly and delicately constituted, that they cannot bear the truth in any form."

The book appeared on the 18th of October, 1842. It was
instantaneously successful in Great Britain, and universally
abused by the American press. Three thousand copies were

LORD MACAULAY (1800–1859)

sold in a week, and four large editions by the end of the year. Dickens made £1,000, of which he was very likely in some need, for he had paid every penny of his expenses in America, and had been shamelessly rooked in some of the hotels. It is quite characteristic of him that he related to Forster in his letters both how he had been overcharged, and also how, at Hartford and Newhaven, where he had found all his expenses paid for him, he stubbornly refused to accept, and would not move until he had received the full account and paid it.

His friends in America approved the book. Longfellow said it was "jovial and good-natured" and could be read "with delight and, for the most part, approbation." Emerson said "it held up bad manners so that churls could see the deformed." In England, Lord Macaulay thought it a failure, but Lord Jeffrey considered Dickens had been "very tender to our sensitive friends beyond the sea" and said his whole heart was with every word.

Much of the work had been done at Broadstairs, whither Dickens went as usual in August. Before that he had conceived the idea of a visit to Cornwall, as he had thought of "opening my new book on the coast of Cornwall, in some dreary iron-bound spot." Directly "American Notes" was finished, off started Dickens, Forster, Maclise, and Stanfield on what turned out to be the most riotous, exuberant, and joyful trip imaginable.

There was no Cornish Riviera express then to transport holiday makers from Paddington to Penzance in six hours. The four friends travelled to Devonshire by rail, and then hired an open carriage. Dickens held the communal purse; Forster looked after the luggage; Stanfield directed the route, aided by "an enormous map, . . . a pocket compass and other scientific instruments," while Maclise, who long ago had established a wonderful reputation among his friends for indolence, "having nothing particular to do, sang songs." "And, Heavens!" wrote Dickens to his American friend, Professor Felton, "if you could have seen the necks of bottles peeping out the carriage pockets . . , witnessed the deep devotion of the post-boys, the wild attachment of the ostlers, the maniac glee of the waiters! . . . I never laughed in my life as I did on this journey. . . . I was choking and gasping and bursting the buckle off the back of my stock, all the way. And Stanfield got into such apoplectic entanglements . . . that we were often obliged to beat him on the back with portmanteaus before we could recover him."

With Dickens' customary thoroughness, he ensured that the party went everywhere and saw everything. They explored every inch of Tintagel, ascended to the height of St. Michael's Mount, rocked on the Logan Rock at St. Buryan, were thrilled by the sunset at Land's End, found the waterfall at St. Wighton, delighted in the beautiful old churches, discovered strange caverns, looked down from high cliffs upon the gleaming waters, descended into the ancient tin and copper mines. The artists sketched wherever they went, and at least two Academy pictures resulted from this holiday, one of which Dickens was so anxious to possess that he purchased it, under a name adopted for the purpose, before the exhibition opened.

He did not, after all, place the scene of his new story in Cornwall; he chose Wiltshire instead.

"Martin Chuzzlewit" was begun in a considerable hurry, and with little notion as to how it would develop and end. Dickens had promised his readers in No. 80 of *Master Humphrey's Clock*, "if it please God, to commence my book in monthly parts, under the old green cover, in the old size and form, and at the same price," on November 1st, 1842. It had been advertised in the first edition of "American Notes" as "a new Tale of English Life and Manners, by 'Boz,'" and the first number was due out in January 1843. The Cornish holiday had been prolonged into the first week of November, and when the party returned to London, Dickens had not even decided upon the title, much less the story. This delay, coupled with Dickens' constitutional inability to construct a machine-made plot, accounts for the shapelessness of the story. He would be a clever man who could follow the narrative of "Martin Chuzzlewit" through its intricate windings, and find any reason in them. Not that that matters in the least. Few now, except children, read Dickens for the sake of the plot.

He had, however, in his mind a clearly defined theme, Selfishness, and an equally defined aim "to exhibit in a variety of aspects the commonest of all the vices; to show how Selfishness propagates itself, and to what a grim giant it may grow from small beginnings." "Martin Chuzzlewit" may therefore be considered the first novel written with a moral purpose. Signs of such purpose, indeed, had never been absent since "Oliver Twist," but this was the first time the book grew out of the purpose, rather than the purpose out of the book. "Nicholas Nickleby," it is true, aimed at and demolished Yorkshire boarding-schools, but in so doing it attacked and defeated an isolated, practical abuse. In "Martin Chuzzlewit" Dickens took up the cudgels for the purpose of attacking a general failing of humanity. Out of that purpose came Mr. Pecksniff.

Mr. Seth Pecksniff, architect and land surveyor, is one of the most difficult of all Dickens' great characters to sum up. "All the Pecksniff family on earth are quite agreed," wrote Dickens, in the preface to the cheap edition of 1848, "that no such character as Mr. Pecksniff ever existed," and risking the obvious deduction, one is inclined to add, or ever could exist. It is not so much that, as many critics have hastened to assert, Mr. Pecksniff is too good to be true, as that he is too true to be human. This criticism is offered in full knowledge of the fact that the "original" of Mr. Pecksniff was at once recognized in literary and artistic circles as being Mr. Samuel Carter Hall, editor of the *Art Union Monthly Journal.*

"Mr. Pecksniff was a moral man: a grave man, a man of noble sentiments, and speech."

To understand that sentence, one has to transport oneself in imagination back to the middle of the nineteenth century, when gravity, noble sentiments, and speech were virtues strenuously cultivated by every self-respecting Victorian father; when the "head of the family" wore stiff cravats and stiff cuffs and top hats and frock-coats; when he was called and thought of as "The Master"; when he was addressed by his children as "Sir" and was stern and unbending in their upbringing, only occasionally condescending to be condescending to them; when his word throughout his household was law, because he was regarded by his wife and his children, his menservants and his maidservants—and himself—as the very fountain head of wisdom and the perfect pattern of righteousness; when religion and morality, far from being topics to be avoided, were the constant subjects of his discourse; and when the slow, ornate, and measured words of counsel and advice which dropped from his lips were eagerly listened to by his inferiors, that is, his entire household, and carefully treasured as being beyond all question authoritative.

It is almost impossible in these later days to conceive the awe and respect with which the Victorian head of the family was regarded, nor the meticulous care with which he played his part. We have long ago laughed pomposity out of fashion; we can hardly bear dignity unless it is coloured with a little jazz. Dickens started the laugh; for he could not bear either pomposity or dignity without a lot of jazz.

When one says that the Victorian head of the family took meticulous care to play well his part of grave and reverend seigneur, it must not be assumed that he was conscious of playing it, that he was a humbug or a hypocrite; he was not. The part he had to play he was carefully educated for, so that he grew up in it; but as Victorian fathers and heads of families were in reality no wiser nor cleverer nor essentially more Christian nor more moral than fathers of to-day, it followed as a matter of course that many a Victorian parent was but a very fallible being behind an iron mask. He presented the correct attitude to the world; he presented it so unfailingly that he came to believe in it himself; but in reality he was but a man of straw, a poor, foolish broken reed, armoured with catchwords and moral tags and religious texts to look imposing.

Or he might be a rogue. The mask of respectability is a favourite and profitable one for rogues, provided they can assume it successfully. Anyone can smell out villainy in the unshaven, ragged vagabond, but it takes most people a long time even to suspect it in a top hat and a frock-coat, when these are accompanied by dignity of manner and rectitude of sentiments.

Take a rogue—a mean, crafty, shallow, lazy, selfish rogue—

endow him with sufficient cunning to think out a way of life that shall enable him to avoid both hard work and the odium which, in a moral and hardworking community, attaches to the obvious rogue; and with sufficient cleverness and histrionic ability to act his part successfully. Let him practise that part until he plays it consummately, until it has become second nature with him, until he cannot leave off playing it, until he has come to much more than half believe in it himself; until he has invested it with a dignity of its own, the dignity that attaches to every supremely artistic achievement, and you have the original of Mr. Pecksniff.

Morality, said Mr. Pecksniff to himself in his early youth (he probably began to work it out at school), morality is a paying game. It is eminently respectable. It is most genteel. One has to be genteel to be moral. The poor can aspire only to honesty and chastity; morality begins with the middle classes. It ends there, too; an aristocrat or a plutocrat has passed beyond the need for it. It is taken for granted that aristocrats and plutocrats are incarnations of all virtue—or all vice; it does not really matter which, since rank or wealth is sufficient in itself. I have neither rank nor wealth; to acquire either would mean an excessive expenditure of energy. It is too fatiguing. Morality, however, involves no such flights. It is snugly and smugly middle-class. It is easy, too. Everyone professes it; all I have to do is to profess it rather better than anyone else. It is universally admired, trusted, and respected. I will be so moral that I will be more admired, more trusted, more respected than all my neighbours. Once establish that reputation, and I will live comfortably on it for the rest of my life.

All this argument is eminently early Victorian: but then Mr. Pecksniff is early Victorian. No other generation could have produced him. To-day he would be driven to become a slate club secretary or a bogus company promoter, both much harder ways of earning a dishonest living. As it was, all he had to do was to set up a genteel establishment in a quiet and beautiful Wiltshire village, near enough to the cathedral city for him to profit by its atmosphere of sanctity, style himself Architect and Land Surveyor—there was no R.I.B.A. in those days to dispute his claim to these titles—build up his reputation for morality, and on the strength of his professions, technical and moral, persuade a sufficient number of gullible parents to entrust their sons to him as resident architectural pupils. When the story opens, he had been doing this last successfully for a number of years. In his carefully laid plans he had not overlooked the possibility of lean periods, and so had established a business side-line to tide over any unfortunate rainy days. He collected rents. It was a genteel occupation, and it enabled him, by personal contact with his neighbours, to impress upon them the perfection of his morality.

In all that has been written of Mr. Pecksniff, it is strange to find so generally overlooked the cleverness, amounting to genius, with which that gentleman chose the scene and nature of his operations. This may be because by the time the story opens he had been so long established in Amesbury (such, we are assured, was his habitat), and had come to play his part so naturally, that even the fact that it is a part, much less that it had ever been planned, can hardly be imagined.

To call Mr. Pecksniff an oily hypocrite, as has been so often done, is superficial criticism. He is a superb artist in hypocrisy; he has elevated hypocrisy into a learned profession; he has almost elevated it into sincerity.

True, he had not escaped making enemies. There were those who said he was like a direction-post, always telling the way to a place and never going there himself. It is the fate of the moral man to excite envy. There were, too, every now and then, distressing scenes with angry pupils who believed themselves cheated and robbed by him. He remained unshaken. He had a perfect defence against all attacks. He forgave his enemies. He added charity to morality and became invulnerable.

Unfortunately, Dickens, with his usual righteous passion for rewards for the good and punishments for the bad in his last number, stripped Mr. Pecksniff of all his possessions and cast him forth to a bankrupt, begging-letter writing and drunken old age. It was, one respectfully submits, a fearful mistake. The Mr. Pecksniff he has painted, the flawless, superhuman Mr. Pecksniff whom he has sustained throughout his previous nineteen numbers, would never have succumbed. He is too great for that. His last words prove it. Ruthlessly lashed by the scorn of old Martin Chuzzlewit's words, beaten to the earth by the old man's cudgel, Mr. Pecksniff's morality triumphs still, bloody but unbowed. In a magnificent farewell, he not only grants his forgiveness to Mr. Chuzzlewit, but adds to it the sublime assurance, "It may be bitterness to you to hear it now, sir, but you will live to seek a consolation in it. May you find a consolation in it when you want it, sir! Good morning!" A superb exit. That man could never descend to begging-letters or drunkenness.

It is a great pity, that "happy" ending which degrades Mr. Pecksniff. It destroys the illusion. For Mr. Pecksniff is illusion. He is not mortal; just as Mr. Pickwick is a reflection of universal benevolence, Pecksniff is a reflection of a common and universal vice, caught and fixed in a peculiarly early Victorian frame. Not even Tom Pinch, his assistant, can bring him down to the level of mankind. Tom Pinch himself is illusion; he is the eternal gull, the credulous, trustful, lovable simpleton whom the kind-hearted will always love and protect, knaves will always defraud and impose upon.

It is due to Dickens' marvellous skill in delineation that both these characters impose upon us throughout the illusion of reality. The details are perfect. Tom Pinch's organ-playing and his vast store of queer, out-of-the-way knowledge make him as real a man as could be desired, until one realizes that his every quality and ability only render him the more perfect foil to that supreme picture of personified hypocrisy, Mr. Pecksniff, the Great Illusion.

If Mr. Pecksniff be illusion, Mrs. Sairey Gamp most emphatically is not. She is of the earth, earthy. She fairly reeks of humanity; unwashed humanity, strongly flavoured with gin. Mrs. Gamp could be seen every day in 1842 in or near Kingsgate Street, High Holborn, waddling along the pavement, complete with her umbrella—"in colour like a faded leaf"—her pattens, and her large bundle, puffing her odorous way towards an imminent birth, a sick-bed, or a recent death. Dickens is, in fact, painting direct from life. "Mrs. Gamp is," he wrote, "a representation of the hired attendant upon the poor in sickness." Not only on the poor, but also on the rich—"eighteen pence a day for working-people, and three and six for gentle-folks—night watching," said Mrs. Gamp with emphasis, "being a extra charge." The ignorant, incompetent, sluttish, and often drunken mid-wife and sick-nurse was a curse from which all classes suffered in those days.

Mrs. Gamp in real life was detestable. She stank, she drank, she slumbered when she ought to have watched, she lost the lives of mothers and children by scores through her filthy hands and habits, she killed frequently other patients by neglect, carelessness, and callous indifference. When her charges were already dead, for she included the laying-out of corpses among her professional bunglings, she was chiefly concerned with what she could make out of the bereaved or steal from the effects of the deceased.

How comes it then that she is ranked, and highly, among Dickens' immortals? For the same general reason that Mr. Wackford Squeers is also of that band. With his inimitable touch—there was never more perfect nickname than that "inimitable"—Dickens, without abating one jot of the obscene sordidness of the real Mrs. Gamp, throws into high relief her humorous aspects, and, perhaps more important still, builds up in her own words, and with a grave ironical seriousness, a perfect picture of the eminence to which she has risen in all the arts and practices of her disgracefully incompetent profession.

Mrs. Gamp is funny. She is funny without knowing it. She is incurably garrulous; she gives herself away completely, and when anyone does that all unconsciously, the result is generally humorous. That does not make all her greatness. Mrs. Gamp is proud. She is proud of her reputation, proud of her ability, proud of her low cunning. She believes utterly in herself; to her mind there never was such a perfectly capable, hard-working, unselfish midwife and layer-out as Mrs. Gamp. Every word that reveals her detestability reveals also her self-admiration. There is no chink in the

"A Deplorable Sceptic," a *Punch* cartoon by Sir John Tenniel featuring Mr. Robert Lowe (Viscount Sherbrooke) and Mr. W. E. Gladstone based on Dickens' characters, Mrs. Gamp and Mrs. Prig

*Reproduced by permission of the proprietors of " Punch"*

armour of her complacency. Any suggestion that she could be in any way improved would pain her most deeply and sincerely —as it did when old Martin Chuzzlewit hinted at "the expediency of a little less liquor, and a little more humanity, and a little less regard for herself, and a little more regard for her patients, and perhaps a trifle of additional honesty." Mrs. Gamp was astounded. She could not understand it. So stunned was she by the shock that her mind could not get past the first accusation before it gave way. She "clasped her hands, turned up her eyes until they were quite invisible, threw back her bonnet for the admission of fresh air to her heated brow; and in the act of saying faintly—'Less liquor!— Sairey Gamp—Bottle on the chimley piece, and let me put my lips to it, when I am so dispoged!' fell into one of the walking swoons. . . ."

It is this marvellous inversion, this showing of Mrs. Gamp through Mrs. Gamp's own self-satisfied eyes, that makes the genius of the characterization. By the invention of the imaginary Mrs. Harris, through whom Sairey Gamp can praise herself without loss of that dignity which always accompanies greatness, Dickens added a superb stroke which put the seal upon the method.

Betsey Prig, "a fair specimen of a Hospital Nurse," as Dickens said, is the natural professional companion of a Sairey Gamp. She is not so eminent in her profession. She is not so fully described. There is no need; one short conversation between the two nurses is quite sufficient. Given Mrs. Gamp, imagination can supply all the rest.

"'Anythin' to tell afore you goes, my dear?' asked Mrs. Gamp, setting her bundle down inside the door, and looking affectionately at her partner.

"'The pickled salmon,' Mrs. Prig replied, 'is quite delicious. I can partick'ler recommend it. Don't have nothink to say to the cold meat, for it tastes of the stable. The drinks is all good.'

"Mrs. Gamp expressed herself much gratified.

"'The physic and them things is on the drawers and mankleshelf,' said Mrs. Prig cursorily. 'He took his

last slime draught at seven. The easy-chair an't soft
enough. You'll want his piller.'"

For a *multum in parvo* that is unbeatable. It only remains to
say that by this picture Dickens practically wiped the Mrs.
Gamps and the Betsey Prigs out of existence, as he had previously done the Wackford Squeers.

It cannot fail to be noticed that Dickens has an unfailing
power of investing all his greatest characters, no matter of
what type they be, with a dignity all their own. From Mr.
Pickwick to Mr. Pecksniff, from Mrs. Jarley to Mrs. Gamp,
they all achieve a grandeur of personality peculiarly fitted to
enable them to rise to the heights of the most difficult situations with which they are confronted. The only occasion on
which any fail to do so are in those dreadful final chapters in
which Dickens, with naïve disregard of all human experience,
deals out his rewards to the virtuous and his punishments to
the wicked. The only finely drawn character so far who lacks
this dignity is Mrs. Nickleby, and it is the very essence of Mrs.
Nickleby that she lacks any sort of dignity.

Mr. Pecksniff has the dignity of the perfect artist, Tom
Pinch has the beautiful dignity of the simple-minded and un-
worldly scholar, Mrs. Gamp has the dignity of the absolutely
self-complacent. Mark Tapley, young Martin Chuzzlewit's
devoted servant and friend, has the dignity of that self-
depreciation which reveals, though it is meant to conceal,
sterling qualities.

Mark Tapley is an inverted Sam Weller. Both originate in
an inn; both have the same splendid devotion, ingenuity, and
capacity for making themselves helpful under the most diverse
and trying conditions; both are true as steel; but whereas
Sam lives, not by work alone, but by wit, and is the very soul
of merriment, Mark's idea of happiness is to be thoroughly
unhappy. "I don't believe," he says, "there was ever a man
as could come out so strong under circumstances that would
make other men miserable, as I could, if I could only get a
chance. But I can't get a chance.—It's my opinion, that
nobody ever will know half of what's in me, unless something
very unexpected turns up."

Of course, the unexpected does turn up. He gets his chance, and Dickens' readers get another immortal.

He goes to America with young Martin Chuzzlewit, and finds a first opportunity in the emigrants' quarters on the outward journey. The description of this journey, incidentally, is a further revelation of Dickens' astonishing powers of observation. He describes the life of the emigrants on board ship as vividly as though he had been a steerage passenger on half a dozen trips across the Atlantic.

"The American portion of this book," wrote Dickens, "is in no other respect a caricature than as it is an exhibition, for the most part, of the ludicrous side of the American character." That is no doubt perfectly true; but it is a cruel picture none the less. Dickens never wrote anything more brutal than these American chapters of "Martin Chuzzlewit." Present-day readers, even American readers, can enjoy wholeheartedly the extraordinary cleverness of these pages, their vivid descriptions and their brilliant satire, though one does discern every now and then even in recent American articles on Dickens, traces of a still unextinguished resentment. It is quite easy to imagine as one follows young Martin Chuzzlewit and Mark Tapley through their doleful experiences in the land of Freedom, the ferocious howl of rage that burst from the United States when these chapters were first published. Among other exhibitions of hatred, it is recorded that the book was burnt publicly on the New York stage.

It mattered not, it made it all the worse, that Dickens was right in his facts. He had, one knows, every particular documented. When it was suggested that the Watertoast Association was a grotesque and impossible caricature, he could retort at once that the account of their proceedings was a literal paraphrase of accounts of proceedings of public associations in America reported in the *Times* of June and July 1843. He could, had he desired, have proved to the hilt the living originals of Colonel Diver, Mr. Jefferson Brick, Major Pawkins, Mr. La Fayette Kettle, General Choke, Mr. Scadder, Mr. Hannibal Chollop, and Mr. Elijah Pogram. He had actually had to endure the two literary ladies on his travels. He had received literally hundreds of letters of the type he printed as from Cyrus Choke, La Fayette Kettle, and Putnam Smif. He had been down the Mississippi to Cairo, and seen for himself the "Valley of Eden," that "earthly Paradise" which unscrupulous real estate agents like Scadder were selling to gullible emigrants like Martin Chuzzlewit, and which he knew to be "a flat morass, bestrewn with fallen timber; a marsh on which the good growth of the earth seemed to have been wrecked and cast away, that from its decomposing ashes vile and ugly things might rise; where the very trees took the aspect of huge weeds, begotten of the slime from which they sprung, by the hot sun which burnt them up; where fatal maladies, seeking whom they might infect, came forth at night, in misty shapes, and creeping out upon the water, hunted them like spectres until day; where even the blessed sun, shining down on festering elements of corruption and disease, became a horror. . . . Eden. . . . The waters of the Deluge might have left it but a week before: so choked with slime and matted growth was the hideous swamp which bore that name."

Save for the picture of Mr. Bevan, the only frank and kindly American Martin Chuzzlewit meets, Dickens never for one instant relents; and even Mr. Bevan, though he does prove that all Americans are not wholly bad, serves to throw into yet higher relief the depravity of the rest. He is out of the main stream of American life, a quiet countryman who likes the cities less every time he sees them. His travels abroad have made him see his country's faults; and he sums these up in the damning verdict that there are in America two classes of society, one of which, "the great mass, asserts a spurious independence, most miserably dependent for its mean existence on the disregard of humanizing convention-alities of manner and social custom, so that the coarser a man is, the more distinctly it shall appear to his taste; while the other, disgusted with the low standard thus set up and made adaptable to everything, takes refuge among the graces and refinements it can bring to bear on private life, and leaves the public weal to such fortune as may betide it in the press and uproar of a general scramble."

This quotation expresses Dickens' considered opinion of the

United States, and it is in the spirit of these words that he penned the American chapters of "Martin Chuzzlewit," which are indeed the "rod in pickle" that he had reserved for the Americans. If ever writer dipped his pen in gall, Dickens did so on this occasion. There is not a single aspect of American life capable of being lampooned which escapes his eye, nor which he does not attack with the utmost virulence. While practically without exception he sheds some ray of kindliness, of pity or of sympathy on his English characters, be they never so villainous, in these American studies there is no gleam of mercy. From the moment Colonel Diver addresses Martin Chuzzlewit on board the *Screw*, and the New York newsboys rush on board with the *New York Sewer*, the *New York Stabber*, the *New York Family Spy*, the *New York Private Listener*, the *New York Peeper*, the *New York Plunderer*, the *New York Keyhole Reporter*, and the *New York Rowdy Journal*, right through to Mark's summing up of the American Eagle on board the boat for England, there is not, except for Mr. Bevan, one single kindly touch, even Mr. Bevan's friends, the Norrises, being cruelly pilloried, in spite of their obvious good qualities.

It makes one shudder to think what kind of pen Dickens would have wielded had the trials of his childhood soured his disposition and ruined his temper. England's greatest and kindliest humorist would have been lost, and in his stead England would have gained her greatest and most virulent satirist. "Gulliver's Travels," admittedly the most savage satire in English literature, is mild compared with what a jaundiced Dickens would have written.

To return to England and to happier themes. There are half a dozen or more minor characters in "Martin Chuzzlewit" who, however much they may be overshadowed by the colossal figures of Mr. Pecksniff and Mrs. Gamp, must on no account be overlooked. The Martin Chuzzlewits, young and old, play most importants parts, but they are among the least attractive of the people in the book; in fact, a more irritating, bumptious, foolishly optimistic and shallow young man than Martin Chuzzlewit junior it would be difficult to find, while old man Martin's doings and character are for ever wrapt in mystery. Jonas Chuzzlewit's "sordid coarseness and brutality" Dickens took it upon himself to explain in the preface to the cheap edition of 1848. "So born and so bred," he wrote, "admired for that which made him hateful, and justified from his cradle in cunning and treachery and avarice; I claim him as the legitimate issue of the father upon whom those vices are seen to recoil . . . their recoil . . . is not a mere piece of poetical justice, but is the extreme exposition of a plain truth." Leave it at that; it explains Jonas Chuzzlewit as well as anything could.

Charity and Mercy Pecksniff are fit issue for such as Mr. Pecksniff; they are among the minor masterpieces of the book. With them, as so often, Dickens uses the method of contrast, and uses it most effectively. There are few kindlier characters than M. Todgers, proprietor of the Commercial Boarding House near the Monument, which "nobody ever found, on a verbal direction, though given within a minute's walk of it." Bailey, "a small boy with a large red head, and no nose to speak of," is one of Dickens' best London street urchins. Poll Sweedlepipe, who "united the two pursuits of barbering and bird-fancying," is obviously a reminiscence of the eccentric barber who used to shave uncle Thomas Barrow in Soho during Dickens' Bayham Street days. Mould, the vampire-like undertaker, with his harem, is priceless; Mr. Chuffey, Anthony Chuzzlewit's old half-witted clerk, is pathetic; Mr. Montague Tigg, or Mr. Tigg Montague, is another of Dickens' glorious shabby-genteel rogues, and he is accompanied by the shadowy Mr. Chevy Slyme, always round the corner, and "whose great abilities seemed one and all to point towards the sneaking quarter of the moral compass."

Both Dickens himself and Forster considered "Martin Chuzzlewit" immeasurably the finest book he had as yet written, and posterity has so far confirmed the verdict as to place it third in popularity among his works, "Pickwick" and "Copperfield" alone taking precedence of it. When first published it was a distinct failure, the sales being only about 20,000 per number, as compared with the fifty to seventy thousand of previous stories.

For these disappointing figures various reasons have been

given, none wholly satisfactory.  The most convincing is that
Dickens' public had grown accustomed to weekly numbers,
and resented the change back to monthly parts, but even that
would hardly account for so sensational a drop in sales.  The
suggestion that his readers had forgotten him owing to his
absence in America will not bear consideration in view of
the lively sale of "American Notes," while any idea that
readers found the story dull until Martin Chuzzlewit and Mark
Tapley went to America is disproved by the circulation
figures.  The proposed emigration only stimulated sales to
the extent of about 2,000 copies, and from first to last the
sales never exceeded 23,000.  Once published in volume form,
however, "Martin Chuzzlewit" rapidly advanced to its present
popularity.  Such unexpected failures of books happen from
time to time in the publishing world, and the case of a book
which goes flatly for quite a long time, and then works
gradually up to the position of a best-seller, is not uncommon.

Unfortunately one of the publishers had not the courage to
wait for the ultimate success of "Martin Chuzzlewit."  Under
the agreement for this novel, Messrs. Chapman and Hall had
contracted to pay Dickens £200 per month during the period
of publication in parts, subject to a reservation, usual in such
agreements, that if the sales were too low to justify this figure,
they were entitled to reduce it to £150.  In June 1843, Mr.
Hall, the junior partner, was injudicious enough to hint that
they might have to consider making this reduction.

Dickens went blind with rage.  It was, indeed, a very
serious blow for him.  He was still considerably in debt to
Messrs. Chapman and Hall over their repurchase of copyrights
on his behalf, and his style of living, though not extravagant,
was based on the theory of a rising, not a falling, income.
Moreover, the prodigal father chose this very inconvenient
moment to recommence his "disappearances."

Dickens' first impulse was to raise money at once, pay
Chapman and Hall, break off relations with them, and give
Mr. Hall, with whom he had previously fallen foul, "a piece
of my mind."  Forster prevailed upon him to do nothing
until the autumn; but in so doing he only succeeded in
delaying the storm.

## CHAPTER VIII

*"We must not ask Dickens what Christmas is, for with all his heat and eloquence he does not know. Rather we must ask Christmas what Dickens is."*—G. K. CHESTERTON.

IN October and November 1843 Dickens, though very hard at work upon "Martin Chuzzlewit," wrote the first and by far the best and most popular of his Christmas stories, "A Christmas Carol."

This short tale needs but little introduction, and less recommendation. There are still many people who read the "Carol" religiously every Christmas Eve. Every one of these, and the great majority of its less regular readers, would echo Thackeray's words when he said of it, "Who can listen to objections regarding such a book as this? It seems to me a national benefit, and to every man or woman who reads it a personal kindness." Lord Jeffrey, though writing perhaps in the heat of the moment, was surely not far wrong when he said, "you have done more good by this little publication, fostered more kindly feelings, and prompted more positive acts of beneficence than can be traced to all the pulpits and confessionals in Christendom since Christmas 1842."

"A Christmas Carol" remains a national benefit in every English-speaking country in the world. It matters not that critics have pointed out its weaknesses as a story, its inferiority to others of Dickens' works. Gissing can protest of the Christmas stories that "not even in the 'Carol' can we look for anything to be seriously compared with the finer features of his novels." Mr. Bernard Darwin may tell us that "In some ways there is nothing strikingly original about the

' Carol.' Superficially at any rate, it has a strong Pick-wickian flavour." He leaves us quite unmoved even when he solemnly proceeds to prove these assertions. We continue obstinately to read, and to love, "A Christmas Carol."

All such criticism is, in fact, beside the point. The "Christmas Carol" is no more to be judged as a literary composition than "Good King Wenceslas" is to be judged by musical and poetical standards. The fact that the words of "Oh come, all ye faithful" are among the world's worst examples of verse makes no difference to the fact that millions of people sing them with great benefit to their feelings every year. "The First Nowel," similarly, will not bear a moment's analysis by a literary critic. Yet these carols remain necessities to us all at Yuletide. They do not make Christmas; it takes a large number of very diverse attributes to make up the sum of Christmas, but Christmas would not really be Christmas without them.

Christmas is, indeed, easily the most complicated of all our great national festivals; it is a positively bewildering tangle of complications. It is impossible to imagine Christmas without turkey and plum pudding and mince-pies (and, until taxation took all the flavour out of strong drink, the wassail bowl); without presents and parties and holly and mistletoe and crackers; without pantomimes; without snow, though it rarely snows at Christmas time; without waits; without the singing of Christmas carols; without the Christmas sermon and the reading or the remembering of the immortal story of Bethlehem. Of these, the last only has direct connection with the feast of the Nativity which the Christmas celebrates; the rest, even the carols, are accretions. Yet, strangely dissimilar enjoyments as may be the over-eating of plum pudding, the pulling of crackers, and the singing of traditional hymns, they are all inspired by and are expressions of the spirit of Christmas, the spirit of "On earth peace, goodwill toward men."

It is as an expression of the spirit of Christmas that Dickens' "Christmas Carol" must be judged; and on that ground the verdict of the public is the only safe guide to follow. It has never for one instant wavered. When the

"Carol" was first published as a small crimson-coloured volume, illustrated by John Leech, just before Christmas 1843, the first edition was sold out on the day of publication, and the public has continued to buy the "Carol" in all sorts of editions, from vest-pocket size to large volumes chiefly consisting of pictures, at every succeeding Christmastide right up to the present day.

Mr. G. K. Chesterton, most brilliant and understanding of Dickens' critics, has summed up excellently the reason why the "Carol" has remained so popular. "The beauty and the real blessing of the story," he says, "do not lie in the mechanical plot of it, the repentance of Scrooge, probable or improbable; they lie in the great furnace of real happiness that glows through Scrooge and everything round him; that great furnace, the heart of Dickens." The "Christmas Carol" is a fairy tale, parable, and sermon all rolled into one, in which everything happens just as it ought to happen in a perfect realization of "On earth peace, goodwill toward men."

Dickens wrote the "Carol" at fever pitch. He worked so hard over it that for weeks he "never left home before the owls went out." He was so overcome by his own emotions that he "wept and laughed and wept again, and excited himself in a most extraordinary manner in the composition," as he told Felton, and, "thinking whereof he walked about the black streets of London, fifteen and twenty miles many a night when all the sober folk had gone to bed." After he had completed it, he "broke out like a madman," and there were "such dinings, such dancings, such conjurings, such blindman's-buffings, such theatre-goings, such kissings-out-of-old years and kissings-in of new ones, [as] never took place in these parts before."

It is no wonder such a man caught the true ring of the Christmas spirit. He was literally possessed of it while he wrote. Was it sudden inspiration, or were there reasons for this extraordinary outburst? Certainly several things had happened during the past few months to predispose his mind to such a theme, and in particular to direct his thoughts more keenly than usual towards the problems of suffering,

BENJAMIN DISRAELI

*From the drawing by Daniel Maclise, R.A., 1833*

want, and privation, and the means of assuaging and relieving these.

Dickens was no armchair philanthropist. His interest in the poor and the needy did not begin and end with writing about them in order to excite other people's sympathies on their behalf. When his own sympathy was aroused over any case of need that he could aid personally he always did so, and put into his efforts all the energy that he put into his writing. A notable instance was his helping of Mrs. Macrone, widow of the publisher. Despite his quarrel with her husband, when he heard, only a few months later, that on Macrone's death she had been left badly off, he found time in one of his busiest periods to contribute a considerable amount of matter to a volume published for her benefit.

Some writers confine their altruism to their books. It was not so with Dickens. His private charity was as overflowing as the charity of his novels. No one will ever know the extent to which he aided a never-ending stream of relatives of three generations: his own, his parents', and his children's. He was ever foremost, as his father had been before him in Chatham days, in aiding deserving public charities.

During 1843 many calls were made upon his sympathies. Forster was ill, off and on, for long periods; and Dickens was constantly making anxious enquiries and trying to do everything possible. In May, John Black, his old editor on the *Chronicle*, who had so early and so generously recognized his abilities, was retired suddenly and rather harshly. Dickens was deeply grieved. "If I could find him out, I would go and comfort him this moment." No sooner said than done; he did find him out, and comforted him with a great dinner at Greenwich, when he "arranged and ordered all to perfection." Within a few weeks he was putting into farewell words his love for Macready, one of his best friends, who was leaving for America. The same summer he exerted himself vigorously on behalf of the children of Edward William Elton, a well-known actor, who was drowned at sea while returning from an Edinburgh engagement.

In the autumn he became tremendously interested in the Ragged School movement, begun this year, which aimed to

provide education for those children who were too destitute
to attend the ordinary schools. He drew the attention of
his friend, Miss Burdett Coutts, for whom he acted for many
years as honorary almoner, to this charitable work, and while
so doing incidentally made one of the most sensible remarks
in the history of education. "I told her, too, that it was of
immense importance that they should be *washed*." It may
seem a small point, but its overlooking defeated many worthy
educational efforts in the nineteenth century.

Finally, in October, he was asked to preside at the opening
of the great Manchester Athenæum; and he chose as the subject of his speech the education of the poor. With Disraeli
and Cobden and many other distinguished men listening,
he told movingly of "thousands of immortal creatures condemned without alternative or choice to tread, not what our
great poet calls the primrose path to the everlasting bonfire,
but one of jagged flints and stones laid down by brutal
ignorance."

It was while on this visit to Manchester that the idea for
"A Christmas Carol" came to him. All the year he had
been portraying the awful results of selfishness and hypocrisy
in Mr. Pecksniff, of avarice and brutality in Jonas Chuzzlewit, while Mrs. Gamp's advent in the summer would naturally
turn his thoughts continually towards the suffering of the
poor in sickness, and so towards the suffering of the poor in
general. Meanwhile, a succession of external events, private
and public, had drawn out his sympathies in various ways,
and culminated in a great public meeting which gave him a
magnificent opportunity to speak out for his own people in
his own proper person. Is it surprising that his great warm
generous heart, so repeatedly touched, had to find relief in
some overwhelming expression of tenderness and love and
sympathy—and of joy, too, for throughout the year he had
had the happiness of being consistently successful in relieving
sorrow and of aiding successful attempts to relieve want and
destroy ignorance? So there came "A Christmas Carol,"
of which Mr. Chesterton rightly says that "The story sings
from end to end like a happy man going home; and, like a
happy and good man, when it cannot sing it yells." Which

THE LEANING TOWER OF PISA

is exactly what Dickens was feeling he had to do when the inspiration of it came to him.

The reason why the idea of the "Carol" came to him in October 1843 is as plain as daylight. In every one of the characters, Scrooge the miser, Bob Cratchit, his clerk, Tiny Tim, the Fezziwigs, the spirits, even old Marley, dead these seven years, can be seen reflected the nature of the events which directed Dickens' thoughts during this year. As for the story itself, imagine the result when the fiercely blazing sympathies of a perfervid reformer who is also a magnificent reporter are purified in the crucible of a child-like imagination nurtured on the "Arabian Nights," and you will discover why the "Carol" is beloved by all who read it.

It is ironic to have to conclude the beautiful story of "A Christmas Carol" with a dismal epilogue of financial disappointment and business quarrels. Yet the truth compels that this should be so; and it is not really surprising. Any writer who has to live by his books is bound to keep a very sharp eye on the amount of money they bring in; and this rule is equally applicable to the author of books with great moral purposes and full of divine sympathy as to the author of catchpenny novels or compilers of compendiums. Dickens had been hard hit over the low sales of "Chuzzlewit," and the unexpectedly meagre profits on the "Carol" proved a crushing blow. "Such a night as I have passed!" he wrote frantically to Forster one Saturday morning in February. "I really believed I should never get up again, until I had passed through all the horrors of a fever. I found the 'Carol' accounts awaiting me, and they were the cause of it. The first six thousand copies show a profit of £230! And the last four will yield as much more. I had set my heart and soul upon a thousand, clear."

Poor Dickens! A sanguine and emotional temperament such as his has grave disadvantages. If it knows raptures of joy far beyond those of ordinary men, it has to pay amply for them by periods of depression and despair such as more equable minds can never experience.

This reverse was terribly overwhelming. It was quite unanticipated; the "Carol" had been an immense success, and had sold splendidly. It was only the publishers' error of spending too much on its production and pricing it too highly to gain adequate return that had reduced the profits. Secondly, it came just after the financial failure of "Chuzzlewit." Thirdly, it hit Dickens at a time when his buoyancy and capacities were at a low ebb after the "agonies" of conceiving "Chuzzlewit," and the hectic fury with which he had written the "Carol." Also, a minor point possibly, but one not to be altogether ignored, it came just as all his "terrific" bills for the previous year were pouring in.

His mind had been very considerably unsettled for the past three months. The lukewarm reception of "Chuzzlewit" had shaken him badly. For the first time in his life he was doubtful of himself. He realized he was over-tired, that he could not go on at the rate he had been doing, that a long and complete rest was essential if he was to continue. Forster suggested a long holiday, but Dickens knew he was past the assistance holidays could give. "You say two or three months," he replied, "because you have been used to see me for eight years never leaving off. But it is not rest enough. It is impossible to go on working the brain to that extent for ever. The very spirit of the thing, in doing it, leaves a horrible despondency behind, when it is done: which must be prejudicial to the mind, so soon renewed and so seldom let alone."

He staggered Forster in November 1843 by proposing to leave England altogether for a period of six to eight months; letting his house in Devonshire Terrace, cutting down his establishment, and living in some place on the continent that combined cheapness and a delightful climate.

The sequence of events which led up to this decision can be clearly traced. For eight years, as Dickens said, he had been drawing heavily upon his mental and spiritual resources. His American experiences must have been terribly exhausting both physically and emotionally, and spiritually must have depressed him to an extent even he did not realize. Immediately he returned to England he threw himself into the exceedingly anxious task of preparing the "American Notes," and almost directly afterwards into a long book which took more out of him than any previous one had done.

GENOA

*After the engraving by E. Finden, 1835*

On top of the mortification of his American experiences
came the bitter disappointment of finding a book he rightly
considered a masterpiece coldly received by the public; and
with that shock there came the dual realization that the
strain of creation was growing too great to bear, yet that
unless he maintained it he would speedily be financially
ruined.  He saw before him, one can well imagine, the terrifying prospect of degenerating into a broken-down writer,
his hold on his public lost, his brain failing, his family poverty-
stricken and finally destitute.  Heaven knows what visions
of Bayham Street and Johnson Street, of Hungerford Market
and the Marshalsea tore their way through his distracted
mind at this period.  He must escape at all costs; he could
not sink to those levels.  Some way out must be found.

He instructed Forster to approach Messrs. Bradbury and
Evans, printers to Messrs. Chapman and Hall.  Eighteen
months previously they had made overtures to him; should
he ever desire to alter his methods of publication they would
be glad to hear from him.  The idea now appealed; he would
be his own publisher, avoid publishers' commissions, control
all expenses of production himself, and so reap increased
profit from his writings.

Messrs. Bradbury and Evans were taken by surprise.
They may also have been influenced by the poor sales of
"Martin Chuzzlewit," or, as Forster suggests, when it came to
the point, lacked confidence in their ability to take over the
rôle of publishers to Dickens.  At any rate, they played for
safety; they made no constructive suggestions, but urged
the advisability of a cheap edition of his published works,
and offered to finance any magazine or periodical Dickens
cared to edit.

Dickens could not face either proposal.  The idea of a
cheap edition appeared to him like "putting myself before
the town as writing tooth and nail for bread"; before the
labour of a new periodical he frankly quailed.  So he announced his decision to Forster; he would withdraw his share
of the subscription from Messrs. Chapman and Hall; he would
tell both them and Messrs. Bradbury and Evans that he
was not likely to do anything for twelve months; he would

J

dump his family in some cheap and salubrious continental
climate; and meanwhile he would himself wander about in
France, Switzerland, and Italy, taking his wife "perhaps to
Rome and Venice, but not elsewhere," the treble purpose
of this vagabondage being rest and recuperation, enrichment
of experience, and the accumulation of material in letters
home to Forster which might furnish the corpus of a "new
and attractive book." Meanwhile, he could quietly meditate
upon a story he had in mind.

With "such insufficient breath as was left" him after
reading this letter, Forster protested. It was like blowing
against a hurricane. The very next day Dickens overwhelmed his objections in a torrent of argument and explanation. His expenses would be halved by this project; he had
it in him to hold his place against fifty writers, if he could
keep his health, but "Chuzzlewit" had warned him that he
must rest; the account of his travels would cost him little
effort, and would at least certainly pay expenses. The move
to France would do the children good, he had already arranged
to leave the baby in England, and he had "a thousand other
reasons."

All Forster could do was to try to delay him in the execution of the project, and this for a short while he succeeded
in doing. Then came the crash of the "Carol's" finances,
and instantly Dickens' mind was made up irrevocably. Retrenchment and economy were now essential; they could not be
achieved in England; he was off abroad, and the date of his
departure was June.

He broke off relations with Messrs. Chapman and Hall,
and came to an agreement with Messrs. Bradbury and Evans
whereby they advanced him £2,800 in consideration of his
assigning to them a fourth share in whatever he wrote during
the next eight years. No interest was to be paid on the loan;
no contracts for books were made. There was an understanding that a Christmas tale would be ready by the end of
the year, but otherwise it was apparently entirely in Dickens'
hands whether he wrote anything at all.

After the usual dinner, which combined a farewell to Dickens
and a celebration of the conclusion of "Martin Chuzzlewit,"

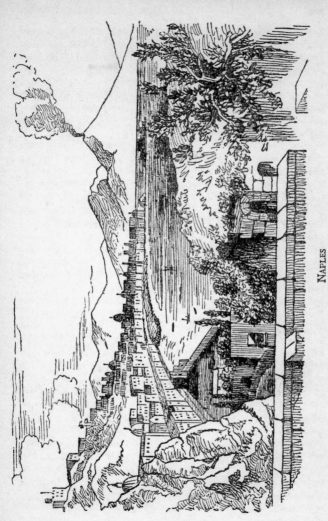

NAPLES

*After the engraving by E. Finden, 1835*

he and his party, consisting of himself, his wife, her sister Georgina, the children, three maids, and a "brave courier," left London on July 1st, and on the 14th arrived at Marseilles, whence Dickens wrote, "Surrounded by strange and perfectly novel circumstances, I feel as if I had a new head on side by side with my old one."

The story of the journey across France from Paris to Marseilles, in "an English travelling carriage of considerable proportions," through Sens, Avallon and Chalons, to Lyons, thence down the "Arrowy Rhone" in "a very dirty vessel full of merchandise" to Avignon, and so by road again to Marseilles, is vividly told in the first three chapters of "Pictures from Italy." It is a description which reveals once more what a marvellous reporter Dickens was.

Though he was travelling the whole time, nothing escaped him, and the narrative is perfectly attuned to the journey. It rattles briskly on through the stages, and pauses only where a few evening hours give the travellers time to stroll round the streets and visit the cathedral. As an example of his powers of observation, one may cite the detailed descriptions of Marseilles in "Pictures from Italy" and the opening chapter of "Little Dorrit." Dickens arrived at Marseilles late at night on the 14th, and by 5 p.m. next day was "steaming out in the open sea" toward Genoa. He did certainly revisit the town two or three times, but even then the descriptions show extraordinarily acute perception, not only of the actual places and people, but of the intangible "atmosphere."

From Marseilles they went on by the *Ss. Marie Antoinette* to Genoa, and landing there drove to the suburb of Albaro, where a house, the Villa Bagnerello, had been taken. Here they were to stay until the end of September.

"The Villa Bagnerello (it sounds romantic, but Signor Bagnerello is a butcher hard by)" was quickly nicknamed by Dickens "The Pink Jail," and was not impressive except as regards its state of dilapidation, and the legion of fleas which "populate the coach house to that extent that I daily expect to see the carriage going off bodily, drawn by myriads of industrious fleas in harness." As compensation it had "one of the most splendid situations imaginable," commanding "the noble bay of Genoa, with the deep blue Mediterranean . . . monstrous old desolate houses and palaces . . . lofty hills . . . with their tops often hidden in the clouds . . . green vineyards . . . bold and picturesque rocks on the seashore." The actual name of the house, though Dickens never used it, was Villa di Bella Vista.

"I don't exactly know what I have done for my country in coming away from it," Dickens wrote to Maclise late in July, "but I feel it is something—something great—something virtuous and heroic. Lofty emotions rise within me, when I see the sun set on the blue Mediterranean. I am the limpet on the rock. My father's name is Turner, and my boots are green."

This semi-comic description of himself probably expressed the exact truth. Dickens did not know why he had left England, even though he had been able to give a thousand good reasons for doing so. He certainly did not know what he had done for his country in leaving it. There is little doubt that he had done himself and his country a great service. Forster calls this moment a turning-point in his career, and there is no reason to question the statement.

He was tired and stale. He had lost his nerve. He was financially embarrassed. He did not know what to write, but knew he had to write to live. Meanwhile he was being drawn into more and more public engagements—in February he had been chairman at great meetings in Liverpool and Birmingham, on the 26th and 28th respectively—and the general nature of these was leading him straight into the ranks of social and educational reformers. He might easily have become absorbed in educational work, in which case he would probably have worn himself out in public speaking, raising money for charities, and general unweariedness of effort. Had he, on the other hand, really started in to write "tooth and nail for bread," he would either have broken down under the strain of serious work, or he would have turned to more trivial and consequently less valuable authorship.

Happily he followed his instinct, broke away from every-

_Tho: Ingoldsby_

THE REV. R. H. BARHAM, "THOMAS INGOLDSBY"
(1788–1845)

thing, escaped out of the country, and became for a few
months a free man. It is characteristic of nearly all great
men, this gift of knowing instinctively what to do in a spiritual
crisis or emergency, not so much for their own personal
benefit as for the ultimate benefit of their life-work.

The actual rest part of this residence abroad had not lasted
long before it was interrupted. It is impossible to imagine
Dickens doing nothing, or even idling industriously, for any
great length of time. By August he had already sent for
his paper and inkstand and the little figures which always
adorned his writing desk, and had begun to think every
morning "with a business-like air" of his Christmas book.

A series of accidents prevented his actually beginning to
write for a while. His youngest daughter, Kate, had a sudden,
sharp illness, and towards the end of August he himself,
running downhill at midnight through the streets of Genoa
to get out of the town before the gates closed, went headlong
over a pole stretched across the street. Though apparently
he had escaped without injury, this accident brought on an
illness exactly reminiscent of his childish days, with the same
"unspeakably agonising pain in the side." Early in September he went to Marseilles to bring back from there across the
Alps his younger brother Frederick, and on the morning after
their arrival at Albaro the latter had the narrowest of escapes
from drowning. He swam out into a strong current, and was
being carried away in full sight of Dickens, the children,
their aunt and their nurse, beyond all hope of recovery, when
happily a fishing boat which happened to be leaving the
harbour struck across to his rescue.

During his stay at Albaro, from mid-July to the end of
September, Dickens did no actual literary work, unless one
includes under that heading private letters written designedly
with a view to later publication. He explored every street,
lane, church, chapel, monastery, palace, theatre, shop,
hill, valley and vineyard, and enquired into every game,
feast, custom and habit in Genoa and the neighbourhood.
He bathed in an "extremely theatrical" costume, and after
an extraordinary manner, going in "whenever he pleased,"
breaking "his head against sharp stones if he went in with

that end foremost," floundering "about till he was all over
bruises," and then staggering out.  He grew a moustache,
and admired and trimmed it daily.  He learnt sufficient
Italian in a month to read anything he wished and to
ask for anything he wanted on his explorations.  He made
friends with the French consul-general, who lived in the next
villa, had reviewed his books in the French papers, and had
an English wife.  Otherwise he sought scarcely any of the
people to whom he had letters of introduction; his interest
was in the real people, the people who lived in their swarms,
like flies, in the filthy, tumbledown rabbit-warrens of the
Genoese streets and slopes.  In these, and in his now numerous
family, he found his rest.  A third son, and fifth child, Francis
Jeffrey, had been born in the January of this year, and Georgina
Hogarth, Kate's sister, had been now for nearly two years
a permanent member of the household.  She was already
the dearly-loved aunty and nurse to the children, and
was beginning to fill for Charles the void left by the death
of her sister Mary.

On the 1st of October the family moved into Genoa for
the winter, Dickens having rented a suite of rooms in the
Palazzo Peschiere, a stately old palace standing on high
ground on the outskirts of the city, covered inside with frescoes
by Michelangelo, and surrounded by lovely gardens with
terraces, balconies, fountains, and groves of camellias and
orange trees.  As for the view, "no custom can impair,"
he said, "and no description enhance, the beauty of the
scene."

Here, in the sound of the bells which clanged and clashed
from the innumerable steeples in the city below him, a din
which at first caused his ideas to "spin round and round till
they lost themselves in a whirl of vexation and giddiness,"
he found what he had been desperately searching for, the
title of his next Christmas story.

The subject had been selected, but the title would not
come, and Dickens was feeling unhappy and out of his element, and longing to be back in Devonshire Terrace.  Then,
on the 6th of October, he scribbled home to Forster a line
from Shakespeare's *Henry IV*, "We have heard THE CHIMES

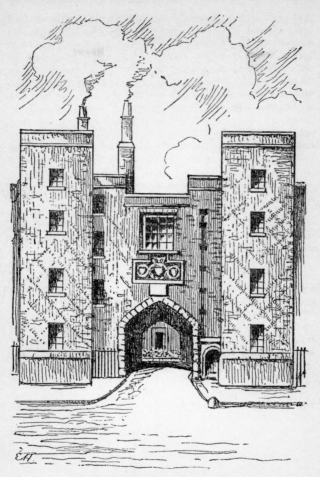

LINCOLN'S INN GATEWAY AS IT WAS

at midnight, Master Shallow!" and within a few days the Master was again at work.

At first he found it difficult to start. He missed London. "Put me down on Waterloo Bridge at eight o'clock in the evening, with leave to roam about as long as I like, and I would come home, as you know, panting to go on. I am sadly strange as it is, and can't settle." Soon this feeling of isolation passed and he was in full swing, "in a regular, ferocious excitement with the 'Chimes'; get up at seven; have a cold bath before breakfast; and blaze away, wrathful and red-hot, until three o'clock or so. . . ."

"Wrathful and red-hot" because this story was to show the other side of the medal. The "Carol" had been gentle and tender, and happy; the "Chimes" was to be gentle and tender, but fierce. What had been accomplished in the "Carol" by kindly methods was to be here achieved by force. The book was to be "a great blow for the poor." Society was to be converted, not this time like Scrooge, by beneficent visions, but with sledge-hammer ones.

The Christmas "annuals" which began with the "Carol" in 1843 and continued until 1848, are Christmas stories only by virtue of their setting. The idea, the spirit of Christmas, gave Dickens a peculiarly apt opportunity to rub in the lessons he was teaching, and the sermons he was preaching all the time. "Ah," he said to Forster, when he had just returned to England from Venice, "when I saw those places, how I thought that to leave one's hand upon the time, lastingly upon the time, with one tender touch for the mass of toiling people that nothing could obliterate, would be to lift oneself above the dust of all the Doges in their graves, and stand upon a giant staircase that Samson couldn't overthrow!"

This theme was the inspiration of all his books. In his greater novels there was room for much embroidery; in his little Christmas tales the theme dominated the stage from start to finish, but the purpose and the design are exactly the same in both. If Christmas be the symbol and festival of Christian charity then Dickens is all Christmas.

He worked at the "Chimes" with "passionate zeal" and

finished with "exultation." "I have worn myself to death," he wrote to Tom Mitton early in November, "in the month I have been at work," but, he added, "I believe I have written a tremendous book, and knocked the 'Carol' out of the field. It will make a great uproar, I have no doubt."

While he was writing the second part a new idea occurred to him. It was so good, so delightful, that he hugged it to himself for several days, no slight feat for Dickens. He just gave Forster the tiniest hint, "I would give a hundred pounds (and think it cheap) to see you read it. . . . Never mind."

A fortnight later there came another hint, more direct this time; he would be in London within the month. He wanted to see proofs and illustrations before publication, and would Forster please not say anything to anybody except "our immediate friends," so that he should not be bothered.

Forster, though he well knew that "all remonstrance would be idle," wrote sagely of the cost and the fatigue; and received the answer he expected. "Notwithstanding what you say, I am still in the same mind about coming to London."

Dickens then confessed that he did not care a hoot about proofs, but that the real reason for the journey was that "unspeakable restless something which would render it almost impossible for me to remain here and not see the thing complete, as it would be for a full balloon, left to itself, not to go up."

Then came the great idea. Dickens wanted Carlyle, of all people, to see the "Chimes" before its publication; and of all things he would best love to read it to him, and to Macready and Stanfield, and Maclise. If Forster was a "real gent," he would get up a little party while Dickens was in London and, conspirator-like, in the midst of it would say innocently, "My boy, would you give us that little Christmas book?" Everybody would be surprised and delighted, and he would consent, and everybody would be entranced, and altogether it would be lovely beyond belief.

It all came off beautifully, according to plan. On December 2nd, at 58 Lincoln's Inn Fields, the reading took place. Carlyle was there, seated on Dickens' right hand, with Stanfield, Laman Blanchard, Douglas Jerrold, Frederick Dickens,

FLORENCE

*After the Engraving by W. Finden, 1835*

William Johnson Fox, Rev. Alexander Dyce, Rev. William Harness, Maclise and Forster. Carlyle listened "with grave attention," Harness and Dyce wept, Fox attended with "rapt solemnity," Stanfield and Maclise with "eager interest"; and all with such delight and approbation that Dickens swore he would not have missed the occasion "for any easily stated or conceived consideration." Maclise had the happy inspiration to sketch the gathering, and either he or some engraver surrounded the head of Dickens with a starry halo. A perfect touch! At the special request of Barham, author of the "Ingoldsby Legends," the reading was repeated on the next night but one.

Three weeks later Dickens was back again at Genoa. During both journeys to and from Italy he contrived, in spite of wintry weather, bad roads, and worse inns, to crowd in a variety of sight-seeings and experiences. Leaving Genoa on the 6th November, he had travelled to England vîa Piacenza, Parma, Modena, Bologna, Ferrara, Venice, Verona, Mantua, Lodi and Milan, to which last place his wife and Georgina Hogarth travelled to spend a couple of days with him. Venice was "above, beyond, out of all reach of coming near, the imagination of a man." He half feared to go to Verona, lest it should put him out of conceit with Romeo and Juliet, but it was "so fanciful, quaint, and picturesque a place" that nothing could have been better.

On his way back by the direct Paris-Marseilles route, he stopped in Paris to visit Macready, visited with him the theatre and the opera, endured there the greatest frost and snow since 1829, and then had a terrible journey by *malle poste* to Marseilles, arriving there fifteen hours late after three days and nights over incredibly bad roads.

On the 10th of January he and his wife started on a tour of Southern Italy, journeying first vîa La Scala, Carrara and Pisa to Rome. On the way Dickens wrote a tenderly beautiful and sympathetic letter to Forster, whose only brother had just died, and signed himself "Your attached and loving friend for life, and far, I hope, beyond it."

The first sight of Rome disappointed him. He entered it on a "dark muddy day"; the Tiber "had looked as yellow as it ought to look," but in Rome "there were no great ruins, no solemn tokens of antiquity to be seen," only "long streets of commonplace shops and houses, such as are to be found in any European town." He had, of course, entered through the modern commercial city.

The impression was soon altered. He quickly discovered and was awed by the Rome of antiquity. The Coliseum in particular moved him as had done nothing else, save perhaps the first view of Niagara; but he found St. Peter's not nearly so impressive as he had hoped. He saw the Carnival, which was "perfectly delirious"; and on his way back from the south revisited Rome for Holy Week.

At Naples, under the auspices of a young English doctor, he "got to understand the low life of Naples . . . almost as well as I understand the do. do. of my own country," except for the language, which he found almost un-understandable. He made the ascent of Vesuvius, starting on "an inexpressibly lovely night without a cloud," climbed to the edge of the crater, "looked down into the flaming bowels of the mountain," and got "burnt from head to foot," to the dismay of his companions, who feared for his life. On the way down three of the party slipped and fell out of sight on a dangerous ice-slope, but fortunately escaped with their lives, though all were injured, and one had not been found when the party left the mountain at midnight.

The weather was so bad that an expedition into Sicily had to be put off. After the second stay in Rome he went on to Florence, ever afterwards to be linked in his mind with Venice and Genoa as one of the three most beautiful and finest of Italian cities.

Early in April he returned to Genoa, and there followed two of the pleasantest months of the whole stay. The weather was beautifully spring-like, the garden "one grove of roses"; he had formed a small circle of friends, and had now all the confidence of a resident of standing.

Meanwhile, all things considered, the "Chimes" had gone off very well. It did not cause quite the uproar he had anticipated, but his friends all liked it, and it sold 20,000 copies in a very short time. The profits on this edition

Ponte Vecchio, Florence, with its shops and covered passage-way

alone were £1,500, and would have been more, save that Messrs. Bradbury and Evans had not all the requisite machinery, and had had to borrow of Messrs. Chapman and Hall of all people!

The story of Trotty Veck, the ticket porter who is so anxious not to misjudge the rich that he has come to misjudge the poor, and to wonder "whether we have any business on the face of the earth or not" or "whether there is any good at all in us, or whether we are born bad," certainly did not oust the "Carol" from popular favour, nor has it done so since. The reason is not far to seek; "A Christmas Carol" really is a Christmas carol; "The Chimes" is a satire. The figures of Alderman Cute—actually drawn from a London alderman who had that year proposed to "put down suicide" —Mr. Filer, and Sir Joseph Bowley, the "Poor Man's Friend," are drawn with venom. That of Fern is hard and bitter. The voice of all the suffering poor speaks out in him with hatred and contempt.

"The Chimes" is indicative of the state of mind Dickens was in when he wrote it. He was vaguely unsatisfied, he knew not with what, save that he had a burning desire to set all things right. Social conditions were all wrong; he could see it even more plainly when he looked at it across the blue Mediterranean, when there was nothing immediate to distract his mind from contemplation of the entire problem of poverty, than when he was in the thick of it.

As a result the reformer triumphed over the humorist in "The Chimes," not to the extent of spoiling the story, but quite decisively and sufficiently to place it far below the "Carol." For Dickens to achieve his happiest efforts, it was necessary that his reforming zeal should be so irradiated with wit and humour that the machinery of purpose was lost sight of. It was in the "Carol"; it was not in "The Chimes." Nevertheless, the latter has retained a certain popularity, ranking second or third among the Christmas stories.

The physical restlessness which had been markedly growing upon Dickens, and which was only one of the signs of his general unsettlement, continued. He did not remain at Genoa more than two months before he was off again, this time for good. The whole party was conveyed by the Great St. Gothard Pass into Switzerland, which Dickens found beautiful, the villages in summer "most charming; most fascinating; most delicious," and the cleanliness wonderful. They stayed at Andermatt, Altdorf and Lucerne, and then made west for Brussels, where Forster, Maclise and Jerrold met them. With these friends they spent a delightful week before returning to England.

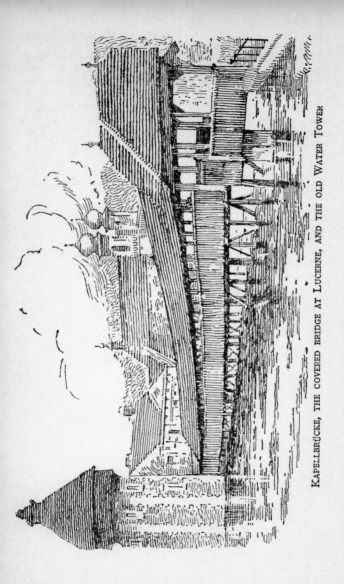

KAPELLBRÜCKE, THE COVERED BRIDGE AT LUCERNE, AND THE OLD WATER TOWER

## CHAPTER IX

"*. . . the happiness I had vaguely anticipated once, was not the happiness I enjoyed, and there was always something wanting.*"—DAVID COPPERFIELD.

ONCE he was back in England, ideas began to ferment in Dickens' head. However much foreign residence and travel might enlarge his experience and widen his sympathies, in London alone could he think properly. He was a Londoner to the core; he was as firmly attached to the grimy, foggy, grey old city, as it was then, as is a homing pigeon to its loft.

The new story had not materialized abroad. So, in London again, forced to consider seriously the immediate earning of a substantial income, and with his mind packed with various and novel impressions, it was natural that he should revert to the idea of a periodical. At the same time, that ideal of universal happiness, at which he had been hammering for eighteen months or more, seized hold of him with renewed force.

It is necessary to inquire into the reasons for this if we are to understand the course of Dickens' life.

There are no people who think harder of happiness than those who have not got it. It is impossible to resist the belief that Dickens was, from about 1842 onwards, forced to contemplation of the ideal of happiness because he was definitely unhappy, and for the greatest and most compelling of causes. He and his wife were drifting apart.

To date his realization of this fact from the time of the American tour is no idle flight of fancy. He himself dated it from an earlier period, but that was in retrospect, when we all see things so much more clearly than at the time. If the two were not spiritually mated, as time proved they were not, the strains and exhaustions of that tour would certainly produce differences and misunderstandings and quarrels between them which would clearly reveal how far apart in temperament and sympathies they stood.

Though Dickens and his wife continued to live together until 1858, it was publicly announced when their separation took place that their relations had been unhappy for many years. Certainly from the time Dickens returned to England from America, he acted more and more like a man who is carrying about with him some secret trouble which is gnawing at his strength, his courage and his hope.

When a man realizes that the wife whom he has loved, and who has loved him, is no longer his spiritual partner, he is filled with blank despair. The whole purpose and meaning seem to drop out of life; he sees the years before him as a mere aching void of loneliness. Even dearly-loved children cannot compensate for his loss; for their love is dependent, and it is protection and support and sympathy which have gone. Manlike, as soon as the first numbing shock is over, he begins desperately to try to fill that void. He plunges into work, into distractions, into pleasure, into vice, according to his temperament. As there is no real substitute for the ineffable blessing of a woman's love, he can never find true satisfaction, never regain complete tranquillity; but he can at least achieve momentary forgetfulness, and even for this he will work himself to death. There is only one thing he cannot face, the gnawing mockery of an utterly purposeless life.

The perpetual physical restlessness, the inability to settle to anything, or to stay anywhere for long, the hesitancy of mind, the doubting of oneself, the sudden projects, the hectic bursts of work, wild whims such as the dash to London to read the "Chimes"—obviously inspired by an unconscious yearning for some stimulus to a waning self-esteem—all these are signs that a man is prey to some deep-rooted unhappiness. Add to these a preoccupation with the ideal of happiness, which will usually manifest itself also in an increased sympathy with private sufferings, and in an ardent temperament, a burning desire to relieve the sufferings of humanity, and the diagnosis may be made almost with certainty.

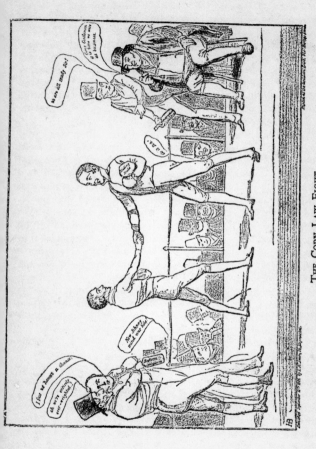

THE CORN LAW FIGHT

Sliding Scale *versus* Fixed Duty. Reading from left, Lord Palmerston (front) and Lord Melbourne, Lord John Russell and Sir Robert Peel, Duke of Wellington and John Bull

*From a cartoon by John Doyle published in 1841*

Happiness had been the theme of both the "Carol" and the "Chimes." It was now to be the whole purpose of a weekly periodical, to be called *The Cricket*, because the cricket is "a cheerful creature that chirrups on the Hearth." It was, of course, domestic happiness that chiefly preoccupied Dickens. He, who had never known that at its best, and but rarely at all, naturally idealized it, and, with his greathearted tenderness, desired it all the more for others now that it seemed irrevocably lost to himself.

The *Cricket* was to have "a 'Carol' philosophy," to "put everybody in a good temper," and to contain a "vein of glowing, hearty, generous, mirthful, beaming reference in everything to Home and Fireside." Incidentally, it was also to chirp, chirp, chirp up to a circulation of unknown hundreds of thousands.

Forster raised objections, on principle, but the scheme was going forward on a modified plan, when suddenly "discussion, project, everything was swept aside by a larger scheme, in its extent and its danger more suitable to the wild and hazardous enterprises of that prodigious year [1845] of excitement and disaster." This was no less than the founding and editing of a daily newspaper.

This was the period of the "hungry forties." The Anti-Corn Law League was setting the country on fire; the long-drawn-out struggle which culminated in the repeal of the Corn Laws and the era of Free Trade and cheap food was swelling to its climax. Dickens proposed to throw himself into the struggle, and to establish a journal "free . . . from personal influence or party bias . . . devoted to the advocacy of all rational and honest means by which wrong might be redressed, just rights maintained, and the happiness and welfare of society promoted."

Forster "put before him, in the strongest form, all the considerations drawn from his genius and fame that should deter him from the labour and responsibility of a daily paper, not less than from the party and political involvements incident to it." Dickens' reply was characteristic, and ominous. Forster's objections weighed with him, *heavily*, but. . . . The times called him to greater effort, offered him a greater opportunity; he could, he thought, "write himself into the hearts of the people," and there was sometimes before him "that possibility of failing health or failing popularity."

His anxiety about his health was not unjustified; he had had to acknowledge that though physically strong and capable of great feats of endurance, constitutionally he was unsound. The attacks of giddiness and headache and pain were recurring with steadily increasing frequency.

His anxiety about his popularity reveals his state of mind. He had already received one severe check, and that while producing his finest work. He had realized at the same time the fearful strain of producing such work, a strain of which Forster says "it may be doubted if ever any man's mental effort cost him more." He was terrified; now that love had passed from his life, what was left but the affection of his public? What indeed? A man like Dickens must have some focus for his energies, or he dissipates them in aimless activities.

Driven on by anxieties and fears and hopes, Dickens plunged this autumn into a very whirlwind of distractions, grave and gay. No sooner was the idea of the weekly periodical abandoned than its title suggested the title and subject for his next Christmas book. Before this was written there came, after the usual Broadstairs holiday, an orgy of private theatricals. The scheme had long been mooted; during the summer a play, Ben Jonson's *Every Man in His Humour*, had been selected, the cast drawn up, and the theatre provisionally booked. For nearly a month before September 21st, the date of production, Dickens flung himself into rehearsals, and was "stage-director, very often stage-carpenter and scene-arranger, property-man, prompter, and bandmaster," in addition to rehearsing his own part, that of the swashbuckling Captain Bobadil. He did everything, arranged everything, managed everybody, and "did the whole of it without an effort." With amateur players that last speaks wonders.

He had a distinguished cast, including Forster, Jerrold, Leech, Mark Lemon, Gilbert A'Beckett, Percival Leigh, Dudley Costello, and Frank Stone, with Stanfield as scene painter. Only Maclise successfully evaded him.

THE NEW STAMP ACT: ALTHOUGH REDUCED TO ONE PENNY, THE
FREEDOM OF THE PRESS REMAINS FETTERED

*A cartoon by Robert Seymour, 1836*

The production was successful beyond all expectations, and created a small sensation in society and the press. A second performance in a larger theatre was called for, and given on behalf of charity. A further play, Beaumont and Fletcher's *Elder Brother*, was produced later in the year.

During October he was busy with "The Cricket on the Hearth," and with the preparation for *The Daily News*, as the new paper was to be called. The story-writing did not go at all well; the exhausting labours of the previous month had induced much ill-health, and Fleet Street was claiming a very great deal of his time. Preparations there did not go too smoothly. Dickens soon found himself "sick, bothered, and depressed." Never for one moment, however, did he consider abandoning the editorship.

The first number of the *Daily News* was announced for January 21st, 1846. The price was to be fivepence. (There was a heavy newspaper tax in those days.) The literary department was to be under the direction of the editor. A brilliant staff had been collected: Forster, of course, Douglas Jerrold, Mark Lemon, W. J. Fox, George Hogarth, Scott Russell, Dudley Costello, and W. H. Wills, afterwards to be so prominent in the direction of *Household Words* and *All the Year Round*. Mr. John Dickens was rescued from retirement to act as head of the reporting department. Charles Dickens was, it goes without saying, working like fury. As editor his salary was to be £2,000 a year. He probably earned a year's salary during the few weeks he was connected with the paper.

Political, social, and literary London was excited over the project. Editorial London experienced some alarm; even the august *Times*, it is said, was not without anxiety as to the effect of this new journal upon its standing. The *Daily News*, with Dickens at its back, Charles Dickens, "than whom there was no more strenuous and commanding figure in the England of Queen Victoria's reign," might easily eclipse all rivals.

The first number dissipated all fears. The *Times* breathed again. Dickens was not England's supreme editor. The

K

*Daily News* would not become the national organ. All of
which Dickens had by this time realized.

On Monday, the 9th of February, "tired to death and quite
worn out," he resigned his editorship. More than a week
previously he had intimated to Forster that he wanted to
talk over leaving the paper, going abroad, and writing a
new book. On Saturday, February 7th, Dickens, his wife,
Georgina Hogarth, Forster, Jerrold and Maclise forgathered
at the Bull Inn at Rochester, and during a week-end spent
in wandering round the old familiar scenes, the momentous
decision was taken. As "Pictures from Italy," or as they
were called, "Travelling Sketches—Written on the Road,"
had commenced in the first number of the *Daily News*,
Dickens could not at once sever all connection with the
paper; but all agreed that the "earliest possible departure
from it was desirable." Actually, he continued to contribute
articles and letters for just over four months.

Thanks to Forster, who had stepped heroically into the
editorial chair, the paper survived. It survives still, its
present name being the *News-Chronicle*.

Dickens had to comfort him, in what must have been a
profoundly disappointing and humiliating experience, the
thought that "The Cricket on the Hearth, a Fairy Tale
of Home," had been a great success, its sale being twice as
great as that of the "Carol" or "The Chimes." It deserved
to be a success; John Peerybingle is altogether lovely, and
the beautiful deception practised by Caleb Plummer on his
blind daughter, who "never knew the ceilings were dis-
coloured, walls blotched . . . wood rotting, paper peeling
off . . . that sorrow and faintheartedness were in the
house . . . [that] they had a master, cold, exacting, and
uninterested," is exquisitely tender pathos. Tilly is deliciously
funny, and so is Mrs. Fielding; and the homely scenes are
painted with a true sympathetic touch. The story is quite
impossible, but then, is it not a fairy tale?

An author, however, finds his satisfaction in the creation
of a book, not in the contemplation of its success. At any
rate Dickens did; and one may imagine that during the
sadly distressed early months of this year none of his published

Oᴘᴘʀᴇssɪᴏɴ ᴏғ ᴛʜᴇ Pʀᴇss: Dʀɪᴠɪɴɢ ʜᴏᴍᴇ ᴛʜᴇ ɴᴇᴄᴇssɪᴛʏ ғᴏʀ ᴛʜᴇ
ᴛᴏᴛᴀʟ ᴀʙᴏʟɪᴛɪᴏɴ ᴏғ ᴛʜᴇ sᴛᴀᴍᴘ ᴅᴜᴛʏ ᴏɴ ɴᴇᴡsᴘᴀᴘᴇʀs

*A cartoon by Robert Seymour, 1836*

works could give him much consolation. He was determined to leave England. A new tale was seething in his mind; in long night walks he was painfully conceiving it, and afterwards he would "joyfully" write it in Switzerland. Yet he was so unsettled at the moment that he actually inquired into his chances of being appointed a paid London magistrate.

The 31st of May saw him en route for Lausanne, in Switzerland, where a pretty little rose-bowered house called Rosemont, situated on the hill above the lake, was taken for six months, with the option of a further six. Before his departure he had been entertained at many farewell dinners, at one of which he made a remark which sums up the whole of one side of his character. "Nothing," said Lord Melbourne, "is ever so good as it is thought." "And nothing," quickly replied Dickens, "so bad." The significance of that retort may be interpreted variously.

The family party, now enlarged by a sixth child, Alfred Tennyson, born the previous October, and shepherded again by the same "brave courier" Roche, travelled via Ostend, Verviers, Coblentz and Mannheim to Strasbourg. Part of the journey was by boat along the Rhine, in beautiful weather. From Strasbourg they trained to Basle; from Basle to Lausanne they travelled in three coaches, and spent three days over the trip. Neuchâtel greatly tempted Dickens, but he decided against it. When he began to write, he would want streets, and Lausanne was only twenty-four miles from Geneva, where sufficient could surely be found.

Lausanne, then as now, was a literary centre as well as a holiday resort, and Dickens soon noticed the abundance of bookshops. He noticed, too, the difficulty of getting about the town, the "streets going up and down hill abruptly and steeply," but the scenery and the countryside could not "be praised too highly, or reported too beautiful." All who have lingered on the banks of the beautiful lake of Geneva and climbed the heights above Lausanne will agree.

The English colony welcomed him very cordially, so that he quickly felt at home. Among those whom he met were some who were to rank among his dearest friends, especially

Mr. and Mrs. de Cerjat, and the Hon. Richard and Mrs. Watson, of Rockingham Castle, Northants, whose home is accurately described as Chesney Wold in "Bleak House."

Within a fortnight work had begun. "An odd shadowy undefined idea . . . that I could connect a great battle-field with my little Christmas story" had taken possession of him. All he was waiting for was the little bronze figures that had to stand on his writing desk before he could compose freely. Meanwhile, he had been far from idle; arrears of correspondence were being cleared off, a paper was being written on Ragged Schools, Miss Burdett Coutts was being advised as to her charities, and a children's version of the New Testament was being prepared for the family's use. Prisons and asylums were being visited; and during the summer he was to become greatly interested in some blind deaf-mutes whom a German doctor was teaching to communicate with the outer world, a feat hitherto considered impossible.

On June 27th he began "Dombey and Son" and continued steadily at it, liking it very much, for a month, breaking off then for a brief mountaineering expedition to Chamonix. He found this place, and Mont Blanc, and the Mer de Glace "above and beyond one's wildest expectations," and could not "imagine anything in nature more stupendous or sublime." This capacity for perpetual surprise must have been of rare help to Dickens. When one is liable to depression or ill-health there is no tonic like a sight or a sensation that drives from the mind every gloomy thought. Dickens retained this capacity throughout life; it is one of the secrets of his extraordinary range and volume of activities.

The Christmas story had been for the time put off, though Dickens had sent home to Forster a suggested title, "The Battle of Life." Nor was "Dombey" resumed until well on in August, the social amenities of Lausanne, at which fresh English visitors were constantly arriving, proving so attractive. Before beginning work in earnest for the winter, there was a great three-day excursion to the Great St. Bernard Pass. There were eleven in the party, with two servants; the Dickenses, Georgina Hogarth, the de Cerjats, the Watsons, two

### THE POOR MAN'S FRIEND

*A cartoon of the Hungry 'Forties by John Leech, 1841. Reproduced by permission of the proprietors of "Punch"*

late and charming arrivals, the Ladies Taylor, and Mr. Haldimand; all "wonderfully unanimous and cheerful."

Travelling vîa Bex and Martigny, the party made the final ascent by mule. Dickens was greatly impressed by the awesome desolation of the scenery and the situation, so much so that next morning, being waked at 5 a.m. by the sound of organ music and chanting in the chapel, he "thought for a moment I had died in the night and passed into the unknown world." "But," he said, "for the Saint Bernard holy fathers and convent in themselves, I am sorry to say that they are a piece of as sheer humbug as we ever learnt to believe in, in our young days."

However, "The brother who carved at our supper could speak some English, and had just had 'Pickwick' given to him!" It was a great pity, thought Dickens, that he had not another of his books with him to present to the monk, who would never understand "Pickwick" and would think him a humbug.

So far at Lausanne, as Forster says, one can see "in all respects at his best the great observer and humorist; interested in everything that commended itself to a thoroughly earnest and eagerly enquiring nature; popular beyond measure with all having intercourse with him; the centre, the very soul, of social enjoyment; letting nothing escape a vision that was not more keen than kindly, and even when apparently most idle, never idle in the sense of his art, but adding day by day to experiences that widened its range and gave freer and healthier play to an imagination always busily at work, alert and active in a singular degree, and that seemed to be quite untiring."

Yet was he happy? While the novelty lasted, at odd moments he could forget; but the history of this and succeeding months and years emphatically denies that he found any lasting happiness.

A new form of uneasiness was attacking him even during this seemingly gay and carefree time. All sorts of ideas for stories were flitting through his mind, without his being able definitely to pin them down, or to decide upon any of them. Thus, the germs of both "The Haunted Man," his

1848 Christmas story, and "A Tale of Two Cities" came to him that summer at Lausanne. As he himself said, "Invention, thank God, seems the easiest thing in the world," but he found an extraordinary difficulty in getting on quickly. In particular, he had "such a preposterous sense of the ridiculous . . . as to be constantly requiring to restrain myself from launching into extravagances in the height of my enjoyment." Again, signs of an unhappily preoccupied mind.

It was not now the case of a brain tired by overwork. He had written little for two years. He put his unsettlement down, indeed, to his long rest, and to his lack of London streets.

He craved for the old familiar distractions. It sounds exactly like a mind adrift, rudderless; in the home port alone could it find relief. "I don't seem able," he wrote to Forster early in September, "to get rid of my spectres unless I can lose them in crowds." What spectres? The imaginary, or the real?

A burst of work and the reading of Number I of "Dombey and Son" to his friends at Lausanne somewhat restored his confidence; and in that moment there developed the idea, at present less than half serious, which was later to result in the fiery orgies of public entertainment which swept innumerable audiences off their feet, and broke down and killed the entertainer. "I was thinking the other day," he wrote, "that in these days of lecturings and readings, a great deal of money might possibly be made (if it were not infra dig.) by one's having Readings of one's own books. . . ."

Soon fresh anxieties and despairs began to crowd upon him. He almost abandoned the Christmas book. He threw aside the first scene and wrestled wildly with an idea that would not come straight. He got it at last, and started again. When a third of the book was written, he again almost gave it up. To manage two stories was an impossibility. He was fearful of wearing himself out.

Dickens fearful of wearing himself out! This is indeed a new man; the Dickens of half a dozen, even four years ago, would not have spoken or thought thus. It was not that he was growing old; he was only thirty-four, a young man who ought to be just rising to the very prime of his strength and powers. It was not age.

To detail the hesitations, doubtings, anxieties, and agonies of spirit of the ensuing months would be merely to repeat what has already been said. They may be summed up in two of his own sentences. "I am sick, giddy, and capriciously despondent. I have bad nights; am full of disquietude and anxiety; and am constantly haunted by the idea that I am wasting the marrow of the larger book, and ought to be at rest."

He fled twice to Geneva, alone, and felt better for it. Meanwhile Forster cheered him by announcing a good sale for Number I of "Dombey and Son": 12,000 copies more than "Chuzzlewit's" opening number had achieved. Yet in his very next letter Dickens sent the conclusion of the "Battle of Life" with the despairing words, "I really do not know what this story is worth." Forster's criticisms led to considerable revision.

During his second visit to Geneva there occurred a small revolution which greatly interested and distracted him, especially in its more comic aspects. "Cannon," he said, "were fired everywhere except at the opposite party"; and he was especially delighted at the blow to the "preposterous, insolent, little aristocracy of Geneva." It is just as well that Dickens did not live in the time of the French Revolution; he would assuredly have become either a Tom Paine or a Scarlet Pimpernel.

The third number of "Dombey and Son" was completed by November 9th. A week later the whole family moved to Paris. By the 21st, Dickens was ranging the streets of Paris, searching for an eligible house, jumping for joy because Forster had secured the assistance of Stanfield and Maclise in addition to the regularly employed illustrators, John Leech and Doyle, for "The Battle of Life," and writing home suggestions for a new periodical. The next day he secured "the most ridiculous, extraordinary, unparalleled, and preposterous" house in the whole world, No. 48, Rue de Courcelles, Faubourg St. Honoré, a cross between a "baby-house, a 'shades,' a haunted castle, and a mad kind of a clock." For the moment everything was glorious; Dombey was booming, the house was delicious, the streets of Paris "wonderfully attractive."

Almost at once came bad news; his well-loved sister, Fanny, wife of Henry Burnett, was reported beyond doubt in consumption. Dickens was terribly upset. Consumption was then the dreadfully incurable disease; it was only a case of waiting for the end. In this instance there was not long to wait; Fanny Burnett passed away in the spring of the following year.

Soon he was arranging to leave Paris for London, three months earlier than his previous intention. A brief dash across the Channel brought mingled vexation and pleasure. "The Battle of Life" had been dramatized, and Mr. and Mrs. Keeley were to present it at the Lyceum on December 21st. Dickens rushed over to London on the 15th, to find all the cast, except the Keeleys, so unutterably bad and slack that he had to read the whole thing through to them. However, it went much better than he expected, and at the same time the book triumphed to the extent of 23,000 copies on the day of publication.

It was on this visit, which only lasted eight days, that Dickens arranged for a cheap edition of his works, in weekly parts at three-halfpence a number. To this edition he prefixed the following simple and moving words: "This cheap edition of my books is dedicated to the English people, in whose approval, if the books be true in spirit, they will live, and out of whose memory, if they be false, they will very soon die." He was quietly confident as to the result, and his confidence has been amply justified. It is above all the spirit of his books which keeps them alive.

On his return to Paris, he threw himself energetically into Number V of "Dombey," the account of the death of little Paul. In January 1847, Forster visited him. It is typical of Dickens that he arranged carefully for his friend's comfort at every stage of the journey on French soil, and wrote him a long letter in his excellent French telling him exactly what to expect. Into a fortnight the two crowded "every variety of sight-seeing, prisons, palaces, theatres, hospitals, the Morgue and the Lazare . . . the Louvre, Versailles, St. Cloud, and all the spots made memorable by the first revolution." They witnessed at least nine plays;

they supped with Alexandre Dumas, met Théophile Gautier, Lamartine, Scribe, David d'Angers, Eugène Sue, Alphonse Karr, and Amadée Pichot. They called upon Chateaubriand, and Victor Hugo, who received Dickens "with infinite courtesy and grace."

A fortnight later Dickens had to tear over to England to supply two additional pages to the number of "Dombey" then in the press, he having miscalculated the amount; a strange error for him, who was wont formerly to be accurate to the very line. Scarcely had he arrived back in Paris than he was recalled by the illness of his eldest son, at that time, owing to the munificence of Miss Burdett Coutts, a scholar at King's College School.

He did not return to Paris, but remained in London. Devonshire Terrace being still let, he took up residence first at the Victoria Hotel, Euston Square, and later in Chester Place, Regent's Park, where his seventh child, Sydney Smith Haldimand, was born on April 18th.

Throughout this year and into the beginning of 1848 the writing of "Dombey and Son" steadily continued. In the spring Dickens took his wife to Brighton to convalesce, and while there pushed forward in his leisure time a grand theatrical venture for the assistance of Leigh Hunt, who was in poverty, and John Poole, a dramatic author also fallen on evil days. Owing to the granting to Leigh Hunt by Lord John Russell of a civil pension of £200 a year, performances in London were cancelled, but not the scheme. Nearly all the players of the previous company were gathered together, and Cruikshank, Augustus Egg, and George Henry Lewes were added to their number. After the usual rehearsal experiences Dickens, for the first time in his life, went "on tour" in the provinces. *Every Man in His Humour*, supported by two farces, was played in Manchester on July 26th, 1847, and in Liverpool on July 28th, at both places with huge success. Maclise nicknamed the company "the splendid strollers," and the nickname stuck.

The receipts were large, but the expenses heavy, so the net profits fell below the £500 which had been hoped for. Immediately, Dickens "startled" Forster by proposing to raise the additional amount by writing an account of the tour by Mrs. Gamp! He actually wrote two sketches, but the necessary help from the artists was not forthcoming, and the project dropped through.

Just before the "tour" Dickens had met in London at Gore House the famous Danish teller of fairy stories, Hans Christian Andersen. The two liked each other at once, and the meeting proved a prelude to a long and close friendship. In a delightful letter written to Andersen soon afterwards, Dickens said, "Whatever you do, do not stop writing, because we cannot bear to lose a single one of your thoughts. They are too true and simply beautiful to be kept safe only in your own head."

For the summer months Dickens went, according to old custom, to Broadstairs, but that pleasant little fishing village was growing popular, and losing its attractiveness for him. He craved the noise and bustle of streets, but he detested street music, and Broadstairs was being overrun by vagrant musicians. "Unless it pours with rain," he wrote, "I cannot write half-an-hour without the most excruciating organs, fiddles, bells, or glee singers. There is a violin of the most torturing kind under the window now (time, ten in the morning) and an Italian box of music on the steps—both in full blast."

At Broadstairs a Christmas story was begun, but the claims of "Dombey" were so pressing that it was put aside, not without doubts and regrets. "I am," he told Forster, "BLOWED if I know what to do." Forster knew all right; and for once his advice on such a question was followed.

The year closed with two big public meetings; the first at Leeds, where he took the chair at a meeting of the Mechanics' Society on December 1st, and spoke powerfully on education; the second at Glasgow, where on the 28th he formally opened the Athenæum, on which occasion "The Inimitable did wonders. His grace, elegance and eloquence enchanted all beholders." So he wrote to Georgina, and the description seems substantially true. During his stay in Scotland he revisited Edinburgh, where there was a state lunch and a public dinner. He learned to his great distress

"Not So Very Unreasonable! Eh?"

John (Lord John Russell): My Mistress says she hopes you won't call a meeting of her creditors; but if you will leave your Bill in the usual way, it shall be properly attended to.

*A cartoon on the Chartist Petition, 1848. Reproduced by permission of the proprietors of "Punch"*

that James Sheridan Knowles, the Irish dramatist, had just gone bankrupt. Immediately plans were put in hand for more "splendid strollings."

Late in March 1848 the writing of "Dombey and Son" was concluded. The last two numbers appeared in April, and at the same time the book was published in volume form.

Dickens had taken "infinite pains" with this story. He had consulted Forster continuously throughout its composition. Its characters had taken a stronger hold upon him than any save those of "The Old Curiosity Shop." He had suffered grievously over the death of little Paul Dombey, spending the night after he had written the chapter containing it wandering "restlessly . . . with a heavy heart," through the streets of Paris. He had taken more than usual care over the illustrations.

In more than one sense he was amply repaid. He believed himself to have done well. His friends and his readers were overwhelmed by it. Thackeray, whose masterpiece, "Vanity Fair," was appearing in monthly numbers at the same time, rushed down to the offices of *Punch* with a copy of Number V of "Dombey" in his pocket, and, throwing it down on the editor's table, exclaimed, "There's no writing against such power as this—one has no chance! Read the chapter describing young Paul's death; it is unsurpassed—it is stupendous." Lord Jeffrey, of course, "cried and sobbed" over the death of Paul Dombey, and declared, "Since the divine Nelly was found dead on her humble couch, beneath the snow and the ivy, there has been nothing like the actual dying of that sweet Paul." "Paul's death," wrote Dickens, "has amazed Paris." Another tribute of a different type, but equally evident of esteem, may well be quoted. "Lawk, ma'am," said a charwoman to Mrs. Hogarth, "I thought that three or four men must have put together 'Dombey!'"

Financially, the book was a very great success. On the first half year, after receiving from his publishers, Messrs. Bradbury and Evans, £100 per month on account, Dickens made a profit of £2,200. From this time onwards he was free from financial fears or embarrassments.

"Dealings with the Firm of Dombey and Son" is a curiously

uneven book. Partly, no doubt, this is to be accounted for
by the fact that it was written in so many different places,
Lausanne, Geneva, Paris, London, Brighton, and Broadstairs. Dickens himself confessed that, while in his fancy
he knew "every stair in the little midshipman's house, and
could swear to every pew in the church in which Florence
was married, or to every young gentleman's bedstead in
Dr. Blimber's establishment," he confusedly imagined Captain
Cuttle hiding from Mrs. Macstinger among the Swiss moun-
tains. Partly, also, one may attribute this unevenness to
Dickens' distressed state of mind during at least the earlier
period of its composition.

A further reason lies in the early incidence of the most
powerful scene in the book, the death of Paul Dombey.
Readers at the time felt that their feelings had been worked
up to such a pitch that whatever followed seemed rather in
the nature of anti-climax. More, Paul's death seemed to
remove the mainspring of the story. Dickens himself, though
he intended this early decease from the start, found difficulty
in getting into the swing of the "new vein" of the story.

Looking at the book to-day, one can criticize it more as
a whole, and perhaps more dispassionately. It is with the
death of little Paul as with the death of little Nell: one feels
it, or one does not, according to temperament; and to-day the
majority of temperaments are inclined not to feel it, though
one does hear of listeners having to switch off the wireless
during the reading of this scene because their emotions overcome them. As a whole, the book is uneven because, while
Dickens created a large number of interesting and amusing
characters, he quite failed of his main purpose.

The theme of the book was to have been Pride. It had
a moral purpose, as had "Martin Chuzzlewit." Whereas,
however, Dickens succeeded magnificently with Mr. Pecksniff,
he failed signally with Mr. Dombey, and still more so with
Edith Granger, the second Mrs. Dombey. There is, indeed,
an air of unreality pervading the whole of the main story,
though curiously enough its plot is the likeliest one he had as
yet conceived; and this unreality degenerates not infrequently
into positive dreariness after the marriage of Mr. Dombey

with Edith. There may be some people who can believe in Mr. James Carker, and in the long-drawn-out account of Edith's mental drift towards elopement; but even their belief can hardly redeem that part of the story from dullness.

Mr. Chesterton, as always, hits the nail on the head when he says that "the story itself is probable; it is the treatment that makes it unreal"; and he goes on to suggest that Dickens "could only make his characters probable if he was allowed to make them impossible. Give him licence to say and do anything, and he could create beings as vivid as our own aunts and uncles. Keep him to likelihood and he could not tell the plainest tale so as to make it seem likely." Surely that is the whole art of characterization in story-telling. It is every author's constant purpose to depart so subtly from likelihood that he creates the impression of perfect naturalness.

There is no character in "Dombey and Son" which dominates the book. Mr. Dombey ought to do so, but he only casts a chill over it. His daughter Florence, like her brother a pathetic child study, is deliberately not made a powerful character. Edith Granger is a puppet from start to finish. Mr. Toots, Major Bagstock and Captain Cuttle probably lay chief claims to our affections, though Susan Nipper does not come far behind, if indeed she be behind at all. Of these four, Toots—dear, stupid, shy Toots, that unfortunate product of Dr. Blimber's educational methods who "when he began to have whiskers he left off having brains"—is the finest creation.

It may safely be asserted that Dickens never touched any laughable creature with more kindliness than Toots. Captain Cuttle with his famous "when found make a note" habit of misquotation, and his real kindheartedness, is another splendid sketch of the honest and deserving poor, and he gathers round him fit companions in Solomon Gills and Jack Bunsby. Incidentally his Little Wooden Midshipman, for so long an adornment of Leadenhall Street, has been moved to the Minories, and may be seen inside the shop at No. 123. Susan Nipper, one may be quite certain, made a perfect wife for Toots, and looked after him and his children with the same sharp devotion that she looked after Florence Dombey.

Major Bagstock, says Mr. Chesterton, "is mountainously

exaggerated, but we all feel that we have met him at Brighton."
Or at Leamington, where he played so important a part, or at
Cheltenham, or wherever else retired army men are found in
lodgings and boarding houses, recalling their past exploits,
real and imaginary. The major is very real indeed, and if
his iteration of "Joey B., Sir . . . Old Joe, Sir . . . old
J. Bagstock, Sir, is tough, Sir, tough, and de-vilish sly!"
grows wearisome, it is nothing to the weariness one experiences
in the company of the ordinary club-room bore.

Paul Dombey is a quaint unusual child, but he does not
remain in the story long enough to stamp his living personality
very deeply upon it. He is, nevertheless, the occasion for
two superb school pictures. Mrs. Pipchin is Mrs. Roylance
of Little College Street, Camden Town, picked up bodily and
given an establishment in Brighton, and no doubt Dickens'
life with that lady is described with a high degree of accuracy
and a somewhat heightened intensity. Whence Dickens
culled Mr. Blimber is more doubtful, though Chichester House,
Chichester Terrace, Brighton, in which a Rev. George Proctor,
D.D., had an academy from 1839 to 1846 has been claimed as
the original of his school. There has been the inevitable
search for the "originals" of the characters of "Dombey and
Son." Two are certain, Mrs. Pipchin and the Little Wooden
Midshipman; success in the search for the rest depends chiefly
upon the optimism and credulity of the searcher.

Among Dickens' pictures of schools that of the Charitable
Grinders must not be forgotten. He had probably learnt a
lot about charity schools when he was enquiring into the
Ragged Schools Movement, and could guess the effect of such
an institution upon Rob the Grinder, alias Biler, the son of
Polly Toodle, Paul Dombey's wet-nurse.

There are the usual delightfully drawn minor characters,
among whom must not be forgotten Miss Tox and Mrs. Chick,
nor any of the Toodles, nor Miss Blimber with her preposterous analyses of character, nor the plaintive Mrs. Wickham,
"a waiter's wife—which would seem equivalent to being any
other man's widow—" nor Peach the Messenger; yet in spite
of all these one has the constant sense of frustration when
reading "Dombey and Son." Nothing is quite as it ought to

be; nothing gives the satisfaction it ought.  Everything seems
rather disjointed, rather forced.  It suggests, in short, the
work of a man whose real mind is absorbed by other and more
painful matters, but who every now and then pulls himself up
short, and determines to be really jolly and cheerful in spite
of everything, and as a start invents Walter Gay, who is as
nice a youngster as one could wish to meet, if only he were not
so abominably and inveterately cheerful.  But all the time
his mind keeps eluding him; and it will be noticed that a story
begun on the theme of pride drifts into one on the theme of
married unhappiness.

One small incident in connection with "Dombey and Son"
deserves record.  A reviewer on the staff of the *Sun* contributed a particularly sympathetic notice of the book, which
so pleased and gratified Dickens that he broke an invariable
rule, and wrote to the paper to express his thanks.  Thus
commenced a long friendship with Mr. Charles Kent, the
reviewer in question, afterwards to become one of "Dickens'
Young Men," and to whom Dickens' last letter was written.

Directly "Dombey and Son" was concluded Dickens threw
himself again with fervour into amateur theatricals.  Shakespeare's house at Stratford-on-Avon was for sale, and a
committee had been formed to secure it for preservation.
The theatrical performances were to endow a curatorship of
the house, which it was proposed should be held in the first
instance by Sheridan Knowles.  Actually, the Stratford
Town Council acquired the house, and the curatorship scheme
had to be abandoned; but the tour, planned and executed on
a much larger scale than the one of the previous year, was
triumphant in every way.

*The Merry Wives of Windsor* was chosen, after much discussion and trial in rehearsals of several other plays, to
alternate with *Every Man in His Humour*, and a farce Dickens
had acted in Doctors' Commons days, *Love, Law, and Physick*,
was also prepared.  Save for Douglas Jerrold, Dickens had
practically the same company as before, with one brilliant
addition, Mrs. Cowden Clarke, author of the famous
*Concordance* to Shakespeare, whom he had persuaded to take
the part of Mistress Quickly in the *Merry Wives*.

Between April 15th and July 20th nine performances were given, the first in London, the last in Glasgow, the others at Birmingham, Manchester, Liverpool, and Edinburgh. Birmingham and Glasgow had two nights each, and in May, a second London performance, at the Haymarket Theatre, was attended by Queen Victoria and the Prince Consort. The total receipts were £2,551.

Dickens, who played as before Bobadil in *Every Man in His Humour*, took the part of Justice Shallow in the *Merry Wives;* and was stage manager, publicity agent, and everything else. "Everywhere," says Forster, "he was the leading figure. In the enjoyment as in the labour he was first. His animal spirits, unresting and supreme, were the attraction of rehearsal at morning, and of the stage at night. . . . There seemed to be no need for rest to that wonderful vitality."

Two days after the last performance, Dickens wrote from Devonshire Terrace to Mrs. Cowden Clarke, "I have no energy whatever, I am very miserable. . . . A real house like this is insupportable, after that canvas screen wherein I was so happy," and, in a postscript, "I am completely *blasé*— literally used up. I am dying for excitement. Is it possible that nobody can suggest anything to make my heart beat violently and my hair stand on end—but no!"

A very illuminating letter.

There followed a real summer holiday at Broadstairs, marred only by a pony-chaise accident to Mrs. Dickens which had, happily, no serious results. The pony bolted down a steep hill, "Kate inside rending the Isle of Thanet with her screams," and crashed at the bottom, fortunately leaving the chaise on the bank.

Towards the end of August he wrote that he was "a mentally matooring of the Christmas book." This was "The Haunted Man," begun the year before and now completed for Christmas publication and dramatization. It was a considerable success in both forms, and is far the poorest of the series.

At the same time Dickens was "mentally matooring" the greatest of all his works, and something very different from all he had written before, "David Copperfield."

## CHAPTER X

*"I wrote a story with a purpose growing, not remotely, out of my experience."*—DAVID COPPERFIELD.

*". . . no one can ever believe this Narrative, in the reading, more than I have believed it in the writing."*—CHARLES DICKENS.

*". . . like many fond parents, I have in my heart of hearts a favourite child.   And his name is DAVID COPPERFIELD."*—CHARLES DICKENS.

No man can sit down to write a true autobiography. He knows too much about himself, and he knows too little.  Because he knows too much, he will, however much he tries to be scrupulously accurate, suppress essential facts; because he knows too little, he will inevitably romance in parts.  However keen his judgment of other people, it invariably breaks down when he tries to assess himself.

Mercifully, Charles Dickens never wrote his autobiography. He began it, and penned a marvellous description of his unhappy days in childhood.  Then, no doubt realizing the impossibility of the task, he abandoned it.  Instead, he wrote "David Copperfield," which is far better.  Had he left to posterity an autobiography, posterity would have been teased to all eternity by the baffling and insoluble problem of separating the fact from the fiction.  As it is, posterity has been quite sufficiently troubled over the sifting of fact from fiction in "David Copperfield"; but, for the cool-headed at any rate, there is always this consolation, that "David Copperfield" is, after all, only a story.

There is, too, a further consolation, and perhaps a better

one; if there is not in "David Copperfield" all Dickens' life, there is certainly all Dickens.

Few great men have ever revealed themselves more fully to the world than did Dickens. Everything he did and said throughout an incredibly active life revealed something of the man. He was incapable of a colourless or neutral action. He was equally incapable of a colourless book; every one he wrote is a forceful expression of his vivid and many-sided personality. He wrote, too, an enormous number of letters, many of very considerable length. Before he was thirty-five years of age he was writing on an average twelve letters a day. A goodly proportion of these has been preserved; and in all save the briefest business communications there is stamped some impress of his personality.

There are three main difficulties confronting any biographer who attempts to assess that personality. There is an over-abundance of evidence; to write a detailed life of Dickens, complete with his letters, his speeches, and analyses of his books, would require a dozen volumes this size. Second, that evidence reveals an extraordinarily complex character. One can, of course, sum him up in a general sentence, as has been done; he was compact of merits and of faults, both magnified by a colossal energy. But analysis of the evidence reveals such a tangle of apparent contradictions and inconsistencies that it is extremely difficult to reduce it to a coherent picture. Third, a very great deal of that evidence is in Dickens' own words, and therefore suffers, and more than ordinarily, from the radical defect of all autobiography.

Dickens wrote always the truth—as he saw it; but the very fact that he saw so much of it, and saw it from so unusual an angle, makes it most difficult to disentangle from his writings the truth as any one of us would see it. This is every whit the same in his letters as in his books. There was never a writer who possessed more abundantly the art of presenting a vividly accurate picture by the conscious use of inaccurate detail. When he desired it for his purpose he was, of course, meticulously accurate, so much so that whenever a critic attempted to cast aspersion on that accuracy, he was mercilessly driven out of the lists by a torrent of proof. When, on the other hand, Dickens desired inaccuracy for his purpose, he could use it just as effectively. The result in either case was the same; a perfect picture of what happened.

He used this inaccuracy constantly in his letters. During his first reading tour, for example, he wrote of his manager that "at Clifton last night, a torrent of five hundred shillings bore Arthur away, pounded him against the wall, flowed on to the seats over his body, and damaged his best dress suit. All to his unspeakable joy." One can imagine the scene perfectly, but it is impossible to take the words literally. That sort of descriptive writing occurs in almost all his letters.

One is perpetually reminded when reading Dickens' novels and letters of the story of one of J. M. W. Turner's gorgeous paintings. "You never saw a sunset like that," objected a prosaic fellow on looking at it. "No," was the quick retort, "but don't you wish you could?"

In "David Copperfield" one gets an epitome of the evidence concerning Charles Dickens. There is in this book sufficient of his real life for one to form a just estimate of its early struggles, its heroic endeavours, its triumphant march to success. There is sufficient of the story of his supreme adventure in love to judge of its effect on him. From the development of David Copperfield's lovable, weak, wayward, strong, energetic and aspiring personality one can form a very good idea of the character of the man Charles Dickens. David Copperfield stops over and over again to review his life and to state the ideals which are inspiring it. Every one of these statements is absolutely true of Charles Dickens. Of these the best is as follows:

"I will only add, to what I have already written of my perseverance at this time of my life, and of a patient and continuous energy which then began to be matured in me, and which I know to be the strong part of my character, if it have any strength at all, that there, on looking back, I find the source of my success. I have been very fortunate in worldly matters; many men have worked much harder, and not succeeded half so well; but I never could have done what I have done, without the habits of punctuality, order, and diligence, without the determination to concentrate myself on one subject at a time, no matter how quickly its successor should come upon its heels, which I then formed. Heaven knows I write this, in no spirit of self-laudation. The man who reviews his own life, as I do mine, in going on here, from page to page, had need to have been a good man indeed, if he would be spared the sharp consciousness of many talents neglected, many opportunities wasted, many erratic and perverted feelings constantly at war within his breast, and defeating him. I do not hold one natural gift, I dare say, that I have not abused. My meaning simply is, that whatever I have tried to do in life, I have tried with all my heart to do well; that whatever I have devoted myself to, I have devoted myself to completely; that in great aims and in small, I have always been thoroughly in earnest. I have never believed it possible that any natural or improved ability can claim immunity from the companionship of the steady, plain, hardworking qualities, and hope to gain its end. There is no such thing as such fulfilment on this earth. Some happy talent, and some fortunate opportunity, may form the two sides of the ladder on which some men mount, but the rounds of that ladder must be made of stuff to stand wear and tear; and there is no substitute for thorough-going, ardent, and sincere earnestness. Never to put one hand to anything, on which I could throw my whole self; and never to affect depreciation of my work, whatever it was; I find, now, to have been my golden rules."

If it be objected that the story of David Copperfield ends while the hero is still a young man, the answer is that in one very real sense the history of Charles Dickens ends with "David Copperfield." He came to the climax of his powers with the writing of this story. His astonishing vitality carried him triumphantly through another twenty years of extraordinarily active life. It enabled him to score one of the greatest successes of Victorian journalism. It enabled him to write many more books, one of which at least, "Great Expectations," must be reckoned among his greatest. It enabled him to carry through his amazing series of public readings. But the story of the growth and development of Charles Dickens, England's greatest master of humour and pathos, ends with "David Copperfield." Hereafter it is the story of a rapidly ageing man, whose powers, though still colossal, and capable of wonderful outbursts of energy and expression, are incapable of further expansion, and are, to a careful observer, perceptibly and inevitably declining. As his sunrise was a blaze of glorious radiance, so was his sunset; but from 1850 it was definitely sunset. After that date, there was nothing new in Dickens.

In "David Copperfield" one gets something more than the story of parts of Dickens' life, and of the ideals which inspired him; one gets a glimpse into the beautiful what-might-have been, in the lovely romance of David's married life with Dora and his final sanctuary within the love and protection of Agnes Wickfield.

In a more literary sense, though still in intimate association with the story of Dickens' life, since all his books are fragments broken from that life, one has in the infinite variety of the "Copperfield" characters, of whom there are more than one hundred, the finest résumé of his range and skill as a creative artist.

Finally, in the story of the genesis and composition of "David Copperfield" one can illustrate, perhaps better than in the case of any other of the novels, the methods by which the Dickens' books were evolved.

In all things, both great and small, Dickens loved regularity and order. "Perhaps there was never a man," says Forster, "who changed places so much and habits so little." Behind all his superficial vagaries, his rushings hither and thither, there was a rigid method of life, the least disturbance from which upset and distressed him. In respect of literary composition, the story of one book is the story of all, save only "Pickwick."

He first "matured" a book, that is, beginning with a vague idea, round which soon gathered a host of other ideas, he turned things over in his mind, till by a process of rejection and clarification he had the general scheme and the main characters clearly designed. During this period of gestation he was invariably restless and uneasy. He battled with his imagination—there is no other word for it—chiefly in long, exhausting walks, frequently taken at night. Suggestions, notes, draft schemes, and questions poured in a stream upon Forster, on whose advice he relied heavily. To a not inconsiderable extent, indeed, Forster may be considered part-author of his books, as his suggestions often modified the plan of the story or the conception of a character. A notable instance of this occurred during the period when "David Copperfield" was struggling to be born; it was Forster who suggested the incorporation into the story of the autobiographical fragment Dickens had written some months previously. This suggestion altered the whole conception of "Copperfield."

When his ideas had become reasonably clear, Dickens went in search of a title and of local colour. Both searches cost him very considerable labour. The original title suggested for the book which was to become "David Copperfield" was "Mag's Diversions, Being the Personal History of MR. THOMAS MAG THE YOUNGER, of Blunderstone House." Many variations of this were tried out; the word "Adventures" was inserted and rejected and inserted again; Blunderstone House became Copperfield House, the name Copperfield being arrived at via Trotfield, Trotbury, Copperboy, and Copperstone. The name of the house was transferred to the hero, while such names as Wellbury, Flowerbury, Magbury, and Topflower were at times inserted in the title only to be discarded. Even when Copperfield had been definitely chosen as the hero's name, Dickens sent Forster a list of six detailed titles, all different from the one finally chosen. At last there emerged "The Personal History, Adventures, Experience, and Observation of David Copperfield the Younger, Of Blunderstone Rookery. (Which He never meant to be Published on any Account.)"

Probably no author was ever more scrupulously accurate over local colour, or worked more diligently to secure that accuracy, than Dickens. Even when he was writing of places he knew intimately, he would revisit them constantly if he were doubtful over details; or he would do so purely and simply to soak himself in their atmosphere. The same care was manifested over descriptions of types of life with which he was thoroughly familiar; he would fortify himself with masses of newspaper cuttings, he would fill huge notebooks with personal observations. Wherever he went, or for whatever purpose, he always devoted a large part of his time to enlarging his experience of matters intimately connected with his books. Few men can ever have explored so comprehensively or so minutely the prisons, hospitals, schools, asylums, and the common life of two continents.

Great Yarmouth became the scene of much of "David Copperfield" quite by accident. A trip to the Isle of Wight had been proposed for the autumn of 1848, but bad weather prevented it, and instead, on Dickens' suggestion, he, John Leech and Mark Lemon went to Norwich and Stanfield Hall —the latter on account of a recent dreadful murder. Norwich proved disappointing; but soon Forster, whom illness had prevented from accompanying the party, heard that "Yarmouth, sir . . . is the strangest place in the wide world: one hundred and forty-six miles of hill-less marsh between it and London. . . . I shall certainly try my hand at it." He had never been there before; and Blunderstone, a village lying some seven or eight miles from Yarmouth, was discovered and investigated on the same journey.

When Dickens actually began to write a story, he almost invariably found much difficulty in getting well started. Over and over there is the same complaint that writing is hanging fire, that he cannot get on fast; often enough that he cannot write a word. Frequently it was not until a quarter or more of the book was written that things really began to go well. Even after that there were dreadful periods when inspiration halted and depression took command.

Not at any time was composition easy. His original manuscripts, some of which may be seen in the British Museum, the Victoria and Albert Museum, and the Dickens House, show innumerable alterations and interlinings. Even when proofs arrived, alterations were still made; Mr. Dick's trouble, in "David Copperfield," did not become Charles the First's head until the proofs were being corrected. The long walks continued throughout; in the afternoon if things were going well, in the silent watches of the night if they were not. Almost always they were taken alone.

Dickens' ordinary writing hours were from about 9 a.m. to 2 p.m. They were absolutely sacred. He might "blaze away" until 3 or 4 p.m. if the mood were on him; no one dared to disturb him. The routine was practically never altered. During his earlier years he sometimes worked at night, occasionally right through the night, but gradually he settled more and more steadily to the long morning. He might have walked the streets throughout the previous night; it was no matter, the morning's composition followed. Generally, on such occasions, it was a hectic burst of writing; he had to unload his mind of the host of thoughts which had piled up during his solitary wanderings.

During his walks and while he was actually writing, Dickens lived utterly in the world of his imagination. Every scene in every detail was vividly present to him as he wrote, every incident acted itself before the eyes of his mind; frequently indeed, he physically acted, before a looking glass, what he was about to set down. His characters were all absolutely alive to him, and he bore the weight of all their emotions. He chuckled, he laughed aloud, he grew indignant or grieved, he sorrowed or wept with the creatures of his fancy.

Finally, on the completion of any book, there came a period of exhaustion and despondency, to relieve which Dickens came more and more frequently to plunge into a whirlwind of distracting activities, usually theatricals. This state, in part of course the natural result of the long strain of exhausting creative work, was often intensified in him by the sorrow of parting company with his characters, who had for so long been so real to him. This sorrow made him not infrequently linger over the conclusion of a book.

The writing of "David Copperfield" went, after the usual slowish start, more easily than had most of his previous books. The reason is plain: Dickens, writing in the first person, as Forster had suggested, quickly found himself writing in his own person. He was not having to go through the strain of projecting himself into the personalities of other people; he was expressing his own feelings and emotions. He was, in parts, writing his autobiography; he was throughout writing an idealized autobiography. David Copperfield was his dream self; he was not only what he had been and was, but also what he might have been.

Forster expressly warns readers against finding too much autobiography in "David Copperfield"; but Forster was a gruff, practical, commonsensical sort of man who probably never fully understood the meaning of the words "spiritual autobiography." He knew Dickens far better than anyone else ever did, but there were depths in Dickens that even he never fathomed, there were implications in Dickens' books that he never came near comprehending.

Though no one but Forster knew at the time of Dickens' experiences in Warren's blacking factory, there was a very general feeling among readers of "David Copperfield" when it was first published that the book contained a considerable amount of autobiographical matter. In the light of all that is known to-day of the novelist's life and character, it is possible to point certainly to various passages, both of fact and of experience, and to say that such-and-such event actually happened to Dickens himself. These passages have been fully referred to in an earlier chapter.

What becomes increasingly possible, as one reads side by side the life of Charles Dickens as recorded by his biographers, and the life of David Copperfield as recorded by himself, is to trace in the latter a true spiritual autobiography. However much the facts of Dickens' life may have been altered for the purpose of the story, his emotional and spiritual growth is very faithfully and completely recorded. "David Copperfield" is the story of Dickens' soul. In it we may see clearly the essential Dickens, the man who won, and has kept, the love of millions of readers.

In this connection, the first point to be noted is the sadness and suffering which pervade "David Copperfield." There is scarcely a life in it that is not deeply touched with tragedy. David passes through a childhood of suffering, and he has to see his beloved child-wife die. Dora can only be married to him after the tragically sudden death of her father; and she realizes before her death her pitiful inadequacy as a wife, and that she could never have made a spiritual partner to David. The good, honest, faithful Peggottys have their simple peace of life destroyed through the loss of little Em'ly. Uriah Heep's life is the record of the poor boy with ability who goes wrong because of a perverted education which has developed a strong inferiority complex. Betsey Trotwood's calm, orderly existence is menaced by a blackmailing husband, Dr. Strong's idyllic absentmindedness by a villainous sowing of suspicion. Mr. Dick, poor soul, is but a half-wit: and under the stress of events comes to realize the fact. The whole Steerforth episode is inexpressibly sad: the story of a brilliant but restlessly unsatisfied mind which brings ruin and desolation upon itself and all connected with it. The Murdstones carry gloom and misery with them wherever they go. Mrs. Copperfield dies heart-broken. The Creakles blight the lives of innumerable children. Martha is a tragic wraith. Miss Mowcher hides under a cheerful countenance an heroic struggle against the disadvantages of physical deformity. Save for the cheery little Omer and Joram group, there are no figures of importance in the story who do not experience to the full the sorrowful side of life. Agnes Wickfield suffers doubly; she suffers the slow agony of watching the gradual degeneration of her father as he gets more and more enmeshed in the web of the crafty Uriah Heep; and she has to crucify at the same time her inextinguishable love for David.

Even Mr. Micawber—greatest comic figure in English literature since Falstaff—is, like Falstaff, tragic. Mr. Micawber is no mere figure of fun; his is the terribly true picture of the man of ability who, as Mr. Chesterton observed, is "too great to succeed." Mrs. Micawber is perfectly right; Wilkins Micawber has exceptional abilities, and all they need is a suitable soil in which to flourish. As she said also, however, those abilities needed room, and there never was room enough for them in England. Dickens has been much blamed for making Mr. Micawber a success in Australia, but surely his instinct was in this instance absolutely right?

In a young, crude colony, peopled with the descendants of ex-convicts and with simple emigrant folk, what more natural than that Wilkins Micawber, a man of presence and of learning, possessing an inimitably impressive literary style and an unrivalled knowledge of the law, should become a District Magistrate and a "distinguished fellow-colonist and townsman of Port Middlebay"? One has only to read actual American or British colonial newspapers of this period to realize how likely was this success of his.

Traddles may perhaps be considered somewhat of an exception to the general rule that tragedy afflicts all lives in David Copperfield, yet even he had to pass through a much-beaten and tearful childhood, was disappointed of his expectations and had to start life with only fifty pounds, and so had a long, hard struggle to make his way in the law, and had to wait many years before he could afford to marry the "dearest girl in the world."

The second point to be noted is that all the tragedy springs directly out of the characters of the persons in the story. It is no question of poor humans being made the sport of the gods; each one who suffers brings that suffering upon himself or herself. "David Copperfield" is a record of the results of human fallibility and weakness; even for the defects of their good qualities people must pay the penalty. David's ardent impulsiveness, Dora's childlike evasion of life, little Em'ly's desire to be a lady, Uriah Heep's insatiable ambition to succeed, Mr. Wickfield's absorption in his one motive, Agnes Wickfield's unlimited capacity for self-sacrifice, Betsey Trotwood's mistake in falling in love with the wrong man, Dr. Strong's absentmindedness, his wife's simplicity, Steerforth's fickleness, Mrs. Steerforth's pride, Rosa Dartle's jealous love, Mr. Micawber's grandiloquent ideas and inconsequential optimism, all bring in their train their penalties, and those penalties fall, not upon themselves alone, but cause suffering also for others. "David Copperfield" was written by a man who had lost all his illusions about human nature, who saw clearly that our follies and our fallibilities are the main cause of all our misfortunes.

But—and herein lies the greatness of the conception of

L

the story and a main key to Dickens' character—it was written by a man who loved human nature all the more because of his keen perception of its weaknesses and the sorrows those bring in their train. It was written, too, by a man who, the more he lost his illusions, the less he lost hope. Dickens never lost hope, never could lose hope, in human nature, in the ultimate triumph of courage and cleanly endeavour, and in the defeat and bafflement of all things ugly and evil. The nineteenth century has often been called the century of hope; Charles Dickens was the supreme optimist of that optimistic century.

He remained an optimist because nothing could ever rob him of his belief in the essential goodness of humanity, because he saw so clearly that environment and indiscipline, both remedial faults, were so largely responsible for people's unhappiness and misery.

In spite of all its sadness and suffering, "David Copperfield" is not a tragedy. It moves steadily and naturally to a peaceful and harmonious close in which wrongs are set right, suffering is put an end to, thoughts of bitterness are seen to die away, steadfast courage and determination gain their due reward, and there is "on earth peace, goodwill toward men." Things would not happen like that in real life? Perhaps not; but that is how Dickens would have life move, and he cannot abandon his hope that that is how it might move. In a story centred in his own life, who shall deny him the satisfaction of weaving the epic of the glorious what-might-have-been, and of the still more glorious what-ought-to-be? His own life had in it sufficient of the heroic, his own spirit was sufficiently unconquerable, his own love and sympathy were sufficiently overflowing, to grant him that right.

There is an almost divine tenderness in "Copperfield." Dickens takes his beloved fellow-creatures, including himself, works out relentlessly the results of their faults and wickednesses, ay, and of their virtues, and then shows them the way out. Faith, hope, and charity—which last word is now so altered from its original meaning that it must be written love—these three will overcome all human tribulations, provided, and only provided, they be accompanied by unflinching determination and energy. With these last characteristics he endows all those his friends in "David Copperfield" who are to work out his glorious purpose: David himself, his aunt Betsey Trotwood, Agnes, Traddles, Dan'l and Clara Peggotty. Even Mr. Dick is given them, so far as his poor half-witted state will allow; and certainly Mr. Micawber is. "I must do Mr. Micawber the justice to say," Traddles acknowledges, "that although he would appear not to have worked to any good account for himself, he is a most untiring man when he works for other people."

It is not an infallible philosophy, of course. The fell power of circumstances will defeat the best of us very often; but without belief in it how could humanity endure? And who shall estimate the beneficent result of a whole-hearted statement of it such as is given in "David Copperfield"?

It remains to say something of the manifestations of Dickens' creative genius in this story. First, one may note that "David Copperfield" is a story of everyday life. It might have happened to any one of us. The melodramatic plot has been left behind. Further, there are few of Dickens' stories which flow along more easily and naturally than this.

In other books one is sometimes exasperated by sudden breaks in the narrative; the story halts suddenly, without apparent reason, to introduce a new set of characters in a new setting. This was no doubt largely the result of serial publication. In "David Copperfield" changes of scene seem to have a happy knack of coming just at the right time.

If in this story, as in all his other stories, Dickens makes liberal use of coincidence to bring his people together, he does not do so more than usually; and is not coincidence one of the remarkable features of normal life? Otherwise, what is there incredible in the life of David Copperfield? It is prosaic and ordinary compared with the life of Charles Dickens.

Dickens has been often scolded for his English; his sentences, we are told, are ungrammatical, prolix, and sometimes cannot be understood. All these criticisms are perfectly true—sometimes. On the other hand, there are passages in Dickens which will rival in beauty and in economy of words those of any other writer, while few can equal his power of piling up an impression of uneasiness, strain, storm and disaster. While the most famous and best, because most sustained, examples of such writing occur in "Barnaby Rudge," "Bleak House," and "A Tale of Two Cities," there are not many short descriptions which can equal that of the storm at Great Yarmouth, when the ship containing Steerforth is wrecked, and Steerforth's dead body is washed ashore. Dickens' description of the Fleet prison in this book is well known; as examples of his power as a writer of English one may mention also the Barkis passages, and in particular the death of Barkis.

Head and shoulders above all the other characters towers the gigantic figure of Mr. Micawber. His "original" was Mr. John Dickens. What Charles Dickens' father thought of his picture as Mr. Micawber has, most unfortunately, never been recorded; but it is safe to hazard a guess that his sense of humour triumphed sufficiently to allow him to be highly gratified. Mr. John Dickens' letter to his son congratulating him upon Mr. Wilkins Micawber would have been a priceless document.

Too much has already been written on the identity of Mr. John Dickens with Mr. Wilkins Micawber. Charles Dickens has been quite sufficiently criticized for making use of his father in this fashion. Some critics have in their indignation made it appear as though Mr. Micawber is a portrait of Mr. Dickens senior. That he certainly is not; Mr. Micawber is a portrait of no one save his inimitable self. If his easy fashion of getting into debt, and his still easier one of paying his debts with I O U's, and his eloquential and literary styles are borrowed from Mr. John Dickens, the picture which results is certainly a great distance away from and far superior to the "original."

"The key of all the great characters of Dickens," says Mr. Chesterton, "is that they are all great fools"; and for once his usually unerring judgment is at fault. The key of all

Dickens' great characters is not that they are fools, but that they are children, and while children and fools are coupled together in the old saying which declares that a special Providence watches over both, that is the only respect in which they are alike.

Mr. Micawber is no fool. He is a man of very considerable ability. It takes no small ability to live upon an income of next to nothing a year, especially if one is hampered by a large and increasing family. Mr. Micawber, it is true, does not always succeed in doing so; he comes to know the inside of a debtors' prison. But he does not remain in that prison, as a man of less ability would have done, and for the rest of the several years that we know him, though harassed incessantly by pecuniary difficulties, with dunning trades-men always on his doorstep, he retains not only his inde-pendence, but, what is far more significant, his incurable buoyancy of spirit, and the "indescribable roll of gentility in his voice."

Misfortune cannot overwhelm Mr. Micawber. He may plunge into the trough of despair, but only to bob up again on the crest of the next wave. No sea of difficulties can drown Mr. Micawber, because he does not, as Hamlet suggested, "take arms against it." He simply floats up and down on the billows, serenely confident that sooner or later the ocean will cast him up on some island of peace and plenty. It does, in Australia, where in an unsophisticated community his undoubted merits receive their due acclamation and reward.

Mr. Micawber lives in a world of phantasy. It is a glorious world, this world of his imagination; it is the world of the romantic child's day-dream, in which everything comes out right in the end, in which kingdoms and palaces and banquets and adoration fall naturally to the dreamer. It is a spacious, exuberantly luxurious, and grandiloquent life; but not an impossible one, provided all the circumstances fall right. In Mr. Micawber's case, unfortunately, they have all fallen wrong.

The humour of Mr. Micawber lies in the fact that he is placed against just the very background which makes his fantastical grandiloquence most ludicrous. As a rich city magnate Mr. Micawber would not be funny at all; he would be insufferably pompous and condescending. As a snugly comfortable clerk he would be humorous, but not markedly so. As a poverty-stricken and debt-ridden shabby-genteel commercial traveller on commission he is irresistible.

Shabby-gentility is usually much more obviously shabby than it is genteel; Mr. Micawber is ineffably more genteel than he is shabby. He wears his rags with an air, carries his debts like a lord, pays them with I O U's like a monarch. He is exactly the child in the backyard playing kings and queens and marble palaces.

Add to all this the fact that Dickens never made a single false stroke in his characterization. There are those who have professed to find great fault in Mr. Micawber's being turned into an amateur detective for the downfall of Uriah Heep. It is a crowning stroke of reality; it is precisely what Mr. Micawber would love to do. What romantically-minded boy has not longed for the chance to play Sherlock Holmes or Sexton Blake in real life?

Due credit must be given to Mrs. Micawber. She is, for her husband, the perfect partner. She will never desert Mr. Micawber, and for that alone she deserves full marks. She both makes him and mars him. She is as optimistic as he, as easily depressed and exalted; she quite successfully prevents him from becoming a "useful" member of society, whenever he seems to tend in that direction, by her invincible belief in him as he is. She schemes uselessly for his advantage, she is quite blind to his weaknesses—and, behind the scenes, she keeps washed and fed the children, holds ferocious creditors at bay, and generally stage-manages an all but impossible situation.

After the immortal Micawbers, and always excepting the fact that David Copperfield, a most lovable and interesting hero, is the mainspring of the story, Miss Betsey Trotwood, Dan'l and Clara Peggotty claim next attention. It has often been said that Dickens could not draw a woman; Betsey Trotwood and Clara Peggotty surely disprove this. True, Betsey Trotwood is in her way an oddity, but it is not a very out-of-the-ordinary way; while about David's old nurse there is nothing of the oddity at all. Both are in their respective ways as true as steel; both are loving and devoted friends, both are kindly and good-hearted. If Betsey Trotwood chooses to hide her good qualities behind a certain angularity of manner and a caustic tongue, so much the better for the story. Her reception of Mr. and Miss Murdstone after the arrival of the poor little dusty and footsore David at Dover is one of the finest touches in the whole book.

The story of little Em'ly does not make the same appeal to twentieth-century as it did to nineteenth-century readers. Our conception of chastity is somewhat less virginal than was theirs; the whole pathos of Em'ly's story lies in the fact that her running away with Steerforth put her hopelessly beyond the pale of all decent society; and to-day to our credit we have altered all that. Yet no changing conception of morality can detract from the nobility of Dan'l Peggotty, who unquestioningly gives up home and occupation and all comfort for an unwearying search for his niece, and who never swerves from his purpose until he has found her and brought her home again. One is inclined to think that Ham Peggotty might have acted rather more charitably towards Em'ly, but there again one is confronted by the moral code of the nineteenth century, than which there are few things more difficult to understand and to forgive to-day.

The story of Dr. Strong and his wife has also rather too much of a nineteenth-century flavour to be altogether palatable at this date. Public feeling is now all against the marrying, unless they desire it, of young girls to elderly and absent-minded scholars; and consequently the flashily attractive Jack Maldon type of would-be seducer has rather dropped out of the picture.

Dr. Strong's school, on the other hand, is strangely modern and anticipates in its "honour" system some very recent and much-admired educational experiments. In this it contrasts forcibly with Mr. Creakle's Salem House, which is one of the really bad old-time private schools which educational reformers of the nineteenth century, including Dickens, and the spread of universal state education, have practically wiped out of existence. Salem House is strongly reminiscent of Dickens' own Wellington House Academy, and over and above the fact that it is marvellously delineated, the chief wonder is that two such attractive and unspoiled characters as David Copperfield and Traddles could emerge from it. Yet the miracle did happen; Dickens survived Wellington House, and several of his schoolfellows there achieved considerable success in after life.

Traddles is one of the neglected heroes of Dickens. The more one studies him the more one loves him. From the chubby boy who was always being beaten by Mr. Creakle yet who invariably smiled through his tears, drew skeletons and became his bright and cheerful self again, to the steady, carefully plodding and successful young lawyer who owes everything to his conscientiousness and hard work, there is nothing but charm in Traddles. There is much more than a hint of Forster in this character.

Steerforth is a common enough type, and true to the life. The boy of brilliant abilities and fascinating manners, who finds achievement so easy that it quickly bores him, and who is condemned to purposelessness by foolishly adoring parents and the possession of too much money, almost invariably makes a mess of things. Dickens had quite sufficient of the Steerforth characteristics himself to make him understand perfectly his unhappy and distracted search for some purpose in life, and to make him deal much more gently with his crime than one would have expected. In his sterner moments, indeed in most moments, Dickens would have had no mercy on what was after all a particularly cruel and heartless seduction; but he knew so well what it could mean to be in Steerforth's case, and he was so dazzled by the romantic boy-hero he had created, that his sympathies outweighed his judgment.

Steerforth's mother calls for little comment; she also is not uncommon, and her behaviour is true to type, even to the invalidism into which she relapsed after her son's departure. Nor is Rosa Dartle so out of line as might at first sight appear, though she carries jealousy to a melodramatic pitch. Littimer is superb throughout, with the exception of his deplorable

mock-repentance in prison. Surely, though, that Middlesex
prison chapter in which Littimer and Uriah Heep are shown
under the benevolent guardianship of Mr. Creakle is only
rather a bad joke on Dickens' part? Or the most charitable
view, it is a huge burst of laughter at some particularly
ridiculous prison system Dickens had visited. It was a pity
to mar a beautiful romance with such a blot of farce. One
has to be prepared for such shocks every now and then in
reading Dickens; he never quite got over the habit of laughing
occasionally in the wrong place.

Uriah Heep, it must be admitted, is in spite of the notoriety
he has gained the least satisfactory of the main characters
in "David Copperfield." The trouble is that he has to grow
up, and Dickens was never too certain about the portrayal of
developing character. His best people are always absolutely
static. Mr. Micawber strides magnificently out of "David
Copperfield" exactly the same man as he strode in; Sam
Weller, Fagin, Mr. Pecksniff, Mrs. Gamp, Mark Tapley, Joe
Gargery, are all full-blown from the moment of their first
appearance; so is Mr. Pickwick, except that he made a
false start. "Age cannot wither, nor custom stale" their
infinite sameness. Uriah Heep as a red-haired boy of fifteen,
with a cadaverous face, "breathing into the pony's nostrils,
and immediately covering them with his hand"—a delicious
touch!—reading Tidd's Practice at night with an immense
admiration for Mr. Tidd, and stealthily wiping his clammy
hands on his pocket-handkerchief, is absolutely convincing;
but Uriah Heep as Mr. Wickfield's partner, as the diabolically
crafty schemer, as a monster of villainy, is frankly impossible.
One cannot believe that he has grown clever enough or
masterful enough to accomplish his misdeeds. His mother
is far better; but she has no need to change. It is curious
that in the same story Dickens succeeds admirably with the
growing-up of Traddles, yet fails notably with Uriah Heep.
David himself is a case apart.

There remain the two heroines, Dora Spenlow and Agnes
Wickfield. About these male opinion will no doubt continue
to differ so long as "David Copperfield" continues to be
criticized. Men will continue to be fascinated by pretty

faces and engagingly childish ways, will fall madly in love
with them, and will neglect the soberer qualities in women
that alone can make a life partnership possible, so long as
women realize the power of prettiness and the value of
ignorance as a means of lightening their responsibilities. No
amount of stories such as that of the Copperfields' housekeep-
ing will prevent the Dora Spenlows of this world from carrying
off most of the prizes of the matrimonial world, nor the
Agnes Wickfields from standing aside to let them. Nevertheless, that is no reason why Agnes should be so ill-treated
as she is by some of Dickens' biographers.

Mr. Bernard Darwin goes so far as to say, "There is no
defending her, I am afraid." What he means is obscure;
women of Agnes Wickfield's type are rare enough, and more's
the pity, but when they are found they are the salt of God's
earth. Dickens knew it; he made a very, very human story
of the marriage of David Copperfield and Dora Spenlow, but
he knew quite well that unless he killed Dora she would kill
David. As it was no part of his purpose to show his hero
being gradually worn out by his wife's inadequacy, having
his love slowly crushed out of existence by her empty childishness, he cut the Gordian knot by granting Dora a beautiful
but timely death, and so freed David to marry the one woman
who was in every way qualified to look after and to cherish
him.

Perhaps it does not often happen like that in real life:
the Dora Spenlows are on the whole noted for longevity;
but it does sometimes, and in this lovely romance, this story
of a clean young life, full of hopeful purpose, fighting its way
upwards in spite of all that threatens to depress and defile
it, surely one would not have it otherwise? In the purifying
of the ardent spirit of David Copperfield Dora plays an
important part, but it is quickly played, and Dickens, great
realist as well as great romanticist, knew that, and ruthlessly
cast her aside the moment her part was done. He had no
interest in Dora Spenlow save as an instrument in the shaping
of his favourite child—or, dare one say, children? He never
said so in words, but one would hazard the guess that Agnes
Wickfield lay nearly as close to his heart as David Copperfield.

## CHAPTER XI

*"Familiar in his mouth as household words."*—SHAKESPEARE, *King Henry V.*

The writing of "David Copperfield" was begun in February 1849. On the 16th of the previous month another son, Henry Fielding, had been born to Dickens. The child was destined to become Sir Henry Fielding Dickens, K.C., Common Serjeant, and to retire after a long and distinguished career in the legal profession.

One humorous incident of this time has specially to be recorded, as Dickens solemnly warned Forster to remember it when writing the author's biography. Mamie and Kate Dickens had taught their father the polka that he might be able to dance it at his son Charley's birthday party. On the night before the event Dickens was suddenly assailed with the fear that he had forgotten his steps, whereupon he jumped out of bed and practised them diligently!

Going to Brighton early in February, Dickens had there the terrifying experience of having both his landlord and his landlord's daughter go mad simultaneously. He and his wife and Mr. and Mrs. John Leech had, after an exciting scene with the lunatics, to retire to the Bedford Hotel.

The first number of "David Copperfield" appeared in May and was celebrated by the inevitable dinner. To this among others came Carlyle who, when asked concerning his health, replied in Mrs. Gummidge's words that he was a "lone lorn creetur' and everything went contrairy with him." This dinner was only one of many during the year; Devonshire Terrace had become a centre of high entertainment, to which aristocrats by birth as well as aristocrats of the intellectual world were proud to be invited.

In June Dickens was again at Broadstairs; but having decided to go elsewhere for the summer, he sailed in July from Ramsgate to Bonchurch, Isle of Wight. At first everything there was delightful; his house was "the prettiest place [he] had ever seen in [his] life, at home or abroad;" there were "views only to be equalled on the Genoese shore of the Mediterranean;" walks, bathing, a waterfall, cheapness, and the society of two dearly-loved friends, the Rev. James and Mrs. White. Unfortunately the relaxing climate of Bonchurch quickly reduced him to limpness, catarrh and exasperation. Though he stubbornly stayed out his time there, he left at the end of September never to return, having pronounced upon the place the awful verdict that "Naples is hot and dirty, New York feverish, Washington bilious, Genoa exciting, Paris rainy—but Bonchurch, smashing."

During this holiday Dickens, who was always interested in hypnotism, made a practical experiment upon his friend John Leech, who became seriously ill as a result of being knocked about by a rough sea while bathing. Thanks chiefly, it would appear, to the crude medical efforts at recovering him, Leech grew steadily worse until one night Dickens hypnotized him into a sleep of over an hour and a half, after which time he began rapidly to recover.

In the autumn the first statement of accounts made it clear that "Copperfield," though universally popular, was not selling so well as "Dombey" had done. Though this did not seriously disturb Dickens and caused him no financial embarrassment, it turned his thoughts more strongly in the direction of the "dim design" which he had originally outlined to Forster while in Paris. This was to edit a cheap, amusing and instructive weekly magazine after the style of Addison's *Spectator*. When he returned to Broadstairs in October, a change which immediately improved the health of the whole family, he began to occupy both his own thoughts and Forster's almost exclusively with this design, having decided that the following spring should see the launching of the periodical.

Charles Dickens could never all his life do without his little bit of magic, whether it were conjuring or hypnotism or super-

BLACK GANG CHINE, ISLE OF WIGHT

*After an Engraving by J. Godfrey, 1856*

natural assistance with his stories and magazines. In *Master Humphrey's Clock* Gog and Magog had in person come to the aid of the quaint little mysterious old man with the almost human timepiece. In the Christmas stories there is no end of spirits and ghostly visitations. There are goblins even in "Pickwick." The wonder is that there were no angels for the *Daily News*.

So now he could not imagine his projected periodical without "a certain SHADOW, which may go into any place by sunlight, moonlight, starlight, firelight, candle light, and be in all houses and all nooks and corners, and be supposed to be cognisant of everything, and go everywhere, without the least difficulty. . . ." Forster successfully laid this poor ghost. As he dryly comments in his biography, "Excellent the idea doubtless . . . but I could not make anything out of it that had quite a feasible look."

The result was that there emerged on Saturday, March 30, 1850, a straightforward miscellany, to be irradiated by the exhilarating personality of Dickens, but quite soberly constructed on the best journalistic lines, and planned "to contribute to the entertainment and instruction of all classes of readers, and to help in the discussion of the more important social questions of the time." It was entitled *Household Words*, the title being drawn from and supplemented by a quotation (slightly inaccurate) from Henry V's stirring speech before Agincourt as recorded by Shakespeare.

Simple though it sounds, the title was not arrived at without the usual heartsearchings. Some fifteen alternatives were considered before *Household Words* was finally chosen, including *The Holly Tree*, *The Robin* and, curiously enough, *Charles Dickens*.

*Household Words* did not suffer the fate of *Master Humphrey's Clock* nor did its editor tire of it as he had done of the *Daily News*. On the contrary, from the start things went well, and it developed into one of the most successful and memorable efforts of nineteenth-century journalism. Published at twopence, it quickly achieved a large circulation and its contents soon became in very truth familiar as household words.

The proprietors were Charles Dickens, who held a half-share, Messrs. Bradbury and Evans, who held a quarter, and Forster and W. H. Wills, who held one-eighth each. All profits and losses were to be shared proportionately. As editor-in-chief Dickens received a salary of £500 per annum, exclusive of his share of the profits. On Forster's suggestion Wills was made sub-editor and manager, at a salary of £5 a week; and he proved the ideal man for the job. Dickens and he got on excellently together; both worked extremely hard and each understood his job and their relationship so well that friction between them was unknown.

*Household Words* did much more than become popular: it became great. Dickens gradually gathered round him a staff of brilliant writers, chiefly young men and women who were proud to work under his editorship, even though all contributions were anonymous. Among these were Mrs. Gaskell, whose famous "Cranford" appeared first in its pages, George Augustus Sala, Henry Morley, R. H. Horne and Wilkie Collins, who was to become the familiar friend of Dickens' later years and was considerably to influence his writing.

Dickens took extraordinary care with contributions, and altered some of them freely. It is recorded that on one occasion he spent four hours making publishable one short story, and that at a time when he was probably among the six busiest men in the country. This editorial care occasionally led to some misunderstandings, and perhaps once or twice a little soreness, when the work of other contributors was attributed to Dickens, and actually published in America under his name. Fortunately the misunderstandings were slight; there have been fewer more loyal or enthusiastic staffs than the little group of "Dickens' Young Men" who contributed to the success of *Household Words*. Few editors have been more exacting of a high standard than was Dickens, but there have been few whose praise was more highly treasured.

The second number of *Household Words* contained the very beautiful sketch by Dickens entitled "A Child's Dream of a Star," the story of a brother and sister who used to sit up together at night to watch their friend, a certain star, rise, and to say good night to it, and of how, when his sister dies,

FORT HOUSE, BROADSTAIRS.

the boy sees in the star's rays a gleaming path up which with other spirits his sister goes to heaven to be received by the angels. It is one of the most tender of all his fancies, and was inspired by the comparatively recent death of his sister Fanny, with whom he had been wont, in Chatham days, to wander through a churchyard at night looking at and talking about the stars.

In Christmas numbers of *Household Words* were printed the charming tales of "The Seven Poor Travellers" and "Boots of the Holly Tree Inn." These Christmas numbers were always special features of *Household Words* to which Dickens gave the most painstaking attention and care. He was rewarded by enormous sales, in some instances exceeding a quarter of a million.

In *Household Words* were printed also "Hard Times" and "The Lazy Tour of Two Idle Apprentices," the latter written in conjunction with Wilkie Collins after a semi-business, semi-pleasure trip of a week in the Lake District, followed by a week-end at Doncaster while the races were on, in October 1857. In its pages appeared also "A Child's History of England," but perhaps the less said about that the better; text-books were not in Dickens' line.

In addition to demanding a high standard from his own contributors, Dickens was always ready to applaud distinguished work in other places, and at times showed remarkable critical acumen. Among others *Household Words* encouraged George Eliot (whom Dickens was sure from the start was a woman), Meredith and Adelaide Anne Procter.

During the thick of the earlier preparations for the weekly Dickens found time to raise the question of the public execution of criminals in two powerful letters addressed to the *Times* in November 1849. Insatiably curious as he always was to learn more of the manners and habits of the lower classes, he attended the execution outside Horsemonger Lane of two notorious murderers, Mrs. Manning and her husband, with "the intention of observing the crowd gathered to behold it." What he saw horrified and disgusted him beyond belief. "I believe that a sight so inconceivably awful as the wickedness and levity of the immense crowd collected at that execution this morning," he wrote, "could be imagined by no man, and could be presented in no heathen land under the sun. The horrors of the gibbet and of the crime which brought the wretched murderers to it faded in my mind before the atrocious bearing, looks, and language of the assembled spectators. When I came upon the scene at midnight the *shrillness* of the cries and howls that were raised from time to time, denoting that they came from a concourse of boys and girls already assembled in the best places, made my blood run cold. . . . When the day dawned, thieves, low prostitutes, ruffians and vagabonds of every kind, flocked on to the ground, with every variety of offensive and foul behaviour. . . . When the sun rose brightly . . . it gilded thousands upon thousands of upturned faces, so inexpressibly odious in their brutal mirth or callousness, that a man had cause to feel ashamed of the shape he wore. . . . When the two miserable creatures who attracted all this ghastly sight about them were turned quivering in the air, there was no more emotion, no more pity, no more thought that two immortal souls had gone to judgment, no more restraint in any of the previous obscenities, than if the name of Christ had never been heard in this world. . . ."

Only a little over eighty years ago! There are people living to-day who can remember such mobs. The picture is a striking reminder of how far we have gone since 1850.

Requested by a correspondent to explain his position more clearly, Dickens in a second letter four days later urged that the execution of criminals should take place within the prison walls, witnessed only by juries empanelled for the purpose, who with the prison authorities should attest the identity of the criminal and the fact of execution and burying. This position was for him a compromise, since he was opposed on principle to capital punishment, but he adopted it as being "the most hopeful," in view of the fact that he feared "many earnest and sincere people" would combine to defeat any attempt to abolish capital punishment.

His compromise cost him some months' estrangement from Douglas Jerrold, a rigid abolitionist. The story of their renewal of friendship is too good to miss. They were one day

GIUSEPPE MAZZINI (1805-1872)

sitting back to back in a club, each with his own friends, neither having made the slightest sign of recognition of the other. All of a sudden Jerrold swung round, held out his hand to Dickens and said, "For God's sake, Dickens, let us be friends again! A life's not long enough for this!"

Thanks to Dickens' letters in the *Times*, and to the agitation they excited, public executions were abolished within a very few years.

During this same autumn Dickens was active on behalf of the Italian refugees who poured into England after the fall of the short-lived Rome Republic of this year. Dickens, who had met the great Italian patriot Mazzini some time previously, was a member of a distinguished committee which raised funds for the refugees, and himself drew up the appeal on their behalf. Over and above his natural sympathy for all in distress, a very characteristic reason for his championship of their cause is found in this appeal, in which he declares them to have "built upon the ruins of a monstrous system which had fallen of its own rottenness and corruption, one of moderation and truth."

With *Household Words* successfully launched and "Copperfield" drawing happily to its close, Dickens, though still a busy enough man, could in the summer of 1850 begin to turn his thoughts again to amusements and diversions. There was a great dinner in June at the Star and Garter, Richmond, in honour of "Copperfield," and, says Forster, "I have rarely seen Dickens happier than he was amid the sunshine of that day." A newcomer to these feasts present on this occasion was Alfred, afterwards Lord, Tennyson, for whose poetry Dickens had a profound respect and love. In July Dickens and Maclise were in Paris, in heat so oppressive that "I can do nothing but lie on the bare floor all day." In August he leased for his summer holiday the house at Broadstairs he had so long desired, Fort House, "a small house without any large rooms, but such a place as a man of moderate means, with an immoderate family of small children, might choose for a summer retreat," as Mr. Edmund Yates described it. Fort House is on the east of the town, on the edge of a small cliff, with fine sands below, and overlooking the harbour. A later resident was to rename it Bleak House, and so create a legend that it was the original of John Jarndyce's house, than which nothing could be farther from the truth.

In September, arrangements were already being made to recommence the "splendid strollings," and November found the old Company down at Knebworth Park, the country residence of Sir Edward Bulwer Lytton, to give three performances of *Every Man in His Humour*. During these days at Knebworth a scheme of some importance was hatched.

Someone suggested that in view of the public interest shown in the company's performances it ought to be possible to devote their attentions to some permanent form of charitable endeavour. Why not raise funds to endow a kind of pensioned lectureship home for deserving authors? The proposal was applauded and, as Forster acidly comments, "too readily assuming what should have had more thorough investigation," the group there and then founded the "Guild of Literature and Art."

Everything was purposely left for the moment very vague as to details. Bulwer Lytton was to write a five-act comedy—which he did—and Dickens a farce—which he did not—and the Guild was to present them and make a lot of money, and then sit down to think out exactly what to do with it. The first part of the scheme developed according to plan except for the farce, from which Dickens was excused, an effort of Mark Lemon's being substituted. This piece, incidentally, Dickens so modified and added to during the following two or three years that it became almost as much his as Lemon's.

Meanwhile there were some private theatricals at Rockingham Castle in January 1851 which revealed Dickens in his maddest, merriest and most energetic mood. He brought down his own private theatre, and instructed a local carpenter in much detail how alterations should be done and how to construct various ingenious stage devices. He had "developed these wonderful ideas," he told Mrs. Watson in a letter, "to the master carpenter at one of the theatres," who had shaken his head "with an intensely mournful air, and said, 'Ah, sir, it's a universal observation in the profession, sir, that it was a great loss to the public when you took to writing books!'" It was on

*Ed Bulwer*      *Alfred Croquis delt.*

EDWARD BULWER, LORD LYTTON

*From the drawing by Daniel Maclise, R.A., 1832*

this occasion that his eldest son, Charley, now an Eton school-boy, first took part in these theatricals.

Throughout the winter preparations were being made for a tremendous inaugural performance of Bulwer Lytton's new comedy, *Not So Bad as We Seem*, at which the Guild of Literature and Art was to be formally launched. The Duke of Devonshire, a munificent patron of the arts and a nobleman in the grand old style, had lent Devonshire House, Piccadilly, for the occasion, and was defraying all expenses.

The performance took place on May 16th, with great éclat. The Queen and the Prince Consort were present, the success was such as had come to be associated with all Dickens' theatrical ventures, and one thousand pounds was raised on the one evening for the Guild. There followed several other performances in London, and during this year and the next many in the provinces—Reading, Bristol, Clifton, Birmingham, Derby, Nottingham, Manchester, Liverpool and Newcastle were all visited, the company carrying its own portable theatre and scenery, and using ordinary concert halls.

This long intermittent tour, says Mr. Ralph Straus, "definitely gave Dickens that craving to *hear* the applause of the public which he never really lost." It gave him also a new bosom friend, Wilkie Collins, to whom he grew increasingly attached, not a little, one gathers, to Forster's displeasure. Though Forster's place as confidential adviser was never usurped, it must have been a bitter pill for the now elderly and always jealously possessive friend of sixteen years' standing to find his companionship neglected in lighter hours for that of the fascinating but vulgar and flighty young Collins. Wilkie Collins receives but slight reference in Forster's "Life," as do others who grew too friendly with Dickens for the biographer's liking.

Dickens, however, felt the need of friendship of a frivolous and distracting nature during these days, for in spite of his brilliant superficial successes things were not going well with him. There is still a certain amount of mystery attached to the story of his separation from his wife, but it is quite certain that they were unhappy together for many years and that throughout the 1850's the domestic troubles which led up to the tragic finale of 1858 were steadily thickening. It is almost certain that Mrs. Dickens had several mental breakdowns before this latter date, and in all likelihood the first of these took place in 1851.

At any rate, when she and her infant daughter Dora, who had been born in August of the previous year, were both seriously ill in the spring, and were taken to Great Malvern for the air, Dickens thought it wiser to refuse an offer from a doctor there to accept his hospitality, on account of what he had observed of his wife's behaviour "when we have been staying in the country houses even of intimate friends."

From Malvern, Dickens was, towards the close of March, hurriedly recalled to London, where his father lay dying. The old man did not recognize him when he arrived, but passed quietly away during the early morning of the 31st. He was buried in Highgate Cemetery, under an inscription written by his son commemorating his "zealous, useful, cheerful spirit."

On the 14th of April, while her father was still in London, the baby Dora also passed away. Dickens was in the chair at a meeting of the General Theatrical Fund when the news was brought. Forster received it, and kept it from his friend until the meeting closed.

He has related his feelings when he heard Dickens, all unconscious of his own loss, speak of actors "having to come from scenes of sickness, of suffering, aye, even of death itself, to play their parts before us," and continue, "how often is it with all of us, that in our several spheres we have to do violence to our feelings, and to hide our hearts in carrying on this fight of life, if we would bravely discharge in it our duties and responsibilities." No one to this day knows to what extent Dickens had to do violence to his own feelings, in order bravely to discharge his duties and responsibilities; but it needs no very shrewd perception to guess that behind the glare and the glitter and the enjoyment of a continuously successful public life there lay oftentimes an aching and despondent heart. Yet never did he give in.

A minor but not inconsiderable trouble of this year was

the move from Devonshire Terrace to Tavistock House, Tavistock Square. Dickens had grown very attached to his residence on the Marylebone Road during the twelve years he had occupied it, so much so that he told Forster after the move that "I seem as if I had plucked myself out of my proper soil when I left Devonshire Terrace, and could take root no more until I return to it." Delays over the repairs and alterations he desired helped to drive him to a state "bordering on distraction." Doubtless they and Dickens' letters drove the architect, his brother-in-law Henry Austin, to much the same state, except that Austin had not on his mind what Dickens had on his.

He was "maturing" another book.

The inevitable restlessness and inquietude which accompanied this period of a book's creation, and which grew in intensity with age, had attacked him at Broadstairs. "I sit down between whiles," he wrote, "to think of a new story, and, as it begins to grow, such a torment of desire to be anywhere but where I am, and to be going I don't know where, I don't know why, takes hold of me, that it is like being *driven away*."

The new story was "Bleak House." In it Dickens was proposing to make a grand assault upon his old enemy the law, and particularly upon the most wasteful, the most dilatory, and the most futile branch of all, the Court of Chancery.

As a picture of the law's delays, "Bleak House" remains unique. As Mr. Bernard Darwin says, "From the moment that we begin with the Court of Chancery in a fog, Chancery gets its grip on the story and never relaxes it." As always when he was attacking a definite abuse, Dickens' story was founded strictly on fact. The case of Jarndyce *v.* Jarndyce, which drags its weary length through the story from end to end, was based upon a suit that began after the death in 1798 of one William Jennens or Jennings, a miser, of Acton in Suffolk, which was still being prosecuted at the time when the story was being written, and continued to be for many years afterwards.

A certain judge having been rash enough to tell Dickens

and others at some public function that the Court of Chancery was "almost immaculate," Dickens' reply in the preface to the edition in volume form was that "everything set forth in these pages concerning the Court of Chancery is substantially true, and within the truth" and if he "wanted other authorities for JARNDYCE AND JARNDYCE" he "could rain them on these pages." The case of Gridley, "the man from Shropshire" who bore his troubles so hardly, was incorporated bodily from a pamphlet sent to him after the first number of "Bleak House" had been published.

As in the case of "David Copperfield," the story of "Bleak House" is one that might have happened to anyone. Even the death by spontaneous combustion of Krook, Dickens was prepared to substantiate. The possibility of Krook's death happening as it did being questioned by a scientist, George Henry Lewes, he retorted in his preface by citing instances of similar deaths, notably one which had been most carefully investigated. There was no tripping Dickens up about his facts.

Yet the insistence upon realism was in a sense a sign of weakness. The essence of the greatness of Dickens' characters lies in their being real, yet above reality, in their peculiarities being heightened so skilfully that, while they impose at every moment an absolute impression of reality, they become more ludicrous, more lovable, or more hateful, than mere humans could be. The supreme genius of Dickens lay in the fact that he brought a race of giants down to earth, gave them local habitations and names and made them so like ordinary people that they are absolutely convincing. As soon as he lost his grip, though ever so slightly, upon this fairyland of his and relied upon stark realism he was still inimitable, he was still the "divine reporter," but his genius was on the decline.

That decline is obvious in "Bleak House." Even Forster is compelled to admit it, loving and somewhat partial critic though he was. He says, quite truly, ". . . this book has suffered by the very completeness with which its Chancery moral is worked out. . . . The Guppys, Weevles, Snagsbys, Chadbands, Krooks, and Smallweeds, even the Kenges,

THOMAS MOORE (1779–1852)

*From a drawing by Daniel Maclise, R.A.*

Vholeses, and Tulkinghorns, are much too real to be pleasant; and the necessity becomes urgent for the reliefs and contrasts of a finer humanity."

Say rather that the necessity becomes urgent for the reliefs and contrasts of a finer super-humanity. What a wonderful story "Bleak House" would have become could we have had a Micawber of the Court of Chancery! Instead, we get Gridley, and Krook, and poor little Miss Flite, true, absolutely true to life—too true to life to rise above it and to show us the greatness of humanity.

With most of what Forster says about the construction of the book one can cordially agree; it is certainly the best-constructed novel Dickens has so far written. Further, as Forster also observes, every character, every trait in every character has a direct bearing upon the central purpose.

In "Bleak House" Dickens builds up step by step, with unflinching realism, an absolutely complete picture of a chaotic muddle. He writes with conscious art, and employs every ounce of his skill as a novelist. There lacks, however, Dickens the creative genius; he is interested only in his characters as subserving his social purpose, the reformation of the Court of Chancery.

This is not to say that the characters in "Bleak House" are uninteresting. Far from it; there are as many in "Bleak House" as in any book, and their range is enormous, from the "honourable, obstinate, truthful, high-spirited, intensely prejudiced" and "perfectly unreasonable" Sir Leicester Dedlock, to the homeless and nameless Jo, the crossing-sweeper; from the inscrutable Mr. Tulkinghorn to the awesome but good-natured Mr. Detective Bucket; from the happy-go-lucky Richard Carstone as he is in the beginning to the crazy Gridley and Miss Flite; from Mr. Chadband to Mrs. Jellyby. Dickens could not help throwing off characters as other writers throw off aphorisms, nor could he help their sparkling with a like brilliance.

Yet in "Bleak House" no great creative figure enters to lift the story from the plane of a very grimy if not actually sordid realism.

In his failing sufficiently to irradiate reality with his

M

magic wand, Dickens made one very grievous error of taste,
for which he was at the time and has been since quite sufficiently scolded. This was in his portrayal of Harold Skimpole,
the "little bright creature" with "no idea of time" and "no
idea of money," who so successfully uses these negative
virtues to sponge upon his friends, and upon John Jarndyce
in particular.

There are in this book two definitely recognizable portraits
of well-known men. Lawrence Boythorn is Walter Savage
Landor, and Harold Skimpole is Leigh Hunt. With regard
to the ethics of the former portrait, opinions may differ;
apparently they did when the book was published. Dickens
said Landor was, if anything, rather pleased with his portrait;
others said he strongly objected to it. At this date it does
not greatly matter; Lawrence Boythorn is a kindly enough
picture, and there would appear to be nothing immoral in
putting your friends into a book providing you are fair to
them.

To Leigh Hunt Dickens certainly was not. He magnified
a certain airiness of manner and an incapacity to manage
financial affairs into qualities that are utterly detestable.
He turned a very charming, deservedly popular man and
a writer of established reputation, into an objectionable
(though still superficially charming) little toady and sponger.
To add to the crime, he was warned, as "Bleak House" was
being written, what he was doing, but beyond altering
Skimpole's name from Leonard to Harold, and toning down
the details ever so slightly, he did nothing. The only
satisfactory feature in a sorry business is that Leigh Hunt
himself did not, until it was pointed out to him, recognize
the picture. It cost Dickens, however, considerable ill-
feeling; Bulwer Lytton in particular was grievously offended.

It was not, of course, the first time Dickens had erred
against good taste in this respect. So long ago as "Nicholas
Nickleby" he had begun with a picture of his mother of
which Mr. J. W. T. Ley, a leading Dickensian authority,
says, "I have been quite unable to find in all my researches
anything to justify any suggestion that Mrs. John Dickens
was anything of the fool that Mrs. Nickleby was." Every-

body had recognized Mr. Samuel Carter Hall in Mr. Pecksniff; and, though nobody liked Mr. Hall, nobody would have accused him of moral obliquity. The case of Mr. Micawber and Mr. John Dickens has been sufficiently discussed. The original of Miss Mowcher wrote to Dickens to protest energetically against her portrait; and Dickens, filled with penitence, turned a malevolent little dwarf into a beneficent one. The saddest case of all was the cruel picture of Maria Beadnell as Flora Finching in "Little Dorrit."

"Well, well, we are all dead now," as a friend of Dickens used to say. The world has forgotten the original of Miss Mowcher, it has forgotten Samuel Carter Hall, it has almost forgotten Leigh Hunt; it remembers Mr. and Mrs. John Dickens and Maria Beadnell only for their connection with Charles Dickens. It will be a long time before it forgets Mr. Micawber or Mr. Pecksniff or Harold Skimpole.

The writing of "Bleak House," which began in November 1851 and continued until August 1853, was rendered difficult by much suffering and depression. At the time when the first number appeared, March 1852, Dickens was finding himself unable to "grind sparks out of this dull blade," and dreading lest he should get behindhand with it. He was restless and discontented; even the birth of his last child, Edward Bulwer Lytton, seemed to upset him. He wrote pettishly a few weeks later to Mr. Cerjat that his wife was "quite well, after favouring me (I think I could have dispensed with the compliment) with No. 10." He had thoughts of stealing away to France or Switzerland, but compromised with Dover for three months. Here he was greatly grieved to hear of the sudden and quite unexpected death of Mr. Watson, and shortly afterwards of the deaths of Count d'Orsay and Mrs. Macready.

From Dover he crossed alone in October to Boulogne to investigate its possibilities as a summer holiday resort. A letter written from there shows both how indefatigably he attended to his multifarious labours, and something of the ideals which made *Household Words* so attractive. "I have thought," he tells Wills, "of the Christmas number, but not very successfully, because I have been (and still am)

constantly occupied with 'Bleak House.' I propose returning
home either on Sunday or Monday, as my work permits,
and we will, immediately thereafter, dine at the office and
talk it over." He then goes on to comment on a poem
submitted to the magazine, and tells Wills it is "at about the
tract-mark ('Dairyman's Daughter,' etc.) of political morality,
and don't think that it is necessary to write *down* to any part
of our audience. I always hold that to be as great a mistake
as can be made."

In the Spring of 1853 the strain of these incessant labours
bore so hardly upon him that his health definitely broke down,
the old pains renewed themselves, he found he could not
recover his elasticity by short rests, and "What with 'Bleak
House,' and *Household Words*, and 'Child's History,' and Miss
Coutts's Homes and the invitations to feasts and festivals,
I really feel as if my head would split like a fired shell if I
remained here [London]."

In June 1853 Dickens left for Boulogne, "thanking
Heaven," says Forster, "for escape from a breakdown."

This was the first really grave warning he had had that
he was beyond all question wearing himself out. There had
been hints, and pretty plain ones, before, but this was unmistakable. The warning was to be repeated over and over
again, ever more seriously and painfully, before the blow at
last fell.

It is difficult at this date to give an adequate picture of
the intensity of his life, so greatly have conditions of life
altered since 1853. He was writing "Bleak House"; he was
editing *Household Words*, being never without a set of proofs,
and writing long letters every few days to Wills which show
that he was reading, altering and rejecting contributions,
looking up references, consulting authorities, etc.; he was
dictating week by week to Miss Hogarth "A Child's History
of England"; he had been for long Miss Coutts's adviser,
secretary and treasurer in connection with her charitable
schemes, which included a home for fallen women which
took up a great deal of his time. All this clerical work, save
only the "Child's History," had to be accomplished without
any of the secretarial aids of to-day; even his numerous letters
were written by hand.

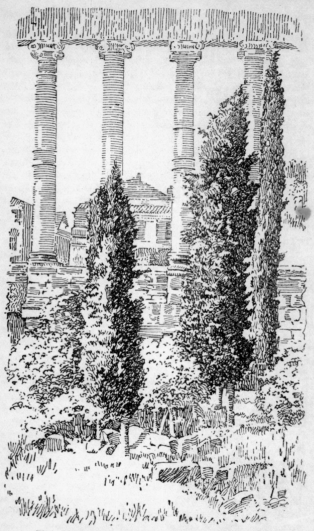

THE TEMPLE OF SATURN, IN THE FORUM, ROME

In addition he was constantly rehearsing plays and travelling to give performances for the Guild of Literature and Art; was regularly in demand at public meetings, dinners and receptions, and as regularly at more private but none the less obligatory functions. All this involved much travelling by rail and road, neither so pleasant, and the latter incredibly slower and more laborious than to-day.

Yet he was still prepared to take on a new and different work. In January 1853, after a great reception at Birmingham, when he was presented with a silver-gilt salver and a diamond ring for his services to the Institution, he promised the following Christmas to give a couple of readings from his books "in aid of the New Midland Institute."

He finished "Bleak House" in August. Financially it had been a great success; its circulation had been steadily maintained at about 40,000, thus, as he said half-regretfully, "beating dear old Copperfield by a round ten thousand or more." Its conclusion was followed by a period of "reaction and prostration of laziness," and a two months' bachelor tour of Italy with Wilkie Collins and Augustus Egg, during which they visited Chamonix, Milan, Genoa, Naples, Rome, Florence and Venice. Early in December he was back in London, his mind full of the Birmingham readings.

On the 27th December he read "A Christmas Carol," on the 29th "The Cricket on the Hearth," on the 30th the "Carol" again, having first insisted that places were to be reserved at popular prices for working men. Six thousand people heard the readings; the enthusiasm was tremendous; between £400 and £500 were made; and applications for similar readings began to pour in from all over the country.

By January 27th, 1854, Dickens found that "After correspondence [from] all parts of England, and every kind of refusal and evasion on my part, I am now obliged to decide this question—whether I shall read two nights at Bradford for one hundred pounds. If I do, I may take as many hundred pounds as I choose."

His decision was a reluctant refusal to accept money: "It was a change," says Forster, "to be justified only when the higher calling should have failed of the old success."

For the present he remained an amateur reader, but the question of signing professional forms was only in abeyance, with Dickens "assenting against his will" that it should so rest.

Before the end of the month he was again reading in public "to a little audience of three thousand five hundred at Bradford." Meanwhile he had already begun "Hard Times."

This story was published in *Household Words* to stimulate the circulation. It succeeded; it more than doubled it. It is difficult to know why, unless the following quotation from a letter written to Mr. Charles Knight supplies the clue: "The English are, so far as I know, the hardest-worked people on whom the sun shines. Be content if, in their wretched intervals of pleasure, they read for amusement and do no worse. They are born at the oar, and they live and die at it. Good God, what would we have of them!" A story written in that spirit may, whatever its literary merit, find an answering note in many a worker's breast. It may very likely be too that Dickens' readings in Birmingham and Bradford had interested in his work numbers of the poorer classes who had before been indifferent to his fame.

"Hard Times" was written in six months—from January to July, 1854. Dickens found the restrictions of short weekly instalments "crushing," but worked savagely at the book and finished it at Boulogne in a state "three parts mad, and the fourth delirious." Ruskin, while according high praise to it, regretted that Dickens chose to "speak in a circle of stage fire." The criticism is just; Mr. Gradgrind, the man of facts who orders his life and that of his family with mathematical precision, and Mr. Bounderby the wealthy banker, are, compared with Dickens' more successful characters, third-rate stagy villains played by a bad company. The only really Dickensian part of the book on a high level is the account of Slearey's circus.

As soon as the book was finished Dickens wrote to Wilkie Collins that he was coming to London for a week, which he proposed to pass in "a career of amiable dissipation and unbounded license in the metropolis," and that if Collins would come and breakfast with him "about midnight—

anywhere—any day, and go to bed no more" until the return to Boulogne, he would "be delighted to have so vicious an associate."

There was more than a suspicion of truth in these exaggerated phrases. Collins was of a different generation from Dickens and Forster, and some of his ideas of pleasure no doubt scandalized the latter. Dickens, one knows, could on occasion enjoy a bit of vulgarity and relish a witty cynicism. In his present excited and jaded state particularly, Collins' sprightly liveliness provided a tonic for him which all Forster's solid worth could not supply.

"There are passages," says Mr. Ralph Straus, "in Dickens's letters to Collins (invariably deleted in the printed versions) which you do not find in his other correspondence." It is, in a way, a pity that those passages are deleted; not that one wants particularly to read them, but because all such suppressions help to give a distorted impression of Dickens. The more Dickens is whitewashed, the more his faults are glossed over, the less like the man who wrote his glorious books does he become. An impeccable Dickens could never have created Mrs. Gamp.

Most of this summer and autumn was spent in Boulogne, to which Dickens had become very attached, and which had taken the place of Broadstairs as the seaside headquarters. In October he returned to London, where the winter months were spent in writing for the Christmas number of *Household Words* "The First (Poor) Traveller" and "The Road," the opening and the concluding parts of "The Seven Poor Travellers"; in giving public readings at Reading, Sherborne and Bradford, the last to "a little fireside party of four thousand"; and in organizing for the second year, and on a much enlarged scale, jolly children's theatricals at Tavistock House.

The children were growing up. Charley had left Eton and was studying in Germany. Even so late an arrival as Edward Bulwer Lytton, now in high favour, and known as Plornishmaroontigoonter or The Noble Plorn, was nearly three, already a comedian of repute, and ready to take his place on any stage. With the help of "Uncle Mark" (Mark

Lemon) and his children, Wilkie Collins and Miss Mary Boyle, quite a large cast could be made up. So year after year these January theatricals took place, and very delightful they were. "First and foremost of that magic circle," wrote Miss Boyle of these days, "was the host himself, always 'one of us,' who invariably drew out what was best and most characteristic in others. . . . I can never forget one evening . . . it seemed like a page cut out of 'A Christmas Carol,' so far, at least, as fun and frolic went."

To what extent Dickens was able to forget his troubles in the incessant stream of distractions and entertainments in which he engaged will never be fully known. While actually writing a book he was certainly lost to the external world, and the contents of his published letters, which rarely flag, suggest that he could equally lose himself in their composition. On the other hand, human experience would point to the fact that a man of powerful and active mind like Dickens could never entirely throw off the painful thoughts which oppressed it; and his behaviour during these years would seem to lend force to this conclusion. The very eagerness with which he pursued distraction would seem evidence of its powerlessness completely to banish his worries. Restlessly active, plunging into work and pleasure alike with an abandon which rises as the years progress, nothing could be found that could satisfy his cravings for long, nothing could rid him permanently of his tormented unsettledness.

## CHAPTER XII

*"There can be no disparity in marriage like unsuitability of mind and purpose."*—MRS. STRONG, in DAVID COPPERFIELD.

THE year 1855 was, Forster records, one of "much unsettled discontent" with Dickens. Forster knew some of the reasons for this, not all. What he did not know was that for a brief month or two Dickens was caught up into the very heart of romance—to have his hopes as cruelly dashed as ever they had been.

Without any warning, there arrived in the early weeks of the New Year a letter from Maria Beadnell! Instantly Dickens' mind went back twenty-two years, and he was a boy again, and she his girlish sweetheart. He replied warmly, too warmly, to Mrs. Winter, as Maria was now. "The associations my memory has with you make the letter more —I want a word—invest it with a more immediate address to me than such a letter could have from anyone else."

Maria replied, and Dickens became more and more infatuated and less and less discreet. Maria, he wrote from Paris in mid-February, was to tell her little daughter that Charles Dickens had "loved her mother with the most extraordinary earnestness." He wrote again and again; and with the reckless abandon of a man so desperately unhappy that his judgment has failed him, poured out sentimental recollections and asseverations which, if they were not actual declarations of present love, were most dangerously near to them. Also, he kept the correspondence a dead secret.

Maria for her part seems to have been equally infatuated. She wrote to tell him that she had always loved him in those far-off days. After that, of course, there was only one thing to be thought of; when and where could they meet? "You open the way," wrote Dickens, "to a confidence between us which still once more, in perfect innocence and good faith, may be between ourselves alone." So they met, in secret, and alone.

Dickens has recorded his impressions of the interview in "Little Dorrit." "Flora, always tall, had grown to be very broad too, and short of breath; but that was not much. Flora, whom he had left a lily, had become a peony; but still that was not much. Flora, who had seemed enchanting in all she said and thought, was diffuse and silly. That was much. Flora, who had been spoiled and artless years ago, was determined to be spoiled and artless now. That was a fatal blow."

Fatal in every sense. The thought of what-might-have-been had preserved in his breast all these years a romantic faith. Now even that dream-like faith was shattered, and he was left face to face with the hideous reality of his life as it was.

Maria did not, or would not, perceive her failure; and persisted with her attentions until Dickens wrote to her pretty straightly and with only bare politeness. After that, presumably that she might still catch some reflected rays of her hero, Mrs. Winter emerged into the open and became friendly with Mrs. Dickens and Miss Hogarth.

In the recoil from this shock, Dickens flung himself impetuously into the political arena, and in a masterpiece of raillery and of rebuke to a "how-not-to-do-it Government," denounced the mismanagement of the Crimean war, and roundly rated the British people. This speech, his first and last as a politician, was delivered at Drury Lane Theatre, and, according to a journalist, "in its conception and in its delivery it was alike inimitable."

*Nullum quod tetigit non ornavit.* On whatever stage he stood it seemed impossible for Charles Dickens not to score an immense personal success. From the moment "Pickwick" began to boom in 1836 to the day of his death in 1870 the applause never died away, and was constantly growing in fervour. With but an occasional slight check to the

sale of one or two of his many books he strode from one
success to another. As reporter, as author, as stage manager
and actor, as public speaker, as public reader his success was
unique. The fascination of his personality conquered instantly
everyone he met. His children—all children—worshipped
him, his friends loved him, his audiences went wild over
him. Yet. . . .

By this time even Dickens himself was finding it necessary
to make excuses for his wild restlessness and unhappiness.
He put it down to his books. "I hold my inventive capacity,"
he told Maria, "on the stern condition that it must master
my whole life, often have complete possession of me, make
its own demand upon me, and sometimes, for months together, put everything else from me. . . . All this I can
hardly expect you to understand—or the restlessness and
waywardness of an author's mind. . . . I am going off; I
don't know where or how far, to ponder about I don't know
what. . . . Once upon a time I didn't do such things you
say. No. But I have done them through a good many
years now, and they have become myself and my life."

To Leigh Hunt he wrote that "when about to begin a book,"
he was "as infirm as Macbeth, as errant as mad Tom, and as
rugged as Timon. I sit down to work," he continued, "do
nothing, get up, and walk a dozen miles, come back and sit
down again, next day go down a Railroad, find a place where
I resolve to stay for a month, come home next morning, go
strolling about for hours and hours, reject all engagements
to have time to myself, get tired of myself, and yet can't
come out of myself to be pleasant to anybody else."

If indeed his books did all this to him, then England
purchased her greatest humorist at a very heavy price. It
was not entirely, or mainly, the books. On one stage—
but it was a private one—the play had broken down completely, and the actors were in despair.

In June 1855 a new type of diversion was eagerly grasped
at. The Tavistock House Theatre, "the smallest theatre in
the world," was thrown open, and for three nights was
crowded with Dickens' distinguished friends. Wilkie Collins
wrote a "domestic melodrama," *The Lighthouse*, and the

Lemon-Dickens farce, *Mr. Nightingale's Diary*, was revived;
Mr. Crummles, alias Charles Dickens, was lessee and manager,
Stanfield painted the scenery, Mr. Francesco Berger was at
the pianoforte, the elder Dickens children, Miss Hogarth,
Frank Stone, Lemon and Collins were in the casts. "The
success was wonderful," says Forster. After one of the performances Lord Campbell told the table that "he had much
rather have written 'Pickwick' than be Chief Justice of
England and a peer of Parliament." Doubtless true; but
much water had flowed under the bridges since the days of
"Pickwick," and the stream was growing ever more turbulent,
was fretting ever more restlessly its banks.

Shortly after this outburst the new book, "Nobody's
Fault," as it was called right up to the eve of publication,
when the title was altered to "Little Dorrit," was taken in
hand in real earnest. It had been begun in May but laid
aside, and even now, after a good start, inspiration came but
fitfully in spite of Folkestone air, and depression was perpetually on the doorstep.

The fitfulness of inspiration is faithfully reflected in the
story itself. "Little Dorrit" is not, for Dickens, a good
book; even Forster admitted that "it made no material
addition to the author's reputation." Isolated parts are
superb; the pen-picture of Marseilles is excellent; the descriptions of the Marshalsea and of the Circumlocution Office can
rank with anything in his works. Anyone who wishes to
know what debtors' prisons were really like in the early nineteenth century can learn from "Pickwick" and "Little
Dorrit" all he wants to know, and find pictures that will
remain in his memory for ever. Of the two, that of the
Marshalsea is if anything the better, as it is more complete
and more sustained; but in point of vividness and accuracy
there is little to choose between them.

The Marshalsea prison was demolished many years ago,
but the district is still redolent with Dickens associations.
Anyone who wanders south across London Bridge into the
Borough will quickly find St. George's Church, to the north
of which stood the prison. He will also find Marshalsea
Road, Dorrit Street, Quilp Street, and on the corner of Lant

Street the "Charles Dickens" elementary school, built over the site of Dickens' boyhood lodging.

As in "Bleak House," none of the characters is dominating, though the Father of the Marshalsea is a very powerful sketch, and Bob is a most human and lovable turnkey. Little Dorrit herself unfortunately suffers from excess of perfection, and one finds it difficult to summon up much enthusiasm about Arthur Clennam and his associates, his adventures in the Circumlocution Office always excepted. Anyone to-day who is perplexed by the fact that the British Civil Service, though obviously quite extraordinarily efficient, is popularly regarded as a byword for inefficiency, will find the reason in the pages of "Little Dorrit." It is an illuminating instance of how Dickens' influence has persisted.

Having decided to winter in Paris, Dickens left for there in October, having previously journeyed up to London to make a magnificent speech at a dinner to Thackeray, who was leaving for a lecturing tour in America.

The death of a friend recalled him to London before the month was out, and during his stay occurred one of these incidents, so slight in themselves, but which give such an insight into the loving and tender side of Dickens. Outside Whitechapel Workhouse one dark rainy night he descried "what seemed to be seven heaps of rags," "seven dumb, wet, silent horrors"—seven homeless girls. He immediately rang the bell for the master of the workhouse, but enquiry proved the casual ward to be full; so Dickens gave each girl a shilling, without, it is recorded, receiving a single "thank you."

He remained in Paris until May 1856, though making frequent journeys to London on business chiefly connected with *Household Words* and to fulfil public reading engagements. One visit, however, concluded very different business. On March 14, 1856, he purchased Gads Hill Place, the house of his childhood ambition, and which he had never given up hope of possessing. It cost him only £1,790.

In Paris he continued steadily at "Little Dorrit," the first number of which, published in December 1855, had scored a success greater even than "Bleak House." For the Christmas number of *Household Words* he wrote three chapters of the

beautiful little story "The Holly Tree Inn," the remainder
being contributed by Wilkie Collins. There was to have
been, apparently, a third author, but his work did not come
up to standard, and Dickens had to do some extra and rather
annoying work. His leisure time he spent in the society of
artists, writers, actors, and musicians, meeting among others
George Sand, whom he found to his surprise to be "a singularly ordinary woman in appearance and manner," and
renewing his acquaintance with Scribe, Auger, Lamartine and
many others distinguished in literary and artistic circles. It
was during this visit that the portrait of him by Scheffer,
which now hangs in the National Portrait Gallery, was
painted.

Dickens was by this time almost as well known in Paris as
in London. He had, indeed, a far-flung international reputation: and many years later Sir Henry Fielding Dickens found
himself treated with great respect in Russia because he was
the son of the illustrious Charles Dickens.

Reputation, however, could avail Dickens little at the
present juncture. He was fancying he had "a digestion, or
a head, or nerves, or some odd encumbrance of that kind"
to which he was "altogether unaccustomed." His "horrid
restlessness" would keep assailing him; as he wrote a page
"it suddenly came into my head that I would get up and
go to Calais. I don't know why: the moment I got there I
should want to go somewhere else."

In May he was back in London, alone. The following
month he had crossed to Boulogne. Here, at any rate, he
seemed to be able to find something of peace and tranquillity.
He put on the blue blouse of the French farmer, gardened,
read amid the roses after his day's work, and enjoyed the
society of his amiable and ambitious little landlord, M. Beau-
court, of whom he said, "I never did see such a gentle, kind
heart."

The summer residence was abruptly and painfully cut short.
An epidemic broke out in Boulogne, attacking among others,
Mr. Gilbert a'Beckett's favourite son. Mr. a'Beckett,
hastening from Paris, was himself ill when he arrived, and
father and son died within forty-eight hours of each other.

Dickens hastily sent his family home, and himself followed shortly afterwards.

"The preparations for the play are already beginning," he wrote to Mamie on October 4th. These were the preparations for another New Year performance at Tavistock House, and were on an unprecedented scale. No expense was spared; the whole house was upside down for months; there was "a painter's shop in the schoolroom: a gasfitter's shop all over the basement, a dressmaker's shop at the top of the house: a tailor's shop in my dressing-room," and later, "four stage carpenters entirely boarding on the premises, a carpenter's shop erected in the back garden, etc. etc." And Dickens? "Calm amidst the wreck, your aged friend glides away on the 'Dorrit' stream, forgetting the uproar for a stretch of hours, refreshing himself with a ten or twelve miles walk, pitches headforemost into foaming rehearsals, placidly emerges for editorial purposes, smokes over buckets of distemper with Mr. Stanfield aforesaid, again calmly floats upon the 'Dorrit' waters."

On the 6th January, 1857, the show began; it lasted four nights; "all London" talked about it, and Dickens himself "doubted if anything so complete as that play would ever be seen again." The play was *The Frozen Deep*, by Wilkie Collins, which gained a remarkable hold upon Dickens. It took a fortnight to put the house straight again. Yet somehow, somewhere amid this chaos large parts of "Little Dorrit," and Dickens' share of *The Wreck of the Golden Mary* were written.

The next excitement was the alterations to Gads Hill. In April Dickens was in Gravesend so as to be able personally to supervise them; and in June he entered into residence.

There followed a stream of visitors, among them Hans Andersen, who thus reported Dickens, "His eyes were bright as ever; the smile on his lips was the same; his frank voice was just as friendly—ay, and if possible, more winning still. He was now in the prime of manhood, in his forty-fifth year; full of youth and life and eloquence, and rich in a rare humour that glowed with kindliness . . . ever genuine, and cheerful, and sympathetic."

In the same month Douglas Jerrold died quite suddenly. Dickens, greatly shocked and grieved, immediately set to work to raise funds for Jerrold's family. Securing Arthur Smith, afterwards to be his business manager on his first reading tours, he formed a committee, and planned theatrical performances, lectures, and readings by himself on behalf of the Jerrolds. Three times he read "A Christmas Carol" at St. Martin's Hall; there were lectures by Thackeray and Dr. W. H. Russell, a noted war correspondent, and a performance of *The Frozen Deep.*

The public performance of *The Frozen Deep* was followed by a request that Dickens should bring his company to Buckingham Palace. Dickens politely refused, but in return invited Queen Victoria to see the play at The Gallery of Illustration, where it had previously been performed. Her Majesty came; and after the play sent for the actor-manager. Dickens sent his excuses. The Queen expostulated and repeated her wish. Dickens repeated his refusal, and there the matter ended.

It is a curious incident. Dickens would not go to Buckingham Palace as an actor because he was not accustomed to go there in real life; he would not be presented to Her Majesty after the play because he was still in actor's costume. If he met his Sovereign, apparently, it must be as one monarch to another.

After London, the provinces. The writing of "Little Dorrit" had been concluded in the summer, and there was nothing now to be done—editorial work being a mere trifle to this giant of labour—but to fill the time with incessant and varied activities. The climax of restlessness was at hand. More money was wanted for the Jerrolds; requests for readings and performances were coming from all over the country, and Dickens set himself to satisfy them in a fury of energy. Forster expostulated, but in vain. "Too late to say, put the curb on," bitterly replied Dickens, ". . . the wrong man to say it to. I have now no relief but in action. I am become incapable of rest. I am quite confident I should rust, break, and die, if I spared myself. Much better to die, doing."

He went on tour. He assumed "an amount of labour in

HOMAGE TO HANS CHRISTIAN ANDERSEN

*Reproduced by permission of the proprietors of "Punch"*

acting and travelling that might have appalled an experienced comedian." His behaviour was remarked upon: "what was highest in his nature had ceased for the time to be highest in his life." The comments are Forster's, who says that all this "expressed but the craving which still had possession of him to get by some means at some change that should make existence easier."

Existence had become very hard. Though he could put on a smiling face and completely deceive Hans Andersen, who loved him a little beyond this side idolatry, he was in fact desperate. His very powers of invention he felt were failing; he, who had found invention so easy, had been compelled to make notes and memoranda for "Little Dorrit"; he was dreading at any moment a break-down; he was perpetually goaded to action by a something, he knew not what—"*Restlessness*, you will say," he told Forster. "Whatever it is, it is always driving me, and I cannot help it." It was more than restlessness; the long tension of twenty years was bursting its bonds at last.

Bit by bit the truth came out. For three years odd words of "home dissatisfactions and misgivings" had been dropping on the ears of Forster, who seems to have been strangely deaf to them. In 1856, Dickens was wildly talking about retiring to a monastery—the St. Bernard—to be alone and to write there a story. The same year he admits in a letter that "I find the skeleton in my domestic closet is becoming a pretty big one."

In 1858, Dickens at last spoke out plainly, first to Collins and then to Forster. In reply to a letter of the latter's touching upon old times, Dickens wrote, "My reference to 'confidences' was merely to the relief of saying a word of what has long been pent up in my mind. Poor Catherine and I are not made for each other, and there is no help for it. It is not only that she makes me uneasy and unhappy, but that I make her so, too—and much more so. She is exactly what you know, in the way of being amiable and complying; but we are strangely ill-assorted for the bond there is between us. . . . I am often cut to the heart by thinking what a pity it is, for her own sake, that I ever fell in her way; and if I were sick and disabled to-morrow, I know how sorry she would be, and how deeply grieved myself, to think how we had lost each other. But exactly the same incompatibility would arise, the moment I was well again; and nothing on earth could make her understand me, or suit us to each other . . . . What is now befalling me I have seen steadily coming, ever since the days you remember when Mary was born, and I know too well that you cannot, and no one can, help me."

There is no need to enlarge upon the matter. Mary was born in 1838. It has been suggested earlier in this book that Dickens had definitely recognized the hopelessness of the position by 1842. Mrs. Dickens had been saying for years before the separation took place that she ought to go away. Dickens had persistently refused, on account of the children. The children were now growing up; the girls, whom specially he wished to protect, were out of their 'teens; why prolong further an unendurable strain?

"There can be no disparity in marriage like unsuitability of mind and purpose." There is the whole position. Dickens was intellectually and physically abnormally active; Mrs. Dickens was intellectually and physically inclined to be indolent. Naturally, the two could not for long work amicably in double harness. Dickens despaired, and sought solace in a furious expenditure of energy. Mrs. Dickens despaired, but had no energy to expend. As the one grew in stature, the other declined. Such cases are hopeless from the start.

Forster was asked to approach Mrs. Dickens. Mrs. Dickens, who probably did not like Forster greatly, asked that Mark Lemon should advise her in the negotiations. The separation was arranged. Mrs. Dickens was to have £600 a year. By her special request Charley was to live with her. She was allowed to see the other children "when, where and how" she wished, but they were to remain with their father and their Aunt Georgy, who for many years already had been as a mother to them.

Unfortunately, a man so well known as Dickens cannot arrange such matters without comment. People talked. Gossip, as always, became slanderous, and presently Dickens' name was being coupled with that of a young actress, Miss Ellen Lawless Ternan, who had acted with him in *The Frozen Deep*. There was no truth in the story.

It needed but that to send Dickens completely off his balance. His reaction was curious, but not surprising. He forgot that he was a private person, and remembered only that he was an "institution," a "great moral force in the land." He wrote a long letter testifying to the length of his domestic unhappiness, saying that he and his wife would have separated long before but for Georgina Hogarth, relating how the separation was arranged, and repudiating the aspersion upon Miss Ternan. This letter he gave to Mr. Arthur Smith, with instructions to show it to "anyone who wished to do me right, or to anyone who may have been misled into doing me wrong."

Mr. Smith obeyed his instructions only too faithfully. A copy of the letter reached the *New York Tribune*, and was published in that newspaper. Its publication stimulated the gossips exceedingly, until Dickens, wild with exasperation at what he called the "violation" of his letter, penned a long vindication of himself and published it on the front page of *Household Words* on June 12th, 1858. There were, he said in effect, so many thousands of people who knew him only through his books, and who might, hearing the scandalous reports being spread about him, come to doubt him and his advocacy of good works. . . . It is no light matter to be a "great moral force."

Had the matter ended there it would still have been a deplorable error, sufficient to have lost any man the respect of his public. Yet, with a resolution akin to madness, Dickens pushed it still further. He sent copies of the article to the other papers for publication. Some printed it, some did not. Among those which did not was *Punch*.

The proprietors of *Punch* were Messrs. Bradbury and Evans; the editor was Mark Lemon. Dickens quarrelled furiously with both. He forbade his children ever to speak to "Uncle Mark" again, or to enter Mr. Evans' house; and he broke off business relations with the firm.

This quarrel involved of course the winding up of *Household Words*, the ownership of which, following a lawsuit and a Chancery decree, was sold by auction in the following year. It was purchased by Mr. Arthur Smith on behalf of Charles Dickens, who had the previous month launched a new periodical, *All the Year Round*, exactly similar in every respect.

It is perhaps the most remarkable tribute paid to Dickens' hold upon his public that his strange actions at this time appear to have done little or nothing to weaken it. A great many people were grieved and upset; there was a certain amount of newspaper criticism, the *Liverpool Mercury* in particular speaking out very plainly; but the great popularity rolled on undiminished. In fact, at this very moment it took on a new and more vigorous lease of life.

In the same month as his separation from his wife was being arranged, Dickens began his blazing career as a professional reader.

## CHAPTER XIII

*" What do you think of my paying for this place, by reviving that old idea of some Readings from my books ?"*—DICKENS to Forster, 5th September, 1857.

"AT the present moment," wrote Dickens to M. de Cerjat in July 1858, "I am on my little Kentish freehold . . . looking on as pretty a view out of my study window as you will find in a long day's English ride. My little place is a grave red brick house, which I have added to and stuck bits upon in all manner of ways, so that it is as pleasantly irregular, and as violently opposed to all architectural ideas, as the most hopeful man could possibly desire. The robbery was committed before the door on the man with the treasure, and Falstaff ran away from the identical spot of ground now covered by the room in which I write. A little rustic ale-house, called the Sir John Falstaff, is over the way—has been over the way, ever since, in honour of the event. Cobham Woods and Park are behind the house; the distant Thames in front; the Medway, with Rochester, and its old castle and cathedral, on one side. The whole stupendous property is on the old Dover Road."

A very pretty little parable of the life of Charles Dickens may be constructed by the imaginatively-minded who are energetic enough to walk from Chatham to Gads Hill via Ordnance Terrace and The Brook.

A few paces up the hill from the station stands Ordnance Terrace, gazing forward over a semi-circular valley which encloses the Chatham dockyards and the Rochester bastions. The view is good, but not too good, for though the house is on a hill, it is only half-way up it, and is rather in a hollow. It is almost the lowest house in the terrace, and by a curious chance, houses above it receive week by week into their furnished apartments the members of the touring companies who are playing at the Chatham Theatre.

There is a sharp descent, both socially as well as physically, to The Brook, Dickens' second Chatham home.

From there one turns westward, and walks through one of the narrowest, crookedest, and most oddly up-and-downish main streets in all England. Part of it is in Chatham, part in Rochester, but it is all one street, and all very similar. It is really very straight, but it wriggles so much that it gives the impression of being very crooked; it is really very flat, but what with its bends and its bumps and its raised pavement at one point and its dip for the railway bridge at another it gives the impression of being very undulating. It is only about two miles long, but it seems like twenty.

Towards the end of it are hidden—in the "old corners" into which young Charles Dickens peeped in his boyhood days— Eastgate House, Watts's Charity, Restoration House, the Cathedral, and finally the Castle. They are all, as it were, tucked away in the pockets of Rochester High Street; even the Castle, though it stands high upon a mound, could quite easily be missed by a young man in a hurry and a sports car. No one, however, can fail to notice the almost startling change that comes over the prospect when one finally emerges from Rochester to be confronted by the great iron-girdered bridge across the Medway.

That bridge is within a minute or so's walk of the Castle. One turns a corner, expecting to see more twisting street, and is amazed to find a broad, dignified arterial road that goes sweeping up the long hill through Strood towards Gravesend and London in a series of magnificent curves.

A mile or more out of Strood it flattens and straightens for a while; then comes another steeper bit to the summit of the hill, and there, on the left-hand side of the road, solid, respectable and eminently English, commanding practically the whole range of the countryside, stands Gads Hill Place. It is a girls' school now, but not noticeably so. There is, happily, no sign of the "show place." It is still a grave and homely residence, pleasantly retired from the road, and not

WATTS'S CHARITY, ROCHESTER, FOUNDED IN 1579

nearly so irregular in appearance as Dickens' letter would suggest. We have, of course, passed through the great bungaloid era in architecture since then. Its exterior is dignified, almost aloof; inside, one understands, as many traces of the Dickens' occupation as possible are retained, even to the mock books and their titles painted on the library door.

The house was built in 1779, and apart from the additions made by Dickens probably looks now much as it did one hundred and fifty years ago. "The Sir John Falstaff" would one imagines, hardly care to be described to-day as "a little rustic alehouse"; both it and "The Leather Bottle" at Cobham a few miles away have had to sacrifice themselves somewhat to fame, but both wear their notoriety with a pleasingly modest air.

At Gads Hill Dickens found at last some measure of peace. "The blessed woods and fields," he told de Cerjat, "have done me a world of good, and I am quite myself again." There, but for the fatal idea of paying for the house by public readings, and the still more fatal glamour of the footlights, he might perhaps have lived to a patriarchal and tranquil old age.

At first he intended to use Gads Hill only as a summer residence; but it grew more and more upon him, and from 1865 became his permanent home. The alterations and additions to the "Kentish Freehold" continued year after year: a whole wing was added to the house, the stables and offices were rebuilt, a well was sunk for water, a tunnel was bored under the Dover Road to lead into the shrubbery opposite, where stood the Swiss chalet, the gift of Fechter, in which from 1865 the Master regularly worked.

"Well, Katey," said Dickens to his daughter in 1870, after building a conservatory he had long set his heart upon, "now you see POSITIVELY the last improvement at Gads Hill." Everybody laughed, because every alteration had been "positively the last." This time the words came sadly true. Within a week the Master had passed away.

Dickens speedily became a highly respected and popular figure in the neighbourhood. He interested himself in the

affairs of the nearby village of Higham, and did all he could
to help the villagers. His meadow became their cricket
ground, himself and his sons the patrons of the club; he
organized for them athletic sports and other festivities out-
of-doors, and theatricals in the house. The well that was
bored at Gads Hill Place was largely for their benefit.

The villagers for their part greatly appreciated the kindly
sympathy he showed. When in 1860 Miss Katie Dickens
was married to Mr. Charles Collins, brother of Wilkie, they
built triumphal arches across the road to the church and
turned out *en masse* to attend the ceremony, while the
village blacksmith fired a salute with a small cannon primed
for the occasion. When Dickens returned from America
they made great preparations for a joyous reception, and
even though he, surfeited with public demonstrations, tried
to avoid them by leaving the train at Gravesend, they were
not to be thwarted, and marched out along the Dover Road
to meet him and to bring him home in triumph.

Among Dickens' most interesting letters is one written
from America shortly towards the end of his second tour.
Racked by illness and suffering daily exquisite pain, lying
but half alive through long hours in order to summon up
sufficient energy for the evening ordeal of reading, he yet found
time and strength to write a long letter to his son Harry (Sir
H. F. Dickens) advising him how to run the Higham cricket
club so as to create and preserve friendly and honest relations
between the members and himself.

At Gads Hill he entertained his friends on a lavish scale.
There was the house, always with some new and interesting
addition, and the estate, constantly growing and constantly
improved, to be shown, and the beautiful countryside with
its delightful old towns and villages, Rochester, Chatham,
Maidstone and Canterbury, Cobham, Chalk, Shorne, and
Cooling, to be explored. The picnics at Gads Hill were
famous; and for his American friends—the Fields—Dickens
turned out upon the Dover Road an old English stage-coach,
complete with red-coated postilions.

Yet his life on his Kentish freehold was in the main quiet
and intensely orderly. When there were no visitors, and

ROCHESTER CASTLE

sometimes when there were, his mornings were given to writing. An early breakfast, an inspection of the house to see everything was in its place, a turn or two in the meadow, and then he would retire to his study or, after its arrival, to the chalet among the trees, where the birds flew in and out as he wrote, and the sun glanced through the branches that rustled over the verandah.

In the afternoons the dogs—Turk, or Linda, or Don, or Sultan, or poor Bumble, "always in scrapes," were whistled out, and they accompanied their master on great joyful walks about the countryside. Dickens soon knew every spot within twelve miles, loving especially the Cobham lanes and Park, and the desolate marsh lands on which stood Cooling Church and its ruined castle.

And when the sun had set there were the nightingales. . . .

There can be little doubt that Dickens would have undertaken his paid public readings even had he never seen Gads Hill. They were foreshadowed from the day he dashed to London to read "The Chimes"; they were certain from the moment he was offered a fee to read at Bradford. Every motive was present to induce him to undertake them. It was not so much that they would bring in large sums of money; they offered him a unique stage which gave him in larger measure and more concentrated form what he needed most in life, excitement and applause. These two words are used in no unkindly sense; Dickens' vitality, mental and emotional, were such that he had constantly to be living at concert pitch, and throughout his life public approval and sympathy were absolute necessities to him. Money was certainly not the main reason for his turning professional reader, though he was eager now to acquire sufficient to endow his family, some members of which were giving already indications of being little able to endow themselves.

The first paid reading was at St. Martin's Hall, London, on April 29th, 1858. Two overwhelmingly successful readings in aid of charity, one at Edinburgh in March, and one in London on April 15th in aid of the Hospital for Sick Children in Great Ormond Street, had finally decided him. The objections Forster and others had urged were swept aside. Dickens

N

told his audience that he felt that it was right that he and his public should meet "on terms of mutual confidence and respect."

From the first there was never any doubt as to the success of the readings. There has never been anything like it. A single man on a bare platform, with a book in one hand and a large paper-knife in the other; in front of him a small reading-table and behind a draping of black cloth, the whole illuminated by a portable gas apparatus—and to hear this man read people all over the British Isles thronged into theatres and halls till they crowded them to the very roof, till they were crushed to the point of suffocation, till they overflowed right on to the reader's platform and hung there clutching the legs of his table.

Large hall or small, it was always the same; more people were turned away than got in. Those who did get in laughed and sobbed and held their breath in tense emotion as the reading proceeded, and cheered themselves hoarse at the end. This account of one is, almost without exception, the account of every reading. "We had a most wonderful night at Exeter," wrote Dickens to Miss Hogarth in August 1858, ". . . it was a prodigious cram, and we turned away no end of people. But not only that, I think they were the finest audience I ever read to. I don't think I ever read, in some respects, as well; and I never beheld anything like the personal affection which they poured out upon me at the end."

Always the same note: practically wherever he went there was the same cram, the same most appreciative audience he had ever met. He never failed them, but always rose to superlative heights in response; and their demonstrations of affection and admiration grew more and more unparalleled. The tale is varied only by incidents such as the smashing of the pay-boxes by the rush of the crowd, or the far more frightening accident at Newcastle-on-Tyne in the winter of 1861, when the gas apparatus fell down, and for a moment there was a fearful danger of panic as well as of fire.

"There were three great galleries crammed to the roof," wrote Dickens next day to his daughter Mamie, "and a panic must have destroyed numbers of people. A lady in the front

ROCHESTER CATHEDRAL

row of stalls screamed, and ran out wildly towards me, and for an instant there was a terrible wave in the crowd. I addressed that lady laughing (for I knew she was in the sight of everybody there), and called out as if it happened every night, 'There's nothing the matter, I assure you; don't be alarmed; pray sit down'; and she sat down directly, and there was a thunder of applause. It took some few minutes to mend, and I looked on with my hands in my pockets; for I think if I had turned my back for a moment there might still have been a move."

It was but rarely that anything went wrong. Dickens' letters during these tours are full of anecdotes, mostly humorous. "Whaa't sart of a hoose, sur?" anxiously enquired the hotel boots on his first visit to Dublin. "Capital!" "The Lard be praised fur the 'onor o' Dooblin!"

Dickens undertook altogether four series of readings, that is, four groups of tours, each extending through two or more years and each followed by a respite of some months. The first series began on April 29th, 1858, and concluded on October 27th, 1859. Most of it took place in 1858; there were sixteen readings at St. Martin's Hall between April and July, followed by eighty-seven in the provinces, including visits to Scotland and Ireland, between August 2nd and November 13th. In all, one hundred and twenty-five paid readings were given in these two years.

The material read was chosen, prepared and rehearsed with scrupulous care. Each reading was timed to take two hours, with an interval of five minutes in the middle. In order to achieve this it was necessary first to piece together a continuous narrative by abridgment of the original text, and over this Dickens expended great pains. There followed long daily rehearsals before a tour, and while the tour was in progress.

There was nothing of the amateur about Dickens; the unbounded success of his readings was due in the first place to his great natural ability both as author and as actor, but it was due also to a preparation which left nothing to chance, to a conscientious and laborious development of his art to the very highest pitch of excellence. During the first few weeks of the first tour Dickens sometimes became hoarse through overstrain of his voice, but he quickly learned to correct that, and from then onwards, as Mr. Straus asserts, "there was not a hall in the Kingdom where every member of his audience could not hear the softest word that came from his lips." As for the art of reading, "Every word came to be learnt by heart; every inflection, every gesture was studied until it was mechanically produced."

The readings chosen for the first series included "A Christmas Carol," "The Chimes," "The Trial" from "Pickwick" "The Story of Paul Dombey," "Boots at the Holly Tree Inn," "The Poor Traveller," and "Mrs. Gamp." Of these, "A Christmas Carol" was first favourite, followed closely by "Pickwick," "Mrs. Gamp," and "Dombey."

For the second series, four fresh readings were prepared but only two were used: an abridgment of "David Copperfield," and "Nicholas Nickleby at the Yorkshire School." Both were hugely successful. For the third he added to his repertoire "Bob Sawyer" and "Dr. Marigold." For the fourth and final series a fatal addition was made, which did much to break Dickens up and hasten his untimely death. This was the murder in "Oliver Twist."

Forster protested vigorously against this last, but unfortunately chose the wrong line of argument. Instead of emphasizing how dangerously fatiguing it would be, he declared the subject "to be altogether out of the province of reading." Dickens' reply to this was, quite reasonably, to give the reading a trial before a small private audience. Unhappily, though opinions were divided, there was sufficient approval to encourage him to give it a public trial. Forster still clung to his mistaken argument, with the result that a "painful correspondence" ensued. "We might have agreed to differ about it very well," wrote Dickens, "because we only wanted to find out the truth if we could, and it was quite understood that I wanted to leave behind me the recollection of something very passionate and dramatic, done with simple means, if the art would justify the theme."

Whether the art did justify the theme cannot now be

HOMES OF THE CANTERBURY WEAVERS

settled. Forster would never admit that it did; on the other hand, Macready declared the reading to be "two Macbeths," and audiences went wild over it. What appears certain is, that coming on top of all his other exertions, it brought Dickens to the verge of a paralytic stroke.

The evil effects of the readings were not manifest for the first few years. During 1858 and 1859, though at times Dickens found it difficult to sleep, and complained once that he seemed "to be always either in a railway carriage, or reading and going to bed," and that he "got so knocked up" that whenever he had a moment to remember it he went to bed "as a matter of course," he was able to declare that: "Although all our people from Smith downwards have given in more or less, at times, I have never been in the least unequal to the work, though sometimes sufficiently disinclined for it."

Arthur Smith, one may be sure, would never have given in but for the fact that he was already a sick man. Dickens had known him as a friend for years; his brother had dramatized "The Cricket on the Hearth" in 1845, and it is probable that the friendship dated from this time. After acting as manager for the Douglas Jerrold performances, he became secretary-manager to Dickens for the first series of readings. He filled the post admirably, revelling in hard work, being equally happy in the thick of correspondence or with his coat off arranging platforms and chairs, and delighting in every sign of success in the readings. Dickens tells the most delicious anecdotes about him. "Arthur . . . had his shirt front and waistcoat torn off last night. He was perfectly enraptured in consequence." What Dickens valued perhaps more than anything else was the "sense I used to have of compactness and comfort about me while I was reading."

Unfortunately, Arthur Smith was two or three times attacked by illness during the first series, and when the time came to open the second, the first six engagements of which he had arranged, he was dangerously ill and not expected to recover. He died less than a month later in October 1861.

Dickens felt his loss grievously; it was, he said, as if his right arm was gone. He went on his tour feeling as if he could only just "open one of the books and screw the text out of myself in a flat dull way." The result was, on the first night at Norwich, one of the exceedingly rare occasions on which a reading fell comparatively flat. Canterbury quickly remedied matters, the audience there giving a response "like the touch of a beautiful instrument," and from then onwards the series, in spite of the somewhat indifferent managership of Mr. Headland, Arthur Smith's successor, marched from one triumph to another.

At Edinburgh in November 1861, "in a gale of wind and fierce rain," one thousand people had to be turned away, while a "steaming wet" audience "never flagged for an instant." In Paris in February 1863, Dickens gave four readings at the British Embassy on behalf of the British Charitable fund, to "such audiences and such enthusiasm" as he had never before seen. "The thing culminated . . . in a two-hours' storm of excitement and pleasure. They actually recommenced," he told Mamie, "and applauded right away into their carriages and down the street."

It was between the conclusion of the second series of readings in June 1863 and the opening of the third in March 1866, that there came an obvious and serious decline in his health. To this in part the exertions and the constant travelling imposed upon him during his tours certainly contributed; but he was, in addition, much moved by the death of his mother, one of his sons, and several friends. Also, he was in a terrible railway accident, in which his life was miraculously spared, but from the shock of which he never properly recovered.

His mother, who had been failing in health for two years, passed away in September 1863, at the age of 73. On the following Christmas Eve Thackeray died. This event was the more distressing to Dickens as it took place only three weeks after the two had become friends again following a five years' estrangement. This long quarrel, which had been magnified by the gossips into a jealous difference between two master novelists, had come to pass through Dickens' defence of one of his "young men," Edmund Yates, who had written (not in *All the Year Round*) a rather too personal article on Thackeray.

On the 7th February, 1864, Dickens' birthday, came the news that his son Walter Savage Landor, an officer in the 26th Native Infantry Regiment, had died at Calcutta on the 31st December, 1863. Almost at the same time Dickens heard of the death of Mrs. White of Bonchurch, which affected him nearly as grievously. In November 1864, the death of John Leech completely unnerved him for a short while.

In February 1865, there came a lameness in his left foot which he put down to frostbite, and persisted in thinking was a local affection, but which was in effect the first outward sign of the danger of paralysis. He had to take to a surgical boot, and give up walking for a time. Then almost on top of this illness came the appalling railway disaster at Staplehurst, near Maidstone, on June 9th.

Dickens had been for a short holiday in France which had appeared very much to recover him, and was on his way home to Gads Hill from Folkestone, when near Staplehurst the express in which he was travelling dashed at full speed on to a bridge where the line was being repaired, and over half the train hurtled into the river beneath.

"I was in the only carriage that did not go over into the stream," Dickens wrote to Milton. "It was caught upon the turn by some of the ruin of the bridge, and hung suspended and balanced in an apparently impossible manner. Two ladies were my fellow-passengers, an old one and a young one.

"This is exactly what passed. You may judge from it the precise length of the suspense: Suddenly we were off the rail, and beating the ground as the car of a half emptied balloon might. The old lady cried out, 'My God!' and the young one screamed. I caught hold of them both (the old lady sat opposite and the young one on my left), and said: 'We can't help ourselves, but we can be quiet and composed. Pray don't cry out.' The old lady immediately answered: 'Thank you. Rely upon me.

Upon my soul I will be quiet.' We were then all tilted down together in a corner of the carriage, and stopped. I said to them thereupon: 'You may be sure nothing worse can happen. Our danger *must* be over. Will you remain here without stirring, while I get out of the window?' They both answered, quite collectedly, ' Yes,' and I got out without the least notion of what had happened. Fortunately, I got out with great caution and stood upon the step. Looking down I saw the bridge gone, and nothing below me but the line of rail. Some people in the other two compartments were madly trying to plunge out of the window, and had no idea that there was an open swampy field fifteen feet down below them, and nothing else! The two guards (one with his face cut) were running up and down on the down side of the bridge (which was not torn up) quite wildly. I called out to them: 'Look at me. Do stop an instant and look at me, and tell me whether you don't know me.' One of them answered: 'We know you very well, Mr. Dickens.' 'Then,' I said, 'my good fellow, for God's sake give me your key, and send one of those labourers here, and I'll empty this carriage.' We did it quite safely, by means of a plank or two, and when it was done I saw all the rest of the train, except the two baggage vans, down in the stream. I got into the carriage again for my brandy flask, and took off my travelling hat for a basin, climbed down the brickwork and filled my hat with water.

"Suddenly I came upon a staggering man covered with blood (I think he must have been flung clean out of his carriage), with such a frightful cut across the skull that I couldn't bear to look at him. I poured some water over his face, and gave him some [to] drink, then gave him some brandy, and laid him down on the grass, and he said, 'I am gone,' and died afterwards. Then I stumbled over a lady lying on her back against a little pollard tree, with the blood streaming over her face (which was lead colour) in a number of distinct little streams from the head. I asked her if she could swallow a little brandy and she just nodded, and I gave her some and left her for somebody else. The next time I passed her she was dead. Then a man . . . came running up to me and implored me to help him find his wife, who was afterwards found dead. No imagination can conceive the ruin of the carriages, or the extraordinary weights under which the people were lying, or the complications into which they were twisted up among iron and wood, and mud and water.''

Ten people were killed and twenty fearfully injured in this dreadful accident. How many were saved from death by what Dickens referred to as his ''—I don't know what to call it—constitutional (I suppose) presence of mind,'' cannot be said, but certainly several owed their lives to him; and the directors of the South-Eastern Railway sent him a Resolution of thanks.

In spite of his remarkable presence of mind at the time— he actually remembered to climb back into his carriage for the manuscript of ''Our Mutual Friend'' which he had left there—he suffered severely from shock for days afterwards, and for the rest of his life was nervous of entering an express train.

His foot troubled him again during the autumn, and by February 1866, he realized himself unwell enough to justify a searching medical examination. The report reassured him. ''Only remarkable irritability of the heart,'' said the specialist. ''I knew well beforehand,'' commented Dickens, ''that the effect could not possibly be without the one cause at the bottom of it, of some degeneration of some function of the heart. Of course I am not so foolish as to suppose that all my work can have been achieved without *some* penalty. . . .''

That, however, was no reason for giving in; and there was every reason for going on. ''I am so undoubtedly one of the sons of Toil—and fathers of children,'' he wrote to Wilkie Collins about this time, ''that I expect to be presently presented with a smock frock, a pair of leather breeches, and a pewter watch, for having brought up the largest family ever known, with the smallest disposition to do anything for themselves."

First his parents, then his brothers and their dependants, and now his children! Can one wonder that in his books Dickens is rather bitter about poor relations?

In the spring of 1866 he contracted with Messrs. Chappells, of Bond Street, from now onwards to be his business managers for all readings, to read "in London, the Provinces, or elsewhere as you and we may agree," for thirty nights at £50 a night. Chappells made all arrangements, paid all expenses, took all responsibility, and all risk.

"The success everywhere," says Forster, "went far beyond even the former successes." At Liverpool three thousand people had to be turned away; at Edinburgh Dickens' reception was such that his staff thought he would never be allowed to begin; at Glasgow placards had to be posted about the town saying that no money would be taken at the doors. Before one-third of the tour was over enough money had been taken to cover all expenses, though Chappells, in addition to paying him most liberally, were lavishly generous in their arrangements for his comfort.

Dickens found that the incessant travelling fatigued him at times, and during May he developed a heavy cold, but otherwise he was generally in good health and spirits. His new manager, George Dolby, was "a man of resources," and he had Wills, his sub-editor, as travelling companion on all his journeys. So satisfied was he that in August he signed a second contract, this time for forty-two readings at £60 a night.

These readings began in January 1867. Their success was, if anything, greater than ever; but now Dickens began to show alarming signs of overstrain. On Monday, January 18th, at Liverpool, he was "taken so faint" after the reading that he had to be laid on a sofa for half an hour. A week later he could hardly hold out against a railway journey of forty minutes. In February he was troubled with a recurrence of "an internal malady that occasionally at long intervals troubles me," and suffered much loss of blood.

Yet in spite of it all he was beginning "to feel myself drawn towards America as Darnay in the 'Tale of Two Cities' was attracted to Paris. It is my Loadstone Rock."

As early as 1859, offers had been made for a reading tour in the United States. Dickens had declined these, as he had also declined in 1862 an offer from Australia of £10,000 for an eight months' tour. The American Civil War had for some years put out of the question any readings on the other side of the Atlantic; but now offers were being renewed, and so vigorously that "every mail brings me proposals."

He had previously declared that only a very large sum paid down before he left England would tempt him to America. Not one but many such guarantees were now being offered, and from responsible people. Chappells, too, were proposing to send him.

By May 1867, Dickens found himself "at bay at last on the American question." Even the death of his old friend Stanfield he felt could not move him as it ought, because of "this spectre of doubt and indecision that sits at the board with me and stands at the bedside."

Early in August, Dolby was sent to America to reconnoitre. Hardly had he gone than Dickens suffered a worse attack of foot trouble than any before. This time his specialist was not reassuring. But in September Dolby returned, and from his report he and Dickens calculated that 80 readings would bring in a net profit of £15,000.

On September 29th, after a long consultation with Forster (who all through sturdily opposed the scheme) and Dolby, Dickens telegraphed to Messrs. Ticknor and Fields, Boston, Mass., that they could go ahead with arrangements for a reading tour in the States. Dolby left at once to complete arrangements, and on the 9th of November Dickens sailed a second time for the United States. He had contradicted rumours in the newspapers as to his ill-health, and had declared that he had never been ill.

He landed in Boston on November 19th, after a somewhat stormy voyage. His reception was as overwhelming as it had been twenty-five years before. He remained five months in the States and made a net profit of £20,000. If the scenes of enthusiasm had been extraordinary in the British

Isles, they were wonderful beyond all description in America. He read chiefly in Boston and New York City, but visited also Philadelphia, Washington, Baltimore, Albany, Portland and other large cities. At Boston thousands of people waited all night outside Ticknor and Fields' offices to purchase tickets for the first readings. And at Boston the trouble with the speculators started.

Though Dickens found the Americans improved out of all recognition on his second visit, they had by no means lost their ability to be "slick." Numbers of them speedily realized that there was good money to be made by speculating on the tickets for admission to Dickens' readings.

The original price of these tickets was two dollars for any seat. Hardly had the sale been concluded in Boston before it was discovered that large numbers of tickets had been purchased by speculators who were now hawking them at enhanced prices. The game quickly became so profitable that large numbers of people began to play it.

Dickens could afford to laugh at this, for the trouble was not his, but Dolby's. Poor Dolby had a dreadful time; everybody blamed him for whatever he did; a newspaper labelled him "pudding-headed Dolby," and he was invariably greeted with a storm of joking and abuse whenever he arrived anywhere to sell tickets.

He never overcame the speculators. He tried selling no more than six tickets to any one person; one speculator, who moved from place to place with Dickens, employed fifty men and so obtained 300 tickets. He refused once to sell tickets to people in caps, the local agent having advised him that speculators wore caps; in five minutes the whole queue was hatted.

By the beginning of 1868 "The noble army of speculators are now furnished," wrote Dickens, "(this is literally true, and I am quite serious), each man with a straw mattress, a little bag of bread and meat, two blankets, and a bottle of whiskey. With this outfit *they lie down in a line on the pavement* the whole night before the tickets are sold. . . . It being severely cold at Brooklyn, they made an immense bonfire in the street—a narrow street of wooden houses!—

which the police turned out to extinguish.  A general fight
then took place, out of which the people farthest off in the
line rushed bleeding when they saw a chance of displacing
others near the door, and put their mattresses in those places,
and then held on by the iron rails.  At eight in the morning
Dolby appeared with the tickets in a portmanteau.  He was
immediately saluted with a roar of 'Halloa, Dolby!  So
Charley has let you have the carriage, has he, Dolby!  How
is he, Dolby?  Don't drop the tickets, Dolby.  Look alive,
Dolby!' etc. etc. etc., in the midst of which he proceeded to
business, and concluded (as usual) by giving universal
dissatisfaction."  Dolby took all this in good part, and his
relations with Dickens (who valued his care and ability most
highly) were ever cordial and affectionate.

As on his British tours, Dickens refused all offers of private
hospitality, living everywhere in hotels with his assistants.
He confined his visiting also within rigid limits, though he
looked up such of the old friends of twenty-five years ago
as were still living.  Irving, Felton, and Prescott were dead,
but he met again Longfellow, Holmes, Emerson and Dana.
He spent much time with Mr. James Fields, who had been
responsible for his coming, and his wife, both of whom were
to rank henceforth among his dearest friends.

He could not, of course, avoid all publicity; he was invited
to the White House, and visited there on his birthday.
There were occasional dinners, and a grand farewell banquet
at Delmonico's in New York on April 18th.  But, long before
that last event took place, it had become apparent that
Dickens was a very sick man indeed.

Travelling from Boston to New York he caught a severe
cold which developed into catarrh, and this never left him
throughout his stay in America.  In December his heart was
troubling him again.  He could not sleep; he had continual
digestive trouble which prevented him from taking any
proper meals.  His foot was painful once more.  The long
railway journeys were trying in the extreme.

During the next two months it is no exaggeration to say
that only the unceasing care of Dolby and Mr. and Mrs.
Fields kept him alive.  Day after day he would lie exhausted

and in pain on a sofa, and it seemed impossible he could ever read at night. Yet night after night he would recover for two hours all his old vitality and strength, and would send thousands of people into ecstasies of delight. Then he would collapse again until the time for the next reading.

In February 1868, he had an unexpected and probably providential holiday. The impeachment of President Johnson so absorbed public attention that Dickens cancelled all readings for a week, and amused himself in the meantime by arranging a great walking match between Dolby and Osgood, the American treasurer for the tour. The formalities were arranged in true Dickensian style. Calling himself "The Gadshill Gasper" and Mr. Fields "Massachusetts Jemmy," Dickens christened Dolby "The Man of Ross" and Osgood "The Boston Bantam," drew up Articles of Agreement for the match, acted as trainer, and wrote a narrative of it. The course was over thirteen miles of slushy road deep in snow; the stakes were four hats, to be presented to the winner at a dinner given by Dickens. Dolby was soundly beaten, Dickens was hugely delighted, much wine was drunk at the dinner; and the indomitable reader was buoyed up for a final series of readings in New York and Boston.

In spite of this tonic, his health was by now in a precarious state. Yet, Dolby has recorded, "Still he persevered with the task he had before him and performed it without one word of complaint, all the time; seldom eating and drinking, and scarcely ever sleeping." By April his diet had become: "At seven in the morning, in bed, a tumbler of new cream and two tablespoonsful of rum. At twelve a sherry cobbler and a biscuit. At three (dinner time), a pint of champagne. At five minutes to eight, an egg beaten up with a glass of sherry. Between the parts, the strongest beef tea that can be made, drunk hot. At a quarter-past ten, soup, and anything to drink that I can fancy." Also, he was taking laudanum in order to get some sleep.

He very nearly gave in. Longfellow and other Harvard men begged him to do so. Dolby, "as tender as a woman and as watchful as a doctor," and George, the man in charge of the gas, mounted guard on the platform whenever he read, dreading at any moment a collapse. By the time he reached Boston he was so lame that he could not walk from the railway station.

Yet the readings were better than ever; and on April 18th he nerved himself for a final magnificent effort. The Press had invited him to dine with them before embarking. Though he was more than half-dead, he made up his mind that nothing should stop him from going.

The dinner was timed for five. Dickens was too ill to get there before six. A newspaper has reported that "At about five o'clock on Saturday the hosts began to assemble, but at 5.30 the news was received that the expected guest had succumbed to a painful affection of the foot. In a short time, however, another bulletin announced Mr. Dickens's intention to attend the dinner at all hazards. At a little after six, having been assisted up the stairs, he was joined by Mr. Greeley, and the hosts forming in two lines silently permitted the distinguished gentleman to pass through. Mr. Dickens limped perceptibly; his right foot was swathed, and he leaned heavily on the arm of Mr. Greeley. He evidently suffered great pain."

His hosts toasted him. He rose to reply; and as they cheered him again and again, all his sickness fell from him as by magic. He spoke to them first as one newspaper man to another. "To the wholesome training of severe newspaper work when I was a very young man," he said, "I constantly refer my first success, and my sons will hereafter testify of their father that he was always steadily proud of that ladder by which he rose."

He followed with a magnificent apology which wonderfully atoned for his blunders of a quarter of a century before:

"I henceforth charge myself, not only here, but on every suitable occasion whatsoever and wheresoever, to express my high and grateful sense of my second reception in America, and to bear my honest testimony to the national generosity and magnanimity . . . on my return to England, in my own person, to bear for the behoof of my countrymen, such testimony to the gigantic changes in this country, as I have hinted at to-night; also to record that wherever I have been, in the smallest places equally with the largest, I have been received with unsurpassable politeness, delicacy, sweet temper, hospitality, consideration, and with unsurpassable respect for the privacy daily enforced upon me by the nature of my avocation here, and the state of my health. This testimony, so long as I live, and so long as my descendants have any legal right in my books, I shall cause to be republished as an appendix to every copy of those two books of mine in which I have referred to America; and this I will do, or cause to be done, not in mere love or thankfulness, but because I regard it as an act of plain justice and honour."

Finally, rising to the greatest heights in a superb peroration, he put forth a magnificent plea for co-operation between the two great Anglo-Saxon races.

"Points of difference there have been, points of difference there probably always will be . . . but broadcast in England is sown the sentiment that those two people are essentially one, and that it rests with them jointly to uphold the great Anglo-Saxon race . . . from the great majority of honest minds on both sides, there cannot be absent the conviction that it would be better for the globe to be riven by earthquake, fired by comet, overrun by iceberg, and abandoned to the Arctic fox and bear, than that it should present the spectacle of these two great nations, each of which has in its own way and hour striven so hard and so successfully for freedom, ever again being arrayed, the one against the other."

A few moments later, again a cripple and a very sick man, he had to be assisted from the hall.

## CHAPTER XIV

*"The tide ran strong; I took care to lose none of it . . ."*
—GREAT EXPECTATIONS.

IT might reasonably have been expected that during these strenuous years of public entertainment Dickens' literary output would have been very severely limited. On the contrary, between 1859 and 1868 he wrote three full-length novels, twenty-eight longish sketches which were published as "The Uncommercial Traveller," three complete short stories, and about twenty-five chapters to various Christmas numbers of *All the Year Round*.

After his break with Messrs. Bradbury and Evans, Dickens returned to his former publishers, Messrs. Chapman and Hall, and while the future of *Household Words* was still in doubt, launched in conjunction with them *All the Year Round*. He wanted at first to call his new magazine *Household Harmony*, and was for some time strangely blind to the obvious objection to this title; but he yielded to persuasion and, after turning over some twenty other titles, finally adapted the Shakespearean quotation, "The story of our lives, from year to year."

The first number of *All the Year Round*, published on April 30th, 1859, contained the opening instalment of "A Tale of Two Cities," and this story continued as a serial in the magazine until November 26th. From June to December it was also being issued in monthly parts by Chapman and Hall, with illustrations—the last he was to do for Dickens—by "Phiz."

"A Tale of Two Cities" has unfortunately achieved a rather factitious popularity of recent years through its having

been considerably over-employed in schools as an examination
text-book or as a reader.    This has resulted in its becoming
for many of the younger generation the only Dickens novel
they have read, which is unfortunate, seeing that it is the
least Dickensian of them all.    Also, since it requires a mature
mind fully to appreciate its finer qualities, this has obscured
to some extent its really remarkable merits.

The idea for the story first came to Dickens as he was
acting in *The Frozen Deep*.    For eighteen months he revolved
it without being able to start.    Various suggested titles,
"Buried Alive," "The Thread of Gold," "The Doctor of
Beauvais," "Memory Carton," will show the trend of his
thoughts.    At last there settled in his mind the idea of
setting himself "the little task of making *a picturesque story*,
rising in every chapter, with characters true to nature, but
whom the story should express more than they should express
themselves by dialogue."

In short, Dickens decided to abandon completely the
rôle in which he had achieved his fame, that of humorist
and unrivalled delineator of character, and to beat the
writers of adventure stories on their own ground.    The
influence of two contemporary writers clearly assisted him
to this decision: Wilkie Collins and Thomas Carlyle.

Collins had shown him what could be done with a closely-
knit plot and how a story could depend upon incident rather
than character; Carlyle had shown him what marvellous
pictures could be woven from the stuff of history.    And he
had the memory of his own "Barnaby Rudge" to encourage
him.

Carlyle's "French Revolution" had, since its publication
in 1837, exercised a peculiar fascination over him.    He read
it and re-read it, and could never sufficiently admire it.    It is
said that he carried a copy wherever he went.    It was quite
natural, therefore, that he should turn to the period of the
revolution as a setting for his adventure story.

It was equally natural that, desirous as ever to be correctly
informed as to his facts, he should apply to Carlyle for help.
He requested from him the loan of a few reference books.
Carlyle, who in spite of his bear-with-a-sore-head reputation

could appreciate a joke, packed up all he had got—two vanloads—and forwarded them to Gads Hill.

Dickens was not in the least dismayed; he read them all.

How far he succeeded in his design of a story of incident is a disputable point; that he succeeded in creating a remarkable story of atmosphere is beyond dispute. As in "Barnaby Rudge" the mutter of the Gordon riots is heard afar off, and gradually swells until it dominates and possesses the book, so in "A Tale of Two Cities" the storm of the French Revolution gathers ominously on every page until, heavy with destruction, it bursts clamant and irresistible to sweep before it everything and everyone in a wild orgy of rage and blind fury.

There is no finer example in our literature of cumulative description. Every scene adds to the effectiveness of the climax and the catastrophe; the Dover Mail toiling through the mist and mud up Shooter's Hill; Mr. Lorry's reverie; the contrasting pictures of unsafe England and starving and plotting France; of Dr. Manette on his release from the Bastille contrasted with Monseigneur's levee and the ride of the Marquis from Paris to his château; trials in England and trials in France; spies in England and spies in France; the quiet life of the Manettes in England, ever and anon disturbed by anxious remembrances and anxious forebodings. Even Mr. Jerry Cruncher's secret, black and midnight trade is faithfully in keeping with the lowering atmosphere of the first half of the book.

Then, when the storm has burst, come descriptive passages as great as any Dickens has ever written: the storming of the Bastille, the death of old Foulon, the burning of the château, Charles Darnay's ride to Paris, life in Paris during the Revolution, the dance of the Carmagnole, Darnay's trial, his re-arrest and re-trial, his escape, the flight to the coast, and Carton's ride on the tumbril to the guillotine— it is a very cascade of marvellous description, penned by an eye-witness who has seen, and suffered all.

This last is no exaggeration. In his preface to "A Tale of Two Cities" Dickens wrote, "Throughout its execution, it has had complete possession of me: I have so far verified what is done and suffered in these pages, as that I have certainly done and suffered it all myself."

In the excitement of finishing the book Dickens wrote to a French friend, M. Regnier, that he hoped it was the best story he had ever written. Few will agree with that sentiment now, and Dickens himself was not long in revoking it. Within twelve months he was to embark upon another story, "Great Expectations," which he was justly to rank after "Copperfield." Perhaps Forster said the last word about "A Tale of Two Cities" when he wrote, "There is no piece of fiction known to me, in which the domestic life of a few simple private people is in such a manner knitted and interwoven with the outbreak of a terrible public event, that the one seems but part of the other. When made conscious of the first sultry drops of a thunderstorm that fall upon a little group sitting in an obscure English lodging, we are witness to the actual beginning of a tempest which is preparing to sweep away everything in France."

Of all the characters in "A Tale of Two Cities" Dickens was most fond of Sydney Carton. It is somewhat difficult to assess Carton because, willy-nilly, one's critical judgment is clouded by the remembrances of Sir John Martin Harvey's wonderful presentation of him in *The Only Way*, incomparably the best stage adaptation of any of Dickens' books. In *The Only Way* Sydney Carton, when played by Martin Harvey, really rose to the heights that Dickens intended him to. In the book he somehow does not. There is a little too much of the besotted jackal about him, a little too much hopelessness, and considerably too much vagueness about his journey to Paris. The final scene is grand—one feels unfortunately too grand for Sydney Carton.

Mr. Lorry is one of the most effective of Dickens' quiet pictures. The whole story of Tellson's bank is excellent in every detail. Dr. Manette, his daughter, and Charles Darnay are, considering their prominent parts in the narrative, but lightly sketched in, and are none of them entirely convincing. In particular, one can hardly credit the strong-charactered, eminently skilled physician who emerges from the wreck of the eighteen-year-buried Bastille prisoner. Yet the home of the Manettes in "the quiet corner of Soho," with its "echoing footsteps of years," is perfectly done.

Much more truly Dickensian characters are Jerry Cruncher, the "Honest tradesman" (and his son), Miss Pross, Madame Defarge and the Vengeance. The brief passages in which Jerry Cruncher proves that Roger Cly was not buried, and Miss Pross and Madame Defarge fight in the deserted Paris lodging are Dickens at his very best, with incident forgotten and his people his only concern.

Thanks to "A Tale of Two Cities" the circulation of *All the Year Round* was from the start very large, and within a short time Dickens had made enough from it to cover all the expenses of its foundation, including the very considerable sum of £3,500 he had paid for *Household Words*. Only once did the circulation flag, in 1861, when a dull serial by Charles Lever, entitled "A Day's Ride, A Life Romance," so depressed it that Dickens was finally driven to advertise the date on which the story would end.

This unfortunate event had a most happy sequel; it turned a short story into "Great Expectations."

Apart from that check *All the Year Round* pursued a triumphant course, and upon Dickens' death was continued by his eldest son, whom he had some years previously taken into the office. Long serials were contributed to it by other eminent writers. These included Wilkie Collins' "Woman in White," "No Name," and "Moonstone"; Bulwer Lytton's "Strange Story"; and Charles Reade's "Hard Cash." Other contributors were Edmund Yates, Percy Fitzgerald, and Charles Lever, not all of whose work was down to the standard of "A Day's Ride."

During 1860 Dickens began to contribute to *All the Year Round* a series of articles written in a personal and intimate manner which were very greatly liked by his readers. There was scattered throughout them a great deal of autobiographical matter, so that it is not surprising to learn that during this year he again had serious thought of writing his autobiography.

In December 1860 the series, comprising seventeen articles, was published under the title of "The Uncommercial

Traveller," with a promise that in the New Year the Traveller would again take the road. In 1865 an enlarged edition containing an additional eleven papers was issued, and after Dickens' death eight more papers were included in the 1875 "Illustrated Library Edition."

Dickens' great interest in the Commercial Travellers' School gave him the idea of the plan of the papers and of the title. "I am," he introduced himself, "both a town traveller and a country traveller, and am always on the road. Figuratively speaking, I travel for the great house of Human Interest Brothers, and have rather a large connection in the fancy goods way. Literally speaking, I am always wandering here and there from my rooms in Covent Garden, London— now about the city streets; now about the country by-roads —seeing many little things, and some great things, which, because they interest me, I think may interest others. These are my brief credentials as the Uncommercial Traveller."

Those interested in comparisons will find an instructive exercise in reading "Sketches by Boz" and "The Uncommercial Traveller" side by side. Many of the titles in the latter work might be inserted in the former without anyone noticing it; for example: "Wapping Warehouse," "Shy Neighbourhoods," "Night Walks," "An Old Stage-coaching House," "A Little Dinner in an Hour." Some sentences, a few paragraphs, could be interchanged. The rest could not; there is thirty years of age, and three hundred years of subtle difference between them.

Before the first series of "The Uncommercial Traveller" was published, a short sketch upon which Dickens was engaged during the autumn of 1860 gave him "such a very fine, new, and grotesque idea" that he half decided to make it the foundation for a serial story. This story he intended at first to publish in the familiar twenty monthly numbers, but the effect of Lever's serial upon the circulation of *All the Year Round* led to a "council of war at the office" in Wellington Street, with the result that "Great Expectations" began in that periodical early in December.

If "A Tale of Two Cities" had been the least Dickensian of all Dickens' novels, "Great Expectations," which followed it

St. Paul's Church, Covent Garden

*After an etching by T. Malton, 1796*

so shortly afterwards, amply proved that the real Dickens was still alive and still capable of rising once more to his greatest heights. There is in it everything that we have come to associate with him at his very best; humour, pathos, rare characterization, strangely real oddities, pictures of low life in London, dramatic turns to the story, and, at the centre, figures who command our respect, our love and our sympathy. In addition we have what Dickens has only once before achieved, a study of the development of the character of a boy through childhood and adolescence.

It was, perhaps, inevitable that from the start comparisons should be made between "Copperfield" and "Great Expectations." Dickens himself read the former book right through to make sure he "had fallen into no unconscious repetitions," and told Forster that he was "affected by it to a degree you would hardly believe." This remark alone would seem to destroy all reason for comparison; yet Forster declared that the way in which Dickens kept "perfectly distinct the two stories of a boy's childhood, both told in the form of autobiography," constituted one of his strongest claims to high rank as a novelist.

It surely constituted nothing of the kind. The two stories are in a different class altogether. When Dickens spoke in the first person as David Copperfield, he was speaking in his own person, and so was hardly in any sense "creating" a character; when he spoke in the first person as Pip in "Great Expectations" he was doing what he had done so many times before, projecting himself into the mind of a being he alone had created, who existed only in his imagination. David Copperfield is unique among the Dickens characters; Pip has to be judged like any other.

He takes a high place, but he does not rank among the greatest even in his own story. Though Dickens throws a pathetic glamour round him in childhood, one cannot resist the feeling that Pip is rather a horrid little snob. He despises dear old Joe Gargery, who is worth a thousand of him, long before he leaves the forge, and he forgets and ignores him afterwards. He is insufferably patronizing to Biddy, who is also far finer in character than he. He hangs round the revolting Miss Havisham because he thinks she is responsible for his "expectations," and is repelled and disgusted to find that these actually come from a convict.

One would have thought that any clean-minded boy might have refused, as soon as he came to years of discretion, to entertain the idea of a fortune coming from a mildewed and degenerate eccentric such as Miss Havisham; but would surely have been proud to receive it from Abel Magwitch. "Wotever I done," says Abel, "is worked out and paid for," and to have been the ideal of a man's life for many years is no light honour, even though that man be a convict.

There is so much to praise in Dickens that it seems a pity to laud him for achievements not entirely praiseworthy. Regarded purely as a study of character, Pip is excellent, because he is absolutely consistent throughout, and is, one presumes, a natural result of such an upbringing as his. Yet, since Dickens set so little store on being regarded as a literary artist and so much on being a portrayer of life, one is bound to consider his characters as human people rather than as artistic creations.

Regarded as a hero for the story, Pip cuts a sorry figure; he is a moral coward and a snob to begin with, and there is no great evidence that he is much better at the end. One regrets that Bulwer Lytton persuaded Dickens to alter the conclusion of the story, which was originally to have left Pip a lonely and solitary man. One regrets still more that Dickens evidently thought he was creating another child-hero "like David."

That blemish apart, one can speak with unstinted praise of the book. Pip's companion, Herbert Pocket, is a delightful boy, much more charming than Pip. The description of Herbert's home is very funny, and very true. Not quite so credible is old Bill Barley, but his daughter Clara is as lovable a girl as Dickens ever drew.

Joe Gargery is one of Dickens' very finest portraits of a simple, honest, loyal and good-hearted man. George Gissing's description of him leaves little to be desired: "A village blacksmith, with heart as tender as his thews are tough; delighting above all things in the society of a little child;

so dull of brain that he gives up in despair the effort to learn his alphabet; so sweet in temper that he endures in silence the nagging of an outrageous wife; so delicate of sensibility that he perspires at the thought of seeming to intrude upon an old friend risen in life."

To the house of Joe Gargery, or rather to the house of Mrs. Joe Gargery, who has so completely become mistress there that Joe has left no more share in the direction than Pip, come two of Dickens' best comics, Uncle Pumblechook and Mr. Wopsle. Of these the former is the superior; Uncle Pumblechook's various attitudes towards Pip are beautifully done. To this house comes later one Biddy, whose relationship to Mr. Wopsle Pip never fathomed, she being granddaughter to Mr. Wopsle's great-aunt, but who is surely a very close literary relative of the Marchioness in "The Old Curiosity Shop."

Incidentally, the school kept by Mr. Wopsle's great-aunt, that "ridiculous old woman of limited means and unlimited infirmity," is no flight of fancy. It can be paralleled down to the last details in the pages of government reports of the first half of the nineteenth century.

Mrs. Joe Gargery would be memorable if only for the three phrases she has immortalized. She has brought Pip up "by hand," and she takes care that of all things he shall not be "pompeyed," while for her almost endemic fits of ill-temper her husband has coined the phrase "on the Rampage."

Miss Havisham is one of the wildest of all Dickens' wild eccentrics. There is quite a lot that is incredible in her manner of living—who renewed the candles, for instance?— but her conduct is quite credible, and so is her aim to train up Estella as an instrument of her revenge upon the falseness of man. Estella is more difficult; if one can accept the theory that any child could have been brought up from infancy in Satis House without losing its wits, one can presumably accept Estella's personality. It is almost equally difficult to believe in what Pip calls, in the last chapter, the "indescribable majesty" and the "indescribable charm" of her beauty. Could any child retain majesty or charm in such an atmosphere?

Pip's journey to London brought him into contact with a group of Dickens' very oldest acquaintances, the legal community of Little Britain, near Newgate. Only two are selected to take prominent parts in the story, but fascinating glimpses are given of law-clerks, petitioners, false witnesses and, best of all, of prisoners in Newgate. It is doubtful whether Dickens was ever happier than when he was prowling about the dusty precincts of the law or round the shabby corridors of a prison.

Of the two main figures Mr. Wemmick the subordinate is far superior to Mr. Jaggers the principal. Mr. Jaggers may have a reputation second to none; he may be able to wear with impunity a hundred-guinea watch and to leave every bolt and bar in his house undone, so greatly is he dreaded by the thieves of London; he may be able to keep in servitude a scarcely tamed savage of a housekeeper; but Mr. Wemmick has a castle in Walworth, with ramparts, a drawbridge and a cannon; Mr. Wemmick has a stone-deaf Aged Parent and a fiancée of wooden build, who wears gowns a little too orange and gloves a little too green; supremest stroke of all, Mr. Wemmick has a Walworth mind and a Little Britain mind— and never the twain must meet.

"Our breakfast was as good as our supper, and at half past eight precisely we started for Little Britain. By degrees, Wemmick got dryer and harder as we went along, and his mouth tightened into a post-office again. At last, when we got to his place of business and he pulled out his key from his coat collar, he looked as unconscious of his Walworth property as if the Castle and the drawbridge and the arbour and the lake and the fountain and the Aged, had all been blown into space together by the last discharge of the Stinger."

That is the sort of touch of which Dickens alone is capable. Abel Magwitch, the convict benefactor of Pip, is one of the most pathetic characters in all Dickens. The story of his life, as he tells it in Chapter XLII, is as sad and as true a record as could well be imagined. His lifelong gratitude to the little boy who saved his life on the marshes by bringing him food, and his savage determination to make him a gentleman, are superbly told. So is his return to England to see the gentleman he has made, to gloat over him, to lavish all the pride of years upon him. Best told of all is the story of his end, the wonderful description of the attempted escape down the Thames, the arrival of the police set on his track by Compeyson, Magwitch's last encounter with his enemy, his trial, and his peaceful end. There was never any fear that Abel Magwitch would be "low." In his way, and considering his life, he was as fine a gentleman as Joe Gargery and a much finer one than Pip.

The country scenes in "Great Expectations" are set in the valley below Gads Hill. Pip's churchyard is that of Cooling, a village some few miles north of Rochester, Joe's forge has been identified in Chalk, and Restoration House in Rochester is still pointed out as the original of Satis House. No one will be surprised to hear that before writing the description of the journey down the Thames Dickens chartered a steamer and travelled down the whole course.

Before concluding "Great Expectations" in August 1861 Dickens had begun his second series of readings. Little literary work was done for the next two years beyond contributions to All the Year Round. In the Christmas number for 1861, "Tom Tiddler's Ground," Dickens created Mr. Mopes, whose portrait was painted direct from an eccentric recluse known as the "Hertfordshire Hermit." The Hermit, it is said, was not pleased about it. In 1862, being in Paris at the time, Dickens founded his contribution to "Somebody's Luggage," that year's Christmas number, on a little French corporal, Bebelle, who became very popular.

In the Christmas number for 1863 he scored one of the greatest of his minor triumphs in the person of Mrs. Lirriper, the lodging-house keeper of 81 Norfolk Street, Strand, who is full of cares and worries and "an old woman and my looks is gone, but that's me, my dear, over the plate-warmer— and considered like." "Mrs. Lirriper's Lodgings" was followed in 1864 by "Mrs. Lirriper's Legacy," which is nearly if not quite as good.

The story of the writing of "Our Mutual Friend," the last

o

long novel Dickens was to complete, is a very sad one, for not only does it show him struggling against ill-health, but also, far more pathetic, against a decay of his powers of which he has become fully conscious.

He had chosen the title as early as 1861. He hoped to start writing in 1862, but could not. He had his ideas, but could make nothing of them. Public readings then intervened to make writing impossible, and it was not until August 1863 that he felt like making a start.

At the moment of starting he was full of his book; but his limitations had become clear to him. "If," he told Forster, "I don't strike while the iron (meaning myself) is hot, I shall drift off again." He was resolved, moreover, not to begin publication until he had completed enough for five monthly numbers.

What a change from the youthful Dickens of twenty-five years ago! Then, provided he could keep one number ahead of the printer, the difficulties of writing and of invention troubled him not a whit. Now, he is an old man, with his story laboriously mapped out and with copious notes to remind him of his characters, painfully writing nearly three numbers in four months, and not daring to go to press without a full five in hand.

"If I were to lose a page of the five numbers I have proposed to myself to be ready by the publication day, I should feel that I had fallen short. I have grown hard to satisfy, and write very slowly. And I have so much—not fiction—that *will* be thought of, when I don't want to think of it, that I am forced to take more care than I once took."

So even the lifelong ability to lose himself in a book has deserted him.

Publication began in May 1864, and within two months it was sadly proved how wise Dickens had been to push on so far in advance. "Although I have not been wanting in industry," he wrote at the end of July, "I have been wanting in invention, and have fallen back with the book. Looming large before me is the Christmas work, and I can hardly hope to do it without losing a number of *Our Friend*. I have very nearly lost one already, and two would take one-half of my whole advance. This week I have been very unwell; am still out of sorts; and, as I know from two days' slow experience, have a very mountain to climb before I shall see the open country of my work."

Why, one might ask, break off at such a time to write an anonymous contribution to a periodical that surely could be trusted to carry on of its own momentum? Because of that fixed determination to be the servant of his public. His readers would expect his work in the Christmas number; and, whatever the cost, they were not to be disappointed.

The death of John Leech about this time further distressed him; and then in 1865 came the really grave illness of February, followed by the Staplehurst railway accident of June.

Of the latter he wrote in his "Postscript in lieu of Preface" to "Our Mutual Friend": "On Friday the ninth of June in the present year Mr. and Mrs. Boffin (in their manuscript dress of receiving Mr. and Mrs. Lammle at breakfast) were on the South Eastern Railway with me, in a terribly destructive accident. When I had done what I could to help others, I climbed back into my carriage—nearly turned over a viaduct, and caught aslant upon the turn—to extricate the worthy couple. They were much soiled, but otherwise unhurt. The same happy result attended Miss Bella Wilfer on her wedding-day, and Mr. Riderhood inspecting Bradley Headstone's red neckerchief as he lay asleep. I remember with devout thankfulness that I can never be much nearer parting company with my readers for ever, than I was then, until there shall be written against my life the two words with which I have this day closed this book—THE END."

What he did not tell his readers was that as one result of the accident he would turn sick and faint as soon as he tried to write a few notes, that he lost a whole number's advance through it, and that he had to write the concluding numbers of "Our Mutual Friend" with the printer round the corner.

Under such circumstances it would not be surprising if "Our Mutual Friend" were an inferior novel. It is; but never was Mr. Chesterton's critical ability more justified than when he said, "Strictly, there is no such novel as 'Nicholas Nickleby.' There is no such novel as 'Our Mutual Friend.'

They are simply lengths cut from the flowing and mixed substance called Dickens—a substance any given length of which will be certain to contain a given proportion of brilliant and of bad stuff."

This definition of "Our Mutual Friend" is perfect. It contains some of the best in Dickens; it contains some of the very worst. From it all his faults can be exemplified; there are in it characters and descriptions which can rank alongside his finest work. From it emerges no giant immortal to stand beside Mr. Micawber, Mr. Pickwick, Sam Weller, Mark Tapley, Mr. Pecksniff, Mrs. Gamp, Joe Gargery; that could only happen when a sustained inspiration possessed Dickens. But Silas Wegg and Mr. Venus, Bella Wilfer and her father (not forgetting Mrs. Wilfer), Gaffer Hexam and Rogue Riderhood, Lizzie Hexam and poor little crippled "Jenny Wren," with her "bad child" of a drunken father, and Sloppy—parents unknown, and "too much of him long-wise, too little of him broadwise," are all people we could not afford to miss.

Nor could one do without the inimitably Dickensian descriptions of the "birds of prey" searching the Thames for dead bodies to rob, of Miss Potterson's riverside "tavern of a dropsical appearance," the Six Jolly Fellowship Porters, of Boffin's Bower, of Mr. Venus's taxidermic and "articulating" shop in Clerkenwell, and of Mr. Silas Wegg's stall near Cavendish Square, with its "little placard, like a kettle-holder, bearing the inscription:

> Errands gone
> On with fi
> Delity by
> Ladies and Gentlemen
> I remain
> Your humble Servt
> Silas Wegg.

Only one other inscription ever written beats that—Mr. Sapsea's in "Edwin Drood."

Nor does this list exhaust the riches of "Our Mutual Friend." There are still the brand-new Veneerings, the

Lammles, Fascination Fledgeby, the Boffins, the Podsnaps, and, very small fry perhaps, but a reminder that Dickens could shine as brilliantly in his tiniest stars as ever he did in his major—the schoolmistress Miss Peecher, "A little pincushion, a little housewife, a little book, a little workbox, a little set of tables and weights and measures, and a little woman, all in one."

Three characters in this book demand mention not so much because they are typically Dickensian as because they are not. These are Bradley Headstone, Eugene Wrayburn, and Mr. Riah.

Bradley Headstone, the pauper boy, of "naturally slow or inattentive intellect," who by determined labour has worked himself up to the position of "highly certificated stipendiary schoolmaster," falls passionately in love with Lizzie Hexam, and Dickens tries to work out what would happen when a man of strong passions who for years has kept those passions under iron restraint finds himself overmastered by them.

Bradley Headstone's story is a tragic and depressing one. Driven mad by love and jealousy, tormented by Eugene Wrayburn and blackmailed by Rogue Riderhood, he ends with murder and suicide. It all seems rather overstrained, yet the conditions of life through which this man had to struggle do not exist to-day, so one dare not say he is not true to life.

In the case of Eugene Wrayburn likewise, one has to postulate that social conditions have so changed that he has become next to impossible in our times. There are still younger sons of good family who are sent into a profession simply because it is fashionable to have a son in that profession, who do nothing, are aimless and bored with life; but it is no longer possible for them to patronize and interfere with the lives of working-class people, because the working classes have achieved a measure of dignity and have secured for themselves some privileges, notably the right to a good education, which to a certain extent preserve them from such patronage and interference. Eugene Wrayburn is a study of a "gentleman" of a bygone age.

Mr. Riah is an apology. A very pretty story attaches to

this gentleman, and one which certainly justifies Dickens as a man, if not as a writer.

In 1863 a Jewish lady, Mrs. Eliza Davies, wrote to Dickens to protest that he had done the Jews "a great wrong" in his picture of Fagin. Dickens replied "that if there be any general feeling on the part of the intelligent Jewish people, that I have done them what you describe as 'a great wrong,' they are a far less sensible, a far less just, and a far less good-tempered people than I have always supposed them to be." He pointed out that Fagin was a Jew, because at the time of the story "that class of criminal almost invariably was a Jew"; that he was called a Jew on account of his race, not his religion; and that the other wicked characters were all Christians.

Mrs. Davies, writing to thank him for the subscription he had enclosed in his letter in reply to her appeal on behalf of the Jewish poor, returned to the attack, and made a good point when she said that though "all the other criminal characters are Christians, they are, at least, contrasted with characters of good Christians."

After that, Dickens felt bound to do something about it; so he created Mr. Riah, the employee of Fascination Fledgeby who is compelled to pose as Pubsey and Co., who loathes his employment because it brings ruin and sorrow to others, and who finally gives it up, though at the time he knows no other means of livelihood.

Mr. Riah is a dear old man who well earns his title of "godmother" on account of his befriending of Lizzie Hexam. Yet one is inclined to agree with the Jewish lady that the character is not entirely satisfactory. Like others of Dickens' "good" people, the goodness is somewhat overdone.

Artistically, the character cannot be justified in the least. But then Dickens was not a literary artist; he was "the servant of the public." One is happy to hear that he and Mrs. Davies remained on such good terms that she became the tenant of Tavistock House when Dickens gave it up.

The mystery of John Harmon, alias Julius Handford, alias John Rokesmith, is best left to those who enjoy solving such puzzles. When Dickens did decide to be involved, he always laid on the complications good and thick; whether from inclination or because the windings of his story compelled him to is not always easy to decide. It always comes out all right in the end, and that is about all one can say for his mysteries.

"Tired with 'Our Mutual,'" wrote Dickens to Forster in September 1865, "I sat down to cast about for an idea, with a depressing notion that I was, for the moment, overworked. Suddenly, the little character you will see, and all belonging to it, came flashing up in the most cheerful manner, and I had only to look on and leisurely describe it."

The little character was Dr. Marigold, a Cheap Jack, "born on the queen's highway, but it was the king's at that time, on a common," a wonderfully fresh, humorous and pathetic study which made "Dr. Marigold's Prescription" one of the most popular of all the Christmas numbers, and later an equally popular reading. Of the eight chapters in this story Dickens contributed Nos. I, VI and VII.

In 1866 he wrote "Mugby Junction," concerning which Dolby says that the idea occurred at Rugby station. Dickens went into the refreshment room, ordered some coffee and stretched out his hand to help himself to milk and sugar. To his surprise these were rudely snatched away from him by the waitress, who insisted that he should first pay for the coffee. A page boy nearby burst out laughing; and was rewarded by being made the Boy at Mugby Junction.

The last Christmas number in which Dickens had any part was "No Thoroughfare" in 1867. This he wrote in conjunction with Wilkie Collins, who shortly afterwards dramatized it.

Before leaving for America, Dickens wrote two short stories for first publication in the States. These were "George Silverman's Explanation" and "Holiday Romance." Each contained about half the material in a monthly number of one of his novels, and for each he received £1,000.

This was not the first time he had received this sum for a short story. In 1860 the *New York Ledger* had tempted him by a similar offer to write "Hunted Down."

The whirligig of time brings its revenges. As a young man Dickens went to America and discovered, to his chagrin, that the non-existence of a world copyright law was losing him a fortune. His books were being published by the scores of thousands without his receiving a penny of profit. He protested, and was abused. Within twenty years America was offering him the highest sums ever paid to an author for literary work.

One thousand pounds for a short story, the work of a few days. One thousand pounds for the right to publish one of his novels. That was what he was receiving in these days.

For money as money, Forster declares, no man cared less than Dickens; but no man knew better than he what lack of money could mean, and he had determined that no one connected with him should suffer from that lack if he could prevent it.

No man ever carried the burden of dependants more cheerfully or manfully than did Dickens. He was, during these years, contributing to his mother's support, supporting his wife, at least one brother and one brother's wife. To all his children he gave the most liberal education possible. He received daily for many years large numbers of requests for subscriptions to public and private charities, and was not slow to respond to cases of genuine need.

He succeeded in his aim that none of his children should know want. He left about £93,000. Not a large fortune: many a pawnbroker has made more; but it was sufficient for his purpose. One can rejoice that he achieved his ambition; one can never cease to deplore that the effort cost him his life.

## CHAPTER XV

*"The more you want of the master, the more you'll find in him."* *

DICKENS had decided before he left America that he would give one final series of readings in the British Isles, "and then read No More." On his informing Messrs. Chappells to this effect, they immediately offered him £6,000 clear of all expenses for a series of seventy-five readings, an offer which matured into a contract to give one hundred readings for a fee of £8,000.

An excellent voyage home in the Cunard liner, the *Russia*, greatly improved the state of Dickens' health; he began to be able to eat properly again, his catarrh left him, and the pain and swelling in his feet diminished. He rested quietly on board, basked in the sunlight and got thoroughly browned. To a couple of half-wits who formed themselves into a deputation (let us hope self-appointed) to ask him to give a public reading to the passengers he quietly replied that sooner than comply he "would assault the captain, and be put in irons."

"Good Lord! seven years younger!" exclaimed his doctor when he saw Dickens on his return to England. So great was his power still to recuperate that it is said that he looked as though he had never had a day's illness. To the keener eyes of the anxious Forster, however, there was apparent an ominous change in him. As he watched him nervously through the summer he noted with distress that "There was manifest abatement of his natural forces, the elasticity of bearing was impaired, and the wonderful brightness of eye

* Said of Dickens by the gas-man at his public readings.

was dimmed at times." The right foot was now affected
as well as the left; and there came one dreadful day when
Dickens, looking at the letters over the shop doors, could
see only parts of them.

Yet at any call upon his energy Dickens could seem for
a brief spell to cast aside all infirmity, and would plunge
into work with all the heartiness of yore. "This indeed was
the great danger," Forster records, "for it dulled the appre-
hension of us all to the fact that absolute and pressing danger
did exist."

The calls were not few nor light. W. H. Wills had been
injured in a hunting accident, so seriously that it was feared
he would never work again. Dickens had to take over not
only the whole of the editing of *All the Year Round* but also its
business management, which formerly he had never touched.
One of his friends, the Rev. Chauncy Hare Townshend,
had died a few months previously leaving a request that
Dickens would edit the papers containing his religious
opinions. The task was a wearisome and unnecessary one,
but apart from the obligation due to friendship, Townshend
had left with the papers a legacy of £1,000.

The readings were to begin in October, and for these there
were of course the usual careful rehearsals. Yet Dickens
found time and energy to go to Paris in June to supervise
rehearsals of a French version of *No Thoroughfare*.

In September he had to say good-bye to his youngest son,
the "Noble Plorn," whom he had decided to send to Australia
to join his elder brother Alfred Tennyson, who was sheep-
farming there with considerable success. "I did not think,"
he said to a friend of this parting, "I could have been so
shaken."

He was, after America, a broken man. Yet, true to the
very last, he lived upon his nerves, and braced himself to
health and strength by the thought of the forthcoming
readings.

The demand for tickets was as great as ever. Dickens
began to read. The enthusiasm of the audiences outstripped
all bounds. Yet somehow a feeling of something wanting
began to obsess him. The farewell tour! Was it not possible

to go right out and beyond all former successes, to score one culminating triumph, to do something starkly simple that should yet reach to the very heights of dramatic art?

The fatal answer came: the murder of Nancy by Bill Sikes. "I have no doubt," wrote Dickens to Forster, "that I could perfectly petrify an audience. . . ."

The reading was prepared: it was rehearsed: it was tried out: it was included in the repertoire, and at once topped the bill. Audiences were petrified . . . and from all over the country came demands from other audiences to be petrified.

The effect of the reading upon audiences was devastating. It was as nothing compared with its effect upon Dickens.

During the daily rehearsals between the private reading on November 14th, 1868, and the first public one on January 5th of the following year, Dickens had concentrated upon "the object of rising from that blank state of horror into a fierce and passionate rush for the end."

He succeeded. He tore himself to bits. Dolby, who like Forster had strenuously opposed the idea of the reading, says, "The terrible force with which the actual perpetration of this most foul murder was described was of such a kind as to render Mr. Dickens utterly prostrate for some moments after its delivery, and it was not until he had vanished from the platform that the public had sufficiently recovered their sense of composure to appreciate the circumstance that the horrors to which they had been listening were but a story and not a reality."

On the morning following the first reading of the Murder, Dolby called upon Dickens, and found him "in a state of great prostration." He knew it was useless to remonstrate; besides, the reading was already advertised for some weeks ahead.

In January, Dickens was reading in Dublin and Belfast. Having only five readings in a fortnight, he benefited greatly by the comparative rest; and then, by all unlucky chances, the engine of the boat-train broke a driving-wheel, and the train only just avoided disaster.

Happily, no one was injured; but Dolby, rejoining Dickens

forty-eight hours later for the next fortnight's trip—a strenuous one—found him warding off illness only by "his strength of will and determination."

Throughout these readings it had been necessary for him to lie on a sofa all day when he had an engagement at night.

On Tuesday, February 16th, Dickens was due to read at St. James's Hall, London. In the morning he went down with the worst attack of foot trouble he had ever experienced, and, despite his reiterated protests, Dr. Beard and Sir Henry Thompson forbade him to read that night or to travel the next day.

Within a week Dickens, provided with a sofa in the train, and personally attended by Mr. Arthur Chappell, was travelling to Edinburgh to give his postponed readings. He had only been there two days when he had to call in a celebrated surgeon, Mr. James Syme, as his foot was bad again.

Mr. Syme allayed his fears by declaring the trouble to be local, due to wet feet and the fatigue of the readings. He advised complete rest. That being impracticable in view of Dickens' engagements, the utmost possible care was to be exercised.

The Edinburgh audience being a particularly responsive one, Dickens worked himself up to such a degree of violence over the Murder reading that he could hardly stagger from it to his room behind the stage. There he lay speechless for minutes on end. Then, after a glass of champagne, he went back to conclude the evening's entertainment.

That night at supper he decided to settle what he should read during the remainder of the tour. When he had arranged four weeks' readings, Dolby asked him if he noticed anything peculiar about them.

"'No,' he replied. 'What is it?'

"'Well,' I said, 'out of four Readings a week you have put down three "Murders."'

"'What of that?'

"'Simply this,' I said, 'the success of this farewell tour is assured in every way, so far as human probability is concerned. It therefore does not make a bit of difference which of the works you read. . . . I am saying this in the interest of your health, and I feel certain that if either Tom or Arthur Chappell were here, he would endorse every word I have said, and would agree with me that the "Carol," "Copperfield," "Nicholas Nickleby," or "Marigold," will produce all the money we can take, and you will be saved the pain of tearing yourself to pieces every night for three nights a week, and to suffer unheard-of torture afterwards, as you have to do. Reserve the "Murder" for certain of the large towns. . . .'

"'Have you finished?' he said angrily.

"'I have said all I feel on that matter,' was my reply.

"Bounding up from his chair, and throwing his knife and fork on his plate (which he smashed to atoms), he exclaimed—

"'Dolby! your infernal caution will be your ruin one of these days!'

"'Perhaps so, sir,' I said. 'In this case, though, I hope you will do me the justice to say it is exercised in your interest.'

". . . Turning round, I saw he was crying (my eyes were not so clear as they might be), and, coming towards me, he embraced me affectionately. . . .

"'Forgive me, Dolby! I really didn't mean it; and I know you are right. . . .'"

"This was the only time," records Dolby, "I ever heard him address angry words to any one. . . ."

The number of "Murders" was cut down, and for a month things went, not well, but as well as could have been hoped. Then came, in March, the death of Sir James Emerson Tennent, which greatly distressed Dickens; and a request that he would attend the funeral.

Dickens loathed funerals, but felt he could not refuse. He therefore arranged to read at York without any intervals for rest, to drive straight from the hall to the station, and to travel through the night to London. He arrived in town "dazed" and worn. Forster was shocked by his appearance.

Still the indefatigable career was pursued. Liverpool gave Dickens a tremendous farewell banquet on the 10th of April, and, the tables being arranged so that it was impossible that the speeches could be heard by most of the six hundred guests, Dickens spent the greater part of the day supervising the hanging of flags round the hall to improve its acoustic properties.

Before this date he had had a request signed by the actors of the chief London theatres to give them a morning reading in London, and had generously consented to give three in May.

In mid-April he set out to read in Lancashire. So ill was he that his "sufferings from fatigue of mind and body gave him such exquisite pain as to bring a return of the sleepless nights he had experienced in America."

From Leeds he slipped down to Chester for a quiet week-end, and one night there was so bad that Dolby "had an instinctive feeling that the travelling career was at an end, if not the Reading career also." Dolby was by now sleeping next door to Dickens wherever he went, and looking in two or three times during the night to see that he was all right.

The next day Dickens asked Dolby what to do, begging him to consider first Chappells' interests. Dolby replied that he should go at once to London to consult Dr. Beard. Impossible; it was Sunday, and the only train had gone. Dickens wrote instead, and carried on with his readings.

He told Beard that he had been extremely giddy, and very uncertain of his footing and of his sense of touch in his left leg, hand and arm. Could this be due to the medicine he was taking?

Beard replied by return of post that there could be no mistaking the symptoms, that they were certainly not caused by the medicine, and that he wished to take him in hand at once.

Dickens read at Blackburn, and went to Blackpool for two days. From there he wrote to Beard to say he was much better, though there was a curious deadness in his left side and he found difficulty in taking hold of things with his left hand. Then he travelled to Preston—to find a telegram announcing Beard's arrival that afternoon.

Directly the doctor came he examined Dickens, and announced that for him to read that night was to invite a paralytic stroke.

Dickens begged to be allowed to try. Beard said in effect, Please yourself—but the result is certain.

It was after five; the doors were to open at seven. Dolby borrowed all the money in the hotel to repay ticket-holders, the manager wired to every place within a radius of twenty miles, the Mayor and Chief Constable of Preston sent mounted police to tell every conveyance coming into the town that the reading was cancelled. Meanwhile Beard took Dickens at once back to London, and the next day called Sir Thomas Watson into consultation.

The result was that Dickens was forbidden ever to travel again to read, or to read even in London for several months.

He went to Gads Hill, rested quietly, and soon began to feel himself again, with the result that he grew worried over the thought of his unfulfilled contract with Chappells. At last he persuaded Sir Thomas Watson to consent to a series of twelve readings in London. It was arranged that these should take place in the opening months of 1870.

Of Chappells, Dickens had the very highest appreciation. "I do believe," he wrote in May 1869, "that such people as the Chappells are rarely to be found in human affairs." They had indeed treated him throughout with the utmost consideration and liberality, and it was his deep sense of gratitude which impelled him to undertake these last readings as some sort of recompense for the inconvenience and financial loss they had suffered through his breakdown.

Meanwhile, with reviving health and spirits came renewed activity. In June came to Gads Hill his American friends the Fields, and for them a regal programme of entertainment was prepared. He showed them Kent, he showed them London; and not merely the London of the tourist. Accompanied by detectives, he and his visitors explored slums, thieves' haunts, doss-houses, and an opium den. Of this last a picture was to be painted by the Master ere the pen dropped from his hand.

For only a month or so later he thought of "Edwin Drood." This last book, never to be finished, upon which he was engaged the day before his death, has been endlessly discussed. A number of attempts have been made to finish it; none is satisfactory, for there has been no Dickens to succeed Dickens.

This is no place to add to that discussion. Suffice to say that Forster was told that the story was to consist of the murder of a nephew, Edwin Drood, by his uncle, Jasper, that the concluding chapters were to be written in the condemned cell, and that the originality of the plot was to consist in the murderer's identity being hidden until the very last moment while he reviewed his career as though it were being told by someone else.

So much for the plot; it is open to any reader to conjecture how it would have been worked out. But the real interest of "The Mystery of Edwin Drood" does not lie in the plot. It lies in the really great group of characters that was emerging —nay, that had emerged in what was written; and in the beautiful and intimate pictures of Rochester, disguised only in name as Cloisterham. In the six numbers of "Edwin Drood" that were completed Dickens showed every indication of rising again to his greatest heights, while a further fragment, discovered by Forster after his death, introduces a fresh set of characters of equal promise.

Mr. Sapsea, auctioneer and estate agent, "fool and jackass," is superb, a giant of the giants. He might have ranked alongside Pickwick, Pecksniff and Micawber. The immortal epitaph he composes for Ethelinda, his "reverential wife," is one of the funniest things Dickens ever wrote.

Mr. Grewgious, Rosa's quaint but kindly guardian, Mr. Bazzard, the clerk of whom he stands so much in awe, Mr. Tartar, the ex-sailor, now resident in Staple Inn, and Mr. Honeythunder, the professional philanthropist who made every room seem too small and who bullied and battered everyone into his opinions, are real Dickens characters who, one feels sure, would have taken a high place among his creations. So is Durdles, the drunken mason, who pays a small boy to pelt him home, and talks of himself in the third person. One remark alone of Durdles makes him great: "If I hide my watch when I am drunk I must be drunk again before I can remember where."

Not less interesting are Miss Twinkleton, mistress of the young ladies' academy at the Nuns' House, who, as soon as her pupils were safely in bed, brushed up her curls and became a much brighter Miss Twinkleton than she had been throughout the day; and Miss Billikin, the lodging-house keeper, who "was put in early life to a very genteel boarding school" where "a poorness of blood flowed from the table which has run through my life."

Though Edwin Drood himself has not perhaps any great claim to fame, his affianced wife, Rosa Bud, always called Rosebud at the Twinkleton academy, and Pussy by her fiancé, is a delicious child, especially when she takes her husband-to-be to buy Turkish Delight, and tells him on parting that she is too sticky to be kissed. Mrs. Crisparkle is a dear old lady. Both Helena and Neville Landless are strangely interesting in their wildness of nature.

It is perhaps unsafe to posit much of Jasper, but had Dickens' avowed intention with regard to him been carried out, he might possibly have developed into a tremendously powerful figure. The Rev. Mr. Crisparkle, not too interesting at first, develops strongly. As for Dick Datchery, there is no saying what he and "the Deputy" might not have achieved together.

The writing of "Edwin Drood" was begun in October and continued steadily until Christmas. It was hard going. Inspiration did not come so freely as in the good old days, and even composition was a difficult and anxious business. Revisions and corrections were numerous.

Just before Christmas, Dickens found to his dismay that the manuscript of the first two numbers he had sent to the printers was "twelve printed pages too short"—just at the very moment when he wanted to drop writing for the time and rehearse for the final readings.

"However," he told Forster, "I turned to it and got it done." Comment on the courage behind those words is superfluous.

In the contract with Messrs. Chapman and Hall for the publication of "Edwin Drood" Dickens required it specially to be inserted "That if the said Charles Dickens shall die during the composition of the said work of 'The Mystery of Edwin Drood,' or shall otherwise become incapable of completing the said work for publication in twelve monthly numbers as agreed," Forster was to determine how much was to be repaid to the firm. It was the first time such a clause had been inserted in any of his agreements.

By contract Dickens was to have received £7,500 for the copyright of "Edwin Drood." This was said to have been the largest sum ever paid to an author for a single book. The profits on all sales after the first 25,000 copies were to be equally divided between author and publishers. Publication began in April, and the sales had reached 50,000 before Dickens' death. £1,000 was paid by his American publishers for advance proofs, and a substantial sum (Dickens left the amount to Baron Tauchnitz) for the Tauchnitz edition printed at Leipzig.

On Christmas Day 1869, Dickens was kept in bed until evening, his foot being bad again, but he recovered quickly enough to give away the prizes on January 6th, 1870, at the Birmingham Midland Institute, of which he was President.

To the delight of himself and everyone present one of the prizewinners was a Miss Winkle. "I have recommended Miss Winkle," Dickens told the audience when the laughing applause had died down, "to change her name."

For the period of his final readings, January to March 1870, Dickens rented from his friends—Mr. and Mrs. Milner Gibson—No. 5 Hyde Park Place, just opposite the Marble Arch.

Of the twelve readings, three were matinées for the special benefit of the actors who some time ago had petitioned him; the remainder were evening entertainments.

Dr. Beard had arranged to be present at all the readings, and examined Dickens carefully during performances. He has recorded that his normal pulse was 72, but that after the first night he never began a reading with one slower than 82, and that after reading it rose alarmingly, twice going as high as 124. It was following the "Murder" that it reached these heights.

During the intervals Dickens would lie for ten minutes prostrate, unable to do more than say a few incoherent words. Members of the audience noted with alarm that he occasionally missed words out and mispronounced others. With

"Pickwick" he had particular difficulty; it became "Picnic," "Peckwicks," "Pickswick"—everything but the correct pronunciation. Dickens noticed this too, and would flash a glance of amused surprise at his family party in the front seats.

It was a desperately anxious time for all who loved Dickens. Yet reading after reading was accomplished without disaster, until finally there came the very last one of all.

This took place on March 15th, at St. James's Hall. The excitement was tense. When Dickens appeared on the platform the entire audience rose as one man and cheered him wildly for several minutes. He read first "A Christmas Carol," then the trial from "Pickwick"; and, says Forster, "probably in all his life he never read so well . . . a subdued tone, as well in the humorous as in the serious portions, gave something to all the reading as of a quiet sadness of farewell."

At the close the audience cheered and applauded tumultuously, and called and called again for him to reappear. As a rule, he never returned to the platform once a reading was over . . . but this was different. He came back, without his book, and said:

"Ladies and gentlemen, it would be worse than idle— for it would be hypocritical and unfeeling—if I were to disguise that I close this episode in my life with feelings of very considerable pain. For some fifteen years, in this hall and in many kindred places, I have had the honour of presenting my own cherished ideas before you for your recognition, and, in closely observing your reception of them, have enjoyed an amount of artistic delight and instruction which, perhaps, is given to few men to know. In this task, and in every other I have ever undertaken, as a faithful servant of the public, always embued with a sense of duty to them, and always striving to do his best, I have been uniformly cheered by the readiest response, the most generous sympathy, and the most stimulating support. Nevertheless, I have thought it well, at the full flood-tide of your favour, to retire upon those older associations between us, which date from much further back than these, and henceforth to devote myself exclusively to the art that first brought us together. Ladies and gentlemen, in but two short weeks from this time I hope that you may enter, in your own homes, on a new series of readings at which my assistance will be indispensable; but from these garish lights I vanish now for evermore, with a heartfelt, grateful, respectful, and affectionate farewell."

In a strained silence he left the platform. Then the applause broke out again, so overwhelmingly that for a brief instant he came back. For a moment longer he faced his beloved public, then kissed his hand to them, and was gone.

Most of the remainder of his life was spent at Gads Hill, quietly writing "Edwin Drood." A few public engagements were unavoidable; but towards the end several had to be cancelled on account of his health.

In March he was summoned to Buckingham Palace to meet Queen Victoria, this being the first and only time in his life he had met Her Majesty in person. He had brought from America a very fine collection of photographs of the Civil War battlefields, which he showed to Mr. (afterwards Sir) Arthur Helps, who mentioned them in conversation with Queen Victoria. Her Majesty expressed a desire to see them, and afterwards to thank Dickens in person for sending them to her.

The interview lasted one and a half hours. During its course Queen Victoria asked Dickens for a set of his books, and requested that she might have them that same afternoon. He begged to have a set specially bound for her.

At the close of the interview Her Majesty picked up a copy of her own book, "Leaves from the Journal of Our Life in the Highlands," saying that "the humblest" of writers would be ashamed to offer it "to one of the greatest," but that it had been suggested to her that he would most value it from her hands. On the fly-leaf Her Majesty had written, "To Charles Dickens, Esq., from Victoria Reg. Buckingham Palace. March 9th, 1870."

He was bidden to attend the next levee, and Miss Dickens

GADS HILL PLACE, WHICH DICKENS PURCHASED IN 1856

was presented to her Majesty at the following drawing-room. Shortly afterwards he was included, by special request of the Prince of Wales, among the guests at a dinner given by Lord Houghton, at which the Prince and the King of the Belgians were present. He was so lame that he could not walk upstairs.

On April 5th he was in the chair at a dinner for the News-vendors' Benevolent and Provident Association, and proposed the toast of "The Corporation of the City of London." On May 2nd he was at the Royal Academy Dinner, where he replied to the toast of "Literature." This was his last public appearance.

In that month he dined with Motley, the historian of the Dutch Republic, and met two great British statesmen, Disraeli and Gladstone, the former at a dinner, the latter at breakfast. On the 17th he was to have attended a royal ball, but when the time came he was too ill to go. These attacks were getting very frequent now.

On May 22nd he met Forster for the last time, at dinner in Hyde Park Place. "He seemed very weary." Yet such was his vitality that he was, between the attacks, superintending the rehearsals of a play to be performed privately at Cromwell House. When the performance took place on June 2nd he acted as stage-manager and prompter, "ringing all the bells and working all the lights," full of "infectious enjoyment." The same day he added a codicil to his will bequeathing his share in *All the Year Round* to his eldest son.

On June 6th the dogs were whistled out for the last time. On June 7th Dickens drove to Cobham Wood with Miss Hogarth, and the two walked round the park. On June 8th he wrote as usual throughout the morning in the chalet; and, quite contrary to his practice, went back to his writing in the afternoon.

At six o'clock he returned to the house for dinner. Miss Hogarth saw that he was in pain. He admitted that for an hour in the afternoon he had been very ill. Dinner began. Dickens talked in odd, incoherent snatches.

He rose from the table, saying he was going immediately to London. Miss Hogarth, alarmed, begged that he would lie down. "Yes," he replied, quite distinctly, "on the ground," staggered, and fell on his left side.

He never spoke again. For almost exactly twenty-four hours, until ten minutes past six on the evening of Thursday, June 9th, 1870, he continued to breathe, but he never recovered consciousness, nor was there any chance of his recovery.

.    .    .    .    .    .    .

He had desired to be buried in some quiet Kentish church-yard, at Cobham, or Shorne, or St. Nicholas under Rochester Castle Wall. All these places were closed for burials. The Dean and Chapter of Rochester Cathedral requested that he might be interred in Rochester Cathedral, but a mightier voice than theirs claimed attention; the voice of the British public.

"Dickens is dead!" Men, women, and children all over the country stopped short in their business or their pleasure when they heard the news, stricken as with a sense of personal loss. In busy streets and market-places, in the quiet shops of little country towns people talked of him with hushed voices; on lonely uplands and in far-off glens unseen tears were dropped when the sad news arrived. From all over the world came the sound of mourning.

"He was almost worshipped," said the *Illustrated London News*, "by the lower-middle classes in our provincial towns—both large and small—was the only author they knew, and the one therefore they were prepared to stand by against all comers."

There was only one burial place for Dickens. The *Times* voiced the feeling of the British people. "Statesmen, men of science, philanthropists, the acknowledged benefactors of their race," it said, "might pass away, and yet not leave the void which will be caused by the death of Dickens. They may have earned the esteem of mankind; their days may have been passed in power, honour, and prosperity; they may have been surrounded by troops of friends; but however pre-eminent in station, ability, or public services, they will

HANS CHRISTIAN ANDERSEN (1805–1875)

*After the portrait by Chr. A. Jensen*

not have been, like our great and genial novelist, the intimate of every household. . . . Westminster Abbey is the peculiar resting place of English literary genius; and among those whose sacred dust lies there, or whose names are recorded on the walls, very few are more worthy than Charles Dickens of such a home. Fewer still, we believe, will be regarded with more honour as time passes, and his greatness grows upon us."

The Dean of Westminster had anticipated the demand thus given eloquent expression, and was already in touch with Dickens' family and executors.

"I emphatically direct," read the instructions in Dickens' will, "that I be buried in an inexpensive, unostentatious, and strictly private manner; that no public announcement be made of the time and place of my burial. . . . I DIRECT that my name be inscribed in plain English letters on my tomb, without the addition of "Mr." or "Esquire." I conjure my friends on no account to make me the subject of any monument, memorial, or testimonial whatever."

These instructions were faithfully obeyed. On the morning of Tuesday, June 14th, a simple, private burial took place in the poets' corner of Westminster Abbey; and to this day the statues of Shakespeare and Chaucer look down upon a plain slab of stone, which differs only from the other slabs in the floor in that on it is inscribed, in plain Roman lettering: CHARLES DICKENS. BORN FEBRUARY THE SEVENTH 1812. DIED JUNE THE NINTH 1870.

Yet the people could not be restrained from paying homage. As soon as the interment was concluded the Abbey was thrown open, and an endless stream of mourners passed by to pay their last tribute. The grave was kept open until Thursday; nor when it was closed did they cease to come.

. . . . . .

"I rest my claims to the remembrance of my country upon my published works, and to the remembrance of my friends upon their experience of me in addition thereto."

So wrote Charles Dickens in his will. It is a fitting epitaph.

In his day, and after his death, his friends testified of him with no uncertain voice. "Among his friends and intimates," said Charles Kent, "no great author has ever been more truly or more tenderly loved."

In 1844 Thomas Carlyle wrote, "I truly love Dickens; and discern in the inner man of him a tone of real music which struggles to express itself as it may, in these bewildered, stupefied, and indeed very crusty and distracted days— better or worse. This which makes him in my estimation one in a thousand." Twenty-six years later Carlyle wrote of him that he was "The good, the gentle, high-gifted, ever-friendly and noble Dickens—every inch of him an honest man."

Of his friendship Marcus Stone said that it was "a more precious inheritance than the wealth of a multi-millionaire." Lady Pollock described him as "the ideal of friendship;" Trollope said he "was perhaps the largest-hearted man" he ever knew; James Payn that he had "never met a man more natural or more charming."

To us of a later generation has been denied the privilege of meeting that ardent personality face to face, of falling under the spell of that compelling charm, of experiencing the deep reality and sincerity of that glowing power of friendship. We can never know the whole of Dickens.

No biographer can hope to present more than a faint reflection of the man Charles Dickens. The richness of any personality can only be realized in personal contact. The best one can do now is to try to tell the strangely varied story of his life as honestly as one can, seeking neither to diminish virtues nor to hide faults, shrinking from no obvious deductions, but refraining from all theories that the facts do not amply justify.

The rest one will leave to Dickens' books, for those are, as he said, his monument, and in them may be read his life. Not perhaps the story of every incident in his crowded and oftentimes perplexing material life, though much of actual happening is recorded, but the whole life of his soul, of the Dickens that caused not only his intimate friends, but the many hundreds of thousands of men, women and children who never looked upon his face nor heard the sound of his voice to love and adore him.

"Take the best out of all Dickens' writings," said Hans Andersen, "combine them into the picture of a man, and there thou hast Charles Dickens." That at least we can all still attempt to do; and it shall go hard with us if we do not discover that the more we want of the Master the more we shall find in him.

## CHAPTER XVI

*"This is the only final greatness of a man ; that he does for all the world what the world cannot do for itself. Dickens, I believe, did it."*—G. K. CHESTERTON.

BRITAIN has just reason to be proud of her novelists. From that day, early in the eighteenth century, when a British journalist conceived the idea of shipwrecking an imaginary Englishman, Mr. Robinson Crusoe, upon an imaginary desert island, and of describing his life and adventures on that island, right down to the present moment, this country has never lacked a constant supply of first-rate novelists.

It does not matter that no one has ever been able quite to decide exactly what a novel is. That fact, indeed, has been rather favourable than otherwise to the British literary genius, which hates to be circumscribed by rules and regulations. Our authors of all kinds have made English literature glorious by their defiance of literary conventions. Shakespeare set at nought the directions for the making of plays handed down from classical times and worshipped reverently by the critics and the lesser dramatists of his day; Mr. Bernard Shaw broke every rule of the theatre when he began to write plays, and has consistently done so ever since, with substantial profit both to the English drama and to himself. Wordsworth and Coleridge found themselves so dissatisfied with the theory of English poetic diction that they evolved a new one, and published the *Lyrical Ballads* in 1798 to exemplify it. Their theory no one troubles about very much now, but everyone reads *The Ancient Mariner*, one of the most wonderful poems in the English language, which was among the results of their experimenting.

In the same way, no English novelist of note, except possibly Charles Reade, has ever sat down obsessed with the thought of how a novel ought to be written; he has sat down to write one just as the spirit moved him. The result, naturally, is that in the history of the English novel one finds an astonishing variety of types.

Daniel Defoe's aim was to make a fictitious story of adventure appear literally true; so he wrote a plain, sober account, minutely realistic, of exactly what might have happened to Crusoe on his desert island. About the same time Dean Swift invented Lemuel Gulliver, sent him to the land of the tiny Lilliputians, to that of the giant Brobdingnagians, to the lands of other fabulous creatures of his imagination, and described his hero's adventures in such detailed yet unexaggerated fashion that violent disputes arose among his readers when it was suggested that Lilliput and Brobdingnag did not exist. "Gulliver's Travels" is a satire, not a novel, but with "Robinson Crusoe" it stamped upon the English novel a characteristic it was never to lose, that of conveying the illusion of reality by painstaking attention to realism in detail.

An elderly bookseller, Samuel Richardson, in the middle of the eighteenth century showed that the novel might be used in an entirely different way. Having been all his life in the habit of writing love-letters for girls unable to write their own, he decided at about the age of fifty to publish a complete letter-writer as a guide for all who wished to undertake what one may call emotional correspondence. To make his book more interesting, he introduced into it a thread of story. Finding his work acceptable he tried again, and at his second attempt produced what is in some respects still the greatest psychological novel that has ever been written. No one who can avoid it ever reads now the interminable "Clarissa Harlowe," but it had in its day an international popularity; and it should not be forgotten that this enormously long book, in which every emotion of the human heart is analysed in detail, is directly responsible for the ever-popular "love story" that is still so eagerly borrowed from the lending library shelves. It was Richardson who first gave women the taste for reading novels.

Richardson's first book, "Pamela," struck one of his contemporaries, a not-too-successful journalist and playwright called Henry Fielding, as a stuffy piece of work, so he set out to write a parody of it. He grew interested in his own book, forgot all about the parody, and after completing "Joseph Andrews" started in all earnestness upon another novel. This was "Tom Jones," which some have called the greatest novel in the language, and which is certainly one of the most English. It marked a very important step in the history of the novel. Fielding found the material for his story in the ordinary life of the English people, and his setting in the English countryside. There is no finer picture extant of the fox-hunting, deep drinking, coarse and hearty squirearchy of the period; nor is there a more breezy open-air atmosphere in any novel. In addition, he showed that the novel could be as much a work of art as a play or a poem. "Tom Jones" has a perfectly-knit plot, and is full of strong and often ironic humour.

The latter part of the eighteenth century and the early part of the nineteenth witnessed a great outburst of novel writing. Dr. Johnson wrote "Rasselas" to pay for his mother's funeral, and produced the first philosophical novel. Oliver Goldsmith gave to the world "The Vicar of Wakefield," a shapeless story that contains some of the most delightful people possible. Laurence Sterne exploited the possibilities of sentimentality and of humour in a series of episodes loosely strung together and called "Tristram Shandy," one of the most extraordinary (and skilful) novels ever written. Tobias Smollett combined adventure and humour in a number of stories which chronicle the exploits of various heroes, the best of which are "Roderick Random," "Peregrine Pickle," and "Humphrey Clinker." The influence of these novels is clear in the earlier works of Charles Dickens, and particularly in the "Pickwick Papers."

Early in the nineteenth century Sir Walter Scott, finding that Byron was ousting him from popularity as a writer of tales in verse, fished out of a drawer an old prose manuscript he had begun long before, completed it, and presented "Waverley" to the world, the first of that wonderful series of historical novels that was to pour from his fertile pen. Meanwhile, in Hampshire, a parson's daughter, in the intervals of keeping house, sewing, calling upon and being called upon by the middle-class society of the neighbourhood (out of which she never moved except for an occasional trip to Bath), had begun to trifle with authorship, first for the amusement of her family, then, one suspects, more for her own, until growing ever more consciously an artist, she had elaborated some half-dozen delicately written and subtly ironic novels which are to-day not so much enjoyed as worshipped by thousands of readers.

No greater contrast could be imagined than there is between Sir Walter Scott and Jane Austen. Scott took all medieval history as his background, and wandered freely through continents and centuries in his books, which are full of the bustle of events, of battle and intrigue and adventure. Jane Austen hardly left her parish; she was content to paint, as she said, on a strip of ivory two inches wide, in minutest detail and in the quietest colours, the domestic lives of the characters of the tiny circle of people in which she moved. Yet her fame is as secure as Scott's.

There comes every now and then in the history of most peoples a time when some writer appears who sums up in his work most of the characteristics of his predecessors, and who transcends them all by the universality of his genius. This has happened at least twice in the history of the English people. It happened with Shakespeare; it happened with Dickens.

It is this universality which distinguishes the very great writer from the merely great. It is his universality which places Shakespeare above all other English writers; it is the same characteristic which places Dickens above all other novelists. It is not so much that Shakespeare and Dickens excel in every particular all other writers, though at their most exalted moments they do; it is rather that whereas the other writers excel only in isolated particulars, Shakespeare and Dickens rise at times to excellence in all particulars, and are capable of more sustained and more frequent flights.

There was as good poetry written by other Elizabethans

P

as by Shakespeare; there were as good plays constructed, as finely drawn characters created by dramatists whose very names are almost forgotten to-day. They are forgotten while Shakespeare is remembered because this universality exalts a writer above mere literary eminence: it exalts him into an expression of the soul of the people to which he belongs. Shakespeare is not simply a great writer; he is the ever-living voice of Elizabethan England. Through him we know the whole spiritual history of one of the greatest periods in our country's existence.

These very great writers invariably appear at a time of national rebirth. Their transcendental qualities have to be drawn out of them by an unusual stress of circumstances. They have to be born into an atmosphere redolent with dissatisfaction of things as they are, an atmosphere into which they can infuse their ardent belief that things can be bettered. A placid, self-contented era can never evoke them.

Nor can they rise until the way has been somewhat cleared for them. The tide of national life must be setting strongly in the new direction. It is not necessary that they shall know this, but it is only when people's minds are ripe for new ideas that their words can sound a responsive echo in a multitude of hearts.

Dickens was born and grew up under ideal circumstances. The long-drawn-out Napoleonic wars ended when he was only three and a half years old, and England was free to embark upon that era of industrial eminence which sounded her fame throughout all corners of the earth and made her the richest nation in the world. His youth was passed in the latter stages of a period of transition, that period which transformed England from an agricultural to an industrial nation.

Such transition periods are invariably accompanied by much misery, especially among the working classes. The country has to adapt itself to the changed circumstances, and always the circumstances move much more swiftly than the process of adaptation. There was probably never more wretchedness and suffering and vice and crime in England, especially in the large cities, than during the first thirty years of the nineteenth century. By a circumstance most fortunate to the development of his native genius, Dickens was, at an impressionable age, plunged into an environment where all this misery could be observed and experienced in its most heightened forms. By an equally fortunate circumstance he was quickly rescued from experiencing it, yet remained in a position to observe it.

He grew up having a foot in both worlds, the old and the new. His preternaturally developed powers of observation kept him perpetually interested in the world in which he was living; his fancy fed upon his memories of England as it had been before the blight of the industrial revolution had fastened upon it.

These memories were the result of his childhood's reading. He had, as has been recorded in this book, literally soaked himself in the works of the eighteenth-century novelists. Anyone who takes the trouble to glance through the works of Defoe, Swift, Fielding, Sterne, Smollett, and of two writers, Addison and Steele, who though not novelists yet excelled in one peculiarly English feature of novel writing, the delineation of character, will realize at once how completely Dickens had absorbed the spirit of these authors and what an enormous debt he owed to them.

This is not to suggest that Dickens was in any sense an imitator. He was not; he was an absolutely original writer, so original that no one has ever successfully followed in his footsteps; but all great writers owe much to their predecessors, and Dickens was no exception to the general rule.

From Defoe and Swift he had learned how the illusion of reality could be conveyed by scrupulous attention to realistic detail, from Fielding a huge enjoyment of bluff, hearty, English good-fellowship, from Smollett the attraction of the bustling chronicle in which a hero is set forth on his road to meet whatever adventures may betide him, from Sterne the handling of humour and pathos, from Goldsmith a whimsical tenderness, from all his authors how to create characters whose personalities will hold the attention of readers and will live in the memory.

Equipped by observation and by reading, and trained as a writer in a newspaper office, Dickens set out to create Dickensland, the most fascinatingly real country ever populated by imaginary people. Almost every place in that country is as easy to locate as one on an ordnance survey map or in a post-office directory; we know the streets and houses in which Dickens' people lived, the inns they stopped at, the churches they got married in, the shops at which they bought their provisions, the lanes in which they walked and the fields in which they played.

At the Bull Inn in Rochester they will still show you the bedrooms in which Mr. Pickwick and his companions slept, the ballroom where Jingle and Tupman danced, and the stairs on which Dr. Slammer challenged Jingle. A few yards along the street you can take tea in the gate-house where Mr. Jasper of "Edwin Drood" lodged with Mr. Tope the Cathedral verger. Dan'l Peggotty's boat-house stands on the muddy flats of the Thames estuary near Gravesend, instead of on the Yarmouth flats, but what does that matter? Everyone knows it is the original home of Dan'l Peggotty and little Em'ly, just as everyone knows that a neat little house on the Broadstairs front, two doors away from the Albion Hotel, is where Betsey Trotwood lived, though Dickens chose to move her to Dover so that David Copperfield could traverse the length of that historic English highway, the old Dover Road. Dover is not envious; it can show you, and does, where David sat down upon some steps in the market-place to rest after his long journey.

There is no illusion whatever about the "local habitations" of Dickens' people. Many of their haunts have been demolished, but many still remain; and all were so accurately described that both those which remain and the sites of those which have been demolished are yearly visited by thousands upon thousands of tourists. It is safe to say that as many people go to look upon the spots where the Fleet and Marshalsea prisons once stood as to gaze upon the little lozenge-shaped graves in Cooling churchyard, or to take lunch at the Leather Bottle Inn at Cobham.

It is when we approach the question of the Dickens characters that we find ourselves faced by one of the greatest riddles in all literary history. Are they real, or are they imaginary? If they are real, in what does their reality consist? It may be best to start with one or two incontestable facts about them, and so work towards the heart of the problem. If we cannot hope to solve that problem, we can at least hope to throw some light upon the secret of Dickens' greatness.

Though no one has yet settled to the satisfaction of anyone else exactly what a novel is, there is one general assertion which may safely be made about the English novel. It must contain interesting people. It will not live unless it does. An English novelist may be careless about plot construction and indifferent about style, but if he can give his readers characters who will hold their attention he is certain of a public.

The history of the English novel is largely the history of a number of characters. Anyone with the most casual acquaintance of those novels which have won fame and reputation during the past two hundred years can recall a dozen of these without hesitation—Tom Jones, Squire Western, Parson Yorick, Uncle Toby, Corporal Trim, Parson Adams, Elizabeth Bennet, Becky Sharp, Jane Eyre, Hardy's Tess and Jude, Wells' Mr. Polly and Kipps, Conan Doyle's Sherlock Holmes (far more interesting than any of his adventures), Galsworthy's Soames Forsyte—not to mention any in the huge Dickens army.

These and many other characters will always keep their authors' memories green. But where are the novelists now who have depended on other sources of strength? There is always a public for the sensational novel, but the "School of Terror" thrillers of the early nineteenth century are as dead as door-nails. There are always readers who demand a cunning plot or an exciting narrative, but Wilkie Collins, who supplied the one, and Charles Reade who gave the other as few men could, are fast fading into oblivion. There will always be a few eclectics for whom the manner of the telling, the style of a story, remains the chief consideration; these will continue to relish the subtle flavour of the prose of Walter Pater and Robert Louis Stevenson, but their numbers will never grow great.

For the vast majority of readers the primary interest in

any novel lies in the characters of the people it contains, and of all English novelists from Defoe to Galsworthy there is none who can be compared with Dickens for creation of interesting people. It has been calculated that there are more than two thousand characters in his books. Mere weight of numbers is not, of course, in itself impressive. What is impressive is that the ordinary reader of Dickens, if questioned about the people in Dickens' books, will find himself so full of information about so many of them that it will take him hours to disgorge his knowledge. It will not be merely a matter of saying something about the outstanding characters, such as Mr. Pickwick, the Wellers, Mr. Micawber, Mrs. Gamp, Mr. Pecksniff, Joe Gargery, Mr. Sapsea (though there are more of these than one would care to describe on a summer's evening), but one is compelled also to recall people who appear but for a brief instant in the story—Mr. Smauker, the Bath footman, for instance, or the second-hand dealer of Chatham to whom David Copperfield sold his coat.

The range and vividness of Dickens' characters is an extraordinarily impressive fact. It is more than that; it is a phenomenon unparalleled in English literary history. The only other comparable instance is that of Shakespeare. Many other novelists have crowded their canvas with figures. Dickens' great contemporary, Thackeray, did so; in our own time H. G. Wells and John Galsworthy have done so, but without the slightest disrespect to these distinguished writers it is possible to say that not one of them can approach Dickens in range, in variety, or in facility of characterization. With them one remembers the main characters who support the story; with Dickens one remembers all the characters.

Shakespeare and Dickens are comparable because each gave through his characters a complete picture of the England of his day. One important qualification, however, must at once be made to that statement. Shakespeare's characterization was more universal than Dickens', because it was able to reveal the common humanity which lies below the surface in all ranks and classes of Englishmen. Shakespeare could enter with equal facility into the emotions of a monarch and those of a peasant, because he realized that monarchs and peasants were both men, moved by the same basic impulses and impelled by the same instincts. He was the more able to do this because during his lifetime all classes of English people were more closely united, more in sympathy with each other than at any other period in our history.

The reverse was the case in Dickens' day. By the early nineteenth century the upper and lower classes of England had grown so far apart that they appeared in effect to be two distinct peoples, as they still do to this day. Dickens was only universal in respect of the lower classes. He truly and fully represented them, and did them incalculable service by explaining them to the upper classes; but he never understood the latter. He was not simply an interpreter of the masses: he was of the masses, and fundamentally he never rose above them.

Though he was for many years an extremely successful and comparatively rich man, though he was on intimate terms of friendship with rich, cultured and educated men and women in Great Britain, France and the United States, he never achieved sympathy with the aristocratic temperament; more strange still, he never appeared, in his books at least, fully to comprehend the psychology of the upper-middle class in which for thirty-five years he moved. His great characters, all his more interesting characters, belong to the lower-middle and lower classes.

This, in one sense, makes his achievement all the more remarkable. The difficulty in character drawing is not to draw sharply contrasted characters, but subtly differentiated ones. Had Dickens been able to draw from the whole range of English society the result would doubtless have been grander, but his task would have been easier, and the picture, one suspects, would have been neither so complete nor so effective. Its outlines would have been blurred by the vastness of the background.

As it was, he drew almost all his people from below a certain level; on the rare occasions when he ventured above that level he usually made a mess of things, as in the cases of Lord Verisopht and Sir Mulberry Hawk in "Nicholas Nickleby." Similarly, in spite of his lengthy residences in France, Italy and Switzerland his attempts at continental characters are conventional and ridiculous. Only once did he make a successful excursion outside his own country, and that was among a people still predominantly Anglo-Saxon. He brought back in his mind from America the materials for one of the most exquisite satires ever written, the American chapters of "Martin Chuzzlewit."

Dickens was, in fact, limited to a comparatively narrow sphere geographically. The great majority of his characters are Londoners, or if they are not Londoners born they usually find their way to the metropolis sooner or later.

We are thus faced with the fact that Dickens, though drawing almost exclusively from the lower-middle and lower classes of English society and in the main from London, not only created some two thousand characters, every one of whom claims attention and no two of whom are alike, but so impressed the reality of these characters upon the whole English-speaking world (to say nothing of foreign countries), that they were welcomed into countless homes with more cordiality than is accorded to long-absent friends and were discussed with more seriousness than the characters of the next-door neighbours. It is here that one begins to approach the real greatness of Dickens.

Just as it is impossible to minimize the vast popularity of Dickens both during and after his lifetime, so it is impossible to minimize the significance of that popularity. No other writer has enjoyed a comparable popularity, because no other has ever so touched and so expressed the soul of a people. Shakespeare has had to be sustained by interpreters, by scholars, poets and dramatists, because Shakespeare, all-embracing though he is, saw life through the eyes of a poet, and his riches are not fully to be enjoyed save by prayer and fasting. Dickens saw life through the eyes of a common man, and his riches lie open to all.

Every one of Dickens' two thousand characters touches at once some responsive chord in our hearts; together those characters fuse into one immense and overwhelmingly true character, our own.

Two main objections are always urged by literary critics

against these characters of Dickens. They say that they are exaggerated, and they say that they are examples of types of character rather than pictures of real people. Those critics, and they are not few in number, who when they have made these objections begin to feel that they are not quite sure about them, are apt to toil laboriously to explain them away. It is far simpler and more straightforward, and considerably nearer the truth, to admit that both objections are substantially correct. Having made that admission, one can then declare that they constitute the highest possible tribute to Dickens' literary ability.

On the one hand there are the allegations that he created types, not people, and that his characters are exaggerated beyond the reality of life as one lives it; on the other there are the indisputable facts of the colossal and sustained popularity of those characters, and an indubitably accurate composite picture of nineteenth-century England. How is one to reconcile these apparent opposites? Only by assuming that Dickens, as an artist, consciously or unconsciously realized the futility of representing people in all detail as they are. By that method fidelity to life is never achieved; all that is achieved is fidelity to the modes of living described. Any reporter with an accurate pencil can do that, but the picture will be out of date in five years.

In museums one may sometimes see in glass cases models of stretches of country on which are illustrated in miniature industries or occupations. The figures, the buildings, the contours and slopes in these models are all distorted; yet when a light is switched on everything falls into perspective and proportion and a perfect picture is revealed. It was so with Dickens; his individual figures are distorted and exaggerated, but, shot through with the radiance of his genius as a writer, they are seen to fall naturally into place, to combine into an accurate and truthful picture.

It in no way detracts from his greatness to suggest that he did not fully realize what he was doing. No great writer ever does; the moment he approaches realization his work begins to deteriorate. No one would be more surprised than Shakespeare, were it possible for him to come alive to-day, to find on what grounds his work is now venerated. It always takes time to discover the full significance, or even the real significance, of a writer's work; and even the author himself, though he usually has a truer sense of what is permanently valuable in his work and what is ephemeral than have most of his contemporaries, can rarely judge accurately what he has done.

It is highly probable that Shakespeare's audiences applauded most vociferously just those parts in his plays which we rightly consider tedious or bombastic, and that they yawned and grew fidgety over the scenes and passages that to-day are seen to reveal his fundamental greatness. Similarly, we have already begun to set aside as second-rate and ephemeral parts of Dickens' work that moved his contemporaries to ecstasies of joyful or sorrowful emotion, and we are discovering new excellencies in him that were but faintly, if at all, revealed to his original readers. Above all, we are beginning to get his characters in true perspective, a thing Dickens never did himself.

To him they were all absolutely real. He worked from start to finish under the impression that he was reproducing real life. He was always comparatively indifferent to criticism of his books as literature; any suggestion as to their falsity to life would instantly provoke him to sensitive fury, and would draw from him the most ingenious and elaborate explanations of their absolute truth.

He knew his people were real. They walked the streets with him, talked with him, poured out their souls to him. He was beside them as they knocked at their front doors; he entered their houses with them and stood at their elbows as they brewed their tea or mixed their bowls of punch; he counted the stairs up which they climbed to their bedrooms, drew back the curtains of their four-poster beds, and blew out their candles for them as they snuggled down between the sheets. Had any one of them at any time lost his umbrella or mislaid his watch-key Dickens could have told him where it was.

Had Dickens really been doing what he thought he was, presenting literal biographies of creatures of his imagination

MR. PICKWICK

*Drawn by Kenny Meadows.  From " Bell's Life in London," 1838*

who were created by fusing the characteristics of actual living people, he would have proved himself a great writer; he would no doubt have achieved a very considerable reputation in his day, but he would have been practically forgotten by now. It was his inimitable ability to catch and fix in human form just those characteristics which make the English people what they are, while suppressing all irrelevant characteristics, that is to distort reality by both exaggeration and diminution without ever losing the illusion of reality that enabled him to write the biography of the soul of the masses of England, a biography that is just as true to-day, and just as well beloved, as it was sixty or eighty years ago.

All great characters in fiction are types. It is only by being types that they can achieve permanence. No absolutely faithful reporter's account of the life and character of any person, however exciting, can remain permanently interesting to a large number of people. In the case of a real person, it may acquire historical interest, but only if it is seen to reflect tendencies and influences of its time. In the case of a fictitious character, it is only when that character is so presented as to show his kinship with eternal strains in human nature that he can retain human affection.

Hamlet is a type; Falstaff is a type. Were they pictures of real people they would have aged and died long ago. Mr. Pickwick is a type: Sam Weller is a type. There are a thousand Mr. Pickwicks, a thousand Sam Wellers, alive to-day. It was the Sam Wellers of the modern world who made the sordid life in the trenches in France and elsewhere during the Great War not merely tolerable but, on occasions, riotously enjoyable and funny.

To say that Dickens' characters are types is by no means to deny them verisimilitude to life. A novelist sets out to present to his readers a number of people who shall through their words and actions and by his descriptions of them exemplify and illustrate certain aspects of character. He knows that if he makes them obviously unreal they will not grip the attention of readers, and his purpose will be nullified because no one will read his book. He knows equally well that if he makes them literally real they will become equally uninteresting. It sounds paradoxical, but it is a fact that to make people seem real in a book one has to make them unreal. The author's success artistically is the measure of his skill in blending reality and unreality, in other words his art in concealing his distortion.

No writer ever hovered so successfully on the border line of reality and unreality as did Dickens. It is impossible to say at any given moment where he crosses the line. It is possible here and there to say definitely that he has crossed it, but that is as far as one can go. Even when one has made this latter assertion, it has to be qualified by saying that even in his apparently wildest moments Dickens may be faithfully reflecting some aspect of human nature. The daily papers are perpetually recording accounts of eccentricities stranger than any that are to be found in Dickens' books.

It is of course dangerous to make any general statement about Dickens' characters, because they vary in degree of verisimilitude to life from the almost photographic to the most grotesque caricature. Mr. Lorry of Tellson's Bank, in "A Tale of Two Cities," is probably as accurate a likeness as any biographer could produce; Jonas Chuzzlewit and Daniel Quilp are about as true to life as a Low cartoon—which, incidentally, is much truer than most people would imagine from a casual glance. There are some aspects of life which the caricaturist can reflect, but which the camera can never record. And Dickens was a superb caricaturist who always conveyed vital truths in his caricatures.

It may perhaps serve as an illustration of Dickens' method if one considers in some detail two of his most famous characters, Mr. Pickwick and Sam Weller. It is Mr. Pickwick's simplicity and kind-heartedness which dominate the pages of the "Pickwick Papers." The characteristics which Dickens wishes to be remembered of this immortal hero, and which he succeeds in impressing upon us to the exclusion of all others, are aptly summarized in two pregnant comments by Sam Weller. After he has rescued his master from the prospect of a chilly night in the corridors of the Ipswich hotel, that worthy observes to him, "You rayther want somebody to look arter you, sir, when your judgment goes

SAMIVEL VELLER

*Drawn by Kenny Meadows.  From "Bell's Life in London," 1838*

out a-wisitin'." Much later on, when Job Trotter, now a poor prisoner in the Fleet, and with Jingle the object of Mr. Pickwick's generosity, tries to express his appreciation of that gentleman's character, Sam takes him up fiercely, and bursts out with the remarkable declaration, "I never heerd, mind you, nor read of in story-books, nor see in picters, any angel in tights and gaiters—not even in spectacles, as I remember, though that may ha' been done for anything I know to the contrairey—but mark my words, Job Trotter, he's a reg'lar thorough-bred angel for all that; and let me see the man as wentures to tell me he knows a better vun."

These are the characteristics which have endeared Mr. Pickwick to generations of readers; they are the only ones in him that really matter, but had they been the only ones mentioned, Mr. Pickwick would have been a mere puppet, no more than a mouthpiece of benevolent simplicity. This is regrettably evident when he is resuscitated in *Master Humphrey's Clock*.

But Mr. Pickwick has other qualities which, had they been emphasized, would have made him appear in a very different light. He can be quite a tyrant to his followers: the directions with which he sends Sam Weller to Bristol after Mr. Winkle show that. For all his simplicity he is capable of coming to a swift decision and of pursuing a resolute course of action with the utmost determination, as Mr. Jingle found to his cost. That he has a keenly developed sense of responsibility is evidenced from the fact that a hard-headed man of business like the elder Mr. Winkle entrusts his son to him for a period of twelve months. He has an iron will; he remains for more than three months in the Fleet Prison, and but for Mrs. Bardell's arrival there, an event which brings his determination and his benevolence into direct conflict, there is every indication that he would have remained there until the day of his death. He is a fiery little man; he verges on half a dozen quarrels in the book, is frequently swelling with indignation, and pursues Messrs. Dodson and Fogg out of Mr. Perker's office with vituperations that do credit to his capacity to get into a white-hot passion, but which strip him of every shred of benevolence.

Had all these aspects of Mr. Pickwick's character been equally developed—not exaggerated—we should have had a very interesting picture of an early nineteenth-century gentleman of leisure, but we should not have had an "immortal." That picture would have gone out of date long ago. But they are not developed; they are simply thrown in, casually, it appears, but really with unerring skill, to create the illusion of reality. They achieve this object perfectly, but they are never allowed to obtrude, to spoil the harmony of the main theme, and it is because we have in Mr. Pickwick a personification of those kindly and simple impulses which exist, however deeply they may sometimes be buried, in the hearts of all of us, that we continue to read about him and to love him. Mr. Pickwick, the type, can never grow old. How completely Dickens succeeds in presenting the type may be judged from the shock that one receives in the last chapter of the book when Mr. Pickwick says, "Nearly the whole of my previous life having been devoted to business and the pursuit of wealth . . ." The statement may be perfectly true, but it introduces a false note. It is difficult to imagine Mr. Pickwick in business; it is quite impossible to think of him pursuing wealth.

Take as further example of this typification that wittiest manservant of all time, Sam Weller. Sam is among the most realistic characters Dickens ever created. He fits exactly into his surroundings; there is not a detail in his appearance, his actions and his attitude to life which is not completely and utterly early nineteenth century. Then why is he as fresh and entertaining to-day as he was one hundred years ago? Because he is the supreme exaggeration of a perennial type. You may meet Sam Wellers to-day all over England; you can hear them cracking their jokes in any big football crowd on any Saturday afternoon, and you can reckon on their kissing their pretty housemaids—or shop-girls; housemaids are rare to-day—in any cinema on Saturday evening. They conceal beneath the same sharp-witted and witty exterior the same capacity for staunch devotion as did Sam; the Great War proved that when the softer conditions of peace-time might have obscured it.

Yet Sam Weller, true to life though he is in every respect,

is both an exaggeration and a distortion—in short, a type.
No Sam Weller in real life is ever quite so continuously witty
on so high a level as is Sam, nor are wit and devotion his
only qualities; they were not the only ones Sam possessed.
Though the fact is never openly mentioned, Sam must have
been an efficient valet. There is never a hint of complaint
from Mr. Pickwick about the way in which his duties are
carried out, though Mr. Pickwick was, one may be sure, a man
who liked all the little attentions of valeting; and surely in
a humorous book Sam's valeting would have been an easy
and attractive source of amusement? To judge from the
errands upon which he is sent, Sam proves himself a very
efficient and intelligent confidential servant. He has also,
but they are always kept quietly in the background and never
allowed to obtrude, other less desirable qualities. He can
grow peevishly irritable even with Mr. Pickwick; he is quite
ready to take part in any street row, even to assault the police;
he gets drunk; he revels in stories and anecdotes which reveal
him as callously indifferent to tragedies that should move one
to sympathy and horror. One dare not enquire with what
kind of stories and jokes he regales the tap-room of nights.

In short, Sam is a tough. He could hardly be anything
else, considering the life he has led. But though all the
necessary touches are supplied to make Sam true to life, we
are scarcely allowed to see, or at least to remember, anything of him but his wit and his devotion to Mr. Pickwick—
always excepted those glorious passages in which he makes
love to Mary, the pretty housemaid. Those passages, it may
be remarked in passing, are easily the most charming love-
scenes in Dickens—and they take a lot of beating outside.

Though all the evidence is supplied of Sam's toughness,
though he asserts it himself—"If you vant a more polished
sort o' feller, vell and good, have him,"—the impression that
is left in the reader's mind of Sam is of an almost feminine
delicacy and tenderness.

This sublime capacity for revealing fundamental aspects
of character while appearing to present complete human
personalities is, and will remain, the chief excellence of Dickens.
This it is which makes him the despair of critics and ensures

for him the love of vast numbers of readers. His people *are* real; they force their reality upon us, they compel our love and our sympathy; and even when the cold searchlight of criticism is thrown upon them it is scarcely possible to say where reality ends and art begins, so perfectly are the two blended. Yet without the art the whole force of the picture would be lost.

It is sometimes urged against Dickens that he does not go below the surface in his characterization, that he is content to portray oddities of manner and habit. While this may be true of some of his less good and less complete characters, it is in the main a very highbrow criticism, possible only from those who can only see that the well-springs of character are tapped when the author minutely analyses every smile and every tear, every aspiration and every sigh. It is besides a criticism which ignores the fact that the lower one descends in the social scale the more completely does behaviour express the character.

What more fundamental bases of English character are there than Mr. Pickwick's kindliness and quiet charity, Sam Weller's cheerful attitude towards life and the invincible loyalty he displays? What is more deeply English than that any mention of that loyalty embarrasses him? What of Mr. Pecksniff's hypocrisy, Mr. Sapsea's complacent pride in himself, Bradley Headstone's blundering persistence, Mrs. Nickleby's muddle-headedness, Dan'l Peggotty's self-sacrifice, Joe Gargery's uncomplaining devotion? One might illustrate by a hundred other examples; to take but one, who like Dickens has ever caught and revealed the fact of the indomitable optimism of the unsuccessful, as he did in Mr. Micawber?

One final criticism of his characterization may be briefly discussed. It is said that his best characters are always static. It is perfectly true. It is a natural consequence of his method. It ensures the permanence of his pictures of human nature. Reference has been made earlier in this book to various instances in which Dickens has attempted the portrayal of developing character, David Copperfield, Uriah Heep, and Pip in particular. It needs only to ask from whom does one gain a clearer insight into human nature, from David

THE GOLDEN CROSS INN, CHARING CROSS, THE MEETING-PLACE
OF PICKWICK AND MR. JINGLE, DEMOLISHED 1830

*From a contemporary engraving*

or from Mr. Micawber, from Pip or from Joe Gargery? As for Uriah Heep, he is perhaps the most notable example in Dickens of the typification blotting out the humanity of a character.

It has been said previously that Dickens never understood the aristocratic temperament or that of the successful and prosperous upper-middle class. It follows that there are some types of character which he never illustrated. He never showed the cool, clear, analytical brain that carries a man to the heights of financial, industrial or legal success. It was beyond his range; his own mind was never cool nor analytical. Nor are many other people's; the type is rare in England. Nor did he show the calm, scholarly, reflective mind, because he was himself the reverse of calm and scholarly. He could not paint a philosopher, because he had himself no philosophy. There are no dignified highbrows in his books (there are plenty of undignified ones), because he never understood the highbrow attitude towards life. Nor does anyone else except the highbrow.

When, however, one says that Dickens could not understand the aristocratic temperament, one has to make a single curious exception. M. le Marquis de St. Evrémonde in "A Tale of Two Cities" is a French aristocrat of the Louis XIV régime to his very finger-tips. One can only assume that Dickens studied him from the outside as an historical type during his researches before writing this book. It seems impossible to believe, in face of all the evidence, that this character was arrived at by his otherwise invariable method of projection of himself into a personality. In support of this theory we have Dickens' own assertion that he found the picture of the Marquis in a book published in Amsterdam.

It was in the painting of those elements in human nature which call forth the common emotions of mankind—laughter, tears, anger, joy, sorrow, pity, sympathy—that Dickens was supreme. He was the Master of feeling; there is no emotion that can be experienced by the great mass of ordinary people which he has not displayed with unerring fidelity through his huge army of strangely-distorted but so truly real characters.

One need not linger here over the faults, real and alleged,

of Dickens as a writer; not because the real faults do not exist, but because he is great enough to carry plenty of them without diminution of his stature. One distinguishing feature of the "universal" writer is his exuberance; he is so full of matter that he has to pour it out regardless of its quality. At times his exuberance carries him to the heights of inspiration, and then he is supreme; at other times it drags him through pages of rant and bombast. This is as true of Shakespeare as it is of Dickens, and in either case one can pardon the turgidity because one never knows when it may be the prelude to divinest inspiration.

A change of fashion is responsible for one of the most serious of Dickens' alleged faults, the so-called "mawkish sentimentality" of his pathetic chapters. Hard modern critics are perhaps rather inclined to overlook how frequently sentimentality has been popular in this country; they overlook also, and this is a much graver error, how deeply it is ingrained in the English character. The English are an intensely sentimental race, far more so than those races whose open expressions of emotion they affect to despise, and except at rare intervals in their history (the present is one of them) they have never made any bones about acknowledging their sentimentality. Even now, one has only to observe the effect upon any cinema audience of an effective "sob-stuff" picture to realize how close beneath the surface this sentimentality of ours still lies.

Another change of fashion leads critics to decry Dickens' habit of moralizing. Again, one is tempted to wonder how little it is understood that the English always have been, not so much a moral race (though they are) as a moralizing one. Alfred the Great moralized; Chaucer moralized; one of the most beautiful poems in the language, the *Faerie Queene*, is nothing but moralizing set in a delicious frame. Shakespeare is full of slabs of morality; many of his best-known and deservedly famous passages are pure sermon. What else can "All the world's a stage," "The quality of mercy," "To be or not to be," or the "few precepts" of Polonius be called? Our habit of moralizing is often traced to the Puritans of the seventeenth century, that unfortunate group of Englishmen to whom it is popular to attribute so many of our less desirable qualities. How many people ever stop to wonder in how many other countries it would have been possible for the Puritans ever to have arisen, much less come to power?

In all fairness to Dickens one must admit, not only that he was born in an age when moralizing was unusually popular, but also that he had plenty to moralize about. There always is in England, the land of good intentions in which action limps so tardily; and there was much more than usual in his day.

A very great deal has been written about Dickens' prose. It is a very important subject, for though no writer ever thought of himself less as a stylist, his prose style was beyond all shadow of doubt a highly decisive factor in his success.

Let us admit at once all its blemishes. It has all the faults incidental to exuberant writing. Dickens is quite capable of penning an ungrammatical sentence. He not infrequently begins in one construction and switches off into another. His relative pronouns often do not refer grammatically to the substantives to which they belong. He piles up long and unwieldy sentences. His punctuation is abhorrent to the modern purist. He is repetitive, both of words and phrases, sometimes to a wearisome degree. He says the same thing two or three times over apparently for the mere pleasure of saying it. In his earlier books particularly he is given to the vices of the so-called "Cockney School" of writers, vices we know to-day as journalese. Eyes are called "optics"; the nose is the organ by which one respires; a mouth is an orifice, and so forth. Straightforward statements of ordinary events are replaced by clumsy circumlocutions. As Dickens was reproved for this fault in the contemporary reviews of "Pickwick" it is perhaps unnecessary further to comment upon it here.

It is more opportune to consider the virtues of Dickens' prose, virtues which are as yet perhaps not as fully recognized as they might be. To say that he could when necessary be as economical of words as any author is merely to pay tribute to his journalistic ability. To add a word about his clarity of description is essential. Mrs. Meynell, among the most fastidious of literary critics, has pointed out his pregnancy of epithet. While at times Dickens seems to scatter adjectives and adverbs with a reckless prodigality, he is not to be confused with those writers who fling epithets on to the page merely for the delight of weltering in words. The distinctness with which his descriptions of places and of people remain in the memory is sufficient evidence that his words are scrupulously chosen. The following description, of Mr. Montague Tigg in "Martin Chuzzlewit," may perhaps serve as illustration. At first sight it appears wordy and over-epithetical; it is only when one tries to take it to pieces and to condense it that one realizes how necessary is every word.

The gentleman was of that order of appearance which is currently termed shabby-genteel, though in respect of his dress he can hardly be said to have been in any extremities, as his fingers were a long way out of his gloves, and the soles of his feet were at an inconvenient distance from the upper leather of his boots. His nether garments were of a bluish gray—violent in its colours once, but sobered now by age and dinginess—and were so stretched and strained in a tough conflict between his braces and his straps, that they appeared every moment in danger of flying asunder at the knees. His coat, in colour blue and of a military cut, was buttoned and frogged, up to his chin. His cravat was, in hue and pattern, like one of those mantles which hair-dressers are accustomed to wrap about their clients, during the progress of the professional mysteries. His hat had arrived at such a pass that it would have been hard to determine whether it was originally white or black. But he wore a moustache—a shaggy moustache too: nothing in the meek and merciful way, but quite in the fierce and scornful style: the regular Satanic sort of thing —and he wore, besides, a vast quantity of unbrushed hair. He was very dirty and very jaunty; very bold and very mean; very swaggering and very slinking; very much like a man who might have been something better, and unspeakably like a man who deserved to be something worse.

It is only when one comes to consider Dickens' prose as a whole that one becomes fully aware of its quality. It is, in short, as Dickensian as his characterization. With individual sentences it is easy to find fault, but when one considers the total effect of a description such as the above, when one reads page after page, chapter after chapter, book after book—for the essential qualities of the style are the same in the last book as in the first—one realizes that here is the one and only vehicle that can possibly carry those queer customers, the Dickens characters. A "straightforward" description of Mr. Montague Tigg would never have described that crooked gentleman; to have said that his trousers were a dingy bluish grey would have been quite inadequate, and to have failed to comment at length upon his moustache would have been to have omitted the essential feature in his make-up. Mr. Montague Tigg was enabled to impose upon people chiefly by virtue of his moustache.

Like Dickens' characters, Dickens' prose is in particulars distorted and exaggerated, but its total effect smooths out into something very straightforward and undeniably effective. Like them, it is compelling; we wind our way through it, get caught up in its rhythm, and find ourselves carried along unresistingly. Though it seems tortuous, there is a strong tide flowing, which ever and again swells into a torrent of words that sweeps everything before it.

Reference has previously been made to Dickens' remarkable capacity for cumulative description, for piling scene upon scene, each rising in intensity, and to his equally remarkable capacity for clothing his characters and their actions in an appropriate atmosphere. It has to be admitted that he carries this latter habit to a fault, that in many instances it becomes a mere trick. It is not necessary, nor is it true to life, that every time something unfortunate is going to happen the sky shall become overcast, the fog come down and the rain begin to fall, nor conversely that the mornings of joyous events shall invariably be bright and sunny. But this is a venial fault, which undoubtedly adds to our enjoyment of the story, and which in any case is easily pardonable when one remembers that the power of whole books derives in large part from a sustained creation of atmosphere.

While one will readily admit that the plots of many of

Dickens' books are cumbrous, shapeless and involved, it is necessary to draw a clear distinction between the plot and the story. The chief interest in his books will always remain his characters, but the actual stories are in themselves absorbing. Even when one has come to know exactly what is going to happen, the narrative carries one on from page to page. There is a never-failing sense of excited anticipation; Dickens is an author whom it is very difficult to leave off reading. Even the incidence of one of the numerous highly dramatic episodes does not provide any excuse for stopping. With other authors one feels that a distinct break in the story has come, and that one can put down the book with a sense of having come to a conclusion. That is impossible with Dickens; he never stops to draw breath. In the opening words of the next paragraph he is off again. The narrative trots briskly on, fresh scenes and fresh characters appear, the hold upon the interest is never relaxed, the reader is swept along, and can only stop when the end of the book is reached. Then one finds oneself experiencing the same reluctance as did Dickens when at the conclusion of each story he had to lay down his pen, the same grief at parting with friends as he did.

The reason for this last is plain. Strictly speaking, no Dickens' novel ever ends, it merely ceases to be written. The affairs of the company are wound up, but the firm goes into voluntary liquidation. There is no reason why any of the stories should not continue indefinitely. Except that there is an official termination (a most unsatisfactory affair) to "Pickwick," that book is as unfinished as "Edwin Drood." The death of little Nell concludes "The Old Curiosity Shop," but the death of Paul Dombey occurs in the first quarter of "Dombey and Son." The only exceptions to this rule are the two historical novels, "Barnaby Rudge," and "A Tale of Two Cities."

We have always this consolation; we can begin again. No one need ever fear to read a Dickens' novel a second time, or twenty times. The flavour grows richer with every re-reading.

---

MADE AND PRINTED BY THE GREYCAINE BOOK MANU-FACTURING  COMPANY  LIMITED,  WATFORD,  HERTS.